Lecture Notes in Computer Science   643
Edited by G. Goos and J. Hartmanis

Advisory Board: W. Brauer   D. Gries   J. Stoer

A. Habel

Hyperedge Replacement: Grammars and Languages

Springer-Verlag
Berlin Heidelberg New York
London Paris Tokyo
Hong Kong Barcelona
Budapest

Series Editors

Gerhard Goos
Universität Karlsruhe
Postfach 69 80
Vincenz-Priessnitz-Straße 1
W-7500 Karlsruhe, FRG

Juris Hartmanis
Cornell University
Department of Computer Science
5149 Upson Hall
Ithaca, NY 14853, USA

Author

Annegret Habel
Department of Mathematics and Computer Science, University of Bremen
Bibliothekstraße, Postfach 33 04 40, W-2800 Bremen 33, FRG

CR Subject Classification (1991): F.4.2–3, G.2.2

ISBN 3-540-56005-X Springer-Verlag Berlin Heidelberg New York
ISBN 0-387-56005-X Springer-Verlag New York Berlin Heidelberg

This work is subject to copyright. All rights are reserved, whether the whole or part of the material is concerned, specifically the rights of translation, reprinting, re-use of illustrations, recitation, broadcasting, reproduction on microfilms or in any other way, and storage in data banks. Duplication of this publication or parts thereof is permitted only under the provisions of the German Copyright Law of September 9, 1965, in its current version, and permission for use must always be obtained from Springer-Verlag. Violations are liable for prosecution under the German Copyright Law.

© Springer-Verlag Berlin Heidelberg 1992
Printed in the United States of America

Typesetting: Camera ready by author/editor
45/3140-543210 - Printed on acid-free paper

Foreword

First approaches to graph transformations, graph grammars and graph languages have been introduced about twenty years ago by several authors in the U.S.A. and Europe in order to model different application areas within Computer Science. Graph grammars can be considered as a generalization of classical Chomsky grammars where strings are replaced by graphs. While in the string case it is obvious how to replace a substring by another one, replacement is no longer trivial in the graph case. Given a graph production with left hand side L and right hand side R, an application of this production to a graph G means to find an occurrence of L in G, to remove L from G and to embed R into the remaining part of G leading to a derived graph H. The main problem is how to construct this embedding. In fact, there have been various different solutions for this embedding problem leading to a variety of graph grammar approaches in the literature.

One of the main influences on this volume has been the algebraic approach developed in Berlin in the early seventies and the NLC (node label controlled) grammars from the school in Leiden built up by G. Rozenberg in the late seventies. The school in Berlin was initiated by H.J. Schneider, M. Pfender and myself in 1973 and mainly influenced by B.K. Rosen (IBM Research, Yorktown Heights), H.-J. Kreowski since about 1975 and Annegret Habel, the author of this volume. She joined our group as a student at the end of the seventies and followed H.-J. Kreowski to Bremen about five years later. In her diploma thesis she provided a most elegant new proof for the "Concurrency Theorem" for graph grammars and a technique for the decomposition of graph productions into atomic parts. She continued this line of research together with two colleagues in Berlin leading to the important concept of amalgamation of graph transformations, an elegant algebraic version of synchronization concepts for graph productions in distributed systems developed by U. Montanari and P. Degano in Pisa.

Influenced by the NLC-school in Leiden, she became interested in context-free graph grammars and languages. In the early eighties it was an open problem how far the rich theory of context-free Chomsky grammars and languages could be generalized to the graph case. In contrast to node replacement in the NLC approach, she joined H.-J. Kreowski investigating edge replacement as a special case of the algebraic approach, where the left hand side of a production consists of a single edge.

Although nice results were obtained in this framework, I was still somewhat sceptical at that time because there were only a few interesting applications of this edge replacement approach. The range of applications, however, becomes significantly larger when hyperedges instead of edges are considered. Hyperedges are allowed to have sequences of source and target nodes instead of just one source and one target node for each edge in a graph. This allows one to model functional expressions, Petri nets, flow diagrams and chemical molecule structures using hyperedge replacement grammars while non-context-free productions are necessary in the framework of usual graphs and graph grammars to model these applications.

Annegret Habel was not only able to generalize the theory of edge to hyperedge replacement system which is presented in this volume but also to find an answer to the open problem from the early eighties: Several major constructions and results known from the classical theory of context-free Chomsky grammars and languages remain valid for hyperedge replacement grammars and corresponding hypergraph languages. This includes closure properties, a Kleene-type characterization of languages, a fixed-point theorem, a pumping lemma, Parikh's theorem, boundedness properties and results concerning the generative power of languages. Although most of these results and their proofs in the graph case are much more sophisticated than those in the string case the presentation by Annegret Habel is significantly clear and complete in contrast to several other publications in the area of graph grammars.

Another important part of this volume is the general theory of decidability concerning graph theoretic properties. In fact, the notion of "compatible properties" includes connectivity, the existence of Eulerian paths and cycles, edge colorability, and several other interesting properties and it is shown that all these properties are decidable for hyperedge replacement grammars. Similar results were obtained in the literature by M. Bauderon and B. Courcelle as well as T. Lengauer and E. Wanke using different approaches.

Last but not least it should be mentioned that this volume is based on the Ph.D. thesis of Annegret Habel and constitutes an important contribution within the ESPRIT Basic Research Working Group "Computing by Graph Transformation". I am very glad that this significant part of the theory of graph grammars and their applications in Computer Science is published by Springer Verlag in this volume of Lecture Notes in Computer Science, which is well recognized in the Computer Science community.

Berlin, July 1992   Hartmut Ehrig

Preface

The area of graph grammars is theoretically attractive and well motivated by various applications. More than 20 years ago, the concept of graph grammars was introduced by A. Rosenfeld as a formulation of some problems in pattern recognition and image processing as well as by H.J. Schneider as a method for data type specification. The four proceedings volumes of the Workshop on Graph Grammars and Their Applications to Computer Science series (Lecture Notes in Computer Science) provide a rich record of the development of this field.

Within graph-grammar theory one may distinguish among several approaches:

- the set-theoretical approach,
- the algebraic approach, and
- the logical approach

(see the overview papers by Nagl, Ehrig, and Courcelle [Na 87, Eh 79+87, Co 89c]). These approaches differ in the method in which graph replacement is described. Specific approaches are

- the node-replacement approach and
- the hyperedge-replacement approach,

concerning the basic units of a hypergraph, nodes and hyperedges.

This monograph is mainly concerned with the hyperedge-replacement approach reviving some ideas from the early seventies which can be found in Feder's [Fe 71] and Pavlidis' [Pa 72] work. Hyperedge-replacement grammars are introduced as a device for generating hypergraph languages including graph languages and string languages (where the strings are uniquely represented as certain graphs). The concept combines a context-free rewriting with a comparatively large generative power. The former is indicated, for example, by a fixed-point theorem and a pumping lemma, the latter by the examples such as the refinement of petri nets, the analysis of flow diagrams, the structural description of molecules, and some typical non-context-free string languages. Hence, we can be confident that this framework combines the theoretical attractivity of a class of context-free grammars and languages with the prospect for nice applications.

This book is a revised, enlarged and updated version of my doctoral dissertation accepted by the University of Bremen. I started to work on it while I was a member of the Theoretical Computer Science group at the Technical University of Berlin; it was finished while I was a member of the Computer Science Department at the University of Bremen. Special thanks are due to my thesis supervisors Hartmut Ehrig and Hans-Jörg Kreowski. They introduced me to the fascinating world of graph grammars, taught me to do research in theoretical computer science, and gave me an environment in which I enjoyed to do creative work. Working in their groups, doing common research, writing joint papers, as well as a feeling of liking and esteem has played a central role in starting and carrying out the research described here.

Additionally, I would like to express my thanks to all those people without whose help this book would not be what it is now. Special thanks are due to Walter Vogler and Clemens Lautemann for many stimulating discussions that we have had during the preparation of joint papers, Peter Padawitz, Udo Hummert, and Detlef Plump for a number of fruitful discussions, numerous suggestions, and constructive comments during the long period of preparing the Ph.D. Thesis, Frank Drewes, Sabine Kuske, Geoff Simmons, and Stefan Taubenberger for their helpful feedback as I revised the manuscript, and all good friends for their general moral support. Finally, let me mention Ingeborg Mayer and Hans Wössner from Springer-Verlag who invited me to submit the manuscript for publication and took care of the production of this book.

I also wish to thank my husband Christopher for helping me throughout this adventure in more ways than I can list here. He suggested me to study theoretical computer science and encouraged me to focus on formal language theory while he was writing his doctoral dissertation in linguistics entitled Aspects of Valuating Grammars. During the time writing my doctoral dissertation he contributed a number of suggestions and — more important than anything else — sound advice. I could not have done it without him.

Bremen, July 1992   Annegret Habel

Contents

General Introduction 1

Chapter I   Introduction to Hyperedge-Replacement Grammars 5
     1   Hyperedges and Hypergraphs 6
     2   Replacement of Hyperedges by Hypergraphs 13
     3   Hyperedge-Replacement Grammars 17
     4   Modifications of HRG's 24
     5   Related Concepts 31
     6   Bibliographic Note 42

Chapter II   Basic Properties of HRG's 43
     1   Parallel Derivations 43
     2   A Context-Freeness Lemma 45
     3   Derivation Trees 51
     4   Bibliographic Note 53

Chapter III   Characterizations of HRL's 55
     1   Closure Properties 56
     2   A Kleene-Type Characterization 63
     3   A Fixed-Point Theorem 67
     4   Bibliographic Note 69

Chapter IV   Structural Aspects of HRL's 71
     1   Simplifications of HRG's 71
     2   A Pumping Lemma for HRL's 78
     3   Applications of the Pumping Lemma 87
     4   Parikh's Theorem for HRL's 94
     5   Bibliographic Note 96

Chapter V Generative Power of HRG's 97
    1   Graph-Generating Grammars of Small Order 97
    2   The Graph-Generating Power of HRG's 101
    3   String-Graph-Generating Grammars of Small Order 107
    4   The String-Graph-Generating Power of HRG's 110
    5   Bibliographic Note 116

Chapter VI Graph-Theoretic Aspects of HRL's 117
    1   Some Compatible Graph-Theoretic Properties 118
    2   A General View of Compatible Predicates 128
    3   Efficient Analysis of Graph Properties 133
    4   A Metatheorem for Graph-Theoretic Decision Problems 136
    5   A Filter Theorem for HRL's 139
    6   Non-Compatible Graph-Theoretic Properties 141
    7   Unsolvable Graph-Theoretic Decision Problems 142
    8   Related Research 143
    9   Bibliographic Note 144

Chapter VII Boundedness Aspects for HRL's 145
    1   Some Compatible Graph-Theoretic Functions 145
    2   A General View of Compatible Functions 156
    3   A Metatheorem for Boundedness Problems 161
    4   Unsolvable Boundedness Problems 167
    5   Related Research 167
    6   Bibliographic Note 168

Chapter VIII Extensions and Variations of HRG's 169
    1   Hypergraph-Replacement Grammars 170
    2   Hypergraph-Replacement Grammars with Application Conditions .. 178
    3   Parallel Hyperedge-Replacement Grammars 182
    4   Figure-Generating Grammars Based on Hyperedge Replacement ... 183
    5   Bibliographic Note 192

Conclusion 193

Bibliography 195

List of Symbols 207

Index 209

General Introduction

Graph grammars and graph languages have been studied since the late sixties and have been motivated by various application areas such as pattern recognition, semantics of programming languages, compiler description, data base systems, specification of data types, developmental biology, etc. (see [CER 79, ENR 83, ENRR 87, EKR 91] for a survey). The general approaches (see, e.g., [Eh 79, Na 79a]) cover lots of potential applications; the more specific approaches (for the special case of node rewriting, see, e.g., Janssens and Rozenberg [JR 80a+b, Ja 83] and, for the case of edge replacement, see the approach in [Kr 77a+79, HK 83+87a]) promise a rich mathematical theory.

In this book, we propose a kind of compromise by introducing hyperedge-replacement grammars reviving some ideas from the early seventies which can be found in Feder's [Fe 71] and Pavlidis' [Pa 72] work. On the one hand, Petri nets, functional expressions, program flow diagrams, molecule structures, and many other complex information structures can be interpreted in a natural way as hypergraphs (the hyperedges of which may have many "tentacles" attached to source and target nodes rather than only two "arms" like the edges of ordinary graphs). On the other hand, the replacement of hyperedges provides a type of context-free rewriting on the level of hypergraphs saving many of the fundamental properties of context-free rewriting on strings and ordinary graphs. Hence, we can be confident that this framework combines the theoretical attractivity of a class of context-free grammars and languages with the prospect for nice applications.

In chapter I, hyperedge-replacement grammars are introduced. They provide a simple mechanism for deriving hypergraphs from hypergraphs by applying productions. In our opinion, hyperedge replacement provides a framework for an attractive hypergraph language theory. Nevertheless, the generative power is large enough to cover hypergraph languages which are interesting from a practical point of view, too.

In chapter II, basic properties of hyperedge-replacement grammars are considered. In particular, it turns out that hyperedge replacement works fully locally without any effect on the context of the hyperedges replaced. Every derivation of a hypergraph H is completely described by corresponding derivations of the hyperedges of H (or, more generally, of an hyperedge-disjoint covering of H).

Some characterizations of hyperedge-replacement languages may illustrate the character of hyperedge replacement. First, Gruska's Kleene-type characterization of context-free string languages in [Gr 71] can be carried over to hyperedge-replacement grammars. Secondly, the hypergraph languages generated by hyperedge-replacement grammars turn out to be the smallest fixed points of their generating productions (when they are considered as systems of language equations). Therefore, the construction of smallest fixed points provides an alternative method of generating hypergraph languages. This generalizes Ginsburg's and Rice's well-known Fixed-Point Theorem for context-free string languages in [GR 62]. These results, discussed in chapter III, are evidence that hyperedge-replacement grammars represent a hypergraph-grammar version of context-freeness.

In chapter IV, structural aspects of hyperedge-replacement languages are investigated. In particular, a Pumping Lemma is stated, which generalizes those Pumping Lemmata known for context-free string and graph languages. Roughly speaking, the lemma says that each sufficiently large hypergraph in a hyperedge-replacement language decomposes into $FIRST \otimes LINK \otimes LAST$ such that $FIRST \otimes LINK^i \otimes LAST$, for $i \geq 0$, belongs to the given language. The crucial part is finding the proper composition $\otimes$ for hypergraphs. The Pumping Lemma can be used to derive several boundedness properties of hyperedge-replacement languages (for example, the boundedness of the connectivity).

In chapter V, the generative power of hyperedge-replacement grammars is studied. On the one hand, it can be shown that many (hyper)graph languages interesting from the point of view of graph theory (for example, series-parallel graphs, outerplanar graphs, partial k-trees, graphs with bandwidth $\leq k$, graphs with cyclic bandwidth $\leq k$, etc.) can be generated by hyperedge-replacement grammars. On the other hand, one may apply the Pumping Lemma (or a derived theorem) to various languages for proving that they cannot be generated by hyperedge-replacement grammars. In particular, it turns out that the generative power of hyperedge-replacement grammars depends strongly on the order (this is the upper bound for the number of "tentacles" a nonterminal hyperedge may have for the attachment to nodes). In other words, the order of hyperedge-replacement grammars induces an infinite hierarchy of classes of hypergraph languages, which remains infinite even if one considers graph or string languages only. The string(-graph) languages include certain non-context-free languages, and the string(-graph) languages of order 2 are just those which can be generated by context-free string grammars.

In chapter VI, some specific graph-theoretic aspects of hyperedge-replacement languages are discussed. Actually, graph-theoretic properties which are "compatible" with the derivation process of hyperedge-replacement grammars are investigated. For example, connectivity, the existence of Eulerian paths and cycles, edge-colorability, and many other properties can be shown to be of this type. If P is such a compatible property, then for all hyperedge-replacement grammars, the following questions turn out to be decidable.

(1) Is there a hypergraph in the generated language satisfying the property P?

(2) Do all hypergraphs in the generated language satisfy the property P?

We refer to this result as a metatheorem because each instantiation of the property yields a particular decision result.

More generally, in chapter VII, "compatible" functions (like the number of nodes and hyperedges, the degree, the number of simple paths, the maximum length of simple paths, the size of a maximum set of independent nodes, etc.) are introduced and a further type of decidability problems, called Boundedness Problems, concerning functions on hypergraphs is investigated. This is as follows:

(3) Are the values of all hypergraphs in the generated language bounded?

It is shown that such a Boundedness Problem is decidable for a class of hyperedge-replacement grammars if the corresponding quantity function is built up by maxima, sums and products and if the function is compatible with the derivation process of the given grammars.

Finally, in chapter VIII, we discuss extensions of hyperedge-replacement grammars to hypergraph-replacement grammars (with application conditions), to parallel hyperedge-replacement grammars, as well as a variation to so-called "figure grammars".

Chapter I
Introduction to Hyperedge-Replacement Grammars

In many fields of computer science it is suitable to represent information by some kind of diagrams rather than by text; in such cases, information processing concerns the manipulation of high-dimensional structures (like graphs and hypergraphs) rather than linear structures (strings). This is the general motivation for developing a graph-grammar and graph-language theory as a counterpart to formal (string-)language theory. Therefore, the research on graph grammars ranges from various applications in pattern recognition, data base systems, semantics of programming languages etc. to the boundary between graph grammars and string grammars (see [CER 79, ENR 83, ENRR 87, EKR 91] for an overview).

It would be easy to introduce a complicated mechanism of graph rewriting so that the general framework becomes nearly unfeasible, but the theoretical achievements are rare and poor, and the best you can achieve are lots of undecidability results. To do somewhat better, many researchers have been looking for simpler special cases of graph rewriting — choosing the atomic items of a graph as key. A majority has proposed various kinds of node replacements (see, e.g., Pratt [Pr 71], Della Vigna and Ghezzi [DG 78], Franck [Fr 78], Janssens and Rozenberg [JR 80a+b, JR 81, Ja 83], Kaul [Ka 83+86], Kreowski and Rozenberg [KR 84], Lichtblau [Li 85+90]), where, in particular, Janssens' and Rozenberg's NLC-approach is most successful (see, e.g., Brandenburg [Ba 83], Turán [Tu 83], Rozenberg and Welzl [RW 86a+b], Engelfriet, Leih, and Rozenberg [EL 88+89+90, ELR 88+91]). A minority has been attracted by the (hyper)edges, the alternative atomic items, and proposed (hyper)edge replacement as a simple way of deriving (hyper)graphs from (hyper)graphs (see, e.g., Feder [Fe 71], Pavlidis [Pa 72], Kreowski, Habel, and Vogler [Kr 77a+79, HK 83+87a+b+c, HKV 89+91], Bauderon and Courcelle [BC 87, Co 90a+b+c], Montanari and Rossi [MR 87], Lengauer and Wanke [LW 88], Lautemann [La 88a+b+90+91], Engelfriet and Heyker [EH 91a+b], Courcelle, Engelfriet, and Rozenberg [CER 91]).

In this chapter, we will give a systematic introduction into hyperedge-replacement grammars reviving some of the ideas from the early seventies, for example those of Feder [Fe 71] and Pavlidis [Pa 72], and relate them to the concepts in the literature. In section 1, hypergraphs are introduced as a generalization of ordinary graphs. Their basic units are hyperedges, i.e. objects, which may have many "tentacles" attached to source and target nodes rather than only two "arms" like the edges of ordinary graphs. Several high-dimensional structures like Petri nets, functional expressions, program flow diagrams, molecule structures, and many other complex information structures can be represented in a natural way by this kind of hypergraphs. The key construction in this book is the replacement of hyperedges of a hypergraph by hypergraphs. A formal definition of hyperedge replacement is given in section 2. Based on this construction, in section 3, so called hyperedge-replacement grammars and languages are introduced. Several examples may illustrate this kind of grammars. These grammars provide a type of context-free rewriting on the level of hypergraphs saving many of the fundamental properties of context-free rewriting on strings and ordinary graphs. Section 4 is concerned with some modifications of hyperedge-replacement grammars (HRG's), which allow us to compare this type of grammars with those in the literature. Finally, in section 5, hyperedge-replacement grammars are related to other graph-grammar formalisms.

1. Hyperedges and Hypergraphs

This section provides the basic notions concerning hyperedges and hypergraphs. In the proposed approach, a hyperedge is an atomic item with an ordered set of incoming tentacles and an ordered set of outgoing tentacles. Incoming tentacles are attached to nodes through a source function. Outgoing tentacles are attached to nodes through a target function.

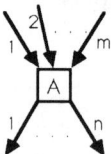

Hyperedges are frequently used in computer science, for instance, as:
1. Functional symbol with arity m and coarity n

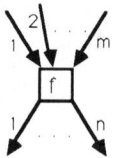

2. Event or transition of a Petri net (with an arbitrary order on the tentacles)

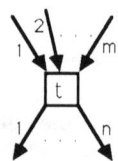

3. Control unit in a flow diagram like statement and decision (with one entry and one exit or two exits, respectively)

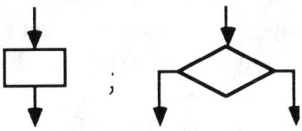

4. Atomic chemical unit like hydrogen, oxygen, and carbon (where the order of the solely incoming tentacles is clockwise and the names of the atoms are the labels)

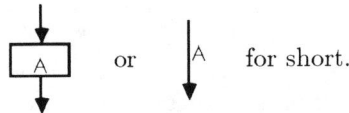

5. Ordinary directed edge (with one incoming and one outgoing tentacle)

$$\boxed{A} \quad \text{or} \quad \downarrow^A \quad \text{for short.}$$

A set of nodes together with a collection of such hyperedges (usually with varying numbers of tentacles) forms a hypergraph if each tentacle is connected with a node.

1.1 Definition (Hypergraphs)

1. Let C be an arbitrary, but fixed set, called set of *labels* (or *colors*). A (directed, hyperedge-labeled) *hypergraph* over C is a system (V, E, s, t, l) where V is a finite set of *nodes* (or *vertices*), E is a finite set of *hyperedges*, $s : E \to V^*$ and $t : E \to V^*$ [1]) are two mappings assigning a sequence of *sources* $s(e)$ and a sequence of *targets* $t(e)$ to each $e \in E$, and $l : E \to C$ is a mapping *labeling* each hyperedge.

2. For $e \in E$, the set of nodes occurring in the sequence $att(e) = s(e) \cdot t(e)$ is called the set of *attachment nodes* of e and is denoted by $ATT(e)$.

3. A hyperedge $e \in E$ is called an (m,n)-*edge* for some $m, n \in \mathbb{N}$ if $|s(e)| = m$ and $|t(e)| = n$ [2]). The pair (m,n) is the *type* of e, denoted by $type(e)$. The set $\{(i,j) \in [m+n]^2 | att_H(e)_i = att_H(e)_j\}$ [3]) is the *relation* of e, denoted by $rel(e)$. In particular, $rel(e) = \emptyset$ if $type(e) = (0,0)$.

---

[1]) For a set A, A^* denotes the set of all strings over A, including the empty string λ; $A^+ = A^* - \{\lambda\}$ denotes the set of all strings over A, except the empty string λ.

[2]) For $w \in A^*$, $|w|$ denotes the *length* of w. For $i \in [1, |w|]$, w_i denotes the i-th symbol in w.

[3]) For $k \in \mathbb{N}$, $[k]$ denotes the set $\{1, \ldots, k\}$ and $[k]^2$ the cartesian product $[k] \times [k]$.

Remark

1. Usually, a directed hyperedge may possess a number of source and target nodes. Instead of the proposed approach — assigning a sequence of source nodes and a sequence of target nodes to each hyperedge —, one may proceed by assigning a set of source nodes and a set of target nodes to each hyperedge (see, e.g., Berge [Be 73]). The consideration of sequences of nodes — instead of sets of nodes — makes it possible to handle a large number of practically relevant examples (e.g., functional expressions, flow diagrams, etc.) in which the order of the tentacles has to be considered.

2. There are no restrictions with respect to the "form" of hyperedges: distinct tentacles of a hyperedge may be attached to the same node. Moreover, there are no restrictions with respect to the labeling of hyperedges; in particular, hyperedges of distinct type may have the same label.

3. In drawings of hypergraphs, a dot (•) represents a node, and a graphical structure of the form

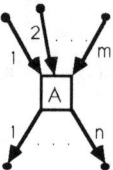

depicts a hyperedge with sources and targets where the label is inscribed in the box, the i-th arrow incoming into the box starts at the i-th source ($i = 1, \ldots, m$) and the j-th arrow outgoing from the box reaches the j-th target ($j = 1, \ldots, n$). In other words, the graphical representation makes use of the one-to-one correspondence between hypergraphs and bipartite graphs.

4. Instead of directed, hyperedge-labeled hypergraphs, we may consider directed hypergraphs in which the nodes as well as the hyperedges are labeled: A *directed, labeled hypergraph* over C is a system (V, E, s, t, l, m) where (V, E, s, t, l) is a directed, hyperedge-labeled hypergraph over C and $m : V \to C$ is a mapping *labeling* each node.

1.2 Example

1. Hypergraphs built up from functional symbols represent functional expressions like

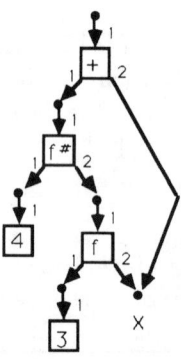

Fig. 1.1. Representation of the functional expression $f^\#(4, f(3, x)) + x$

2. A Petri net is usually represented as a directed bipartite graph. If the transitions (depicted by □) together with their incoming and outgoing edges (ordered arbitrarily) are interpreted as hyperedges, Petri nets, i.e., directed bipartite graphs, turn out to be hypergraphs.

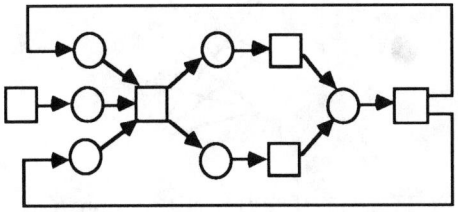

Fig. 1.2. A Petri net

3. Putting control units together in the usual way, one gets flow diagrams as hypergraphs.

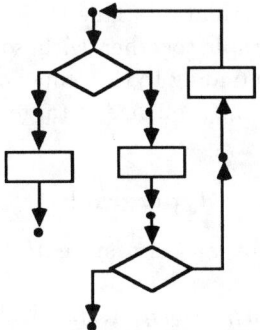

Fig. 1.3. Representation of a flow diagram

4. A chemical molecule like natural rubber is a hypergraph if each connection between two atoms is interpreted as a node with two incident tentacles.

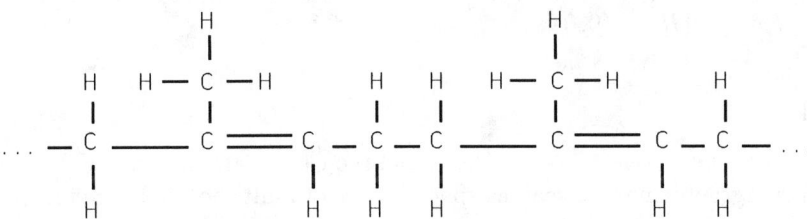

Fig. 1.4. Representation of a chemical molecule

5. An undirected graph like the complete bipartite graph $K_{3,4}$ is a hypergraph if each undirected edge abbreviates two directed (1,1)-edges in opposite directions with a special invisible label.

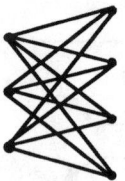

Fig. 1.5. The bipartite graph $K_{3,4}$

Hyperedges do not only play a static part as building blocks of hypergraphs, but also a more dynamic part as place holders for hypergraphs. However, before a hypergraph can take the place of a hyperedge, it needs some preparation. While a hyperedge is attached to its source and target nodes according to the conventions, a hypergraph must be equipped with such information. This leads to the concept of a multi-pointed hypergraph which is a hypergraph together with some "external" nodes given by a sequence of begin nodes (corresponding to the sequence of source nodes) and a sequence of end nodes (corresponding to the sequence of target nodes).

1.3 Definition (Multi-Pointed Hypergraphs)

1. A *multi-pointed hypergraph* over C is a system $H = (V, E, s, t, l, begin, end)$ where (V, E, s, t, l) is a hypergraph over C and $begin, end \in V^*$. Components of H are denoted by V_H, E_H, s_H, t_H, l_H, $begin_H$, end_H, respectively. The set of all multi-pointed hypergraphs over C is denoted by $\mathcal{H}_C$.
2. For $H \in \mathcal{H}_C$, the set of nodes occurring in the sequence $ext_H = begin_H \cdot end_H$ is called the set of *external nodes* of H and is denoted by EXT_H. The set of all other nodes is said to be the set of *internal nodes* and is denoted by INT_H.
3. $H \in \mathcal{H}_C$ is said to be an (m,n)-*hypergraph* for some $m, n \in \mathbb{N}$ if $|begin_H| = m$ and $|end_H| = n$. The pair (m,n) is the *type* of H, denoted by $type(H)$. The set $\{(i,j) \in [m+n]^2 | ext_{H,i} = ext_{H,j}\}$ is the *relation* of H, denoted by $rel(H)$. In particular, $rel(H) = \emptyset$ if $type(H) = (0,0)$.

Remark

1. There is a one-to-one correspondence between hypergraphs and (0,0)-hypergraphs so that hypergraphs may be seen as special cases of multi-pointed hypergraphs. Somewhat ambiguously, we speak about hypergraphs instead of multi-pointed hypergraphs provided that the pointedness of the nodes is of a secondary importance.
2. There are no restrictions with respect to the distinguished nodes, i.e. the *begin* and *end* nodes of a multi-pointed hypergraph H; in particular, the sequence $ext_H = begin_H \cdot end_H$ may have repetitions.

1.4 Example

The *begin*-component of a functional expression indicates its arity, the *end*-component its coarity. The *begin*-component of a flow diagram indicates its entries, the *end*-component its exits.

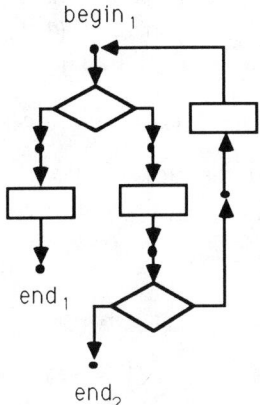

Fig. 1.6. Representation a flow diagram with one entry and two exits

1.5 Definition (Singletons, Handles, and Frames)

1. $H \in \mathcal{H}_C$ is said to be a *singleton* if $V_H = EXT_H$ and $|E_H| = 1$ [4]. In this case, $e(H)$ refers to the single hyperedge of H and $l(H)$ to its label.
2. A singleton H with $E_H = \{e\}$, $s_H(e) = begin_H$, and $t_H(e) = end_H$ is said to be a *handle*. If $l_H(e) = A$, $type(e) = (m,n)$ for some $m,n \in \mathbb{N}$, and the nodes in $ext_H = begin_H \cdot end_H$ are pairwise distinct, then H is said to be an (m,n)-*handle* induced by A and is denoted by $(A,(m,n))^\bullet$ or $A(m,n)^\bullet$.
3. $H \in \mathcal{H}_C$ is said to be a *frame* if $V_H = EXT_H$ and $E_H = \emptyset$.

Remark

1. Given $H \in \mathcal{H}_C$, each hyperedge $e \in E_H$ induces a handle $e^\bullet$ by restricting the mappings s_H, t_H, and l_H to the set $\{e\}$, restricting the set of nodes to those occurring in $s_H(e)$ and $t_H(e)$, and choosing $begin_{e^\bullet} = s_H(e)$ and $end_{e^\bullet} = t_H(e)$.
2. For each $H \in \mathcal{H}_C$, $frame(H) = (EXT_H, \emptyset, s, t, l, begin_H, end_H)$ with the empty mappings s, t, and l is a frame.

---

[4] For a finite set A, $|A|$ denotes the number of elements in A.

Graphs and strings may be considered as special cases of (multi-pointed) hypergraphs.

1.6 Definition (Graphs and String Graphs)

1. An (m,n)-hypergraph H over C is said to be an (m,n)-*graph* if $|V_H| \geq 1$ and all hyperedges of H are $(1,1)$-edges. The set of all $(1,1)$-graphs over C is denoted by $\mathcal{G}_C$.
2. A $(1,1)$-hypergraph H over C is called a *string graph* if it is of the form

$$H = (\{v_0, v_1, \ldots, v_n\}, \{e_1, \ldots, e_n\}, s, t, l, v_0, v_n)$$

where $v_0, v_1, \ldots, v_n$ are pairwise distinct, $s(e_i) = v_{i-1}$, and $t(e_i) = v_i$ for $i = 1, \ldots, n$. If $w = l(e_1)\ldots l(e_n)$, then the $(1,1)$-hypergraph is called the *string graph* induced by w and is denoted by $w^\bullet$.

Remark

1. Graphs are drawn as usual, i.e., an ordinary $(1,1)$-edge is drawn as

$$\xrightarrow{A} \quad \text{instead of} \quad \xrightarrow{1}\boxed{A}\xrightarrow{1}.$$

2. A string graph of the form

$$\bullet \xrightarrow{a_1} \bullet \xrightarrow{a_2} \bullet \xrightarrow{a_3} \cdots \xrightarrow{a_n} \bullet$$

provides a unique graph representation of the string $a_1 a_2 a_3 \ldots a_n \in C^+$.

1.7 Definition (Subhypergraphs, Morphisms, and Isomorphic Hypergraphs)

1. Let $H, H' \in \mathcal{H}_C$. Then H is called a *subhypergraph* of H', denoted by $H \subseteq H'$, if $V_H \subseteq V_{H'}$, $E_H \subseteq E_{H'}$, and $s_H(e) = s_{H'}(e)$, $t_H(e) = t_{H'}(e)$, $l_H(e) = l_{H'}(e)$ for all $e \in E_H$. Note that nothing is assumed about the relation of the distinguished nodes.
2. Let $H, H' \in \mathcal{H}_C$. A *hypergraph morphism* h from H to H', denoted by $h : H \to H'$, consists of a pair of mappings $h = (h_V : V_H \to V_{H'}, h_E : E_H \to E_{H'})$ satisfying the conditions $h_V^*(s_H(e)) = s_{H'}(h_E(e))$, $h_V^*(t_H(e)) = t_{H'}(h_E(e))$ [5], and $l_H(e) = l_{H'}(h_E(e))$ for all $e \in E_H$.
3. A hypergraph morphism $h : H \to H'$ is said to be an *isomorphism* from H to H' if $h_V : V_H \to V_{H'}$ and $h_E : E_H \to E_{H'}$ are bijective mappings, $h_V^*(begin_H) = begin_{H'}$, and $h_V^*(end_H) = end_{H'}$. If there is an isomorphism from H to H', H and H' are *isomorphic*, denoted by $H \cong H'$. The class of all hypergraphs isomorphic to a hypergraph H is denoted by $[H]$.

---

[5] For a mapping $f : A \to B$, the free symbolwise extension $f^* : A^* \to B^*$ is defined by $f^*(a_1 \ldots a_k) = f(a_1) \ldots f(a_k)$ for all $k \in \mathbb{N}$ and $a_i \in A$ ($i = 1, \ldots, k$).

Hypergraphs in the sense of definitions 1.1 and 1.3 are sometimes called *concrete*. In general, the specific sets of nodes and hyperedges chosen to define a hypergraph precisely are irrelevant. Therefore, we shall not distinguish between isomorphic hypergraphs.

1.8 Definition (Hypergraph Languages)

1. A set $L \subseteq \mathcal{H}_C$ of multi-pointed hypergraphs is called a *hypergraph language* over C if it is *closed under isomorphisms*, i.e., if $H \in L$ and $H \cong H'$, then $H' \in L$. In particular, $L \subseteq \mathcal{H}_C$ is said to be *finite* if the number of non-isomorphic hypergraphs in L is finite.
2. $L \subseteq \mathcal{H}_C$ is said to be *homogeneous* if $type(H) = type(H')$ and $rel(H) = rel(H')$ for all $H, H' \in L$. In this case, $type(L)$ and $rel(L)$ denote the type and the relation of the hypergraphs in L, respectively.

2. Replacement of Hyperedges by Hypergraphs

The key construction in this book is the replacement of some hyperedges of a hypergraph by hypergraphs yielding an expanded hypergraph. Given multi-pointed hypergraphs H and R, a hyperedge e in H may be replaced by R, whenever e and R "fit together", i.e., whenever e and R are of the same type and, whenever the i-th and the j-th external node of R are the same, then the i-th and the j-th attachment node are the same, too. The replacement may be done in two steps:

(1) Remove the hyperedge.
(2) Add the hypergraph except the external nodes and hand over each tentacle of a hyperedge (of the replacing hypergraph) which is attached to an external node to the corresponding source or target node of the replaced hyperedge.

The construction is rather simple as the following sketch shows.

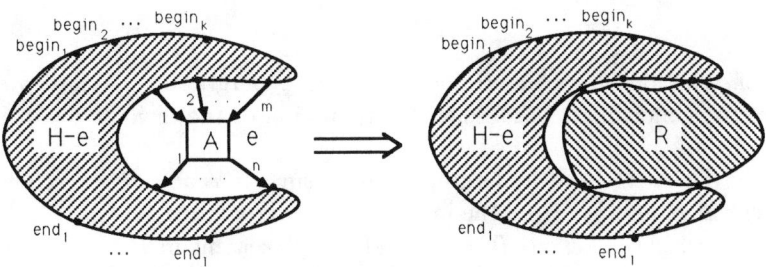

Fig. 2.1. Replacement of a hyperedge

As a natural generalization, an arbitrary number of hyperedges may be replaced simultaneously.

2.1 Definition (Hyperedge Replacement)

1. Let $H \in \mathcal{H}_C$ be a multi-pointed hypergraph and $B \subseteq E_H$ be a set of hyperedges to be replaced. A mapping $repl : B \to \mathcal{H}_C$ is said to be a *base for replacement* if for all $b \in B$, $type(repl(b)) = type(b)$ and $rel(repl(b)) \subseteq rel(b)$.

2. Let $H \in \mathcal{H}_C$, $B \subseteq E_H$, and $repl : B \to \mathcal{H}_C$ be a base for replacement. Then the *replacement* of B in H by $repl$ yields a multi-pointed hypergraph X given by

- $V_X = V_H + \sum_{b \in B}(V_{repl(b)} - EXT_{repl(b)})$ [1],
- $E_X = (E_H - B) + \sum_{b \in B} E_{repl(b)}$,
- each hyperedge keeps its label,
- each hyperedge of $E_H - B$ keeps its sources and targets,
- each hyperedge of $E_{repl(b)}$ (for all $b \in B$) keeps its internal sources and targets and the external ones are handed over to the corresponding sources and targets of H, i.e.,

$$\left. \begin{array}{l} s_X(e) = handover^*(s_{repl(b)}(e)) \\ t_X(e) = handover^*(t_{repl(b)}(e)) \end{array} \right\} \text{ for all } b \in B \text{ and } e \in E_{repl(b)}$$

where $handover : V_{repl(b)} \to V_X$ is defined by
$handover(v) = v$ for $v \in V_{repl(b)} - EXT_{repl(b)}$,
$handover(x_i) = s_i$ $(i = 1, \ldots, m)$ for $begin_{repl(b)} = x_1 \ldots x_m$ and $s_H(b) = s_1 \ldots s_m$,
$handover(y_j) = t_j$ $(j = 1, \ldots, n)$ for $end_{repl(b)} = y_1 \ldots y_n$ and $t_H(b) = t_1 \ldots t_n$,

- $begin_X = begin_H$ and $end_X = end_H$.

3. The multi-pointed hypergraph X is denoted by $REPLACE(H, repl)$. If $B = \{e_1, \ldots, e_n\}$ and $repl(e_i) = R_i$ for $i = 1, \ldots, n$, then we also write $H[e_1/R_1, \ldots, e_n/R_n]$ instead of $REPLACE(H, repl)$.

Remark

1. The construction above determines a unique hypergraph X. More precisely, X is unique up to isomorphism because the construction of the disjoint union is unique up to isomorphism.

2. Let $h : H \to H'$ be a hypergraph morphism. If $repl : B \to \mathcal{H}_C$ is a base for replacement in H and $h_E(B)$ is the image of B under h, then $repl' : h_E(B) \to \mathcal{H}_C$ with $repl'(h_E(e)) = repl(e)$ for $e \in B$ is a base for replacement in H'. Vice versa, if $repl' : B' \to \mathcal{H}_C$ is a base for replacement in H' and for each $e \in B'$, the sequence $ext_{repl(e)}$ does not contain repetitions, then $repl : h_E^{-1}(B') \to \mathcal{H}_C$ with $repl(e) = repl(h_E(e))$ for $e \in h_E^{-1}(B')$ is a base for replacement in H.

---

[1] The sum symbols "+" and "$\sum$" denote the disjoint union of sets; the symbol "−" denotes the set-theoretical difference.

2.2 Example

1. The replacement of the (1,2)-edge e in the hypergraph H by the (1,2)-hypergraph R yields the hypergraph X (see Fig. 2.2 and 2.3).

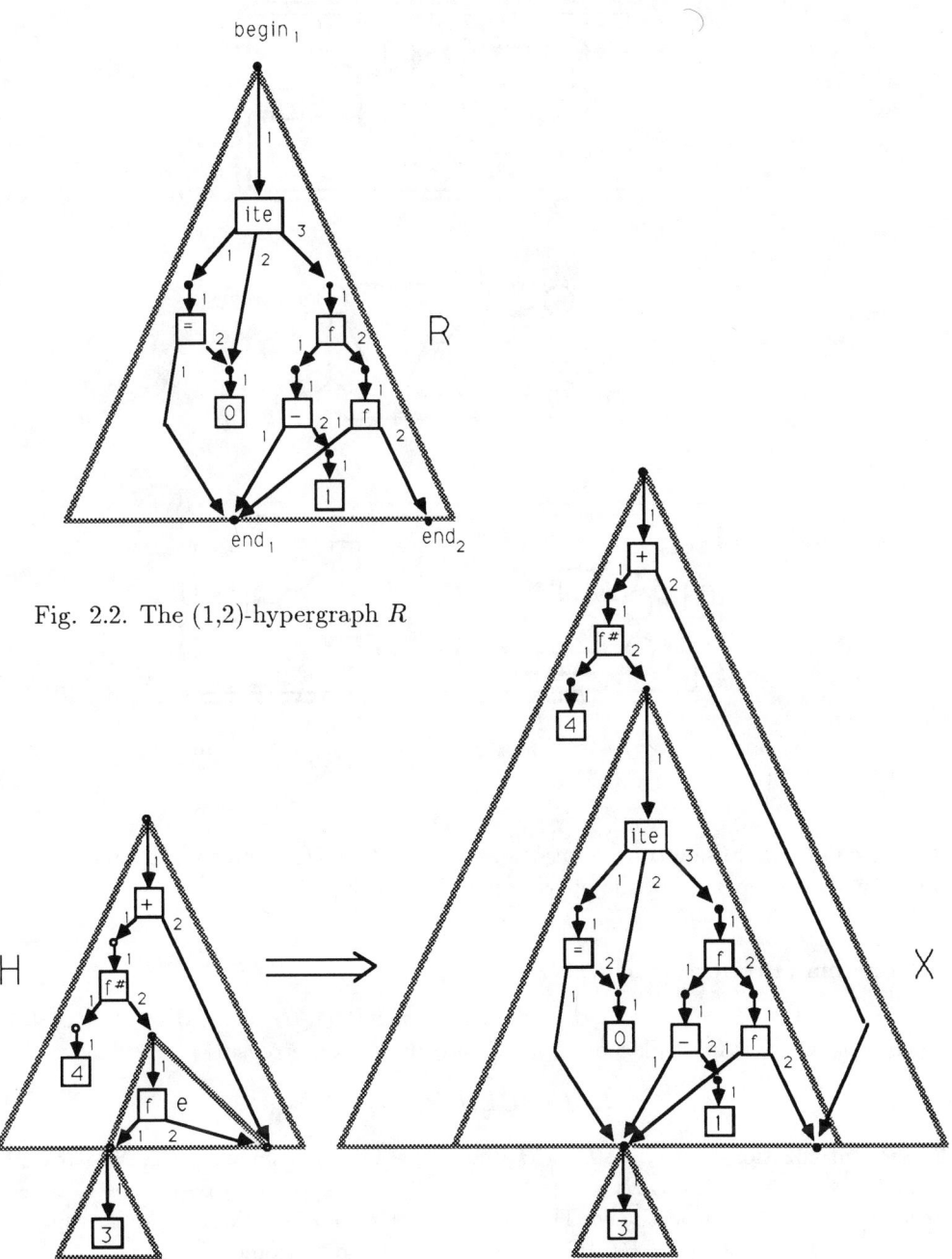

Fig. 2.2. The (1,2)-hypergraph R

Fig. 2.3. Replacement of the (1,2)-edge e in H by R

2. Net refinements in the sense of Valette [Va 79] and Suzuki and Murata [SM 80] are hyperedge replacements. For instance, the replacement of the transition t in the net N by the net R yields the net N' (see Fig 2.4).

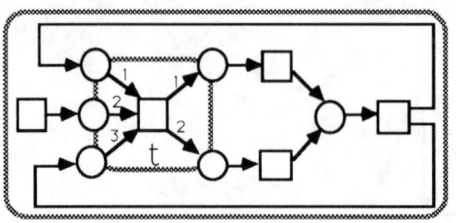

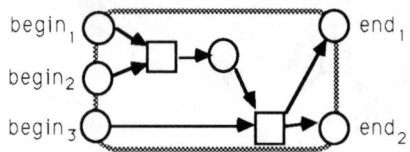

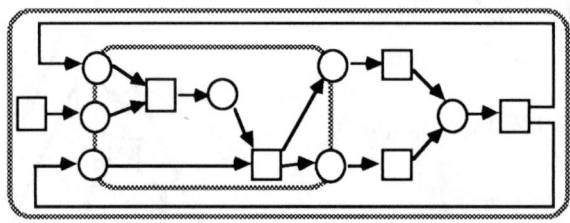

Fig. 2.4. Nets N, R, and N'

The core of the following considerations is the $REPLACE$ operation. Therefore, let us mention some properties of the operation $REPLACE$.

2.3 Lemma (Properties of $REPLACE$)

1. Identity. Let $H \in \mathcal{H}_C$, $B \subseteq E_H$, and let $repl : B \to \mathcal{H}_C$ defined by $repl(e) = e^\bullet$. Then $repl$ is a base for replacement in H and (up to isomorphism)

$$REPLACE(H, repl) = H.$$

2. Sequentialization. Let $repl : B \to \mathcal{H}_C$ be a base for replacement in H. Moreover, let $B_1, B_2 \subseteq B$ such that $B_1 \cup B_2 = B$, $B_1 \cap B_2 = \emptyset$, and $repl_1, repl_2$ be the restrictions of $repl$ to B_1 and B_2, respectively. Then $repl_1$ is a base for replacement in H, $repl_2$ is a base for replacement in $REPLACE(H, repl_1)$, and (up to isomorphism)

$$REPLACE(H, repl) = REPLACE(REPLACE(H, repl_1), repl_2).$$

3. Parallelization. Let $repl_1 : B_1 \to \mathcal{H}_C$ be a base for replacement in H and $repl_2 : B_2 \to \mathcal{H}_C$ be a base for replacement in $REPLACE(H, repl_1)$ with $B_2 \subseteq E_H - B_1$. Then $repl : B_1 \cup B_2 \to \mathcal{H}_C$ given by $repl(e) = repl_i(e)$ for $e \in B_i$ ($i = 1, 2$) is a base for replacement in H and (up to isomorphism)

$$REPLACE(REPLACE(H, repl_1), repl_2) = REPLACE(H, repl).$$

4. Confluence. Let $repl_1 : B_1 \to \mathcal{H}_C$, $repl_2 : B_2 \to \mathcal{H}_C$ be bases for replacement in H and $B_1 \cap B_2 = \emptyset$. Then $repl_2$ is a base for replacement in $REPLACE(H, repl_1)$, $repl_1$ is a base for replacement in $REPLACE(H, repl_2)$, and (up to isomorphism)

$$REPLACE(REPLACE(H, repl_1, repl_2)$$
$$= REPLACE(REPLACE(H, repl_2), repl_1).$$

5. Associativity. Let $repl_1 : B_1 \to \mathcal{H}_C$ be a base for replacement in H, $repl_2 : B_2 \to \mathcal{H}_C$ be a base for replacement in $REPLACE(H, repl_1)$ with $B_2 \cap (E_H - B_1) = \emptyset$, and for $e \in B_1$, $repl_{2,e} : B_{2,e} \to \mathcal{H}_C$ be the restriction of $repl_2$ to the set $B_{2,e} = B_2 \cap E_{repl_1(e)}$. Moreover, let $repl : B_1 \to \mathcal{H}_C$ defined by $repl(e) = REPLACE(repl_1(e), repl_{2,e})$ be a base for replacement in H. Then (up to isomorphism)

$$REPLACE(REPLACE(H, repl_1), repl_2) = REPLACE(H, repl).$$

Proof

Lemma 2.3 immediately follows from Definition 2.1. $\square$

3. Hyperedge-Replacement Grammars

In this section, we introduce hyperedge-replacement grammars generalizing context-free graph grammars as described in [Kr 77a+79] and context-free string grammars. They can be seen as hypergraph-manipulating and hypergraph-language generating devices and turn out to be closely related to other concepts in computer science (see section 5).

Based on hyperedge replacement, one can derive multi-pointed hypergraphs from multi-pointed hypergraphs by applying productions of a simple form.

3.1 Definition (Productions and Derivations)

1. Let $N \subseteq C$ be a set of *nonterminals*. A *production* over N is an ordered pair $p = (A, R)$ with $A \in N$ and $R \in \mathcal{H}_C$. A is called the *left-hand side* of p and is denoted by $lhs(p)$, R is called the *right-hand side* and is denoted by $rhs(p)$.
2. Let $H, H' \in \mathcal{H}_C$, $p = (A, R)$ be a production, and $e \in E_H$ a hyperedge such that $l_H(e) = A$ and $repl : \{e\} \to \mathcal{H}_C$ given by $repl(e) = R$ is a base for replacement. Then H *directly derives* H' by p (applied to e) if H' is isomorphic to $H[e/R]$. We write $H \underset{p,e}{\Longrightarrow} H'$, $H \underset{p}{\Longrightarrow} H'$, or $H \underset{P}{\Longrightarrow} H'$ provided that $p \in P$.

3. A sequence of direct derivations $H_0 \underset{p_1,e_1}{\Longrightarrow} \ldots \underset{p_k,e_k}{\Longrightarrow} H_k$ is called a *derivation of length* k from H_0 to H_k. The derivation is shortly denoted by $H_0 \overset{*}{\underset{P}{\Longrightarrow}} H_k$ provided that $p_1, p_2, \ldots, p_k \in P$ or just by $H_0 \overset{*}{\Longrightarrow} H_k$. If the length of the derivation is of interest, we write $H_0 \overset{k}{\underset{P}{\Longrightarrow}} H_k$ or $H_0 \overset{k}{\Longrightarrow} H_k$. Additionally, in the case $H_0 \cong H_0'$, we speak of a *derivation* from H_0 to H_0' *of length 0*.

Using the concepts of productions and derivations, hyperedge-replacement grammars (HRG's) and languages (HRL's) can be introduced in a straightforward way.

3.2 Definition (Hyperedge-Replacement Grammars and Languages)

1. A *hyperedge-replacement grammar* is a system $HRG = (N, T, P, Z)$ where $N \subseteq C$ is a set of *nonterminals*, $T \subseteq C$ is a set of *terminals*, P is a finite set of *productions* over N and $Z \in \mathcal{H}_C$ is the *axiom*.
2. The *hypergraph language* $L(HRG)$ generated by HRG consists of all terminal labeled hypergraphs which can be derived from Z by applying productions of P:

$$L(HRG) = \{ H \in \mathcal{H}_T \mid Z \overset{*}{\underset{P}{\Longrightarrow}} H \}.$$

3. A hypergraph language $L \subseteq \mathcal{H}_C$ is said to be a *hyperedge-replacement language* if there is a hyperedge-replacement grammar HRG with $L(HRG) = L$.
4. Two hyperedge-replacement grammars HRG and HRG' are said to to be *equivalent* if $L(HRG) = L(HRG')$.

Remark

1. Hyperedge-replacement grammars as introduced above are based on the replacement of hyperedges. It turns out that hyperedge replacement works fully locally without any effect on the context of the hyperedges replaced (see chapter II, section 2). To emphasize this aspect, hyperedge-replacement grammars are sometimes called context-free hypergraph grammars (see, e.g., [HK 87c]).
2. Even if one wants to generate graph languages (or string-graph languages) rather than hypergraph languages, one may use nonterminal hyperedges because the generative power of hyperedge-replacement grammars increases with the maximum number of tentacles of a hyperedge involved in the replacement (see chapter V).
3. It is not assumed that N and T are disjoint sets. Hence hyperedges with terminal labels may be rewritten. The terminals only serve as a filtering mechanism to define the generated languages, they do not influence the derivation process at all.
4. The set $L(HRG)$ is closed under isomorphisms. Hence, $L(HRG)$ is a hypergraph language in the sense of definition 1.8. Moreover, $L(HRG)$ is homogeneous. Therefore, non-homogeneous languages cannot be generated by the grammars introduced above.

3.3 Example (Control-Flow Graphs)

Control-flow graphs of "semi-structured" programs, which are used for data flow analysis by Farrow, Kennedy and Zucconi [FKZ 76], can be generated by the hyperedge-replacement grammar specified as follows. Consider the following productions, given in a kind of Backus-Naur Form:

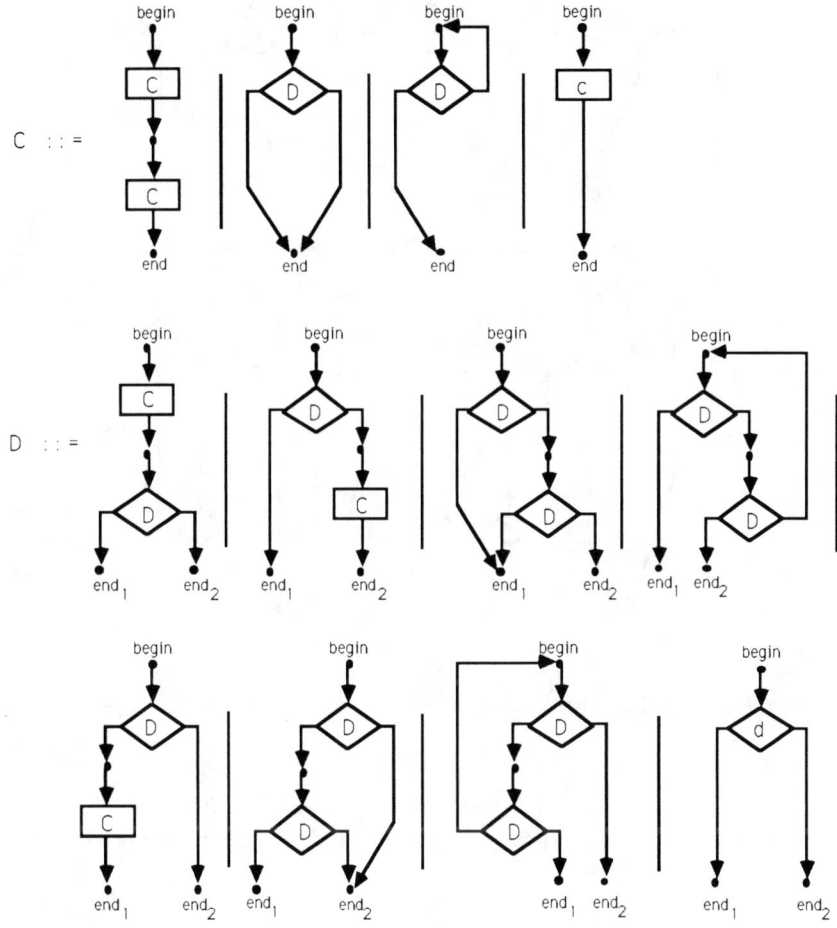

Fig. 3.1. Productions for generating semi-structured control-flow graphs

where the numbering of tentacles is omitted, because it can easily be added. The number of incoming tentacles is always one and the number of outgoing tentacles is one or two. In the latter case, the tentacles may be counted from left to right. C and D are the nonterminal symbols, c and d are the terminal symbols. A (1,1)-handle induced by C is the axiom. The generated hypergraphs are of type (1,1), this means that they possess a uniquely determined *begin*-node and a uniquely determined *end*-node.

An example of a derivation in this grammar, deriving a multi-exit loop, is given in Fig. 3.2.

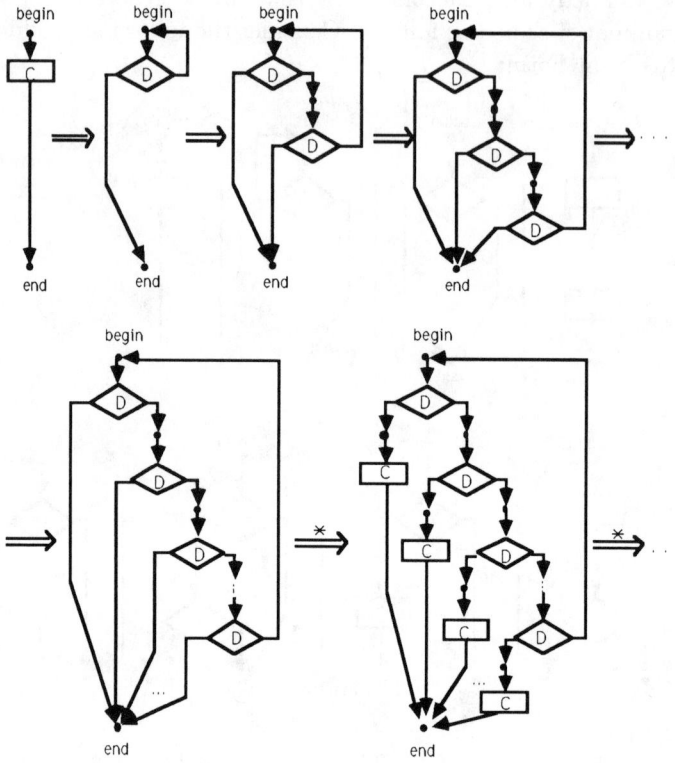

Fig. 3.2. Derivation of a semi-structured control-flow graph

Furthermore, let us mention that the rooted *context-free flow-graph grammars* considered by Lichtblau [Li 90+91] may be interpreted as special hyperedge-replacement grammars.

3.4 Example (Chemical Structures)

The following hyperedge-replacement grammar HRG_{CHEM} generates multi-pointed hypergraphs which describe the chemical structures of the natural rubber molecules. The example stems from Feder [Fe 71], where it is given in terms of so-called plex grammars.

The productions of HRG_{CHEM} are as follows:

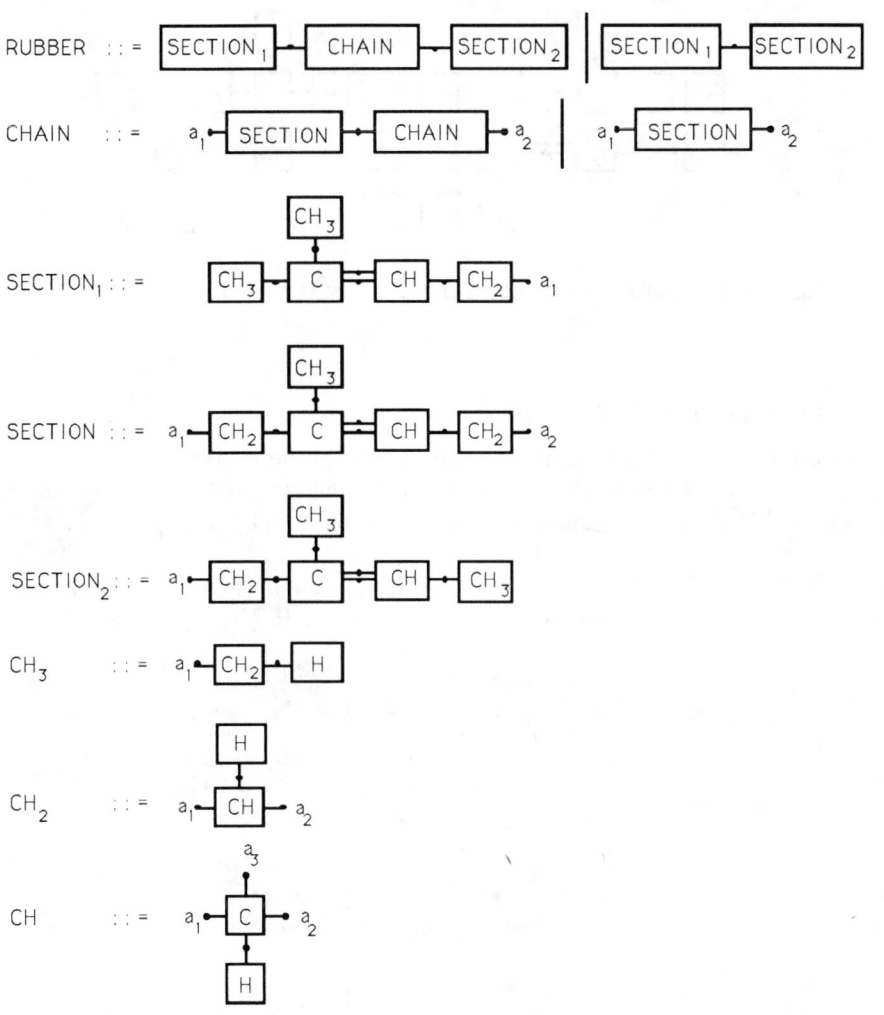

Fig. 3.3. Productions of of the grammar HRG_{CHEM}

The numbering as well as the directions of the arrows are omitted, because they are not significant. The attaching points, i.e. the external nodes, are indicated by a_1, a_2 and a_3, respectively. Each hyperedge with label $CHAIN$ or $SECTION$ possesses two attaching points; hyperedges with label $SECTION_1$ or $SECTION_2$ possess one attaching point; and the hyperedges with label CH_3, CH_2, and CH possess one, two, and three attaching points, respectively. Finally, the hyperedges with label C and H possess four and one attaching point, respectively. $RUBBER$, $CHAIN$, $SECTION$, $SECTION_1$, $SECTION_2$, CH_3, CH_2, and CH are the nonterminal symbols, C and H (designating the carbon atom and the hydrogen atom) are the terminal symbols. Distinguishing a (0,0)-handle induced by $RUBBER$ as axiom, we obtain a hyperedge-replacement grammar, which generates the set of all (0,0)-hypergraphs representing the chemical structure of natural rubber molecules.

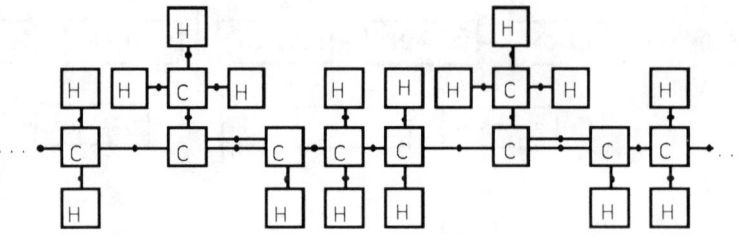

Fig. 3.4. Part of a hypergraph generated by the grammar HRG_{CHEM}

3.5 Example (k-Bipartite Graphs)

An undirected graph without multiple edges is said to be *bipartite* if its node set V can be partitioned into two non-empty sets V_1 and V_2 such that no pair of two nodes in the same set are adjacent. More specific, it is said to be *k-bipartite* if $|V_1| = k$.

The set $kBIP$ of all k-bipartite graphs ($k \geq 1$) can be generated by a hyperedge-replacement grammar HRG_{kBIP}. The productions of HRG_{kBIP} are as follows:

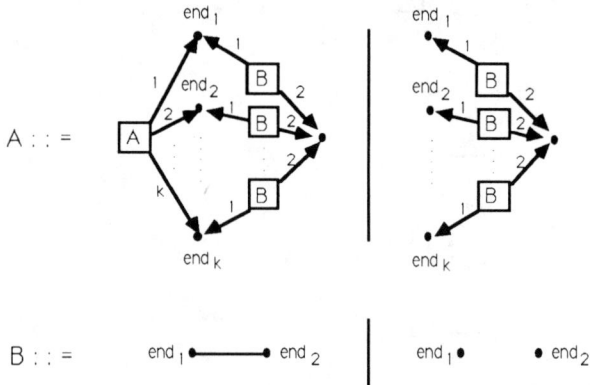

Fig. 3.5. Productions of the grammar HRG_{kBIP}

A and B are nonterminals and there is only one terminal label. (Hence terminal hyperedges are sufficiently represented by unlabeled ones.) Finally, a $(0, k)$-handle induced by the symbol A is used as axiom of HRG_{kBIP}.

This example demonstrates that hyperedge-replacement grammars are a useful tool for generating sets of graphs. Other graph languages characterized by certain graph-theoretic properties can be generated by hyperedge-replacement grammars, too. Hence the framework may be of some interest even from a graph-theoretic point of view. Further examples like outerplanar graphs, k-trees, graphs of bandwidth $\leq k$, graphs of cyclic bandwidth $\leq k$, etc. are given in chapter V. A detailed discussion of graph-theoretic aspects of hyperedge-replacement grammars can be found in chapter VI.

3.6 Example (String Graphs)

Consider the hyperedge-replacement grammar $HRG = (N, T, P, Z)$ where $N = \{S, A\}$, $T = \{a, b, c\}$, Z is a (1,1)-handle with label S and P consists of the following productions:

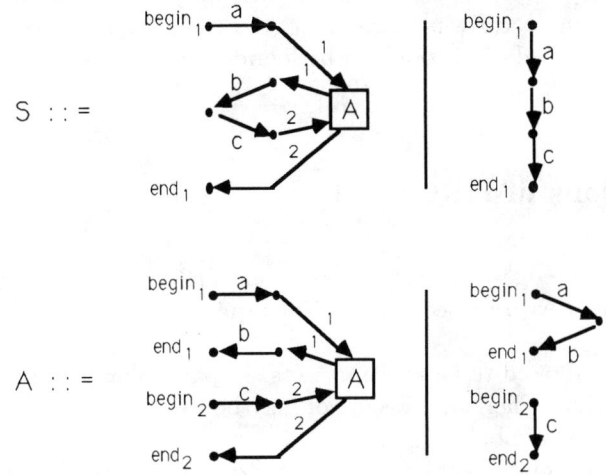

Fig. 3.6. Productions of the grammar HRG

Starting from the axiom Z, the application of the second production yields the string graph $(abc)^\bullet$. By applying the first production, then applying the third production $n-1$ times, followed by an application of the fourth production, we obtain the following derivation:

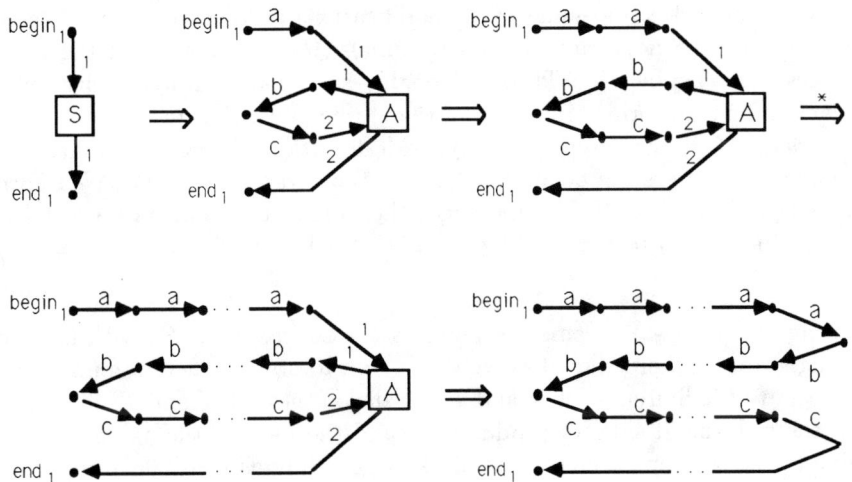

Fig. 3.7. Derivation of a string graph

Furthermore, the only hypergraphs in $L(HRG)$ are string graphs of the form $(a^n b^n c^n)^\bullet$ for $n \geq 1$. Thus, $L(HRG) = \{(a^n b^n c^n)^\bullet | n \geq 1\}$.

As this example shows, hyperedge-replacement grammars are a powerful tool for generating string-graph languages. In particular, they can be used to generate some string-graph languages whose corresponding string languages are not context-free. Further examples and a detailed discussion can be found in chapter V.

4 Modifications of HRG's

In section 3, a hyperedge-replacement grammar $HRG = (N, T, P, Z)$ has been defined in a general manner with respect to different aspects.

(1) N and T are allowed to be arbitrary sets. In particular, it is not required that the sets are disjoint. Therefore, a symbol may be used as nonterminal symbol as well as as a terminal symbol.
(2) There are no requirements with respect to the labelings of the hyperedges. In particular, hyperedges of different types may be equally labeled. This gives more flexibility when modelling with this kind of grammars (see, e.g., overloading of operation symbols).
(3) There are no requirements with respect to the "form" of the hyperedges. In particular, different tentacles of a hyperedge may be attached to the same node. This situation occurs, e.g., in the grammar for generating semi-structured control-flow graphs.

In this section, we describe some basic modifications of hyperedge-replacement grammars concerning the nonterminals and terminals, the labelings, and the form of the hyperedges. The Typification Theorem roughly says that each hyperedge-replacement grammar can be transformed into an equivalent one in which same-labeled nonterminal hyperedges are of the same type. The Type-Modification Theorem says that the type of nonterminal hyperedges can be modified in a suitable way. Finally, the Well-Formedness Theorem says that "deformed" hyperedges (i.e., hyperedges having tentacles attached to the same node) can be replaced by so-called "well-formed" ones.

Comparing hyperedge-replacement grammars $HRG = (N, T, P, Z)$ with usual context-free string grammars, one may observe that — up to now — there are no requirements with respect to the finiteness of N and T, the disjointness of N and T, the labels occurring on the right-hand sides of productions, and the form of the axiom. The decision to define hyperedge-replacement grammars as generally as possible is important when modelling application domains with these grammars. In particular, the fact that N and T are not required to be disjoint turns out to be useful. Considering, for example, the grammar generating chemical structures, one may distinguish the symbols C and H as the only terminal symbols. On the other hand, one may be interested in distinguishing, for example, C and H as well as CH, CH_2, and CH_3 as terminal symbols. If the set of terminals and the set of nonterminals are allowed to overlap, the set of productions can be retained. Otherwise, we have to modify the set of productions in an unnatural way: we are forced to duplicate some symbols and to consider different versions of a production (where the terminal resp. nonterminal version of a symbol occurs) or to consider additional productions which allow us to interpret the symbols as terminals.

4.1 Theorem (Normal-Form Theorem)

For each hyperedge-replacement grammar $HRG = (N, T, P, Z)$, an equivalent grammar $HRG' = (N', T', P', Z')$ can be constructed such that N' and T' are finite, N' and T' are disjoint, for every $p \in P$, the right-hand side of p is a hypergraph over $N' \cup T'$, and Z' is a handle over N'.

Notation

Hyperedge-replacement grammars satisfying the conditions of theorem 4.1 are said to be *usual* hyperedge-replacement grammars.

Proof

Let $HRG = (N, T, P, Z)$ be a hyperedge-replacement grammar. Then an equivalent grammar HRG' is constructed satisfying the conditions of theorem 4.1. First, an equivalent grammar with a handle as axiom is designed. Then, the sets of nonterminals, terminals, and productions are restricted in a suitable way. Finally, some relabelings are done for obtaining a grammar in which nonterminals and terminals are disjoint.
1. Let S_1 be a new symbol not occurring in HRG and $HRG_1 = (N_1, T, P_1, Z_1)$ where $N_1 = N \cup \{S_1\}$, $P_1 = P \cup \{(S_1, Z)\}$, and Z_1 is a handle with $frame(Z_1) = frame(Z)$ and $l(Z_1) = S_1$. Then $L(HRG_1) = L(HRG)$.
2. Let $HRG_2 = (N_2, T_2, P_2, Z_1)$ where $N_2 \subseteq N_1$ and $T_2 \subseteq T$ are the sets of nonterminals and terminals, respectively, occurring in Z_1 or any production and $P_2 \subseteq P_1$ is the set of productions whose right-hand sides are labeled in $N_2 \cup T_2$. Then N_2 and T_2 are finite because the set P_1 is finite and each hypergraph in the grammar has only a finite number of hyperedges. Moreover, $L(HRG_2) = L(HRG_1)$ because $P_2 \subseteq P_1$ and each production of P_1 which occurs in a derivation from Z_1 to a hypergraph $H \in \mathcal{H}_T$ turns out to be a production in P_2 as well.
3. Finally, we construct a hyperedge-replacement grammar $HRG_3 = (N_3, T_3, P_3, Z_1)$ in which N_3 and T_3 are disjoint. For this purpose, we create a new symbol $\bar{x}$ for each symbol $x \in N_2 \cap T_2$. Let $N_3 = \{x \in N_2 | x \notin T_2\} \cup \{\bar{x} | x \in N_2 \cap T_2\}$, $T_3 = T_2$, and P_3 be obtained according to the following rule: For each production in P_2 there is a corresponding production in P_3 in which each symbol $x \in N_2 \cap T_2$ is replaced by the corresponding symbol $\bar{x} \in N_3$. Moreover, for each x-labeled hyperedge e in the old grammar, there is a production $(\bar{x}, X)$ with $X = e^{\bullet}$ in the new grammar. Then $L(HRG_3) = L(HRG_2)$. Moreover, HRG_3 satisfies the conditions of theorem 4.1. □

Considering the definition of hyperedge-replacement grammars, one may wonder why there are no restrictions with respect to the labelings of the hyperedges on the right-hand sides of the productions. This is important for various reasons. On the one hand, several problems can be easily modeled (e.g., overloading of operation symbols is allowed). On the other hand, when writing productions for a grammar, one does not have to check syntactic conditions concerning the labeling. Whenever there is a production (A, R) of type (m, n) and a A-labeled hyperedge of different type, then the production cannot be applied to the hyperedge. With respect to proofs, it is often useful to assume that same-labeled nonterminal hyperedges are of the same type. This situation can be obtained by modifying the grammar in a suitable way.

In the following, we consider hyperedge-replacement grammars in which each nonterminal symbol has an associated type. For simplicity, the definition of a "typed" grammar is based on usual hyperedge-replacement grammars.

4.2 Definition (Typed Grammars)

A usual hyperedge-replacement grammar $HRG = (N, T, P, Z)$ is said to be *typed* if there is a mapping $ltype : N \to \mathbb{N} \times \mathbb{N}$ such that for all hypergraphs H in the grammar (i.e., the right-hand sides of productions as well as the axiom) and all hyperedges $e \in E_H$ with label in N, $ltype(l_H(e)) = type(e)$, and for all productions $(A, R) \in P$, $ltype(A) = type(R)$.

4.3 Theorem (Typification Theorem)

For each hyperedge-replacement grammar, an equivalent typed grammar can be constructed.

Proof

Let $HRG = (N, T, P, Z)$ be a hyperedge-replacement grammar. By theorem 4.1, we may assume that HRG is usual. We will construct a grammar $HRG' = (N', T, P', Z')$ with the set $N' = N \times TYPE$ where $TYPE \subseteq \mathbb{N} \times \mathbb{N}$ denotes the set of all types occurring in the grammar, i.e., the types of the hyperedges as well as the types of the hypergraphs in the grammar. P' and Z' are obtained with the help of the translation t that adds type information to all those hyperedges which are labeled in N, formally defined as follows. For every hypergraph $H \in \mathcal{H}_C$, $t(H)$ is the hypergraph $(V_H, E_H, s_H, t_H, l, begin_H, end_H)$ where l is defined by $l(e) = (l_H(e), type_H(e))$ if $l_H(e) \in N$ and $l(e) = l_H(e)$ otherwise.

Now set $P' = \{((A, type(R)), t(R)) | (A, R) \in P\}$ and $Z' = t(Z)$. Then HRG' is typed. Moreover, $L(HRG) = L(HRG')$. This may be seen as follows. If $H \in \mathcal{H}_C$, $e \in E_H$, and $repl : \{e\} \to \mathcal{H}_C$ with $repl(e) = R$ is a base for replacement in H, then $t(H[e/R]) = t(H)[e/t(R)]$. From this follows (by induction on the length of derivations) that for each derivation $Z \stackrel{*}{\Longrightarrow} H$ in HRG, there is a derivation $Z' \stackrel{*}{\Longrightarrow} H'$ in HRG' with $H' = t(H)$ and, on the other hand, for each derivation $Z' \stackrel{*}{\Longrightarrow} H'$ in HRG', there is a derivation

$Z \stackrel{*}{\Rightarrow} H$ in HRG with $t(H) = H'$. Since t is the identity of hypergraphs in $\mathcal{H}_T$, this proves $L(HRG) = L(HRG')$. □

Remark

1. Let $HRG = (N, T, P, Z)$ be a typed hyperedge-replacement grammar and $ltype : N \to \mathbb{N} \times \mathbb{N}$ the corresponding type function. Then, for $A \in N$, $A^\bullet$ denotes the handle $(A, ltype(A))^\bullet$ induced by A and the type of A.

2. A hyperedge-replacement grammar $HRG = (N, T, P, Z)$ is said to be *completely typed* if there is a mapping $ltype : N \cup T \to \mathbb{N} \times \mathbb{N}$ such that for all hypergraphs H in the grammar and all hyperedges $e \in E_H$, $ltype(l_H(e)) = type(e)$, and for all productions $(A, R) \in P$, $ltype(A) = type(R)$. Using the same ideas as in the proof above, it can be shown that for each hyperedge-replacement grammar HRG, there is a completely typed grammar HRG' such that $L(HRG)$ is equal to $L(HRG')$ up to the added type information.

As the grammar for generating semi-structured control-flow graphs shows, it is adequate to distinguish between incoming tentacles and outgoing tentacles of a hyperedge. With respect to the generated language, it turns out that for nonterminal hyperedges, it is relevant that there is a tentacle attached to a node, but not whether it is an incoming one or an outgoing one.

4.4 Theorem (Type-Modification Theorem)

Let $HRG = (N, T, P, Z)$ be a typed hyperedge-replacement grammar and $B \in N$ a symbol of type (m, n) for some $m, n \in \mathbb{N}$. Let $m', n' \in \mathbb{N}$ such that $m' + n' = m + n$. Then there is an equivalent typed hyperedge-replacement grammar $HRG' = (N, T, P', Z')$ in which B is of type (m', n') and all other symbols retain their type.

Proof

Let $HRG = (N, T, P, Z)$ be a typed hyperedge-replacement grammar. We will construct a new grammar $HRG' = (N, T, P', Z')$. The (obvious) idea is to change the type of the B-labeled hyperedges as well as the type of the right-hand sides of B-productions. P' and Z' are obtained with the help of the translations $mod, mod' : \mathcal{H}_C \to \mathcal{H}_C$ that change the type of B-labeled hyperedges of type (m, n) and the type of (m, n)-hypergraphs, respectively. Formally, mod and mod' are defined as follows. For every hypergraph $H \in \mathcal{H}_C$, $mod(H)$ is the hypergraph $(V_H, E_H, s, t, l_H, begin_H, end_H)$ with $s(e) = first_{m'}(att_H(e))$ and $t(e) = last_{n'}(att_H(e))$ if $l_H(e) = B$ and $type(e) = (m, n)$ and $s(e) = s_H(e)$ and $t(e) = t_H(e)$ otherwise. Accordingly, for every hypergraph $H \in \mathcal{H}_C$, $mod'(H)$ is the hypergraph $(V_H, E_H, s_H, t_H, l_H, begin, end)$ where $begin = first_{m'}(ext_H)$ and $end = last_{n'}(ext_H)$ if $type(H) = (m, n)$ and $begin = begin_H$ and $end = end_H$ otherwise. ($first_{m'}(w)$ denotes the sequence of the first m' symbols of w; $last_{n'}(w)$ denotes the sequence of the last n' symbols of w.)

Now let $P' = \{(A, mod(R))|(A, R) \in P, A \neq B\} \cup \{(B, mod'(mod(R)))|(B, R) \in P\}$ and $Z' = mod(Z)$. Then HRG' is a typed grammar in which B is of type (m', n'). Moreover, $L(HRG) = L(HRG')$. This may be seen as follows. If $H \in \mathcal{H}_C$, $e \in E_H$, and $repl : \{e\} \to \mathcal{H}_C$ with $repl(e) = R$ is a base for replacement in H, then $mod(H[e/R]) = mod(H)[e/mod'(mod(R))]$ if $l_H(e) = B$ and $mod(H[e/R]) = mod(H)[e/mod(R)]$ otherwise. From this follows (by induction on the length of derivations) that for each derivation $Z \stackrel{*}{\Rightarrow} H$ in HRG, there is a derivation $Z' \stackrel{*}{\Rightarrow} H'$ in HRG' with $H' = mod(H)$ and, on the other hand, for each derivation $Z' \stackrel{*}{\Rightarrow} H'$ in HRG', there is a derivation $Z \stackrel{*}{\Rightarrow} H$ in HRG with $mod(H) = H'$. Since mod is the identity on hypergraphs in $\mathcal{H}_T$, this proves that $L(HRG) = L(HRG')$. □

As the grammar for generating semi-structured control-flow graphs (example 3.3) shows, it is sometimes suitable to distinguish between tentacles of a hyperedge attached to the same node. With respect to the generated language, it turns out that for nonterminal hyperedges, it is relevant that there is a tentacle attached to a node, but not whether there is more than one tentacle with this property. Although it is often adequate to use "deformed" hyperedges, i.e., hyperedges with tentacles attached to the same node, a grammar with deformed hyperedges can be modified in such a way that all occurring hyperedges are "well-formed" in the sense that different tentacles of a hyperedge are attached to different nodes. (Note that in the case of the grammar for control-flow graphs, we obtain a grammar which no longer has a natural interpretation.)

4.5 Definition (Well-Formed Grammars)

1. A hypergraph $H \in \mathcal{H}_C$ is said to be *repetition-free* if $ext_{H,i} \neq ext_{H,j}$ for all $i, j \in [1, |ext_H|]$ with $i \neq j$. Accordingly, a hyperedge $e \in E_H$ is said to be *repetition-free* if $att_H(e)_i \neq att_H(e)_j$ for all $i, j \in [1, |att_H(e)|]$ with $i \neq j$.
2. A hyperedge-replacement grammar $HRG = (N, T, P, Z)$ is called *repetition-free* if all right-hand sides of productions in P are repetition-free. It is said to be *well-formed* if it is repetition-free and all hyperedges in the grammar which are labeled in N are repetition-free.

4.6 Theorem (Well-Formedness Theorem)

For each hyperedge-replacement grammar, an equivalent well-formed grammar can be constructed.

Proof

Let $HRG = (N, T, P, Z)$ be a hyperedge-replacement grammar. By the Typification Theorem given in 4.3, we may assume that HRG is typed. We will construct a well-formed hyperedge-replacement grammar $HRG'' = (N'', T, P'', Z'')$ in two steps.

We first construct a hyperedge-replacement grammar $HRG' = (N', T, P', Z')$ by deforming the right-hand sides of the productions in all possible ways and adding relation information to those hyperedges which are labeled in N.

Let N' be the set of all pairs (A, rel) where $A \in N$, $ltype(A) = (m, n)$, and rel is an equivalence relation on $[m + n]$.

P' and Z' are obtained with the help of two operations. The first operation deformes a hypergraph according an equivalence relation. Let $H \in \mathcal{H}_C$, $type(H) = (m, n)$, and rel be an equivalence relation on $[m+n]$ with $rel(H) \subseteq rel$. Let $\sim_{rel}$ be the corresponding equivalence relation on EXT_H given by $ext_{H,i} \sim_{rel} ext_{H,j}$ if and only if $(i, j) \in rel$ and $\approx_{rel}$ be the extension of $\sim_{rel}$ to V_H. Then H/rel denotes the *quotient hypergraph* of H with respect to $\approx_{rel}$, i.e., $H/rel = (V, E_H, s, t, l_H, begin, end)$ where V is the quotient set of V_H through $\approx_{rel}$ with natural mapping $nat : V_H \to V$, $s(e) = nat^*(s_H(e))$ and $t(e) = nat^*(t_H(e))$ for $e \in E_R$, $begin = nat^*(begin_H)$ and $end = nat^*(end_H)$. The translation r adds relation information to those hyperedges which are labeled in N, formally defined as follows. For every hypergraph $H \in \mathcal{H}_C$, $r(H)$ is the hypergraph $(V_H, E_H, s_H, t_H, l, begin_H, end_H)$ with $l(e) = (l_H(e), rel_H(e))$ if $l_H(e) \in N$ and $l(e) = l_H(e)$ otherwise.

Now let P' be the set of all productions $((A, rel), r(R/rel))$ where (A, R) is a production in P and rel is an equivalence relation satisfying $rel(R) \subseteq rel$. Furthermore, let $Z' = r(Z)$. Then $L(HRG) = L(HRG')$. This may be seen as follows. If $H \in \mathcal{H}_C$, $e \in E_H$, and $repl : \{e\} \to \mathcal{H}_C$ with $repl(e) = R$ is a base for replacement in H, then $rel(R) \subseteq rel_H(e)$, $rel(r(R/rel_H(e))) = rel_H(e)$, and $r(H[e/R]) = r(H)[e/r(R/rel_H(e))]$. From this follows (by induction on the length of derivations) that for each derivation $Z \overset{*}{\Rightarrow} H$ in HRG, there is a derivation $Z' \overset{*}{\Rightarrow} H'$ in HRG' with $H' = r(H)$ and, on the other hand, for each derivation $Z' \overset{*}{\Rightarrow} H'$ in HRG', there is a derivation $Z \overset{*}{\Rightarrow} H$ in HRG with $r(H) = H'$. Since r is the identity of hypergraphs in $\mathcal{H}_T$, this proves $L(HRG) = L(HRG')$.

In a second step, we construct a well-formed grammar $HRG'' = (N'', T, P'', Z'')$ with $N'' = N'$ by redefining the sequences of attachment nodes for hyperedges which are labeled in N' as well as the sequences of external nodes.

The translation $w : \mathcal{H}_C \to \mathcal{H}_C$ redefines the sequences of attachment nodes of hyperedges which are labeled in N', formally defined as follows. For every hypergraph $H \in \mathcal{H}_C$, $w(H)$ is the hypergraph $(V_H, E_H, s, t, l_H, begin_H, end_H)$ where for a hyperedge $e \in E_H$ with $l_H(e) \in N'$ and $type(e) = (m, n)$, $s(e) = att_H(e)'_1 \ldots att_H(e)'_m$ and $t(e) = att_H(e)'_{m+1} \ldots att_H(e)'_{m+n}$ where $att_H(e)'_1 = att_H(e)_1$ and for $j > 1$, $att_H(e)'_j = att_H(e)_j$ if there is no $i \in [1, j-1]$ with $(i, j) \in rel(e)$ and $att_H(e)'_j = \lambda$ (the empty string) otherwise. Analogously, the translation $w' : \mathcal{H}_C \to \mathcal{H}_C$ redefines the sequences of external nodes. For every hypergraph $H \in \mathcal{H}_C$ with $type(H) = (m, n)$, $w'(H)$ is the hypergraph $(V_H, E_H, s_H, t_H, l_H, begin, end)$ with $begin = ext'_{H,1} \ldots ext'_{H,m}$ and $end = ext'_{H,m+1} \ldots ext'_{H,m+n}$ where $ext'_{H,1} = ext_{H,1}$ and for $j > 1$, $ext'_{H,j} = ext_{H,j}$ if there is no $i \in [1, j-1]$ with $(i, j) \in rel(H)$ and $ext'_{H,j} = \lambda$ otherwise.

Now let $P'' = \{(A, w'(w(R))) | (A, R) \in P'\}$ and $Z'' = w(Z')$. Then HRG'' is well-formed. Moreover, $L(HRG') = L(HRG'')$. This may be seen as follows. If $H \in \mathcal{H}_C$, $e \in E_H$, and $repl : \{e\} \to \mathcal{H}_C$ with $repl(e) = R$ is a base for replacement in H, then $rel_H(e) = rel(R)$, $rel_{w(H)}(e) = rel(w'(w(R)))$, and $w(H[e/R]) = w(H)[e/w'(w(R))]$. From this follows that for each derivation $Z' \stackrel{*}{\Rightarrow} H'$ in HRG', there is a derivation $Z'' \stackrel{*}{\Rightarrow} H''$ in HRG'' with $H'' = w(H')$ and, on the other hand, for each derivation $Z'' \stackrel{*}{\Rightarrow} H''$ in HRG'', there is a derivation $Z' \stackrel{*}{\Rightarrow} H'$ in HRG' with $w(H') = H''$. Since w is the identity of hypergraphs in $\mathcal{H}_T$, this proves $L(HRG') = L(HRG'')$. □

Remark

A hyperedge-replacement grammar HRG is said to be *completely well-formed* if it is repetition-free and all hyperedges in the grammar are repetition-free. Using the same ideas as in the proof above, it can be shown that for each hyperedge-replacement grammar HRG, there is a completely well-formed grammar HRG' such that $L(HRG)$ is equal to $L(HRG')$ up to the representation and labeling of the non-repetition-free hyperedges.

At the end of this section, let us use the Type-Modification Theorem and the Well-Formedness Theorem for modifying a grammar into a grammar in which all nonterminal hyperedges are *stars*, i.e., well-formed hyperedges with outgoing tentacles only.

4.7 Corollary (Normal-Form Theorem)

For each hyperedge-replacement grammar $HRG = (N, T, P, Z)$, there is an equivalent *star-replacement grammar* $HRG' = (N, T, P', Z')$, i.e., a well-formed and typed hyperedge-replacement grammar in which each nonterminal hyperedge of the grammar is a star.

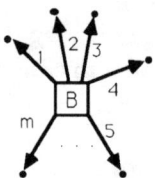

Proof

Let $HRG = (N, T, P, Z)$ be a hyperedge-replacement grammar. By Theorem 4.3, we may assume that HRG is typed. Now consider a nonterminal $B \in N$ of type (m, n) where $m, n \in \mathbb{N}$. By the Type-Modification Theorem 4.4, we can construct an equivalent typed grammar in which B is of type $(0, m + n)$. By repeating this process for all nonterminals of the grammar, we get an equivalent typed grammar in which each nonterminal is of type $(0, k)$ for some $k \in \mathbb{N}$. By the Well-Formedness Theorem, the obtained grammar can be modified to a well-formed one. In this grammar, each nonterminal hyperedge is a star. □

Remark

Star-replacement grammars are special hyperedge-replacement grammars with a lot of nice properties: For each star-replacement grammar $HRG = (N, T, P, Z)$, there is a mapping $rank : N \to I\!N$ such that each hypergraph H occurring in the grammar is labeled according to $rank$, i.e., $rank(l_H(e)) = type(e)_2$ for all $e \in E_H$ with $l_H(e) \in N$, and each production $(A, R) \in P$ is built according to $rank$, i.e., $rank(A) = type(R)_2$. ($rank$ corresponds to the mapping $ltype$ and assigns the second component of $ltype(A)$ to a symbol $A \in N$. $type(e)_2$ and $type(R)_2$ denote the second components of $type(e)$ and $type(R)$, respectively.) Furthermore, each right-hand side R of a production is equipped with a *single* sequence ext_R ($= end_R$) of *pairwise distinct* nodes and each nonterminal hyperedge e in a hypergraph H of the grammar is attached to a *single* sequence $att_H(e)$ ($= t_H(e)$) of *pairwise distinct* nodes.

5. Related Concepts

Graph grammars have been developed as an extension of the concept of formal grammars on strings to grammars on graphs. Among string grammars, context-free grammars have proven to be extremely useful in practical applications and powerful enough to generate a wide spectrum of interesting formal languages. It is therefore not surprising that analogous notions have been developed also for graph grammars. Corresponding to the different graph-grammar formalisms in the literature, and to the differing opinions about what the term "context-free" means, a number of different types of graph grammars have been given this predicate (cf., Feder [Fe 71], Pavlidis [Pa 72], Della Vigna and Ghezzi [DG 78], Janssens and Rozenberg [JR 80b], Slisenko [Sl 82], Habel and Kreowski [HK 83+87a+c], Montanari and Rossi [MR 87], Bauderon and Courcelle [BC 87], Lengauer and Wanke [LW 88], Lautemann [La 88b], Engelfriet [En 89+91]). Among the most general, there are the so-called boundary node-label controlled graph grammars of Rozenberg and Welzl [RW 86a] based on node-replacement and the hyperedge-replacement grammars. In the following, some relationships between the different types of grammars are discussed.

5.1 Context-Free String Grammars

Direct derivations in context-free string grammars can be simulated by direct derivations in hyperedge-replacement grammars using the one-to-one correspondence between strings and string graphs. Let $p = (A, v)$ be a context-free string production with $A \in N$ ($N \subseteq C$) and $v \in C^+$; let $u, w \in C^*$; and let $uAw \longrightarrow_p uvw$ denote the resulting derivation step. Furthermore, let $(uAw)^\bullet$, $(uvw)^\bullet$, and $v^\bullet$ be the string graphs corresponding to uAw, uvw, and v, respectively. Then the production $p^\bullet = (A, v^\bullet)$ is applicable to $(uAw)^\bullet$ with the result $(uvw)^\bullet$. This situation is depicted by the following diagram:

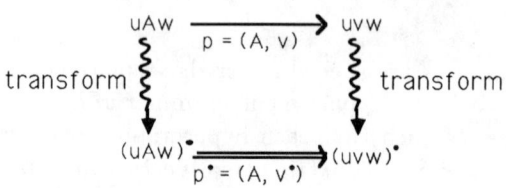

Obviously, each context-free string grammar $G = (N, T, P, S)$ (without λ-productions) induces a hyperedge-replacement grammar $G^\bullet = (N, T, P^\bullet, S^\bullet)$ with $P^\bullet = \{p^\bullet | p \in P\}$ such that there is a one-to-one correspondence between the derivations in G and the ones in $G^\bullet$; the graph language $L(G^\bullet)$ generated by $G^\bullet$ is obtained from the string language $L(G)$ generated by G just by transformation:

$$L(G^\bullet) = L(G)^\bullet = \{w^\bullet | w \in L(G)\}.$$

In this sense, hyperedge-replacement grammars generalize context-free string grammars. Hence, some results of the string case can be directly carried over to the hypergraph case — for example all undecidability results known for context-free string grammars. In chapter V, we will discuss further aspects of the relationship between context-free string grammars and hyperedge-replacement grammars.

5.2 Feder's Plex Grammars

Feder [Fe 71] studies so-called plex grammars. His approach is based on the following idea: In conventional string derivations, each terminal and non-terminal symbol may appear in a string with a symbol to its left or right. Each symbol can be visualized as having two "attaching points", a left one and a right one, at which it may join to or associate with other symbols. A more general symbol can be envisaged as having an arbitrary number, n, of attaching points for joining to other symbols. A symbol of this type is called an n *attaching-point entity*, abbreviated NAPE. Structures formed by interconnecting such entities are called *plex structures*. (The word "plex" is derived from the word "plexus", meaning, "an interwoven arrangement of parts").

A Fe-structure $S = (\Psi, \Gamma, \Delta)$, where the prefix Fe refers to Feder, is a system consisting of a *component list* Ψ, a *joint list* Γ, and a *tie-point list* Δ.

- The component list is a string of the form $\Psi = a_1 \ldots a_m$ where, for $i = 1, \ldots, m$, a_i is a single NAPE, called *component*.
- The joint list Γ specifies the way in which the NAPEs of the component list are interconnected. A joint list is divided into fields. Each *field* is a string of the form $\gamma = \gamma_1 \ldots \gamma_m$, where, for $i = 1, \ldots, m$, γ_i is a natural number including 0. Each field specifies a *joint*: an entry γ_i in the i-th position of a field indicates that attaching point γ_i of the NAPE a_i connects at the joint. If the i-th component is not involved at the particular joint, then 0 appears in this position. (Each field must contain at least two non-null identifiers.)
- The tie-point list is also divided into fields. Each *field* is of the form $\delta = \delta_1 \ldots \delta_m$, where, for $i = 1, \ldots, m$, δ_i is a natural number including 0. The tie-point fields

specify *tie-points* in the same way that the joint-list fields specify joints. (Each tie-point list field must contain at least one non-null identifier.)

To achieve a complete specification, it is required that every attaching point of every NAPE must either connect with another NAPE or be one of the tie-points, i.e., every attaching point of every NAPE must be referenced in at least one field. (Additional requirements are necessary to guarantee that each attaching point of a NAPE is used in at most one field.)

Fe-productions $p = (L, R)$ consist of two Fe-structures L and R possessing the same number of tie-points. The correspondence between the tie-points of L and R is given by the ordering of the fields. In particular, a Fe-production is said to be *context-free* if the component list of L consists of one component only, the component list of R is non-empty, and R is "connected". A Fe-production $p = (L, R)$ is applied to a connected substructure of a structure G in the following way: Exchange the connected substructure L of G for R.

It turns out that Fe-structures and Fe-productions correspond directly to multi-pointed hypergraphs and hypergraph productions. Each such direct Fe-derivation $G \longrightarrow_p H$ corresponds to a direct derivation in the sense of hypergraph replacement if the Fe-structures G, H, L, and R are transformed to multi-pointed hypergraphs by a component-to-hyperedge interpretation, called *interpret*. The operation *interpret* interprets each n attaching-point entity A of the component list of a Fe-structure X by a A-labeled hyperedge with n tentacles and each field of the joint- or tie-point list as a node. Moreover, each field determines all tentacles of hyperedges attached to the node. Finally, the tie-point list determines some distinguished nodes. For example,

$$S = (\underbrace{\langle CH_2\rangle\langle C\rangle\langle CH_3\rangle\langle CH\rangle\langle CH_2\rangle}_{\text{component list}}, \underbrace{(21000, 02100, 03020, 04010, 00031)}_{\text{joint list}}, \underbrace{(10000, 00002)}_{\text{tie}-\text{point list}})$$

is an Fe-structure. It is shown diagrammed as follows:

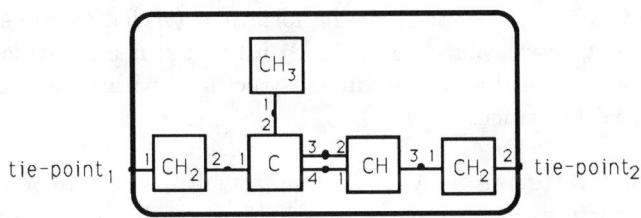

The relationship between both kinds of derivations is represented by the following commutative diagram.

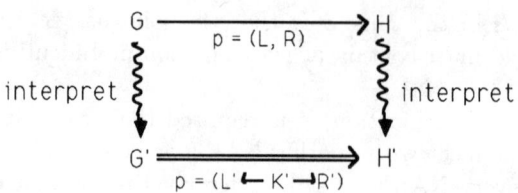

where $L' = interpret(L)$, $R' = interpret(R)$, and K' is the discrete hypergraph which contains one node for each tie-point of L (resp. R). This leads to a corresponding relation between both kinds of grammars and their generated structures. It turns out that (unrestricted) plex grammars as investigated by Feder can be considered as a special case of hypergraph-replacement grammars in the sense of the Berlin approach (see, e.g., Ehrig [Eh 79] and chapter VIII). Moreover, context-free plex grammars can be viewed as hyperedge-replacement grammars.

5.3 Pavlidis' Context-Free Graph Grammars

Pavlidis [Pa 72] studies so-called m-th order context-free graph grammars and gives some topological characterizations of sets of graphs which can be generated by this kind of grammars.

An *m-th order structure* is an entity which is connected to the rest of a graphical structure by m nodes. Pavlidis thinks of such elements as polygons which are attached to each other through their nodes. Such structures are closely related to the NAPEs proposed by Feder [Fe 71]. In the following, a structure composed from higher-order structures possessing some distinguished nodes is said to be a Pa-structure, where Pa refers to Pavlidis. Rewriting such an m-th order structure corresponds to replacing it by another Pa-structure connected to the rest of the structure by exactly m nodes.

An *m-th order context-free graph grammar* is a system $GG = (N, T, P, Z)$ where

- N is a set of nonterminal structures: nodes, branches, triangles,..., polygons with m nodes,
- T is a set of terminal structures: nodes and branches,
- P is a finite set of productions of the form $p = (A, R)$, where A is a k-th order nonterminal structure (for some $1 \leq k \leq m$) and R is a Pa-structure (containing possibly both terminal and nonterminal structures) with k distinguished nodes,
- Z is an initial Pa-structure.

Obviously, each Pa-structure may be seen as a multi-pointed hypergraph where the nodes of the structures are the nodes of the hypergraph and the structures are respesented by hyperedges attached to the nodes of the structures. It turns out that m-th order context-free graph grammars as introduced by Pavlidis can be viewed as hyperedge-replacement grammars generating graph languages.

5.4 Della Vigna's and Ghezzi's Context-Free Graph Grammars

Della Vigna and Ghezzi [DG 78] study a special kind of node-replacement graph grammars based on the graph-grammar model described by Pratt [Pr 71]. Pratt uses "context-free" graph grammars as the basic grammar form out of which "pair grammars" are constructed. (Pair grammars are used to define translations between string and graph representations of programs and data.) Della Vigna and Ghezzi work on the model of Pratt in order to develop a theory on "context-free graph grammars" similar to that of context-free string grammars. Their context-free graph grammars work as follows:

DG-graphs $G = (V, E, s, t, l_V, l_E, in, out)$, where the prefix DG refers to Della Vigna and Ghezzi, are connected graphs (V, E, s, t, l_E) with an additional node labeling $l_V : V \to C$ and with two distinguished nodes in and out. DG-productions $p = (A, R)$ consist of a nonterminal $A \in N$ and a DG-graph R. A DG-production $p = (A, R)$ is applied to a node v of a graph G with $l_V(v) = A$ in the following way:

(1) Remove the node v from G.
(2) Add the right-hand side R disjointly.
(3) Edges originally coming into v become incoming edges of in of R; edges originally going out from v become outgoing edges of out of R.

Each such direct DG-derivation $G \longrightarrow_p H$ corresponds to a direct derivation in the sense of hyperedge replacement if the DG-graphs G, H, and R are tranformed to $(1,1)$-graphs by a node-to-edge stretching, called $stretch$. The operation $stretch$ replaces each labeled node v of a DG-graph X by two unlabeled nodes v_s and v_t and a connecting edge e such that incoming and outgoing edges as well as labels are inherited according to the following picture. (Note that in_s becomes $begin$ and out_t becomes end.)

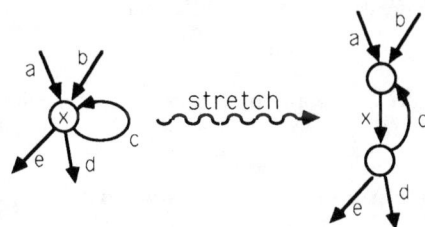

The relationship between both kinds of derivations is represented by the following commutative diagram:

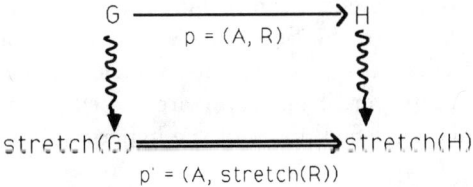

This leads to a corresponding relation between both kinds of graph grammars and their generated graph languages. It turns out that node-replacement grammars as introduced by Pratt and investigated by Della Vigna and Ghezzi can be considered as a special case of our (hyper)edge-replacement grammars. This applies in particular to Della Vigna's and Ghezzi's investigations of context-free graph grammars. Hence it is no longer mysterious that the Pumping Lemmata in [DG 78] and [Kr 79] look so similar although they are formulated for graph languages which contain quite different kinds of graphs and are generated by quite different kinds of derivations — at first sight.

5.5 Slisenko's Context-Free Graph Grammars

Slisenko [Sl 82] studies a special kind of node-replacement graph grammars which work as follows: Sli-graphs $G = (V, E, \varphi, l)$, where the prefix Sli refers to the author, are undirected graphs (V, E, φ) with a node labeling $l : V \to C$. A *star graph* is a triple $R^* = (R, B, b)$, where R is a Sli-graph, B is a set of so-called boundary edges (disjoint from the edges of R), and $b : B \to V_R$ is a mapping assigning a node to each edge in B. A star graph $R^* = (R, B, b)$ is said to be *simple* if its kernel, R, consists of a single node without edges. A Sli-production $p^* = (L^*, R^*)$ consists of a simple star graph L^* the kernel of which is labeled by a symbol $A \in C$ and a star graph R^* with the same boundary set as L^*.

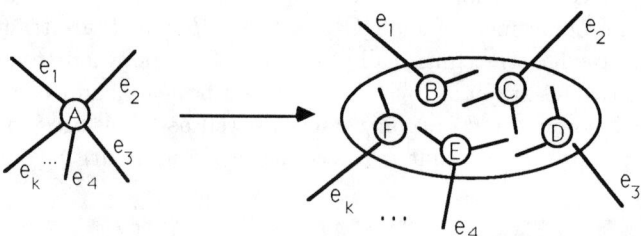

A Sli-production $p^* = (L^*, R^*)$ is applied to a node v of a Sli-graph G with $l(v) = A$ in the following way:

(1) Remove the node v from G.
(2) Add the right-hand side R disjointly.
(3) Each edge $e \in B$ originally incident to v becomes incident with $b(e)$ of R.

Each such direct Sli-derivation $G \longrightarrow_{p^*} H$ corresponds to a direct derivation in the sense of hyperedge replacement if the Sli-graphs G, H, and the star graph R are transformed to hypergraphs by a node-to-hyperedge transformation, called *transform*. The operation *transform* replaces each edge e of a Sli-graph X by a node $\bar{e}$ and each A-labeled node v of X with k incident edges $e_1, \ldots, e_k$ by an A-labeled hyperedge $\bar{v}$ with k tentacles attached to $\bar{e}_1, \ldots, \bar{e}_k$. Moreover, if $e_1, \ldots, e_k$ are the edges of the boundary set, then $\bar{e}_1, \ldots, \bar{e}_k$ become the distinguished nodes of the hypergraph.

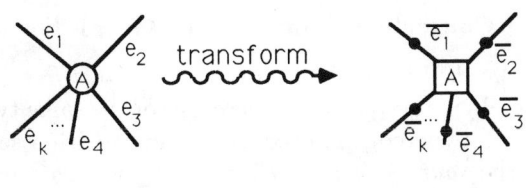

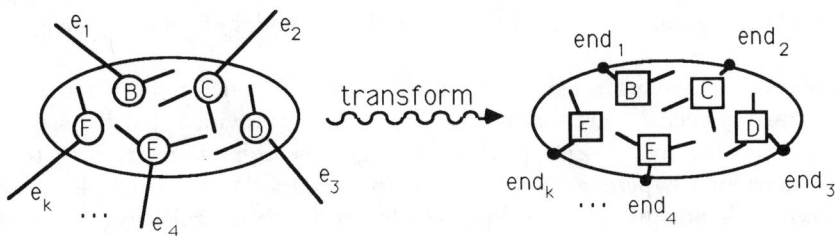

The relationship between both kinds of derivations is represented by the following commutative diagram. (A denotes the label of the simple star graph L^* and $R' = transform(R^*)$).

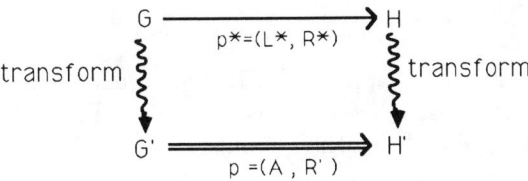

This leads to a correspondence between both kinds of graph grammars and their generated graph languages. It turns out that node-replacement grammars as investigated by Slisenko can be considered as a special case of our hyperedge-replacement grammars.

5.6 Montanari's and Rossi's Context-Free Hypergraph Grammars

Montanari and Rossi [MR 87] consider particular classes of networks of constraints, called *hierachical networks*. Formally, a network of constraints is seen as a hyperedge-labeled hypergraph whose nodes are variables and whose hyperedges with k tentacles represent k-ary constraints ($k \geq 1$) and thus are labeled by k-ary relations on some finite universe. To describe classes of networks of constraints they use context-free hypergraph grammars. Their grammar model is essentially the same as the one of hyperedge-replacement grammars. The main difference between their definition and the one developed in this book is that for each hyperedge, they do not have functions s and t to identify the source and the target nodes of a hyperedge; they only have one *connection function* c which returns the k-tuple of nodes connected by the hyperedge.

5.7 Bauderon's and Courcelle's Context-Free Graph Grammars

Bauderon and Courcelle [BC 87] define a notion of *context-free graph grammar* based on the substitution of a hypergraph for a hyperedge (of the same type) in a hypergraph. They deal with directed, hyperedge-labeled hypergraphs with a sequence *src* of distinguished nodes called the *sources*. The labels of the hyperedges are chosen in a ranked alphabet, i.e., in a set C each element of which has an associated integer (in $I\!N$) that they call its *type*. The type is defined by a mapping $ltype : C \to I\!N$. The type of the label of a hyperedge must be equal to the number of nodes of that hyperedge.

Each context-free hypergraph grammar in the sense of Bauderon and Courcelle may be seen as a star-replacement grammar in the sense of 4.7 (provided that the sequences *src* do not have repetitions). Moreover, their hypergraphs are more restrictive: terminal as well as nonterminal hyperedges are required to be stars. As the examples in section 3 have shown, it is adequate to consider also hypergraphs in which the hyperedges are allowed to possess source nodes as well as target nodes: For modelling petri nets, it is important to distiguish the preset and the postset of each transition. For representing function expressions, it is adequate to distinguish the argument list and the value list. For representing flow diagrams, it is necessary to differentiate between the *begin* and the *end*. These possibilities with respect to modelling are not given in the approach of Bauderon and Courcelle. However, from a theoretical point of view, the approaches are equivalent.

Finally, let us mention that the approach of Bauderon and Courcelle is mainly oriented to the Berlin approach to graph grammars (see, e.g., [Eh 79]). Therefore, it is not surprising that hyperedge-replacement grammars in [BC 87] and [HK 87b+c] look so similar.

5.8 Lengauer's and Wanke's Cellular Graph Grammars

Lengauer and Wanke [LW 88, Wa 89] consider efficient ways of analyzing families of hierarchical engineering designs, using methods from the area of graph grammars. Their work is based on a slightly different version of hyperedge-replacement grammars which they call context-free cellular graph grammars. A *context-free cellular graph grammar* is a list of *cells* $(C_1, \ldots, C_k)$ ($k \geq 1$). Each cell C_i is a graph equipped with some hyperedges which are labeled with a set of indices of the index set $\{1, \ldots, k\}$. The indices refer to the cells which can be replaced for the hyperedge. (It is required that the hyperedge and the the cell corresponding to an index are of the same type.) The generated language of a context-free cellular graph grammar is the set of all cells without hyperedges which can be derived from the cell C_k. It is easy to see that each context-free cellular graph grammar induces a hyperedge-replacement grammar which generates graphs only.

5.9 Algebraic Approach to Graph Grammars

Let $p = (A, R)$ be a production of type (m, n), and $H \Longrightarrow_p H'$ by $p = (A, R)$ be a direct derivation. Then all the hypergraphs can be grouped together in the way depicted in the following figure, where L is the (m, n)-handle induced by A, K is the discrete hypergraph with m *begin* nodes and n *end* nodes (without hyperedges) and D is obtained from H just by removing the hyperedge which is subject of the replacement. The arrows denote how the hypergraphs are included into each other according to the construction. It is simple to see that squares (1) and (2) form pushout or gluing diagrams so that hyperedge replacement turns out to be a special case of the algebraic approach to (hyper)graph grammars (see, e.g., Ehrig [Eh 79]).

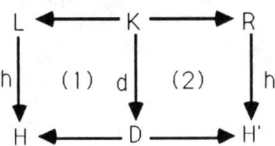

Hence, all results known in the algebraic approach (also called "Berlin approach") apply to hyperedge-replacement grammars.

5.10 Node-Label Controlled Graph Grammars

Janssens and Rozenberg [JR 80a+b] introduce a kind of node-replacement grammars called *node-label controlled* (NLC) grammars. This kind of grammars rewrites single nodes only and establishes connections between the embedded graph and the neighbors of the rewritten node on the basis of the labels of the involved nodes only. This model belongs to one of the most investigated models (see, e.g., Janssens and Rozenberg [JR 81], Brandenburg [Br 83], Turán [Tu 83], Janssens [Ja 83], Janssens, Rozenberg, and Welzl [JRW 86]). Unfortunately, for this kind of grammar, the order of rewriting two nonterminal nodes in a graph may influence the result. Therefore, arbitrary NLC grammars cannot be considered as "truly context-free". Several ways of enforcing context-freeness in NLC grammars have been investigated so far.

1. Janssens and Rozenberg in [JR 80b] restrict NLC grammars to so-called *context-free* NLC grammars. In [Ja 83], this kind of grammars are called *neighborhood-uniform* NLC grammars, short NUNLC grammars, because the embedding is done "uniformly" with respect to neighborhoods within the whole rewriting process. In addition to these investigations, so-called *Church-Rosser* NLC grammars are considered in [JKRE 82]. These are NLC grammars with an additional restriction that guarantees that the graph resulting from a derivation is independent of the order in which the direct derivation steps are performed. As shown in [JKRE 82], the context-free NLC grammars studied in [JR 80b] turn out to be special Church-Rosser NLC grammars.

2. Rozenberg and Welzl in [RW 86a] restrict NLC grammars to so-called *boundary* NLC grammars, short BNLC grammars. The "boundary" restriction means that all graphs

involved (i.e., the axiom and the right-hand sides of productions) are such that two nonterminally labeled nodes are never connected by an edge. Due to the boundary restriction, BNLC grammars are closer to context-free grammars than arbitrary NLC grammars, and thus have nicer properties with respect to normal forms, decidability, and complexity of recognition (see [RW 86a+b]).

3. Engelfriet and Leih [EL 90] investigate *boundary* eNCE (or B-eNCE) grammars, of which the BNLC grammars are a special case. These B-eNCE grammars enjoy all the nice properties of the BNLC grammars, while they are much easier to handle and understand. (eNCE grammars are straightforward generalizations of NCE grammars (see [JR 82]) and can be used to generate sets of graphs which are node- as well as edge-labeled. The e stands for "edge-labeled" and NCE for "neigborhood controlled embedding".)

4. Finally, let us mention that Courcelle in [Co 87] introduces and investigates so-called *context-free* NLC grammars. Courcelle calls a rewriting system *context-free* if it is *confluent* (two rewriting steps concerning distinct positions can be done in any order, giving the same result) and *associative*. Although NUNLC and BNLC grammars look context-free (they are confluent), they turn out to be not context-free in the sense of Courcelle because they are not necessarily associative.

Some authors have started to investigate the relationships between node-label controlled graph grammars and hyperedge-replacement grammars.

1. Lautemann in [La 88b] shows that each language generated by a BNLC grammar of bounded nonterminal degree can be generated by a hyperedge-replacement grammar, too. Conversely, Vogler in [Vo 90] shows that each set of simple graphs generated by a hyperedge-replacement grammar can be generated by an "enriched" BNLC grammar of bounded nonterminal degree (up to node labels).

2. Engelfriet and Rozenberg in [ER 90] compare the generating power of the boundary edNCE graph grammars and the hyperedge-replacement grammars. It turns out that boundary edNCE graph grammars of bounded nonterminal degree and hyperedge-replacement grammars have the same power for generating sets of graphs.

5.11 Handle Node-Label Controlled Graph Grammars

While in NLC grammars, the left-hand side of each production is required to be a single node, Main and Rozenberg [MR 87] examine the extension of NLC grammars where the left-hand side of each production is a *handle*, i.e., a graph with exactly two labeled nodes, and one edge connecting the nodes. The way that a handle NLC grammar generates a set of graphs is based on the mechanism of ordinary NLC grammars. Roughly speaking, the rewriting process of this kind of grammars works as follows: Given a graph μ and a production $H := \alpha$ (where H is a handle and α is a node-labeled graph) of the grammar, a derived graph is obtained as follows:

(0) Choose an occurrence of the handle H in μ, called the mother handle. (The set of nodes which are directly connected to the mother handle is called the *neighborhood*.)
(1) Delete the mother handle (and its incident edges) from μ and call the resulting graph μ'.
(2) Add a copy of α (the daughter graph) to the graph μ'.
(3) Introduce new edges between μ' and the daughter graph according to the following rule: For each pair (Y, Z) in the connection relation C of the grammar, connect every Y-labeled node in the daughter graph with every Z-labeled node in the neighborhood of the mother handle.

Although in edge-replacement grammars as well as in handle NLC grammars an edge (respectively an edge together with its endpoints) is replaced, there are important differences.

(1) Handle NLC grammars are based on node-labeled graphs while edge-replacement grammars are based on edge-labeled graphs.
(2) In handle NLC grammars, the handle as well as its incident edges are deleted. Only the nodes in the neighborhood of the handle remain preserved. In edge-replacement grammars, only the edge is deleted; the endpoints of the edge remain preserved.
(3) Handle NLC grammars have the power of recursive enumerability; edge-replacement grammars do not yield this, because they use a very restrictive mechanism to embed a graph.
(4) Handle NLC grammars do not have the finite Church-Rosser Property; edge-replacement grammars have this property, an essential property with respect to context-freeness.

5.12 Edge-Label Controlled Graph Grammars

Main and Rozenberg ([MR 90]) introduce a graph-grammar model based on edge replacement, where both the rewriting and the embedding mechanisms are controlled by edge labels. The model of edge-label controlled (ELC) graph grammars is influenced by the model of node-label controlled (NLC) graph grammars as well as by the research on edge-replacement grammars (see [HK 83+87a]). Roughly speaking, the rewriting process of this kind of grammars works as follows: Given a graph μ and a rule $A := (\alpha, \alpha_{source}, \alpha_{target})$ of the grammar, a derived graph is obtained by the following steps:

(0) Choose an edge e (mother edge) with label A.
(1) Delete e as well as its source, its target, and its neighborhood edges yielding a new graph μ'.
(2) Add a copy of α (the daughter graph) to the graph μ'.
(3) Introduce new edges between μ' and the daughter graph according to the labels of the original neighborhood edges, the labels of edges in the daughter graph which are neighborhood edges with respect to nodes of α_{source} and α_{target}, and the connection relation of the grammar. Establish some new internal edges in the daughter graph (provided that originally there were edges parallel to the mother edge).

It is not surprising that the model under consideration is "too powerful" in the sense that it generates the whole class of recursively enumerable graph languages. But, by suitable restrictions, one obtains a graph-grammar model that is — more or less — that of edge-replacement grammars. (Note that edge-replacement grammars as considered in [HK 83+87a] allow loops, i.e., edges from a node to itself. There are several sensible ways to handle loops with edge-label controlled graph grammars, but none of these methods corresponds to the treatment given in [HK 83+87a].)

6. Bibliographic Note

Hyperedge-replacement grammars were first introduced in [HK 87c]. The kind of introduction chosen in sections 1 to 3 is similar to the one in [HK 87b].

Chapter II
Basic Properties of HRG's

As shown in the previous chapter, several graph-grammar approaches equipped with the predicate "context-free" may be seen as special hyperedge-replacement grammars. In this chapter, we will present some properties of hyperedge-replacement grammars which provide evidence that hyperedge-replacement grammars represent a graph-grammar version of context-freeness.

In section 1, we generalize the notion of derivations to that of parallel derivations. These allow the replacement of an arbitrary collection of hyperedges instead of a single hyperedge. It turns out that parallel derivations can be sequentialized yielding the same hypergraph. Thus, they do not increase the generative power. In section 2, we show that hyperedge replacement works fully locally without any effect on the context of the hyperedges replaced. On the one hand, given a derivation of the form $H \stackrel{*}{\Longrightarrow} H'$ and a subhypergraph G of H, we are able to extract the part of the derivation concerning G yielding a subderivation $G \stackrel{*}{\Longrightarrow} G'$ where G' is a subhypergraph of H'. On the other hand, we may consider the subderivations induced by the handles of the hyperedges in H, called fibres of the derivation, and combine them to a derivation of H. It turns out that this procedure again yields the derivation $H \stackrel{*}{\Longrightarrow} H'$. Therefore, each derivation is uniquely determined by the fibres of the initial hyperedges and the context of these hyperedges. If the replacement of a hyperedge would influence the context, we could not get this general result. Finally, in section 3, we present a notion of a derivation tree for hyperedge-replacement grammars. These derivation trees are quite similar to derivation trees for context-free string grammars, which are an essential element of the theory of context-free string grammars; they represent derivations in a hyperedge-replacement grammar. The main problem is given by the graphical structure of a hypergraph. While in a string graph there is an order on the (hyper)edges, we do not have such an order when considering hypergraphs.

1. Parallel Derivations

For technical reasons we are going to generalize the notion of derivations to that of parallel derivations, which allows the simultaneous replacement of an arbitrary collection of hyperedges instead of a single hyperedge. We use the notion of a production base to determine the choice of hyperedges to be replaced as well as the assignment of productions to be applied.

1.1 Definition (Parallel Derivations)

1. Let $H \in \mathcal{H}_C$, $B \subseteq E_H$, and P be a set of productions. A mapping $prod : B \to P$ is called a *production base* in H if $l_H(b) = lhs(prod(b))$ all $b \in B$ and $repl : B \to \mathcal{H}_C$ given by $repl(b) = rhs(prod(b))$ is a base for replacement in H.

2. Let $H, H' \in \mathcal{H}_C$ and $prod : B \to P$ be a production base in H. Then H *directly derives H' in parallel* (by $prod$) if H' is isomorphic to $REPLACE(H, repl)$ where $repl : B \to \mathcal{H}_C$ is given by $repl(b) = rhs(prod(b))$ for all $b \in B$. In this case, we write $H \Rightarrow H'$ by $prod$, or $H \Rightarrow H'$.

3. A sequence of direct parallel derivations $H_0 \Rightarrow \ldots \Rightarrow H_k$ by $prod_1, \ldots, prod_k$ is called a *parallel derivation of length k* from H_0 to H_k and is denoted by $H_0 \overset{*}{\Rightarrow} H_k$. If the length of the derivation shall be stressed, we write $H_0 \overset{k}{\Rightarrow} H_k'$. Additionally, in the case $H_0 \cong H_0'$, we speak of a *parallel derivation* from H_0 to H_0' of length 0.

4. A direct parallel derivation $H \Rightarrow H'$ by the empty base $prod : \emptyset \to P$ is called a *dummy*. A parallel derivation is said to be *valid* if at least one of its steps is not a dummy.

Remark

1. A direct parallel derivation from H to H' by the production base $prod : B \to P$ with $B = \{e_1, e_2, e_3, e_4\}$ and $prod(e_i) = (A_i, R_i)$ ($i = 1, \ldots, 4$) is depicted in in the following figure.

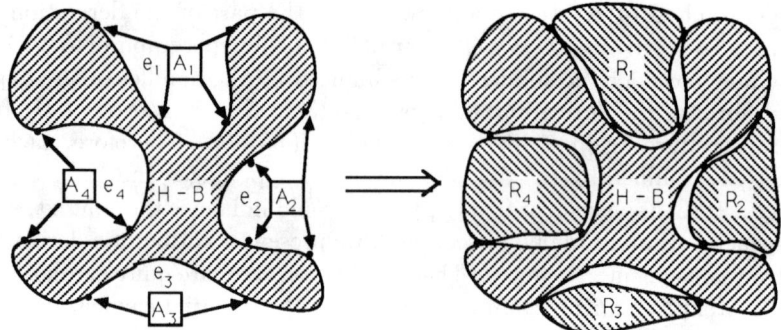

Fig. 1.1. A direct parallel derivation

2. Direct parallel derivations have some significant properties: On the one hand, the definition of a direct parallel derivation includes the case that all hyperedges are replaced in one step. On the other hand, the definition includes the case that no hyperedge is replaced. Besides these two extremes, a non-empty proper subset of hyperedges may be replaced.

3. Direct parallel derivations generalize the usual "sequential" derivations in the following sense: For each direct derivation $H \Longrightarrow H'$ by $p \in P$ applied to e, there is a direct parallel derivation $H \Rightarrow H'$ by $prod : \{e\} \to P$ with $prod(e) = p$.

1.2 Sequentialization Theorem

Let $H \Rrightarrow H'$ by $prod: B \to P$ be a direct parallel derivation. Then, for each enumeration $e_1, \ldots, e_n$ of the elements in B, there is a derivation $H = H_0 \Longrightarrow \ldots \Longrightarrow H_n = H'$ by $prod(e_1), \ldots, prod(e_n)$.

Remark

The Sequentialization Theorem follows immediately from the properties of $REPLACE$ presented in chapter I, 2.3. The derivations resulting in the Sequentialization Theorem are called *sequentializations* of the given parallel derivation.

1.3 Corollary

For each parallel derivation $H \stackrel{*}{\Rrightarrow} H'$, there is a "sequential" derivation $H \stackrel{*}{\Longrightarrow} H'$.

Remark

Corollary 1.3 is an immediate consequence of the Sequentialization Theorem. From the viewpoint of generative power, "$\stackrel{*}{\Longrightarrow}$" and "$\stackrel{*}{\Rrightarrow}$" do not have to be distinguished because of corollary 1.3 and remark 1.1(3). Hence, from now on, we use the symol "$\stackrel{*}{\Longrightarrow}$" for both kinds of derivations.

2. A Context-Freeness Lemma

Most of the results presented in this book (as, e.g., the Fixed-Point Theorem and the Pumping Lemma) are mainly based on some fundamental aspects of hyperedge-replacement derivations. Roughly speaking, hyperedge-replacement derivations cannot interfere with each other as long as they handle different hyperedges. This is shown in three steps. The Restriction Lemma provides a procedure for restricting a derivation to a subhypergraph. The Joint-Embedding Lemma states that a collection of derivations of the form $H(e) \stackrel{*}{\Longrightarrow} H'(e)$ can be simultaneously applied to H leading to a single derivation $H \stackrel{*}{\Longrightarrow} H'$ provided that the hypergraphs $H(e)$ and the hyperedges e in H "fit together". Finally, it is shown that by first restricting a derivation to each subhypergraph induced by a hyperedge, and then joining them again, we obtain the original derivation. In other words, hyperedge-replacement derivations can be distributed to the handles of the hyperedges without losing information.

2.1 Assumption

Let P be a fixed set of productions and DER be the class of all (parallel) derivations by productions of P.

2.2 Restriction Lemma

Let $H_0 \Longrightarrow \ldots \Longrightarrow H_k$ by $prod_1, \ldots, prod_k$ be a derivation where, for $i = 1, \ldots, k$, $prod_i : B_i \to P$ is a production base in H_{i-1}. Moreover, let $H'_0 \subseteq H_0$. Then there is a derivation $H'_0 \Longrightarrow \ldots \Longrightarrow H'_k$ by $prod'_1, \ldots, prod'_k$ where, for $i = 1, \ldots, k$, $prod'_i$ is the restriction of $prod_i$ to $B'_i = B_i \cap E_{H'_{i-1}}$ and $H'_i \subseteq H_i$.

Notation

The resulting derivation is denoted by $RESTRICT(der, H'_0)$ where der refers to the given derivation.

Remark

1. The explicit construction works as follows: Let $H_0 \Longrightarrow H_1$ by $prod_1 : B_1 \to P$ be the first derivation step. Let $B'_1 = B_1 \cap E_{H'_0}$ and $prod'_1$ be the restriction of $prod_1$ to B'_1. Then $prod'_1$ is a production base in H'_0 and $H'_0 \Longrightarrow H'_1$ can be constructed such that $H'_1 \subseteq H_1$. Hence this restriction step can be iterated. Note that the constructed derivation is of the same length as the original one. But the restriction may lead to a derivation with dummy steps.
2. If the right-hand sides of the productions of P are repetition-free, we get a slightly *generalized version* of the Restriction Lemma saying that whenever there is a morphism $h_0 : H'_0 \to H_0$, then there is a derivation $H'_0 \Longrightarrow \ldots \Longrightarrow H'_k$ by $prod'_1, \ldots, prod'_k$ where, for $i = 1, \ldots, k$, $prod'_i : h_{i-1,E}^{-1}(B_i) \to P$ is given by $prod'_i(e) = prod_i(h_{i-1,E}(e))$ for $e \in h_{i-1,E}^{-1}(B_i)$ and there is a morphism $h_i : H'_i \to H_i$.
3. Let $der \in DER$ be a derivation from H to H' and $B \subseteq E_H$. Then der induces a mapping $fibre : B \to DER$ given by $fibre(e) = RESTRICT(der, e^\bullet)$ for all $e \in B$. For $e \in B$, the derivation $fibre(e)$ is said to be the *fibre* of der induced by e.

Proof

The Restriction Lemma is proved by induction on the length of the derivation. The basis, $k = 0$, obviously holds. Assume now that the statement holds for some $k \geq 0$. Let $H_0 \Longrightarrow \ldots \Longrightarrow H_{k+1}$ by $prod_1, \ldots, prod_{k+1}$ be a derivation of length $k+1$. Then, we may cut off the last derivation step and obtain a derivation of length k. By the inductive hypothesis, there is a derivation $H'_0 \Longrightarrow \ldots \Longrightarrow H'_k$ by $prod'_1, \ldots, prod'_k$ where, for $i = 1, \ldots, k$, $prod'_i$ is the restriction of $prod_i$ to $B'_i = B_i \cap E_{H'_{i-1}}$ and $H'_i \subseteq H_i$. In particular, $H'_k \subseteq H_k$ and, hence, $E_{H'_k} \subseteq E_{H_k}$. On the other hand, $B_{k+1} \subseteq E_{H_k}$. Let now $B'_{k+1} = B_{k+1} \cap E_{H'_k}$ and $prod'_{k+1}$ be the restriction of $prod_{k+1}$ to B'_{k+1}. Then $prod'_{k+1}$ is a production base in H'_k. Thus, there is a direct derivation $H'_k \Longrightarrow H'_{k+1}$ by $prod'_{k+1}$ where $H'_{k+1} = REPLACE(H'_k, repl'_{k+1})$ and $repl'_{k+1}$ is the base for replacement induced by $prod'_{k+1}$. Then we get

$$V_{H'_{k+1}} = V_{H'_k} + \sum_{e \in B'_{k+1}} INT_{rhs(prod'_{k+1}(e))}$$

$$\subseteq V_{H_k} + \sum_{e \in B_{k+1}} INT_{rhs(prod_{k+1}(e))} = V_{H_{k+1}},$$

$$E_{H'_{k+1}} = E_{H'_k} - B'_{k+1} + \sum_{e \in B'_{k+1}} E_{rhs(prod'_{k+1}(e))}$$

$$\subseteq E_{H_k} - B_{k+1} + \sum_{e \in B_{k+1}} E_{rhs(prod_{k+1}(e))} = E_{H_{k+1}}.$$

The latter holds because $E_{H_k} - B_{k+1} \supseteq (E_{H_k} - B_{k+1}) \cap E_{H'_k} = E_{H'_k} - (B_{k+1} \cap E_{H'_k}) = E_{H'_k} - B'_{k+1}$. Hence, $H'_{k+1} \subseteq H_{k+1}$. Therefore, there is a derivation $H'_0 \Longrightarrow \ldots \Longrightarrow H'_{k+1}$ by $prod'_1, \ldots, prod'_{k+1}$, which possesses the desired properties. This completes the inductive step. □

2.3 Joint-Embedding Lemma

Let $H \in \mathcal{H}_C$, $B \subseteq E_H$, and $fibre : B \to DER$ be a mapping assigning a derivation $fibre(e)$ of the form $H_0(e) \Longrightarrow \ldots \Longrightarrow H_k(e)$ by $prod_{1,e}, \ldots, prod_{k,e}$ with $H_0(e) = e^\bullet$ to each $e \in B$. Then there is a derivation $H_0 \Longrightarrow \ldots \Longrightarrow H_k$ by $prod_1, \ldots, prod_k$ starting from $H = H_0$, where, for $i = 1, \ldots, k$, $prod_i$ is the extension of the production bases $prod_{i,e} : B_{i,e} \to P$ to the set $B_i = \sum_{e \in B} B_{i,e}$ and $H_i \supseteq H_i(e)$ for $e \in B$. Moreover, for $i = 0, \ldots, k$, $H_i = REPLACE(H, repl_i)$ where $repl_i : B \to \mathcal{H}_C$ is defined by $repl_i(e) = H_i(e)$ for all $e \in B$.

Notation

The resulting derivation is denoted $EMBED(H, fibre)$.

Remark

1. There is a slightly *generalized version* of the Joint-Embedding Lemma not requiring $H_0(e) = e^\bullet$: Whenever $H_0(e)$ is a hypergraph satisfying $type(H_0(e)) = type_H(e)$ and $rel(H_0(e)) \subseteq rel_H(e)$, then there is a derivation $H_0 \Longrightarrow \ldots \Longrightarrow H_k$ by $prod_1, \ldots, prod_k$, where, for $i = 1, \ldots, k$, $prod_i$ is the extension of the $prod_{i,e}$, and, for $i = 0, \ldots, k$, $H_i = REPLACE(H, repl_i)$, where $repl_i : B \to \mathcal{H}_C$ is defined by $repl_i(e) = H_i(e)$ for all $e \in B$.
2. The common length of the derivations composed by $EMBED$ is not a serious restriction because each derivation can be lengthened by dummy steps.
3. For a one-element set B, the Joint-Embedding Lemma is a reformulation of the Embedding Lemma in Kreowski [Kr 77b] for the case of hyperedge replacement.

Proof

The Joint-Embedding Lemma is proved by induction on the length of the derivations.

The basis, $k = 0$, obviously holds. $repl_0(e) = H_0(e) = e^{\bullet}$ for $e \in B$ implies $H_0 = H = REPLACE(H, repl_0)$. Assume now that the statement is true for some $k \geq 0$. Let, for $e \in B$, $H_0(e) \Longrightarrow \ldots \Longrightarrow H_{k+1}(e)$ by $prod_{1,e}, \ldots, prod_{k+1,e}$ be a derivation of length $k+1$ with $H_0(e) = e^{\bullet}$. Separating the last derivation step for each derivation, we get derivations of length k. By the inductive hypothesis, the derivations can be embedded into H yielding a derivation $H_0 \Longrightarrow \ldots \Longrightarrow H_k$ by $prod_1, \ldots, prod_k$, with $H_0 = H$ where, for $i = 1, \ldots, k$, $prod_i$ is the extension of the production bases $prod_{i,e} : B_{i,e} \to P$ in $H_i(e)$ to the set $B_i = \sum_{e \in B} B_{i,e}$. Moreover, for $i = 0, \ldots, k$, $H_i = REPLACE(H, repl_i)$, where $repl_i : B \to \mathcal{H}_C$ is given by $repl_i(e) = H_i(e)$. In particular, we have $H_k = REPLACE(H, repl_k)$, where $repl_k : B \to \mathcal{H}_C$ is given by $repl_k(e) = H_k(e)$. Then $E_{H_k(e)} \cap E_{H_k(e')} = \emptyset$ for $e \neq e'$. Consider now the direct derivations $H_k(e) \Longrightarrow H_{k+1}(e)$ by $prod_{k+1,e} : B_{k+1,e} \to P$ ($e \in B$). Then $B_{k+1,e} \cap B_{k+1,e'} = \emptyset$ for $e \neq e'$. Let $prod_{k+1}$ be the extension of the production bases $prod_{k+1,e}$ in $H_k(e)$ to the set $B_{k+1} = \sum_{e \in B} B_{k+1,e}$. Then $prod_{k+1}$ is a production base in H_k. Hence, there is a direct derivation $H_k \Longrightarrow H_{k+1}$ by $prod_{k+1}$. Moreover, we have

$$H_{k+1} = REPLACE(H_k, repl'_{k+1})$$
$$= REPLACE(REPLACE(H, repl_k), repl'_{k+1})$$
$$= REPLACE(H, repl_{k+1})$$

where $repl'_{k+1} : B_{k+1} \to P$ is the base for replacement in H_k induced by $prod_{k+1}$, $repl_{k+1} : B \to \mathcal{H}_C$ is the base for replacement in H given by

$$repl_{k+1}(e) = REPLACE(repl_k(e), repl'_{k+1,e})$$
$$= REPLACE(H_k(e), repl'_{k+1,e})$$
$$= H_{k+1}(e),$$

and $repl'_{k+1,e} : B_{k+1,e} \to \mathcal{H}_C$ is the restriction of $repl'_{k+1}$ to $B_{k+1,e}$. Note that $prod_{k+1}$ is the extension of the production bases $prod_{k+1,e} : B_{k+1,e} \to P$, $repl'_{k+1}$ is the base for replacement induced by $prod_{k+1}$, and $repl'_{k+1,e}$ is the restriction of $repl'_{k+1}$ to $B_{k+1,e}$. Hence, $repl'_{k+1,e}$ is the base for replacement induced by $prod_{k+1,e}$. This completes the inductive proof. □

2.4 Context-Freeness Lemma

1. Let der be a derivation from H to H'. Then there is a set $B \subseteq E_H$ such that the mapping $fibre : B \to DER$ given by $fibre(e) = RESTRICT(der, e^{\bullet})$ for all $e \in B$ allows one to reconstruct the derivation der as $EMBED(H, fibre)$, i.e., up to isomorphism [1])

$$EMBED(H, fibre) = der.$$

---

[1]) Let $H_0 \Longrightarrow \ldots \Longrightarrow H_k$ by $prod_1, \ldots, prod_k$, $H'_0 \Longrightarrow \ldots \Longrightarrow H'_k$ by $prod'_1, \ldots, prod'_k$ be two derivations, where, for $i = 1, \ldots, k$, $prod_i : B_i \to P$ and $prod'_i : B'_i \to P$. Then the derivations are said to be *equal (up to isomorphism)* if there are isomorphisms $f_i : H_i \to H'_i$ ($i = 0, \ldots, k$) such that for $i = 1, \ldots, k$, $f_{i-1,E}(B_i) = B'_i$ and $prod_i(e) = prod'_i(f_{i-1,E}(e))$ for all $e \in B_i$.

2. Let $H \in \mathcal{H}_C$, $B \subseteq E_H$, and $fibre: B \to DER$. Then the fibres can be extracted from the embedding derivation $EMBED(H, fibre)$, i.e., for all $e \in E_H$, up to isomorphism

$$RESTRICT(EMBED(H, fibre), e^\bullet) = fibre(e).$$

Remark

Roughly speaking, the first statement of the Context-Freeness Lemma says that derivations in hyperedge-replacement grammars can be decomposed into "thin fibres" (where each one starts from the subhypergraph induced by a hyperedge) without losing information.

Proof

1. Let $H = H_0 \Longrightarrow \ldots \Longrightarrow H_k$ by $prod_1, \ldots, prod_k$ be a derivation, where, for $i = 1, \ldots, k$, $prod_i : B_i \to P$ is a production base in H_{i-1}, and let $B = E_H$. Moreover, let $e^\bullet = H_0(e) \Longrightarrow \ldots \Longrightarrow H_k(e)$ by $prod_{1,e}, \ldots, prod_{k,e}$ be the restriction of the derivation to $e^\bullet$ where, for $i = 1, \ldots, k$, $prod_{i,e}$ is the restriction of $prod_i$ to the set $B_{i,e} = B_i \cap E_{H_{i-1}(e)}$ and $H_i(e) \subseteq H_i$. Joint embedding of these derivations into H yields a derivation $H = H_0' \Longrightarrow \ldots \Longrightarrow H_k'$ by $prod_1', \ldots, prod_k'$ where, for $i = 1, \ldots, k$, $prod_i'$ is the extension of the $prod_{i,e}$ to the set $B_i = \sum_{e \in B} B_{i,e}$. Then we have $H_0' = H = H_0$ and, if $H_i' = H_i$ and $i < k$, then $prod_{i+1}' = prod_{i+1}$ (the extension of the restrictions of a mapping equals the mapping). Therefore, $H_{i+1}' = H_{i+1}$ (up to isomorphism). This completes the first part of the proof.

2. Let $H \in \mathcal{H}_C$, $B \subseteq E_H$, and, for $e \in B$, $H_0(e) \Longrightarrow \ldots \Longrightarrow H_k(e)$ by $prod_{1,e}, \ldots, prod_{k,e}$ be a derivation with $H_0(e) = e^\bullet$. Let $H_0 \Longrightarrow \ldots \Longrightarrow H_k$ by $prod_1, \ldots, prod_k$ be the joint embedding of the derivations into H and, for $e \in B$, $H_0'(e) \Longrightarrow \ldots \Longrightarrow H_k'(e)$ by $prod_{1,e}', \ldots, prod_{k,e}'$ with $H_0'(e) = e^\bullet$ be the restriction to $e^\bullet$. Then $H_0'(e) = e^\bullet = H_0(e)$ and, if $H_i'(e) = H_i(e)$ and $i < k$, then $prod_{i+1,e}' = prod_{i+1,e}$ (the restrictions of an extenstion of mappings equal the original mappings). Therefore, $H_{i+1}'(e) = H_{i+1}(e)$ (up to isomorphism). This completes the second part of the proof. □

The results presented in the following chapters are mainly based on the first statement of the Context-Freeness Lemma. We will use it in the following recursive version concerning hypergraphs which are derivable from handles.

2.5 Theorem (Decomposition of Derivations)

Let $F, H \in \mathcal{H}_C$ and F be a handle. Then there is a derivation $F \stackrel{k+1}{\Longrightarrow} H$ for some $k \geq 0$ if and only if there is a direct derivation $F \Longrightarrow G$ and, for each $e \in E_G$, there is a derivation $e^\bullet \stackrel{k}{\Longrightarrow} H(e)$ with $H(e) \subseteq H$ such that $H = REPLACE(G, repl)$ with $repl(e) = H(e)$ for $e \in E_G$.

Proof

Let $F \stackrel{k+1}{\Longrightarrow} H$ be a derivation of length $k+1$. Then the derivation is of the form $F \Longrightarrow G \stackrel{k}{\Longrightarrow} H$. Now one may construct the fibres $fibre(e) : e^\bullet \stackrel{k}{\Longrightarrow} H(e)$ of $G \stackrel{k}{\Longrightarrow} H$ induced by e. Then $H(e) \subseteq H$. By the Context-Freeness Lemma, we know that $EMBED(G, fibre) = G \stackrel{k}{\Longrightarrow} H$. Therefore, $REPLACE(G, repl) = H$ where $repl$ is the base for replacement with $repl(e) = H(e)$ for $e \in E_G$.

Conversely, let $F \Longrightarrow G$ be a direct derivation and for $e \in E_G$, $fibre(e) = e^\bullet \stackrel{k}{\Longrightarrow} H(e)$ be a derivation with $H(e) \subseteq H$. Moreover, let $REPLACE(G, repl) = H$ where $repl$ is the base for replacement with $repl(e) = H(e)$ for $e \in E_G$. Then the embedding of the derivations $fibre(e)$ into G yields a derivation $EMBED(G, fibre) = G \stackrel{k}{\Longrightarrow} H'$ with $H' = REPLACE(G, repl) = H$. Therefore, there is a derivation $F \Longrightarrow G \stackrel{k}{\Longrightarrow} H$ of length $k+1$. □

Remark

1. The situation may be illustrated as follows.

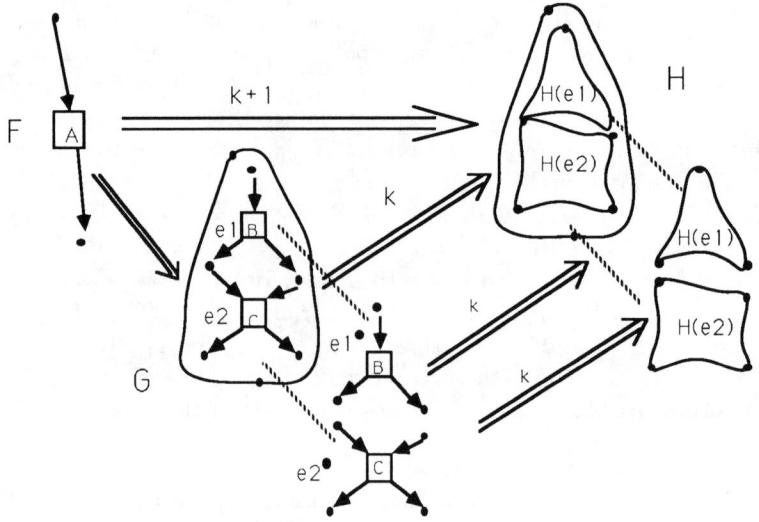

Fig. 2.1. Decomposition of a derivation

2. Given a hypergraph $H \in \mathcal{H}_C$, each derivation of H induces a decomposition of H into smaller hypergraphs: Let H be a hypergraph and $F \stackrel{k+1}{\Longrightarrow} H$ be a derivation of H from the handle F. Then the derivation decomposes into a direct derivation $F \Longrightarrow G$ and derivations $e^\bullet \stackrel{k}{\Longrightarrow} H(e)$ with $H(e) \subseteq H$ ($e \in E_G$). For $e \in E_G$, the derivation $e^\bullet \stackrel{k}{\Longrightarrow} H(e)$ may be valid or not. In the first case, it has the same form as the original derivation, but it is shorter than the original one. In the latter case, $H(e)$ is isomorphic to $e^\bullet$ and, hence, a handle.

3. Derivation Trees

The systematic use of trees to illustrate derivations is an important device that greatly sharpens our intuition. Since we use this concept in formal proofs, it is necessary to have precise definitions. We introduce the notion of derivation trees and discuss the relationship between derivation trees and derivations.

3.1 Definition (Derivation Trees and Their Results)

Let P be a set of productions.
1. The set $HANDLE(P)$ of all *handles* induced by P is defined as follows.
(a) If $(A, R) \in P$ and $e \in E_R$, then $e^\bullet \in HANDLE(P)$.
(b) If $H \in HANDLE(P)$, $type(H) = (m, n)$, and rel is an equivalence relation on $[m+n]$ with $rel(H) \subseteq rel$, then the quotient hypergraph H/rel is in $HANDLE(P)$.
2. The set $TREE(P)$ of all *derivation trees* over P together with the mappings $root, result : TREE(P) \to \mathcal{H}_C$ are recursively defined as follows.
(a) If $H \in HANDLE(P)$, then $(H) \in TREE(P)$ and $root((H)) = result((H)) = H$.
(b) If $H \in HANDLE(P)$ is a handle, $(A, R) \in P$ is a production applicable to the hyperedge e in H, and $tree : E_{H[e/R]} \to TREE(P)$ is a mapping assigning a derivation tree $tree(e')$ with $root(tree(e')) = e'^\bullet$ to each hyperedge e' in $H[e/R]$, then $(H, (A, R), tree) \in TREE(P)$ is a derivation tree over P, $root((H, (A, R), tree)) = H$, and $result((H, (A, R), tree)) = REPLACE(H[e/R], result \circ tree)$.

Remark

Derivation trees may be represented as labeled hypergraphs. Then their nodes are labeled by handles and their hyperedges are labeled by productions. A derivation tree $T = (H, (A, R), tree)$ with $root(T) = H$, $tree(e_i) = T_i$, and $root(tree(e_i)) = H_i$ ($e_i \in E_{H[e/R]}$) has the following shape.

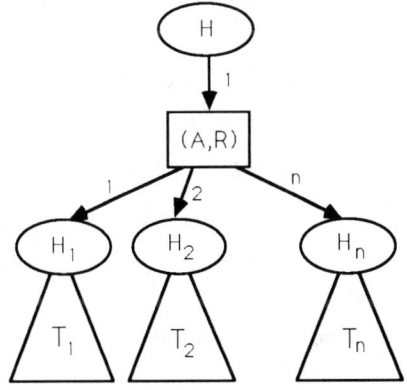

Fig. 3.1. A derivation tree $(H, (A, R), tree)$

We shall now show that a derivation tree is an adequate representation for derivations by showing that for every derivation from a handle H to a hypergraph H' there is a derivation tree with root labeling H and result H', and conversely.

3.2 Lemma

For each derivation $H \stackrel{*}{\Longrightarrow} H'$ by P starting from a handle $H \in HANDLE(P)$, there is a derivation tree T over P with $root(T) = H$ and $result(T) = H'$.

Proof

The statement is proved by induction on the length of a derivation. If $H \stackrel{*}{\Longrightarrow} H'$ is a zero-step derivation, then $H = H'$ (up to isomorphism). If, moreover, $H \in HANDLE(P)$, then (H) is a derivation tree over P, $root((H)) = H$, and $result((H)) = H = H'$. Assume now that the statement holds for some $k \geq 0$. If $H \stackrel{*}{\Longrightarrow} H'$ is a k+1-step derivation by P starting from $H \in HANDLE(P)$ with hyperedge e, then the derivation is of the form $H \Longrightarrow R' \stackrel{k}{\Longrightarrow} H'$. If the first derivation step is a dummy, then $H \cong R'$, $R' \stackrel{k}{\Longrightarrow} H'$ can be modified into a derivation $H \stackrel{k}{\Longrightarrow} H'$, and, by the inductive hypothesis, there is a derivation tree over P with the desired properties. Otherwise, there is a production $(A, R) \in P$ such that $A = l_H(e)$, $type(R) = type_H(e)$, $rel(R) \subseteq rel_H(e)$, and $R' = H[e/R]$. We now consider the fibres $e^\bullet \stackrel{k}{\Longrightarrow} H'(e)$ of $R' \stackrel{k}{\Longrightarrow} H'$ induced by $e \in E_{R'}$. By the inductive hypothesis, for each derivation $e^\bullet \stackrel{k}{\Longrightarrow} H'(e)$ of length k, there is a derivation tree $tree(e)$ over P with $root(tree(e)) = e^\bullet$ and $result(tree(e)) = H'(e)$. Now $(H, (A, R), tree)$ is a derivation tree over P. Moreover, $root((H, (A, R), tree)) = H$ and $result((H, (A, R), tree)) = REPLACE(H[e/R], result \circ tree)$. By the Context-Freeness Lemma, we have $REPLACE(H[e/R], result \circ tree) = H'$. Thus, the derivation tree $(H, (A, R), tree)$ has the desired properties. This completes the inductive proof. □

We will now obtain the converse of lemma 3.2. That is, for every derivation tree over P there is a derivation by P.

3.3 Lemma

For each derivation tree T over P, there is a derivation $H \stackrel{*}{\Longrightarrow} H'$ by P with $H = root(T)$ and $H' = result(T)$.

Proof

The statement is proved by structural induction. If T is a derivation tree over P of the form (H) with $H \in HANDLE(P)$, then there is a zero-step derivation $H \stackrel{0}{\Longrightarrow} H$ by P and $H = root(T) = result(T)$. If T is a derivation tree over P of the form $(H, (A, R), tree)$, then there is a direct derivation $H \Longrightarrow H[e/R]$ by $(A, R) \in P$ applied to $e \in E_H$. Moreover, by the inductive hypothesis, for each derivation tree $tree(e)$

over P, there is a derivation $e^{\bullet} \stackrel{*}{\Longrightarrow} result(tree(e))$ by P. Embedding of these derivations into the hypergraph $H[e/R]$ yields a derivation $H[e/R] \stackrel{*}{\Longrightarrow} H'$ by P with $H' = REPLACE(H[e/R], result \circ tree)$. Thus, there is a derivation $H \Longrightarrow H[e/R] \stackrel{*}{\Longrightarrow} H'$ by P with $H = root(T)$ and $H' = result(T)$. □

We can combine lemma 3.2 and 3.3 into the following theorem.

3.4 Theorem

Let P be a set of productions. Then, for all $H \in HANDLE(P)$, there is a derivation $H \stackrel{*}{\Longrightarrow} H'$ by P if and only if there is a derivation tree T over P with $root(T) = H$ and $result(T) = H'$.

Proof

The proof follows immediately from the lemmata 3.2 and 3.3. □

4. Bibliographic Note

Parallel derivations were introduced by Ehrig and Kreowski ([Kr 77a+b, Eh 79]); the constituent parts of the Sequentialization Theorem can be found, e.g., in [Kr 77a+b] and [Eh 79]. The Context-Freeness Lemma was first formulated and proved for edge-replacement grammars (see [HK 83+87a]); a formulation for hyperedge-replacement grammars can be found in [HK 87c]. Finally, derivation trees in the sense of definition 3.1 are closely related to rule trees as introduced and investigated by Kreowski [Kr 86+87a].

Chapter III
Characterizations of HRL's

In this book, we view (hyper)graph grammars mainly as language-generating devices. Therefore it is very interesting to have characterizations of the class of languages that can be generated by hyperedge-replacement grammars. In this chapter, two well-known characterizations of context-free string languages are generalized and adapted to hyperedge-replacement grammars. Gruska [Gr 71] and Yntema [Yn 71] developed a context-free analogon to Kleene's characterization of regular languages. Ginsburg and Rice [GR 62] proved that context-free languages are the least fixed points of their generating productions (considered as a system of language equations). For both results we present hyperedge-replacement grammar versions providing alternative mechanisms for generating hyperedge-replacement languages.

The chapter is organized as follows. In section 1, we define some operations, called substitution and iterated substitution, and show that hyperedge-replacement languages are closed under these operations. Both operations turn out to be essential with respect to section 2 as well as to section 3. In section 2, a Kleene-Type Characterization of hyperedge-replacement languages is given. Roughly speaking, it says that the class of all hyperedge-replacement languages is the smallest class of hypergraph languages which contains all finite (homogeneous) languages and is closed under substitution and iterated substitution. Finally, in section 3, a Fixed-Point Theorem is stated saying that hyperedge-replacement languages are the least fixed points of their generating productions (considered as a system of language equations).

In the following, we assume that for any hypergraph H, the sequence ext_H of external nodes does not contain repetitions. This is no rigorous restriction (c.f., the Well-Formedness Theorem). All results may be formulated and proved for the general case. Nevertheless, the proofs become more simple, when we assume that the right-hand sides of productions as well as the axiom of a hyperedge-replacement grammar are repetition-free and that the hypergraph languages consist of repetition-free hypergraphs.

General Assumption

In the following, let $\mathcal{H}_C$ denote the set of all *repetition-free* hypergraphs over C. Furthermore, let $\mathcal{L}_C$ denote the class of all languages of *repetition-free* hypergraphs over C.

1. Closure Properties

In this section, we consider some operations under which the set of hyperedge-replacement languages (HRL's) is closed. The operations are useful not only in constructing or proving that certain languages are hyperedge-replacement languages but also in proving certain languages not to be hyperedge-replacement languages.

First, we will consider so-called X-substitutions. For each symbol $A \in X$, let $SUB(A)$ be a particular hypergraph language. Then we may replace *all* hyperedges e in a hypergraph $H \in L$ with labels in X, respectively, by hypergraphs $R(e)$, where $R(e)$ is an arbitrary hypergraph in $SUB(l_H(e))$. The result of this replacement process is a hypergraph language, denoted by $SUB(L)$.

1.1 Definition (X-Substitution)

Let $X \subseteq C$ be a finite set of symbols. Then a mapping $SUB : X \to \mathcal{L}_C$ is said to be an X-*substitution*. $SUB : X \to \mathcal{L}_C$ is extended to languages $L \in \mathcal{L}_C$ by defining

$$SUB(L) = \bigcup_{H \in L} \left\{ REPLACE(H, repl) \mid repl(e) \in SUB(l_H(e)) \text{ for } e \in E_{H,X} \right\}$$

where, for $H \in \mathcal{H}_C$, $E_{H,X} = \{e \in E_H \mid l_H(e) \in X\}$ and $repl : E_{H,X} \to \mathcal{H}_C$ is a base for replacement in H.

Remark

Each X-substitution $SUB : X \to \mathcal{L}_C$ induces a set of productions over X, denoted by $P(SUB)$, which is given by $P(SUB) = \{(A, R) \mid A \in X \text{ and } R \in SUB(A)\}$.

Using similar arguments as in the string case we get the following closure property.

1.2 Theorem (Closure Under X-Substitution)

For all finite sets $X \subseteq C$, the hyperedge-replacement languages over C are closed under X-substitution. That is, if L is a hyperedge-replacement language and $SUB : X \to \mathcal{L}_C$ is an X-substitution assigning a hyperedge-replacement language $SUB(A)$ to each $A \in X$, then $SUB(L)$ is a hyperedge-replacement language as well.

Proof

Let $HRG = (N, T, P, Z)$ be a usual hyperedge-replacement grammar generating L and for $A \in X$, $HRG(A) = (N(A), T(A), P(A), Z(A))$ be a usual hyperedge-replacement grammar generating $SUB(A)$. Without loss of generality, we may assume that the set of symbols occurring as nonterminals and the set of symbols occurring as terminals are disjoint and that the sets of nonterminals of the grammars are pairwise disjoint. Furthermore, we may assume that $X \subseteq T$. (Otherwise, we consider $X' = X \cap T$ and the restriction of SUB to X', SUB'. For this substitution, $SUB'(L(HRG)) = SUB(L(HRG))$.) We will construct a grammar $HRG' = (N', T', P', Z')$ generating $SUB(L(HRG))$ with help of a new set $\bar{X} = \{\bar{A} | A \in X\}$ of symbols and a relabeling of hyperedges with a label in X. For a hypergraph $R \in \mathcal{H}_C$, let $\bar{R}$ denote the hypergraph in which each symbol $A \in X$ is replaced by the corresponding symbol $\bar{A} \in \bar{X}$.

Now let $HRG' = (N', T', P', Z')$ be the hyperedge-replacement grammar with

- $N' = N \cup \bar{X} \cup N(X)$
  where $N(X) = \bigcup_{A \in X} N(A)$,
- $T' = (T - X) \cup T(X)$
  where $T(X) = \bigcup_{A \in X} T(A)$,
- $P' = \bar{P} \cup Q \cup P(X)$
  where $\bar{P} = \{(A, \bar{R}) | (A, R) \in P\}$,
  $Q = \{(\bar{A}, Z(A)) | A \in X\}$, and
  $P(X) = \bigcup_{A \in X} P(A)$,
- $Z' = Z$.

Then $L(HRG') = SUB(L(HRG))$. This may be seen as follows.

First, let $H' \in SUB(L(HRG))$. Then, there is a hypergraph $H \in L(HRG)$ and a base for replacement $repl : E_{H,X} \to \mathcal{H}_C$ with $repl(e) \in SUB(l_H(e))$ such that $REPLACE(H, repl) = H'$. By $H \in L(HRG)$, there is a derivation $Z \stackrel{*}{\Rightarrow} H$ by P and a corresponding derivation $Z \stackrel{*}{\Rightarrow} \bar{H}$ by $\bar{P}$. Since $repl : E_{H,X} \to \mathcal{H}_C$ is a base for replacement in H and for $e \in E_{H,X}$, $SUB(l_H(e))$ is generated by $HRG(l_H(e))$, there is a direct derivation step $\bar{H} \Longrightarrow \hat{H}$ by $prod : E_{\bar{H},\bar{X}} \to Q$ with $prod(e) = (\overline{l_H(e)}, Z(l_H(e)))$ for $e \in E_{\bar{H},\bar{X}} = E_{H,X}$. Furthermore, there are derivations $Z(l_H(e)) \stackrel{*}{\Rightarrow} repl(e)$ by $P(l_H(e))$. Using the generalized version of the Joint-Embedding Lemma, we get a derivation $\hat{H} \stackrel{*}{\Rightarrow} \hat{H}'$ by $P(X)$ where $\hat{H}' = REPLACE(\hat{H}, repl)$. Since the axioms $Z(l_H(e))$ are repetition-free handles (c.f. general assumption) and $type(Z(l_H(e))) = type(e)$ ($e \in E_{H,X}$), the hypergraphs H, $\bar{H}$, and $\hat{H}$ only differ in the labels of the hyperedges. By this reason, $\hat{H}' = REPLACE(\hat{H}, repl) = REPLACE(H, repl) = H'$. Now

$$Z \stackrel{*}{\underset{\bar{P}}{\Longrightarrow}} \bar{H} \underset{Q}{\Longrightarrow} \hat{H} \stackrel{*}{\underset{P(X)}{\Longrightarrow}} H'$$

forms a derivation of H' by P'. Moreover, H' is labeled over $(T - X) \cup T(X)$. Thus, $H' \in L(HRG')$.

For the converse, let $H' \in L(HRG')$ and $Z \stackrel{*}{\Longrightarrow} H'$ be a derivation of H' by P'. Then the derivation can be transformed in a suitable way. We make use of the fact that "sequentially independent" derivation steps can be interchanged. In the special case of hyperedge replacement, two consecutive steps are sequentially independent if and only if the hyperedge which is replaced in the second step is not just created in the first step.

Consequently, derivation steps using productions $\bar{P} \cup Q$ are sequentially independent of previous derivation steps using productions of $P(X)$ $((N(X) \cup T(X)) \cap (N \cup \bar{X}) = \emptyset)$ and derivation steps using productions $\bar{P}$ are sequentially independent of previous derivation steps using productions of Q $((N(X) \cup T(X)) \cap N = \emptyset)$. Hence, there is a derivation of the form

$$Z \underset{\bar{P}}{\overset{*}{\Longrightarrow}} \bar{H} \underset{Q}{\overset{*}{\Longrightarrow}} \hat{H} \underset{P(X)}{\overset{*}{\Longrightarrow}} H'.$$

For the derivation $Z \underset{\bar{P}}{\overset{*}{\Longrightarrow}} \bar{H}$ by $\bar{P}$, there is a corresponding derivation $Z \overset{*}{\Longrightarrow} H$ by P. Moreover, H is labeled over T because H' is labeled over $T' = (T - X) \cup T(X)$ and $\bar{H}$ is labeled over $(T - X) \cup \bar{X}$. Hence $H \in L(HRG) = L$. For each $e \in E_{\bar{H},N(X)}$ ($= E_{H,X}$), there is a derivation $Z(l_H(e)) \overset{*}{\Longrightarrow} H'(e)$ by $P(l_H(e))$ (see the generalized version of the Restriction Lemma; furthermore, we make use of the assumption that the sets of nonterminals of distinct grammars are pairwise distinct.) $H'(e)$ is labeled over $T(l_H(e))$ because H' is labeled over $T' = (T - X) \cup T(X)$. Thus, $H'(e) \in L(HRG(l_H(e))) = SUB(l_H(e))$. By the Context-Freeness Lemma, $H' = REPLACE(H, repl)$ with $repl(e) = H'(e)$ ($e \in E_{H,X}$). Thus there is a hypergraph $H \in L$ and a base for replacement $repl : E_{H,X} \to \mathcal{H}_C$ with $repl(e) \in SUB(l_H(e))$ such that $REPLACE(H, repl) = H'$. This means $H' \in SUB(L)$. □

Remark

1. An *X-homomorphism* $HOM : X \to \mathcal{L}_C$ is an X-substitution such that $HOM(A)$ contains a single hypergraph for each A. Since an X-homomorphism is a special type of X-substitution, hyperedge-replacement languages are closed under X-homomorphisms.
2. Hyperedge-replacement languages are closed under *concatenation*. For making this precise, we define a concatentation operation on homogeneous hypergraph languages. Let L_1, L_2 be homogeneous hypergraph languages of types (m_1, n_1) and (m_2, n_2), respectively, and rel be an equivalence relation on $[(m_1 + m_2) + (n_1 + n_2)]$. Then the concatenation of L_1 and L_2 with respect to rel is given by

$$L_1 \oplus_{rel} L_2 = \{H_1 \oplus_{rel} H_2 | H_1 \in L_1 \text{ and } H_2 \in L_2\}$$

where, for $H_1 \in L_1, H_2 \in L_2$, $H_1 \oplus_{rel} H_2$ is the quotient hypergraph $(H_1 + H_2)/\approx_{rel}$ of $H_1 + H_2$ with respect to the equivalence relation $\approx_{rel}$ induced by rel (see chapter I, proof of theorem 4.6). In this context, $H_1 + H_2$ denotes the disjoint union of H_1 and H_2 with $begin_{H_1+H_2} = begin_{H_1} \cdot begin_{H_2}$ and $end_{H_1+H_2} = end_{H_1} \cdot end_{H_2}$.
Now the closure result can be obtained as follows. Let, for $i = 1, 2$, L_i be a hyperedge-replacement language and $Z(A_i) = (A_i, (m_i, n_i))^\bullet$ be the handle induced by a symbol $A_i \in C$ and the type of L_i. Then $L_1 \oplus_{rel} L_2 = SUB([Z(A_1) \oplus_{rel} Z(A_2)])$ [1] with $SUB(A_i) = L_i$ for $i = 1, 2$. Obviously, $[Z(A_1) \oplus_{rel} Z(A_2)]$ is a finite hyperedge-replacement language. Now the closure of hyperedge-replacement languages under $\{A_1, A_2\}$-substitution implies the closure under the concatenation $\oplus_{rel}$.

---

[1] Remember that $[H]$ denotes the class of hypergraphs isomorphic to $H \in \mathcal{H}_C$.

3. Finally, hyperedge-replacement languages (of the same type) are closed under *union*. This may be seen as follows: For $i = 1, 2$, let L_i be a hyperedge-replacement language of type (m, n) and $Z(A_i) = (A_i, (m, n))^\bullet$ be the handle induced by the symbol $A_i \in C$ and the type of L_i. Then $L_1 \cup L_2 = SUB([Z(A_1)] \cup [Z(A_2)])$ with $SUB(A_i) = L_i$ for $i = 1, 2$. Obviously, $[Z(A_1)] \cup [Z(A_2)]$ is a finite hyperedge-replacement language. Now the closure of hyperedge-replacement languages under $\{A_1, A_2\}$-substitution implies their closure under union.

1.3 Definition (Iterated X-Substitution)

Let $SUB : X \to \mathcal{L}_C$ be an X-substitution. Then the *iterated X-substitution* of SUB, denoted by $SUB^* : X \to \mathcal{L}_C$, is defined by

$$SUB^*(A) = \bigcup_{n=0}^{\infty} SUB^n(A)$$

where $SUB^0(A) = \emptyset$ and $SUB^{i+1}(A) = SUB^i(SUB(A))$ for $i \geq 0$.

Remark

1. For each X-substitution $SUB : X \to \mathcal{L}_C$, SUB^* is an X-substitution as well. Therefore, the extension to languages $L \in \mathcal{L}_C$ is defined. It is straightforward to show that

$$SUB^*(L) = \bigcup_{n=0}^{\infty} SUB^n(L)$$

where $SUB^0(L) = L \cap \mathcal{H}_{C-X}$ and $SUB^{i+1}(L) = SUB^i(SUB(L))$ for $i \geq 0$.
2. For $A \in X$, $L \in \mathcal{L}_C$, and $n \in \mathbb{N}$, $SUB^n(A) \subseteq SUB^{n+1}(A)$ and $SUB^n(L) \subseteq SUB^{n+1}(L)$.

Before we show that hyperedge-replacement languages are closed under iterated X-substitution, we present a lemma which demonstrates the close relationship between iterated X-substitution and parallel derivations by productions induced by the substitution mapping.

1.4 Lemma (Iterated X-Substitution & Parallel Derivations)

Let $X \subseteq C$, $SUB : X \to \mathcal{L}_C$ an be X-substitution assigning a homogeneous [2]) hypergraph language to each $A \in X$, $P(SUB)$ be the set of productions induced by SUB, and $Z : X \to \mathcal{H}_C$ be the mapping assigning the handle $Z(A) = (A, type(SUB(A)))^\bullet$ to each $A \in X$. Then, for $A \in X$ and $L \in \mathcal{L}_C$,

---

[2]) Remember that a language L is homogeneous if $type(H) = type(H')$ and $rel(H) = rel(H')$ for all $H, H' \in L$.

$$SUB^*(A) = \left\{ H \in \mathcal{H}_{C-X} \,\middle|\, Z(A) \underset{P(SUB)}{\overset{*}{\Longrightarrow}} H \right\}, \text{ and}$$

$$SUB^*(L) = \bigcup_{H \in L} \left\{ H' \in \mathcal{H}_{C-X} \,\middle|\, H \underset{P(SUB)}{\overset{*}{\Longrightarrow}} H' \right\}.$$

Proof

The proof of the first statement is based on two claims.

Claim 1. If $H \in SUB^n(A)$, then $H \in \mathcal{H}_{C-X}$ and there is a derivation $Z(A) \underset{P(SUB)}{\overset{n}{\Longrightarrow}} H$.

Proof of Claim 1 (by induction on n). The basis is trivial; $SUB^0(A) = \emptyset$ and for $H \in SUB^1(A) = SUB^0(SUB(A))$, $H \in SUB(A) \cap \mathcal{H}_{C-X}$ and $Z(A) \Longrightarrow H$ by $(A, H) \in P(SUB)$ is a direct derivation. Assume that the statement is true for some $n \geq 1$ and let $H \in SUB^{n+1}(A)$. Then, $H \in SUB^n(SUB(A))$, i.e., there is some $R \in SUB(A)$ and some base for replacement $repl : E_{R,X} \to \mathcal{H}_C$ with $repl(e) \in SUB^n(l_R(e))$ such that $H = REPLACE(R, repl)$. Since $Z(A) = (A, type(SUB(A)))^\bullet$ and $R \in SUB(A)$, there is a direct derivation $Z(A) \Longrightarrow R$ by $(A, R) \in P(SUB)$. Moreover, by the inductive hypothesis, for all $e \in E_{R,X}$, $repl(e) \in \mathcal{H}_{C-X}$ and there is a derivation $Z(l_R(e)) \overset{n}{\Longrightarrow} repl(e)$ by productions of $P(SUB)$. Joint Embedding of these derivations into R yields a derivation $R \overset{n}{\Longrightarrow} H'$ by productions of $P(SUB)$ with result $H' = REPLACE(R, repl) = H$. Now $H \in \mathcal{H}_{C-X}$ and there is a derivation $Z(A) \overset{n+1}{\Longrightarrow} H$. This completes the inductive proof.

Claim 2. If $Z(A) \underset{P(SUB)}{\overset{n}{\Longrightarrow}} H$ is a derivation with $H \in \mathcal{H}_{C-X}$, then $H \in SUB^n(A)$.

Proof of Claim 2 (by induction on the length of the derivation). For zero-step derivations $Z(A) \overset{0}{\Longrightarrow} H$, we have $H \cong Z(A) \notin \mathcal{H}_{C-X}$. For one-step derivations $Z(A) \overset{1}{\Longrightarrow} H$ with $H \in \mathcal{H}_{C-X}$, $H \cong R$ for some production $(A, R) \in P(SUB)$; therefore, $H \in SUB(A) \cap \mathcal{H}_{C-X} = SUB^0(SUB(A)) = SUB^1(A)$. Assume that the statement is true for n-step derivations ($n \geq 1$) and let $Z(A) \overset{n+1}{\Longrightarrow} H$ by $P(SUB)$ be a $n+1$-step derivation with $H \in \mathcal{H}_{C-X}$. Then the derivation is of the form $Z(A) \Longrightarrow R' \overset{n}{\Longrightarrow} H$. If the first derivation step is a dummy, then $R' \cong Z(A)$ and the remaining derivation $R' \overset{n}{\Longrightarrow} H$ can be transformed into a derivation $Z(A) \overset{n}{\Longrightarrow} H$. By the inductive hypothesis, $H \in SUB^n(A) \subseteq SUB^{n+1}(A)$. Otherwise, $R' \cong R$ for some production $(A, R) \in P(SUB)$. Without loss of generality, $R' = R$. By the general assumption, all right-hand-sides of productions in $P(SUB)$ are repetition-free. Now, by the generalized version of the Restriction Lemma, for each $e \in E_{R,X}$, there is a derivation $Z(l_R(e)) \overset{n}{\Longrightarrow} H(e)$ with $H(e) \in \mathcal{H}_{C-X}$. By the inductive hypothesis, $H(e) \in SUB^n(l_R(e))$. Furthermore, $repl : E_{R,X} \to \mathcal{H}_C$ with $repl(e) = H(e)$ for $e \in E_{R,X}$ defines a base for replacement in R and $REPLACE(R, repl) = \bar{H}$. Thus, $H \in SUB^n(SUB(A)) = SUB^{n+1}(A)$. This completes the inductive proof.

Now, the first statement follows directly from claim 1 and claim 2:

$$SUB^*(A) = \bigcup_{n=0}^{\infty} SUB^n(A)$$

$$= \bigcup_{n=0}^{\infty} \left\{ H \in \mathcal{H}_{C-X} | Z(A) \underset{P(SUB)}{\overset{n}{\Rightarrow}} H \right\}$$

$$= \left\{ H \in \mathcal{H}_{C-X} | Z(A) \underset{P(SUB)}{\overset{*}{\Rightarrow}} H \right\}.$$

The proof of the second statement makes use of the fact that SUB^* is an X-substitution, the first statement, as well as the Context-Freeness Lemma.

$$SUB^*(L) = \bigcup_{H \in L} \left\{ REPLACE(H, repl) | repl(e) \in SUB^*(l_H(e)) \text{ for } e \in E_{H,X} \right\}$$

$$= \bigcup_{H \in L} \left\{ REPLACE(H, repl) | Z(l_H(e)) \underset{P(SUB)}{\overset{*}{\Rightarrow}} repl(e) \in \mathcal{H}_{C-X}, e \in E_{H,X} \right\}$$

$$= \bigcup_{H \in L} \left\{ H' \in \mathcal{H}_{C-X} | H \underset{P(SUB)}{\overset{*}{\Rightarrow}} H' \right\}.$$

Remember the following. If $H \in \mathcal{H}_C$, $fibre(e) = Z(l_H(e)) \overset{*}{\Rightarrow} repl(e)$ are derivations by $P(SUB)$ with $repl(e) \in \mathcal{H}_{C-X}$ ($e \in E_{H,X}$), and $REPLACE(H, repl) = H'$, then $EMBED(H, fibre) = H \overset{*}{\Rightarrow} H'$ is a derivation by $P(SUB)$ and $H' \in \mathcal{H}_{C-X}$. Vice versa, if $H \overset{*}{\Rightarrow} H'$ is a derivation by $P(SUB)$ and $H' \in \mathcal{H}_{C-X}$, then there are derivations $fibre(e) = Z(l_H(e)) \overset{*}{\Rightarrow} repl(e)$ by $P(SUB)$ with $repl(e) \in \mathcal{H}_{C-X}$ ($e \in E_{H,X}$) such that $REPLACE(H, repl) = H'$. □

1.5 Theorem (Closure Under Iterated X-Substitution)

For all finite sets $X \subseteq C$, the hyperedge-replacement languages over C are closed under iterated X-substitution. That is, if L is a hyperedge-replacement language and $SUB : X \to \mathcal{L}_C$ is an X-substitution assigning a hyperedge-replacement language $SUB(A)$ to each $A \in X$, then $SUB^*(L)$ is a hyperedge-replacement language as well.

Proof

Let $HRG = (N, T, P, Z)$ be a usual hyperedge-replacement grammar generating L and for $A \in X$, $HRG(A) = (N(A), T(A), P(A), Z(A))$ be a usual hyperedge-replacement grammar generating $SUB(A)$. Without loss of generality, we may assume that the set of symbols occurring as nonterminals and the set of symbols occurring as terminals are disjoint and that the sets of nonterminals of the grammars are pairwise disjoint. Furthermore, we may assume that $X \subseteq T$. (Otherwise, we consider $X' = X \cap T$ and the restriction of SUB to X', SUB'. For this substitution, $SUB'^*(L(HRG)) = SUB^*(L(HRG))$.) We will construct a grammar $HRG' = (N', T', P', Z')$ generating $SUB^*(L(HRG))$ with help of a new set $\bar{X} = \{\bar{A} | A \in X\}$ of symbols and a relabeling of hyperedges with a label in X. For a hypergraph $R \in \mathcal{H}_C$, let $\bar{R}$ denote the hypergraph in which each symbol $A \in X$ is replaced by the corresonding symbol $\bar{A} \in \bar{X}$.

Now let $HRG' = (N', T', P', Z')$ be the hyperedge-replacement grammar with

- $N' = (N \cup N(X)) \cup \bar{X}$
  where $N(X) = \bigcup_{A \in X} N(A)$,
- $T' = (T \cup T(X)) - X$
  where $T(X) = \bigcup_{A \in X} T(A)$,
- $P' = \bar{P} \cup (Q \cup \bar{P}(X))$
  where $\bar{P} = \{(A, \bar{R}) | (A, R) \in P\}$,
  $Q = \{(\bar{A}, Z(A)) | A \in X\}$,
  $\bar{P}(X) = \bigcup_{A \in X} \bar{P}(A)$, and $\bar{P}(A) = \{(B, \bar{R}) | (B, R) \in P(A)\}$,
- $Z' = Z$.

Then $L(HRG') = SUB^*(L(HRG))$. This may be seen as follows.

First, let $H' \in SUB^*(L(HRG))$. Then, by lemma 1.4, there is a hypergraph $H \in L(HRG)$ and a derivation $H \stackrel{*}{\Longrightarrow} H'$ by $P(SUB)$. Furthermore, $H' \in \mathcal{H}_{C-X}$. By $H \in L(HRG)$, there is a derivation $Z \stackrel{*}{\Longrightarrow} H$ by P and a corresponding derivation $Z \stackrel{*}{\Longrightarrow} \bar{H}$ by $\bar{P}$. Now we consider the derivation $H \stackrel{*}{\Longrightarrow} H'$ by $P(SUB)$. This derivation is of the form

$$H = H_0 \underset{P(SUB)}{\Longrightarrow} H_1 \underset{P(SUB)}{\Longrightarrow} \cdots \underset{P(SUB)}{\Longrightarrow} H_n = H'.$$

For each production $(A, R) \in P(SUB)$, $R \in SUB(A) = L(HRG(A))$, there is a derivation $Z(A) \stackrel{*}{\Longrightarrow} R$ by $P(A)$ and a corresponding derivation $Z(A) \stackrel{*}{\Longrightarrow} \bar{R}$ by $\bar{P}(A)$. Furthermore, there is a direct derivation $(\bar{A}, type(R))^\bullet \Longrightarrow Z(A)$ by Q. Combining these derivations in a suitable way, we get a derivation

$$(\bar{A}, type(R))^\bullet \underset{Q}{\Longrightarrow} Z(A) \underset{\bar{P}(A)}{\stackrel{*}{\Longrightarrow}} \bar{R}$$

Now each direct derivation step $H_i \Longrightarrow H_{i+1}$ by $P(SUB)$ may be replaced by a derivation $\bar{H}_i \stackrel{*}{\Longrightarrow} \bar{H}_{i+1}$ by $Q \cup \bar{P}(X)$. This yields a derivation

$$\bar{H} = \bar{H}_0 \underset{Q \cup \bar{P}(X)}{\stackrel{*}{\Longrightarrow}} \bar{H}_1 \underset{Q \cup \bar{P}(X)}{\stackrel{*}{\Longrightarrow}} \cdots \underset{Q \cup \bar{P}(X)}{\stackrel{*}{\Longrightarrow}} \bar{H}_n = \bar{H}'.$$

Composing the derivations, we obtain a derivation

$$Z \underset{\bar{P}}{\stackrel{*}{\Longrightarrow}} \bar{H} \underset{Q \cup \bar{P}(X)}{\stackrel{*}{\Longrightarrow}} \bar{H}_n = \bar{H}'.$$

$\bar{H}'$ is labeled over $(T - X) \cup T(X)$. Furthermore, we know that $H' \in \mathcal{H}_{C-X}$. Thus, $\bar{H}' = H'$ and H' is labeled over $(T \cup T(X)) - X = T'$. Hence, $H' \in L(HRG')$.

Conversely, let $H' \in L(HRG')$. Then there is a derivation $Z \stackrel{*}{\Rightarrow} H'$ by productions of P' and $H' \in \mathcal{H}_{T'}$. Making use of the fact that sequentially independent derivation steps can be interchanged, the derivation can be transformed into a derivation of the form

$$Z \stackrel{*}{\underset{\bar{P}}{\Rightarrow}} \bar{H} = \bar{H}_0 \stackrel{*}{\underset{Q \cup \bar{P}(X)}{\Rightarrow}} \bar{H}_1 \stackrel{*}{\underset{Q \cup \bar{P}(X)}{\Rightarrow}} \cdots \stackrel{*}{\underset{Q \cup \bar{P}(X)}{\Rightarrow}} \bar{H}_n = H'$$

where $\bar{H}$ is labeled over $(T - X) \cup \bar{X}$ and for $i = 1, \ldots, n - 1$, $\bar{H}_i$ is labeled over $(T - X) \cup (T(X) - X) \cup \bar{X}$. For the derivation $Z \stackrel{*}{\Rightarrow} \bar{H}$ by $\bar{P}$, there is a corresponding derivation $Z \stackrel{*}{\Rightarrow} H$ by P with $H \in \mathcal{H}_T$, i.e., $H \in L(HRG) = L$. Each derivation $\bar{H}_i \stackrel{*}{\Rightarrow} \bar{H}_{i+1}$ by $Q \cup \bar{P}(X)$ can be transformed into a derivation

$$\bar{H}_i \underset{Q}{\Rightarrow} \hat{H}_i \stackrel{*}{\underset{\bar{P}(X)}{\Rightarrow}} \bar{H}_{i+1}.$$

Now we consider the restrictions of the derivation. For a hyperedge e with label $l(e)$ in $\bar{X}$, the restriction of the derivation to $(l(e), type(e))^\bullet$ yields a derivation of the form

$$(l(e), type(e))^\bullet \underset{Q}{\Rightarrow} Z(l(e)) \stackrel{*}{\underset{\bar{P}(l(e))}{\Rightarrow}} \bar{H}_{i+1}(e)$$

where $\bar{H}_{i+1}(e)$ is labeled over $(T(l(e)) - X) \cup \bar{X}$. Since $\bar{P}(l(e))$ and $P(l(e))$ differ only in labels, there is a derivation $Z(l(e)) \stackrel{*}{\Rightarrow} H_{i+1}(e)$ by $P(l(e))$ where $H_{i+1}(e)$ is labeled over $T(l(e))$. Hence $H_{i+1}(e) \in L(HRG(l(e))) = SUB(l(e))$ and $(l(e), H_{i+1}(e)) \in P(SUB)$. Therefore, for each derivation $\bar{H}_i \stackrel{*}{\Rightarrow} \bar{H}_{i+1}$ by $Q \cup \bar{P}(X)$, there is a direct derivation $H_i \Rightarrow H_{i+1}$ by $P(SUB)$. Composing these derivations, we obtain a derivation $H_0 \stackrel{*}{\Rightarrow} H_n$ by $P(SUB)$. Moreover, $H_n = \bar{H}_n = H'$ because H' is labeled over $T' = (T \cup T(X)) - X$. Now $H \in L$, $H \stackrel{*}{\Rightarrow} H'$ is a derivation by $P(SUB)$, and $H' \in \mathcal{H}_{C-X}$. Therefore, by lemma 1.4, $H' \in SUB^*(L)$. □

2. A Kleene-Type Characterization

Kleene [Kl 56] characterized the regular string languages as the smallest class of string languages which contains all finite string languages and is closed under concatenation and star iteration. Gruska [Gr 71] and Yntema [Yn 71] (independently) generalized this result to context-free string languages using symbol substitution and symbol iteration. We are going to develop a similar characterization for hyperedge-replacement languages. The crucial operations in our characterization are A-substitution and iterated A-substitution which are special cases of substitution and iterated substitution considered in section 1.

A type of substitution that is of specific interest is that in which a single symbol A is the object of substitution. In this case, we speak of A-substitution and iterated A-substitution where the symbol A refers to the set $X = \{A\}$. Moreover, we will use a notation in which the functional value of the substitution mapping SUB, $SUB(A)$, becomes "visible".

2.1 Notation

Let $SUB : \{A\} \to \mathcal{L}_C$ be an A-substitution and $K, L \in \mathcal{L}_C$. Then $SUB_A(K, L)$ and L^A denote the sets $SUB_A(K, L) = SUB(K)$ and $L^A = SUB^*(A)$, where $SUB(A) = L$. $SUB_A(K, L)$ is said to be the A-*substitution* in K by L; L^A is called the *iterated A-substitution* of L into L.

2.2 Theorem (Properties of HRL's)

(1) Finite, homogeneous hypergraph languages over C are HRL's.
(2) For all $A \in C$, the class of HRL's over C is closed under A-substitution.
(3) For all $A \in C$, the class of HRL's over C is closed under iterated A-substitution.

Proof

(1) Let $L \in \mathcal{L}_C$ be a finite, homogeneous hypergraph language and $T \subseteq C$ the set of labels used. Then L can be generated by a hyperedge-replacement grammar $HRG = (\{S\}, T, P, Z)$ where S is a symbol not in T, Z is the handle induced by the symbol S and the type of L, and $P = \{(S, choose([R])) | R \in L\}$ where $choose : \{[H] | H \in L\} \to L$ is a mapping which chooses a hypergraph $choose([R]) \in [R]$ for each class $[R] \subseteq L$. By finiteness of L and choice of one hypergraph of each class of isomorphic hypergraphs, P becomes finite. By homogeneity of L, all productions of P can be applied to Z. Since direct derivations are unique up to isomorphism, exactly the hypergraphs of L can be generated. This proves the first statement. Statements (2) and (3) follow immediately from the theorems 1.2 and 1.5 of the previous section. □

On the one hand, hyperedge-replacement languages are closed under symbol substitution and iterated symbol substitution (see theorems 1.2 and 1.5 as well as theorem 2.2). On the other hand, we can show that each hyperedge-replacement language can be constructed from finite, homogeneous hypergraph languages by symbol substitution and iterated symbol substitution. This leads to the following Characterization Theorem for hyperedge-replacement languages.

2.3 Theorem (Characterization Theorem)

The class of all hyperedge-replacement languages over C is the smallest class CFL of homogeneous hypergraph languages satisfying the following conditions:
(1) If $L \in \mathcal{L}_C$ is finite and homogeneous, then $L \in CFL$.
(2) If $K, L \in CFL$ and $A \in C$, then $SUB_A(K, L) \in CFL$.
(3) If $L \in CFL$ and $A \in C$, then $L^A \in CFL$.

Proof

Let L be an arbitrary hyperedge-replacement language over C, $T \subseteq C$ be the finite set of symbols used, and $HRG = (N, T, P, Z)$ be a typed and well-formed hyperedge-replacement grammar generating L. Let $A_1, \ldots, A_n$ be an enumeration of the nonterminals of HRG with $A_i \neq A_j$ for $i \neq j$ and $A_1 = l(Z)$. Now the proof is organized in the following way:

(a) On the one hand, we inductively define hypergraph languages $L_{i,j} \in CFL$ ($1 \leq i \leq j \leq n$) making use of HRG and the order on the nonterminals.

(b) On the other hand, we define hyperedge-replacement grammars $HRG_1, \ldots, HRG_n$ with regard to HRG such that, for $i = 1, \ldots, n$, $L(HRG_j) = L_{j,j}^{A_j}$ and $HRG = HRG_1$. Then, for $j = 1, \ldots, n$, $L(HRG_j) \in CFL$ and, in particular, $L(HRG) \in CFL$.

Based on these ideas, the proof proceeds as follows.

(a) For $1 \leq i \leq j \leq n$, we define the languages $L_{i,j}$ by double downward induction from n:

$$L_{i,n} = \{R' \in \mathcal{H}_{N \cup T} | (A_i, R) \in P \text{ and } R \cong R'\} \quad \text{for } 1 \leq i \leq n.$$

$$L_{i,j-1} = SUB_{A_j}(L_{i,j}, L_{j,j}^{A_j}) \quad \text{for } 1 \leq i < j \leq n.$$

Obviously, the languages $L_{i,n}$ are finite, homogeneous languages and, hence, are in CFL. The languages $L_{i,j-1}$ ($1 \leq i < j \leq n$) are constructed from languages in CFL by symbol substitution and iterated symbol substitution, and, hence, are in CFL (see theorem 2.2). Hence, all languages $L_{i,j}$ (with $1 \leq i \leq j \leq n$) are in CFL.

(b) Let us now define the hyperedge-replacement grammars HRG_j closely related to $HRG = (N, T, P, Z)$: For $1 \leq j \leq n$, let $HRG_j = (N_j, T_j, P_j, Z_j)$ be the hyperedge-replacement grammar with

- $N_j = N - \{A_i | 1 \leq i < j\}$,
- $T_j = \{A_i | 1 \leq i < j\} \cup T$,
- $P_j = \{(A, R) \in P | A \in N_j\}$, and
- $Z_j = A_j^\bullet$.

Note that $HRG = HRG_1$ and, hence, $L(HRG) = L(HRG_1)$. To complete the proof of the theorem, it remains to show that $L(HRG_j) = L_{j,j}^{A_j}$ for $1 \leq j \leq n$. This is a direct consequence of the following claim.

Claim.

$$L_{i,j} = \{H \in \mathcal{H}_{T_{j+1}} | \exists (A_i, R) \in P_i : R \underset{P_{j+1}}{\overset{*}{\Longrightarrow}} H\} \quad \text{for } 1 \leq i \leq j \leq n.$$

$$L_{j,j}^{A_j} = L(HRG_j) \quad \text{for } 1 \leq j \leq n.$$

(For the sake of simplicity, we assume that $T_{n+1} = N \cup T$ and $P_{n+1} = \emptyset$.)

Proof of the claim. We will use an upward induction for $k = n - j$ to n and a downward induction for j from n.

Basis step. Let $k = 0$, that is, $j = n$. Then, for $1 \leq i \leq n$, we have

$$L_{i,n} = \left\{ R' \in \mathcal{H}_{N \cup T} | (A_i, R) \in P \text{ and } R \cong R' \right\}$$
$$= \left\{ H \in \mathcal{H}_{T_{n+1}} | \exists (A_i, R) \in P_i : R \underset{P_{n+1}}{\overset{*}{\Longrightarrow}} H \right\}$$

because $T_{n+1} = N \cup T$ and $P_{n+1} = \emptyset$. Defining $P(A_n, L_{n,n})$ as $\{(A_n, R) | R \in L_{n,n}\}$, using lemma 1.4, and remembering that $P(A_n, L_{n,n}) = P_n$ (up to isomorphism), we get

$$L_{n,n}^{A_n} = \left\{ H \in \mathcal{H}_{C - \{A_n\}} | A_n^{\bullet} \underset{P(A_n, L_{n,n})}{\overset{*}{\Longrightarrow}} H \right\}$$
$$= \left\{ H \in \mathcal{H}_{T_n} | A_n^{\bullet} \underset{P_n}{\overset{*}{\Longrightarrow}} H \right\}$$
$$= L(HRG_n).$$

Inductive step. Assume now that the statements are true for some $k \geq 0$, that is, for some $j \leq n$. Moreover, let $1 \leq i < j$. Then, by definition of $L_{i,j-1}$, definition 1.1, lemma 1.4, and the inductive hypothesis,

$$L_{i,j-1} = SUB_{A_j}(L_{i,j}, L_{j,j}^{A_j})$$
$$= \left\{ H \in \mathcal{H}_{T_{j+1} - \{A_j\}} | \exists G \in L_{i,j} : G \underset{P(A_j, L_{j,j})}{\overset{*}{\Longrightarrow}} H \right\}$$
$$= \left\{ H \in \mathcal{H}_{T_j} | \exists G \in \mathcal{H}_{T_{j+1}} \exists (A_i, R) \in P_i : R \underset{P_{j+1}}{\overset{*}{\Longrightarrow}} G \text{ and } G \underset{P_j}{\overset{*}{\Longrightarrow}} H \right\}$$
$$= \left\{ H \in \mathcal{H}_{T_j} | \exists (A_i, R) \in P_i : R \underset{P_j}{\overset{*}{\Longrightarrow}} H \right\}.$$

($P(A_j, L_{j,j})$ denotes the set of productions induced by A_j and $L_{j,j}$.) Let us mention that the last equality holds because — on the one hand — $P_{j+1} \subseteq P_j$ and — on the other hand — each derivation of the form $R \underset{P_j}{\overset{*}{\Longrightarrow}} H$ by P_j can be transformed into a derivation $R \underset{P_{j+1}}{\overset{*}{\Longrightarrow}} G \underset{P_j}{\overset{*}{\Longrightarrow}} H$ where $G \in \mathcal{H}_{T_{j+1}}$. In the case $i = j - 1$, we have

$$L_{j-1,j-1}^{A_{j-1}} = \left\{ H \in \mathcal{H}_{C - \{A_{j-1}\}} | A_{j-1}^{\bullet} \underset{P(A_{j-1}, L_{j-1,j-1})}{\overset{*}{\Longrightarrow}} H \right\}$$
$$= \left\{ H \in \mathcal{H}_{T_{j-1}} | A_{j-1}^{\bullet} \underset{P_{j-1}}{\overset{*}{\Longrightarrow}} H \right\}$$
$$= L(HRG_{j-1}).$$

(On the one hand, we use lemma 1.4, properties of $L_{j-1,j-1}$ shown above and the fact that $P_j \subseteq P_{j-1}$. On the other hand, we use the fact that each derivation $A_{j-1}^{\bullet} \underset{P_{j-1}}{\overset{*}{\Longrightarrow}} H$ by P_{j-1} with $H \in \mathcal{H}_{T_{j-1}}$ can be transformed into a derivation of the form $A_{j-1}^{\bullet} = H_0 \underset{P_{j-1}}{\overset{*}{\Longrightarrow}} H_1 \underset{P_{j-1}}{\overset{*}{\Longrightarrow}} \ldots \underset{P_{j-1}}{\overset{*}{\Longrightarrow}} H_n = H$ where $H_i \in \mathcal{H}_{T_j}$ and $H_i \underset{P_{j-1}}{\overset{*}{\Longrightarrow}} H_{i+1}$ is a derivation of the form $H_i \underset{P_{j-1}}{\Longrightarrow} H_i' \underset{P_j}{\overset{*}{\Longrightarrow}} H_{i+1}$ ($i = 0, \ldots, n-1$).) This completes the inductive proof. □

3. A Fixed-Point Theorem

We are going to present a Fixed-Point Theorem for hyperedge-replacement languages. Ginsburg and Rice [GR 62] proved that context-free string languages are the least fixed points of their generating productions (considered as a system of language equations). We present a similar result for hyperedge-replacement languages. The construction of the least fixed points provides an alternative method for generating hyperedge-replacement languages.

3.1 Definition (Systems of Equations, Solutions, and Least Fixed Points)

1. Let $N, T \subseteq C$ be disjoint sets of symbols. An N-substitution $EQ : N \to \mathcal{L}_{N \cup T}$ is called a *system of equations* over N. N is said to be the set of *indeterminates* or *unknowns* of EQ.

2. Let $EQ : N \to \mathcal{L}_{N \cup T}$ be a system of equations over N. An N-substitution $L : N \to \mathcal{L}_T$ is a *solution* (or a *fixed point*) of EQ if, for all $A \in N$,

$$L(A) = L(EQ(A)).$$

3. $L : N \to \mathcal{L}_T$ is a *least fixed point* of EQ if L is a solution of EQ, and, if L' is any other solution of EQ, then $L(A) \subseteq L'(A)$ for all $A \in N$.

3.2 Lemma (Existence and Uniqueness)

Every system of equations $EQ : N \to \mathcal{L}_{N \cup T}$ has a unique least fixed point.

Proof

Let $L(A) = \{H \in \mathcal{H}_T |$ for all solutions L' of $EQ : H \in L'(A)\}$ for all $A \in N$. Then it is straightforward to show that L is a solution and that $L(A) \subseteq L'(A)$ for all solutions L'. Thus L is the unique least fixed point of EQ. □

We shall now characterize the least fixed point of a system of equations.

3.3 Lemma (Characterization of Least Fixed Points)

Let EQ be a system of equations over N. Then the least fixed point of EQ, denoted EQ^*, is given by

$$EQ^*(A) = \bigcup_{n=0}^{\infty} EQ^n(A)$$

where $EQ^0(A) = \emptyset$ and $EQ^{i+1}(A) = EQ^i(EQ(A))$ for $i \geq 0$.

Proof

It is straightforward to show that the following set equation is valid:

$$EQ^*(A) = EQ^*(EQ(A))$$

for all $A \in N$. Thus EQ^* is a solution of EQ. To show that EQ^* is the least fixed point of EQ, we precede as follows. Let L be an arbitrary solution of EQ. By induction, we can prove the following:

$$EQ^n(A) \subseteq L(A).$$

Obviously, $EQ^0(A) = \emptyset \subseteq L(A)$. Moreover, $EQ^1(A) = EQ(A) \cap \mathcal{H}_T \subseteq L(EQ(A)) = L(A)$, because L is an N-substitution and a solution of EQ. Assume now that for all $A \in N$, $EQ^n(A) \subseteq L(A)$ and consider a hypergraph $H \in EQ^{n+1}(A)$. Then $H \in EQ^n(EQ(A))$ and can be written as $H = REPLACE(R, repl)$ where $R \in EQ(A)$ and $repl(e) \in EQ^n(l_R(e))$ for $e \in E_R$ with $l_R(e) \in N$. By the inductive hypothesis, $repl(e) \in L(l_R(e))$ for e with $l_R(e) \in N$. Thus, $H \in L(EQ(A))$. Since L is a solution of EQ, we obtain $H \in L(A)$. This completes the inductive proof.

Now, for all $n \in \mathbb{N}$, $EQ^n(A) \subseteq L(A)$, i.e., $EQ^*(A) \subseteq L(A)$. Summarizing, EQ^* is a solution of EQ, and if L is any other solution of EQ, then $EQ^*(A) \subseteq L(A)$ for all $A \in N$. Consequently, EQ^* is the least fixed point of EQ. □

Remark

Note that $EQ^* : N \to \mathcal{L}_T$ is the iterated N-substitution of EQ. As a consequence, we have the following situation. If the assigned languages, $EQ(A)$, are hyperedge-replacement languages, then the constructed languages $EQ^*(A)$ are hyperedge-replacement languages, too. In particular, if for all $A \in N$, $EQ(A)$ is finite and homogeneous, then for all $A \in N$, $EQ^*(A)$ is a hyperedge-replacement language.

There is a relationship between the least fixed point of the system of equations EQ associated with a hyperedge-replacement grammar HRG and the language family L generated by HRG.

3.4 Definition (Associated Equation System & Generated Language Family)

Let $HRG = (N, T, P, Z)$ be a typed hyperedge-replacement grammar. The *system of equations*, $EQ : N \to \mathcal{L}_{N \cup T}$, *associated with* HRG is defined as $EQ(A) = \{R' | (A, R) \in P \text{ and } R \cong R'\}$. The *language family* $L : N \to \mathcal{L}_T$ *generated by* HRG is given by $L(A) = \{H \in \mathcal{H}_T | A^\bullet \stackrel{*}{\underset{P}{\Longrightarrow}} H\}$.

Remark

Typedness of $HRG = (N, T, P, Z)$ ensures the existence of a mapping $\_^\bullet : N \to \mathcal{H}_N$ assigning the handle $A^\bullet$ induced by the symbol A and the type of A to each $A \in N$. This allows to define the language family generated by HRG in the above way.

3.5 Fixed-Point Theorem

Let $HRG = (N, T, P, Z)$ be a typed hyperedge-replacement grammar, $EQ: N \to \mathcal{L}_{N \cup T}$ be the associated system of equations, and $L: N \to \mathcal{L}_T$ the generated language family. Then L is the least fixed point of EQ.

Proof

Let $HRG = (N, T, P, Z)$ be a typed hyperedge-replacement grammar, $EQ: N \to \mathcal{L}_{N \cup T}$ be the system of equations associated with HRG, and $L: N \to \mathcal{L}_T$ the language family generated by HRG. By lemma 1.4 and the relationships between $P(EQ)$ and P,

$$EQ^*(A) = \left\{ H \in \mathcal{H}_T \mid A^\bullet \underset{P(EQ)}{\overset{*}{\Rightarrow}} H \right\} = \left\{ H \in \mathcal{H}_T \mid A^\bullet \overset{*}{\underset{P}{\Rightarrow}} H \right\} = L(A)$$

for all $A \in N$, i.e., $EQ^* = L$. By lemma 3.3, EQ^* is the least fixed point of EQ. Therefore, L is the least fixed point of EQ. □

Remark

1. The Fixed-Point Theorem for hyperedge-replacement languages generalizes Ginsburg's and Rice's well-known Fixed-Point Theorem for context-free string languages in [GR 62] as well as the Fixed-Point Theorem for context-free graph languages given in [HK 83+87a]. A similar theorem for a slightly different notion of hyperedge-replacement grammar has been established by Bauderon and Courcelle [BC 87]. The proof given in [BC 87] makes use of the fact that a set of hypergraphs can be generated by a hyperedge-replacement grammar if and only if it is "equational", whereas in this book, the Fixed-Point Theorem is proved "directly" without use of other results.
2. The construction of least fixed points provides an alternative method for generating hyperedge-replacement languages.

4. Bibliographic Note

The results on hyperedge-replacement languages presented in this chapter (expressed in a slightly different way) may be seen as adaptions of the results for edge-replacement languages given in [HK 87a].

Chapter IV
Structural Aspects of HRL's

In this chapter, we present a number of necessary conditions for a hypergraph language to be a hyperedge-replacement language. Besides a Pumping Lemma (which is in the spirit of the well-known Pumping Lemma for context-free string languages), a so-called Connectivity Theorem and a Minimum-Degree Theorem are presented. These theorems give necessary but not sufficient conditions for sets of hypergraphs generated by hyperedge-replacement grammars. They can be used to show that certain sets of hypergraphs cannot be generated by this kind of grammars. Moreover, a version of Parikh's Theorem for hyperedge-replacement languages is presented.

The chapter is organized as follows: In section 1, we consider some simplifications of hyperedge-replacement grammars which will be useful in the following. In section 2, we state a Pumping Lemma which generalizes those Pumping Lemmata known for context-free string and graph languages. It says roughly that each sufficiently large hypergraph belonging to a hyperedge-replacement language decomposes into $FIRST \otimes LINK \otimes LAST$ such that $FIRST \otimes LINK^k \otimes LAST$ for $k \geq 0$ belongs to the given language. The crucial part is to find the proper composition $\otimes$ for hypergraphs. Section 3 is concerned with graph-theoretic properties — like the connectivity and the minimal degree — of the generated (hyper)graphs. In section 4, we present a theorem expressing the semilinearity of hyperedge-replacement languages under the Parikh mapping.

1. Simplifications of HRG's

In this section, we consider — similar to context-free string grammars — "reduced" hyperedge-replacement grammars which do not possess "empty productions" or "single productions". Furthermore, we show that for each typed hyperedge-replacement grammar there is an equivalent reduced grammar without empty productions and single productions. The proofs are similar to the corresponding proofs in the string case. This is due to the frequent use of the Context-Freeness Lemma (chapter II, 2.4).

We first undertake the task of eliminating those symbols from a grammar which are not used: Let $HRG = (N, T, P, Z)$ be a typed hyperedge-replacement grammar. A symbol $A \in N$ turns out to be *irrelevant* (or *useless*) — insofar as the language $L(HRG)$ is concerned — if no terminal hypergraph can be derived from the handle $A^\bullet$ induced by A or if A does not occur in any hypergraph derived from the axiom Z. Useless symbols of this kind can be removed from the grammar HRG without effect on $L(HRG)$.

1.1 Definition (Reduced Grammars)

A typed hyperedge-replacement grammar $HRG = (N, T, P, Z)$ is said to be *reduced* iff $P = \emptyset$ or, for all $A \in N$,
- there is a derivation $A^\bullet \overset{*}{\Rightarrow} H$ from the handle $A^\bullet$ induced by A to some terminal hypergraph $H \in \mathcal{H}_T$;
- there is a derivation $Z \overset{*}{\Rightarrow} G$ from the axiom to some hypergraph $G \in \mathcal{H}_{N \cup T}$ possessing a hyperedge with label A.

Remark

For simplicity, reducedness is defined for typed grammars only. More generally, we could define it for arbitrary grammars. But this does not seem to be significant because handles with same label but different type may behave differently with respect to the question "Is there a terminal hypergraph derivable from the handle?" and hyperedges with same label but different type may behave differently with respect to the question "Is there a production applicable to the hyperedge?"

1.2 Theorem (Reducedness Theorem)

For each hyperedge-replacement grammar, an equivalent reduced grammar can be constructed effectively.

Proof

Let $HRG = (N, T, P, Z)$ be a hyperedge-replacement grammar. By the Typification Theorem given in chapter I, 4.3, we may assume that HRG is typed. Now an equivalent reduced hyperedge-replacement grammar $HRG'' = (N'', T, P'', Z)$ is constructed in two steps. First, the set of nonterminals is restricted to those from (the handles of) which a terminal hypergraph can be derived. In the second step, the set of remaining nonterminals is restricted to those which are accessible from the axiom of the grammar. (Note that the procedure is similar to the corresponding proof in the string case (cf. [HU 69], theorems 4.2+4.3).)

Step 1. Let $HRG = (N, T, P, Z)$ be typed. First, we construct the set

- $N_T = \left\{ A \in N \mid A^\bullet \underset{P}{\overset{*}{\Rightarrow}} H \text{ for some } H \in \mathcal{H}_T \right\}$.

For this purpose, we define sets N_k for $k \in I\!N$ recursively as follows:

- $N_0 = \emptyset$,
- $N_{k+1} = N_k \cup \{A \in N \mid (A, R) \in P \text{ and } l_R(e) \in N_k \cup T \text{ for all } e \in E_R\}$ for $k \geq 0$.

Then we have $N_T = \bigcup_{k=0}^{\infty} N_k$: For $k \in I\!N$, $A \in N_k$ implies $A \in N_T$ and, conversely, if $A^\bullet \stackrel{k}{\Longrightarrow} H \in \mathcal{H}_T$, then $A \in N_k$. Since $N_k \subseteq N_{k+1} \subseteq N$ for all $k \in I\!N$ and N is finite, there is some $l \in I\!N$ such that $N_l = N_{l+1}$. By definition, this means $N_l = N_{l+1} = N_{l+2} = \ldots$, so $\bigcup_{k=0}^{\infty} N_k = N_l$. Obviously, all N_k up to the smallest possible l can be constructed effectively. So we are done.

Now let $HRG' = (N', T, P', Z)$ be the hyperedge-replacement grammar with $N' = N_T \cup \{l(Z)\}$, $P' = \{(A, R) \in P \mid A \in N_T, R \in \mathcal{H}_{N_T \cup T}\}$ if $l(Z) \in N_T$ and $P' = \emptyset$ otherwise. Surely, HRG' satisfies the property that $P' = \emptyset$ or, if $A \in N'$, then $A^\bullet \stackrel{*}{\Longrightarrow} H$ for some $H \in \mathcal{H}_T$. Furthermore, it is straightforward to verify that $L(HRG') = L(HRG)$.

Step 2. Consider $HRG' = (N', T, P', Z)$ as constructed in step 1. Then we have to remove all symbols which are not accessible from the axiom Z. Therefore, we construct the set

- $N'_{access} = \left\{B \in N' \mid Z \stackrel{*}{\underset{P'}{\Longrightarrow}} G \text{ with } l_G(e) = B \text{ for some } e \in E_G\right\}$.

For this purpose, we define sets N'_k for $k \in I\!N$ recursively as follows:

- $N'_0 = \{l(Z)\}$,
- $N'_{k+1} = N'_k \cup \{B \in N' \mid A \in N'_k, (A, R) \in P', \text{ and } l_R(e) = B \text{ for some } e \in E_R\}$.

Then we have $N'_{access} = \bigcup_{k=0}^{\infty} N'_k$. Since the sets N'_k are monotonically increasing subsets of N' and since N' is finite, there is some $l \in I\!N$ such that $N'_l = N'_{l+1}$. By definition, this means $N'_l = N'_{l+1} = N'_{l+2} = \ldots$. Thus, $\bigcup_{k=0}^{\infty} N'_k = N'_l$. Clearly, all N'_k up to the smallest possible l can be constructed effectively. So we are done.

Now let $HRG'' = (N'', T, P'', Z)$ be the hyperedge-replacement grammar with $N'' = N'_{access}$ and $P'' = \{(A, R) \in P \mid A \in N'', R \in \mathcal{H}_{N'' \cup T}\}$. Then HRG'' turns out to be reduced. Furthermore, it is straightforward to verify that $L(HRG'') = L(HRG')$. □

We get the following result as corollary of the proof of theorem 1.2.

1.3 Corollary (Emptiness Problem)

For hyperedge-replacement grammars, the *Emptiness Problem* is decidable, i.e., there is an algorithm for determining whether the language of a hyperedge-replacement grammar is empty or not.

Proof

Let $HRG = (N, T, P, Z)$ be a hyperedge-replacement grammar generating L. By the Typification Theorem (see chapter I, theorem 4.3), we may assume that HRG is typed. Moreover, we assume that Z is repetition-free (see chapter III, general assumption). Now we construct the set $N_T = \{A \in N | A^\bullet \stackrel{*}{\Longrightarrow} H \text{ for some } H \in \mathcal{H}_T\}$ as in the proof of theorem 1.2. Then $L = L(HRG) \neq \emptyset$ if and only if $l(Z) \in N_T$. □

It is often convenient to eliminate productions which produce neither nodes nor hyperedges. Productions of this type are called empty productions.

1.4 Definition (Empty Productions)

A production (A, R) is said to be *empty* if there are no internal nodes and no hyperedges in the right-hand side of the production, i.e., $INT_R = \emptyset$ as well as $E_R = \emptyset$.

Given a hyperedge-replacement grammar $HRG = (N, T, P, Z)$, we are going to eliminate empty productions. However, if $frame(Z)$ is in $L(HRG)$, then clearly it is impossible to have no empty productions.

1.5 Theorem (Elimination of Empty Productions)

For each hyperedge-replacement grammar, an equivalent grammar can be constructed in which either
(a) there are no empty productions, or
(b) there is exactly one empty production of the form $(l(Z), frame(Z))$ where Z denotes the axiom of the grammar and the label of Z, $l(Z)$, does not appear on the right-hand side of any production.

Notation

Hyperedge-replacement grammars satisfying the condition (a) or (b) are said to be *grammars without empty productions*.

Proof

Let $HRG = (N, T, P, Z)$ be a hyperedge-replacement grammar. By the Typification Theorem (see chapter I, theorem 4.3), we may assume that HRG is typed. Then we construct an equivalent hyperedge-replacement grammar $HRG' = (N', T, P', Z')$ without empty productions using more or less the same ideas as in the string case (see, e.g., [AU 72], theorem 2.14, [HU 69], theorem 4.11). First, we construct the set

- $FRAME = \left\{A \in N | A^\bullet \stackrel{*}{\underset{P}{\Longrightarrow}} frame(A^\bullet)\right\}$.

For this purpose, we define sets $FRAME_k$ for $k \in \mathbb{N}$ recursively. A nonterminal A is included in $FRAME_k$ if there is a derivation $A^\bullet \stackrel{*}{\Longrightarrow} frame(A^\bullet)$ of length $\leq k$. Note that $A^\bullet \not\cong frame(A^\bullet)$ for all $A \in N$ so that $FRAME_0$ does not contain any symbol.

- $FRAME_0 = \emptyset$;
- $FRAME_{k+1} = FRAME_k \cup$
  $\{A \in N | (A, R) \in P, INT_R = \emptyset, \text{ and } l_R(e) \in FRAME_k \text{ for } e \in E_R\}$.

Since $FRAME_k \subseteq FRAME_{k+1} \subseteq N$ for all $k \in \mathbb{N}$ and N is finite, there is some $l \in \mathbb{N}$ such that $FRAME_l = FRAME_{l+1}$. $FRAME_l = FRAME_{l+1}$ implies $FRAME_l = FRAME_{l+m}$ for all $m \geq 1$. Now all $FRAME_k$ up to the smallest possible l can be constructed effectively. Furthermore, $FRAME = FRAME_l$ may be verified, i.e., $FRAME$ can be constructed effectively.

Now $HRG' = (N', T, P', Z')$ is constructed according to the following rules:

(a) If (A, R) is in P and $B \subseteq \{e \in E_R \mid l_R(e) \in FRAME\}$,
    then $(A, R - B)$ is in P' provided that $R - B$ [1]) is not a frame.
(b) If $l(Z) \in FRAME$, add the productions $(S', frame(Z))$ and (S', Z) to P' where S' is a new symbol with $ltype(S') = type(Z)$. In this case, choose $N' = N \cup \{S'\}$ and $Z' = S'^\bullet$. Otherwise, choose $N' = N$ and $Z' = Z$.

Then HRG' is a typed hyperedge-replacement grammar satisfying the condition (a) or (b). It is straightforward to verify that $L(HRG') = L(HRG)$. □

Typed hyperedge-replacement grammars without empty productions are *monotone* in the following sense: Let $HRG = (N, T, P, Z)$ be a typed hyperedge replacement grammar. Then, for each production $(A, R) \in P$, the *monotony condition* $size(A^\bullet) \leq size(R)$ [2]) is satisfied with the possible exception of the production $(l(Z), frame(Z))$ where the label of the axiom, $l(Z)$, does not appear on the right-hand side of any production. This observation has a nice consequence with respect to the Membership Problem for hyperedge-replacement grammars.

1.6 Corollary (Membership Problem)

For hyperedge-replacement grammars, the *Membership Problem* is decidable, i.e., there is an algorithm for determining whether, given a hyperedge-replacement grammar $HRG = (N, T, P, Z)$ and a multi-pointed hypergraph $H \in \mathcal{H}_T$, H is in $L(HRG)$ or not.

---

[1]) Let $H \in \mathcal{H}_C$ and $B \subseteq E_H$. Then $H - B$ denotes the multi-pointed hypergraph $(V_H, E_H - B, s, t, l, begin_H, end_H)$ where s, t, and l are the restrictions of the mappings s_H, t_H, and l_H to the set $E_H - B$, respectively.

[2]) For $H \in \mathcal{H}_C$, $size(H)$ denotes the number of nodes and hyperedges in H, i.e., $size(H) = |V_H| + |E_H|$.

Proof

Let $HRG = (N, T, P, Z)$ be a hyperedge-replacement grammar. By the Typification Theorem (see chapter I, theorem 4.3) and theorem 1.5, we may assume that HRG is a typed grammar without empty productions. Let $H \in \mathcal{H}_T$. Suppose that $size(H) = k$ for some $k \in \mathbb{N}$. Then — analogously to the string case — the set $L(HRG)_k = \{H \in L(HRG) | size(H) \leq k\}$ can be constructed effectively (up to isomorphic samples). Now $H \in L(HRG)$ if and only if $H \in L(HRG)_k$. □

Another transformation on hyperedge-replacement grammars — which turns out to be useful — is the removal of productions of the form (A, R) where R is a nonterminal singleton. Productions of this type do not produce any node; they produce a single nonterminal hyperedge. Therefore, they are called single productions.

1.7 Definition (Single Productions)

A production (A, R) over N is said to be a *single production* if R is a singleton with label in N.

Given a hyperedge-replacement grammar $HRG = (N, T, P, Z)$, we are going to eliminate single productions.

1.8 Theorem (Elimination of Single Productions)

For each hyperedge-replacement grammar, an equivalent grammar without single productions can be constructed.

Proof

Let $HRG = (N, T, P, Z)$ be a hyperedge-replacement grammar. By the Typification Theorem (see chapter I, theorem 4.3) and theorem 1.5, we may assume that HRG is a typed grammar without empty productions. We now construct a hyperedge-replacement grammar $HRG' = (N, T, P', Z)$ without single productions using more or less the same methods as in the string case (see, e.g., [AU 72], theorem 2.15, [HU 69], theorem 4.4).

First, we construct the set

- $SING(A) = \left\{ H \in \mathcal{H}_N \,\middle|\, A^\bullet \underset{P}{\overset{*}{\Longrightarrow}} H \text{ and } H \text{ is a singleton} \right\}$ for all $A \in N$.

This may be done as follows: Define sets $SING(A)_k$ for $A \in N$ and $k \in \mathbb{N}$ recursively. For a singleton H, H is in $SING(A)_k$ if there is a derivation $A^\bullet \overset{*}{\Longrightarrow} H$ of length $\leq k$ and the label of H is in N. Note that $A^\bullet \overset{0}{\Longrightarrow} A^\bullet$ for all $A \in N$, so $A^\bullet$ already appears in $SING(A)_0$.

- $SING(A)_0 = [A^\bullet]$,
- $SING(A)_{k+1} = SING(A)_k \cup$
  $\{H[e/R] \mid H \in SING(A)_k,\ e \in E_H,\ \text{and}\ (l_H(e), R) \in P \text{ is a single production}\}$.

Since $SING(A)_k \subseteq SING(A)_{k+1} \subseteq N$ for all $k \in N$ and N is finite, there is some $l(A) \in I\!N$ such that $SING(A)_{l(A)} = SING(A)_{l(A)+1}$. This implies $SING(A)_{l(A)} = SING(A)_{l(A)+m}$ for all $m \geq 1$. Now all $SING(A)_k$ up to the smallest possible $l(A)$ can be constructed effectively. Furthermore, $SING(A) = SING(A)_{l(A)}$ may be verified. Hence, $SING(A)$ can be constructed effectively for all $A \in N$.

Now let $HRG' = (N, T, P', Z)$ be the hyperedge-replacement grammar with

$$P' = \{(A, H[e/R]) \mid H \in SING(A),\ e \in E_H,\ (l_H(e), R) \in P \text{ is not a single production}\}.$$

Then P' is a finite set of productions because P is a finite set and, for each $A \in N$, $SING(A)$ consists of a finite number of non-isomorphic hypergraphs. (A production set is said to be *finite* if the number of productions with non-isomorphic right-hand sides is finite.) By inspection, the new grammar $HRG' = (N, T, P', Z)$ is typed and has neither empty nor single productions. It is straightforward to verify that $L(HRG') = L(HRG)$.
□

1.9 Definition (Proper and Cycle-Free Grammars)

1. A hyperedge-replacement grammar $HRG = (N, T, P, Z)$ is said to be *proper* if it is typed, well-formed, reduced, and possesses neither empty nor single productions.
2. A typed hyperedge-replacement grammar $HRG = (N, T, P, Z)$ is said to be *cycle-free* if there is no non-trivial derivation (at least one production is applied) of the form $A^\bullet \stackrel{*}{\Longrightarrow} R$ where $A \in N$ and $R \in \mathcal{H}_N$ is a singleton with label A.

Now we get the following result as corollary of the theorems above.

1.10 Corollary

1. For each hyperedge-replacement grammar, an equivalent proper grammar can be constructed effectively.
2. Each proper hyperedge-replacement grammar is cycle-free.

Proof

The first statement follows directly from the Typification Theorem, the Well-Formedness Theorem (both given in chapter I), and the theorems 1.2, 1.5, and 1.8. The second statement is an immediate consequence of the fact that for proper grammars the application of a non-terminating production leads to a hypergraph with increased size; the size cannot be reduced again by applying further productions.
□

2. A Pumping Lemma for HRL's

The main result presented in this section is a Pumping Lemma for hyperedge-replacement languages. Roughly speaking, it says that each sufficiently large hypergraph belonging to a hyperedge-replacement language can be decomposed into three hypergraphs $FIRST$, $LINK$, and $LAST$, so that a suitable composition of $FIRST$, $LAST$, and k samples of $LINK$ for each natural number k yields also a member of the language. This theorem generalizes the well-known Pumping Lemma for context-free string languages — also named Bar-Hillel Lemma or uvwxy Lemma (cf., e.g., [BPS 61], [HU 69]) — and it is closely related to the Pumping Lemma for context-free graph languages given in [Kr 79].

For a precise formulation of the Pumping Lemma for hyperedge-replacement languages we use an operation which allows to compose hypergraphs in a suitable way.

2.1 Definition (Composition and Iterated Composition)

1. Let $X \in C$ and $m, n \in \mathbb{N}$. Then $H \in \mathcal{H}_C$ is said to be $X(m,n)$-*handled* if there is a unique (m,n)-edge $e \in E_H$ with label X, i.e., $l_H(e) = X$. In this case, e is called the $X(m,n)$-*handle* of H; the hypergraph without the $X(m,n)$-handle, $H - e$, is denoted by H_0.

2. Let $H \in \mathcal{H}_C$ be a multi-pointed hypergraph with $X(m,n)$-handle e and let $H' \in \mathcal{H}_C$ be an (m,n)-hypergraph. Then the multi-pointed hypergraph $H[e/H']$ is called the *composition* of H and H' with respect to e and is abbreviated by $H \otimes H'$.

3. Let $H \in \mathcal{H}_C$ be an $X(m,n)$-handled (m,n)-hypergraph. Then for $k \in \mathbb{N}$, $H^k \in \mathcal{H}_C$ is recursively defined as follows:
(a) $H^0 = X(m,n)^\bullet$;
(b) $H^{i+1} = H \otimes H^i$ for $i \geq 0$.

Remark

1. The composition of a multi-pointed hypergraph H with $X(m,n)$-handle e and an (m,n)-hypergraph H' with respect to e can be constructed by removing e from H and inserting H' instead of it. This can be depicted as follows:

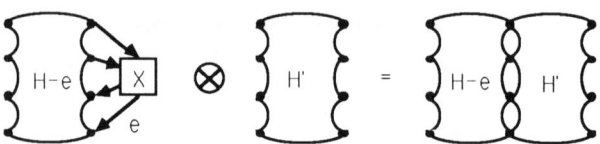

2. Let $H \otimes H'$ be the result of the composition of H and H' with respect to the $X(m,n)$-handle e in H. Then $H_0 = H - e$ is a subhypergraph of $H \otimes H'$. Moreover, there is a morphism $embed : H' \to H \otimes H'$ where $embed_V : V_{H'} \to V_{H \otimes H'}$ is defined by $embed_V(begin_{H',i}) = s_H(e)_i$, $embed_V(end_{H',j}) = t_H(e)_j$ for $begin_{H',i}, end_{H',j} \in EXT_H$

and $embed_V(v) = v$ otherwise, and $embed_E : E_{H'} \to E_{H \otimes H'}$ is defined by $embed_E(e) = e$ for all $e \in E_{H'}$.

3. $\otimes$ is an associative operation in the following sense: Let $F, G, H \in \mathcal{H}_C$ such that $(F \otimes G) \otimes H$ and $F \otimes (G \otimes H)$ are defined. Then $(F \otimes G) \otimes H = F \otimes (G \otimes H)$ (up to isomorphism).

4. The (m,n)-hypergraph $X(m,n)^\bullet$ plays a distinguished role with respect to the composition defined above. It has the property of being a unit:
  (a) Let H be an (m,n)-hypergraph. Then $X(m,n)^\bullet \otimes H = H$ (up to isomorphism).
  (b) Let $H \in \mathcal{H}_C$ be $X(m,n)$-handled. Then $H \otimes X(m,n)^\bullet = H$ (up to isomorphism).

5. Let H be an $X(m,n)$-handled (m,n)-hypergraph. Then, for all $k \in \mathbb{N}$, H^k is an $X(m,n)$-handled (m,n)-hypergraph. Intuitively, H^k is created from k samples of the hypergraph H which are composed with each other. This can be depicted as follows:

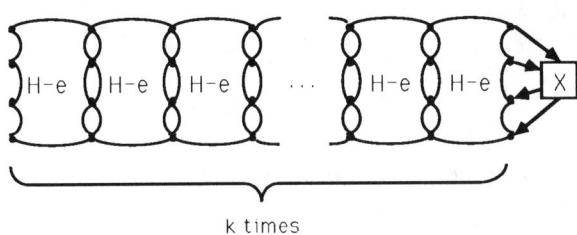

One more prerequisite is required for our Pumping Lemma. Hyperedge-replacement grammars can be classified according to the upper bounds of the numbers of external nodes in the right-hand sides of their productions, which will be called orders. Actually, we are going to formulate a Pumping Lemma for each order. The resulting classification of hyperedge-replacement languages will be subject of a more detailed study in chapter V.

2.2 Definition (Order)

1. A hyperedge-replacement grammar $HRG = (N, T, P, Z)$ is said to be of *order r* (for some $r \in \mathbb{N}$) if for all $(A, R) \in P$, $|EXT_R| \leq r$. The class of all hyperedge-replacement grammars of order r is denoted by $\mathcal{HRG}_r$; the class of all hyperedge-replacement grammars is denoted by $\mathcal{HRG}$.

2. A hyperedge-replacement language L is of *order r* (for some $r \in \mathbb{N}$) if there is a hyperedge-replacement grammar HRG of order r with $L(HRG) = L$. The class of all hyperedge-replacement languages of order r is denoted by $\mathcal{HRL}_r$; the class of all hyperedge-replacement languages is denoted by $\mathcal{HRL}$.

Remark

Obviously, we have $\mathcal{HRL}_0 \subseteq \mathcal{HRL}_1 \subseteq \mathcal{HRL}_2 \subseteq \mathcal{HRL}_3 \subseteq \ldots$. It will be shown that all of the inclusions are proper (see chapter V).

2.3 Theorem (Pumping Lemma)

Let L be a hyperedge-replacement language of order r (for some $r \in \mathbb{N}$). Then there exist constants p and q depending only on L such that the following is true: For each multi-pointed hypergraph H in L with $\text{size}(H) > p$ [1)] there are
- a symbol $X \in C$,
- natural numbers $m, n \in \mathbb{N}$,
- an $X(m,n)$-handled multi-pointed hypergraph $FIRST$,
- an $X(m,n)$-handled (m,n)-hypergraph $LINK$, and
- an (m,n)-hypergraph $LAST$

such that
(1) $H = FIRST \otimes LINK \otimes LAST$,
(2) $\text{size}(LINK \otimes LAST) \leq q$,
(3) $\text{extsize}(LINK) \leq r$,
(4) $\text{intsize}(LINK) > 1$ ($LINK$ is non-trivial),
(5) for $k \in \mathbb{N}$, $FIRST \otimes LINK^k \otimes LAST$ is in L.

Remark

1. The multi-pointed hypergraph H is composed of the hypergraphs $FIRST_0$, $LINK_0$, and $LAST$. This can be depicted by

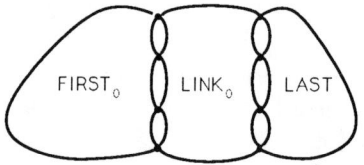

Since $LINK$ and $LAST$ are of the same type, $LAST$ — instead of $LINK$ — may be composed with $FIRST$. Moreover, $LINK$ — instead of $LAST$ — may be composed with $LINK$. Hence pumping is possible. The pumped hypergraphs have the shape

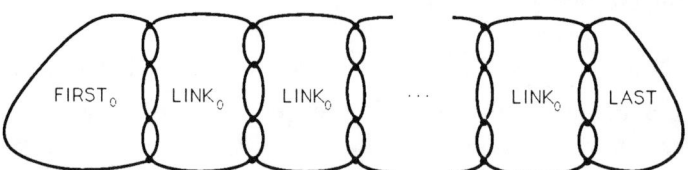

2. In some sense, the pictures are intuitive simplifications, because they suggest that $FIRST_0$, $LINK_0$, and $LAST$ are connected hypergraphs — but they do not have to be connected in general (see example 2.4).

[1)] For $H \in \mathcal{H}_C$, $\text{size}(H)$ denotes the number of nodes and hyperedges in H, i.e., $\text{size}(H) = |V_H| + |E_H|$. More specific, $\text{extsize}(H)$ denotes the number of external nodes in H and $\text{intsize}(H)$ the number of internal nodes and hyperedges, i.e., $\text{extsize}(H) = |EXT_H|$ and $\text{intsize}(H) = |INT_H| + |E_H|$.

3. Note that the number of external nodes of the $LINK$-component is bounded by r. This requirement restricts the number of possible decompositions of H.
4. Property (4) guarantees that the pumped multi-pointed hypergraphs are different from the given one and from each other.
5. The Pumping Lemma states that for sufficiently "large" hypergraphs "pumping" is possible without leaving the class of hypergraphs under consideration. In theorem 2.3, we consider the size of hypergraphs. Similarly, we may consider the number of nodes or the number of hyperedges as relevant counting units. Replacing the condition "$size(H) > p$" by "$|V_H| > p$" or "$|E_H| > p$", respectively, we obtain weaker versions of the Pumping Lemma.
6. The pumping property is a necessary condition for a hypergraph language to be a hyperedge-replacement language. One of the main uses of the Pumping Lemma is to prove that specific hypergraph languages are not in $\mathcal{HRL}_r$ or not in $\mathcal{HRL}$ (see Chapter V).

Proof (of the Pumping Lemma)

Let L be a hyperedge-replacement language of order r. By corollary 1.10, we may assume that L is generated by a proper grammar $HRG = (N, T, P, Z)$ of order r. (Note that the transformations of grammars presented in section 1 do not influence the order: If a grammar is of order r, then the transformed grammar is of order r as well.) Now choose

$$p = \max{}^n + c \quad \text{and} \quad q = \max{}^{n+1} + c$$

where $c = \max\{extsize(R) | R = Z \text{ or } (A, R) \in P\}$ denotes the maximum number of external nodes occurring in Z or a right-hand side of a production in P, $\max = \max\{intsize(R) | R = Z \text{ or } (A, R) \in P\}$ denotes the maximum number of internal nodes and hyperedges occurring in Z or a right-hand side of a production in P, and n denotes the number of elements in N.

In the following we will show that each multi-pointed hypergraph H in L with $size(H) > p$ can be decomposed into multi-pointed hypergraphs $FIRST$, $LINK$, and $LAST$ such that pumping in the sense of the theorem is possible. Let H be a multi-pointed hypergraph in L with $size(H) > p$ and $der : Z \Longrightarrow H_1 \Longrightarrow \ldots \Longrightarrow H_m = H$ be a derivation of H in HRG. Without loss of generality, we may assume that der is a canonical derivation, i.e., in each derivation step all nonterminal hyperedges are replaced and there are no dummy derivation steps. Then we can find a sequence of productions $p_1, \ldots, p_m$ such that for each $i = 1, \ldots, m - 1$, p_i and p_{i+1} are dependent in der, i.e., the nonterminal hyperedge replaced by p_{i+1} is just generated by p_i in the preceding direct derivation step of der. The left-hand sides of those productions form a sequence of nonterminals $A_1, \ldots, A_m$. If the length m of the derivation der is greater than the number n of nonterminals in N (and this is guaranteed by $size(H) > \max{}^n + c$, see claim 2 below), at least two items in this sequence must be equal. Then choose $A_k = A_l$ with $1 \leq k < l \leq m$ and $m - k \leq n$. Consequently, one nonterminal $A = A_l$ occurs in a multi-pointed hypergraph derived from the handle with label $A = A_k$. Such a situation provides a self-embedding property (c.f. [HU 69], 4.5).

We will decompose the derivation of H in a suitable way. Let us mention that the derivation $Z \stackrel{*}{\Rightarrow} H_{k-1} \stackrel{*}{\Rightarrow} H_{l-1} \stackrel{*}{\Rightarrow} H_m$ can be transformed into an equivalent derivation $Z \stackrel{*}{\Rightarrow} H'_{k-1} \stackrel{*}{\Rightarrow} H'_{l-1} \stackrel{*}{\Rightarrow} H_m$ where H'_{k-1} and H'_{l-1} are terminal up to one nonterminal hyperedge e_k and e_l, respectively, with label A. Let now $A^\bullet \stackrel{*}{\Rightarrow} G_{l-1} \stackrel{*}{\Rightarrow} G_m$ be the restriction of $H'_{k-1} \stackrel{*}{\Rightarrow} H'_{l-1} \stackrel{*}{\Rightarrow} H_m$ to $l_{H'_{k-1}}(e_k)^\bullet$. Then G_{l-1} is terminal up to one nonterminal hyperedge e_l with label A. Finally, let $A^\bullet \stackrel{*}{\Rightarrow} F_m$ be the restriction of the derivation $G_{l-1} \stackrel{*}{\Rightarrow} G_m$ to $l_{H'_{l-1}}(e_l)^\bullet$. This situation may be depicted as follows:

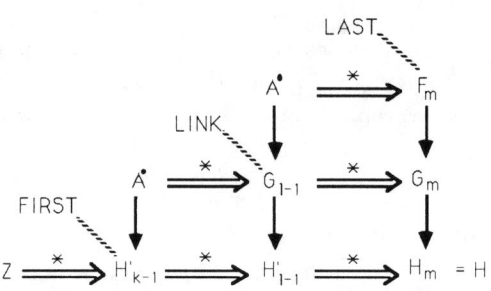

By the Context-Freeness Lemma, we have $H_m = H'_{k-1}[e_k/G_m]$ and $G_m = G_{l-1}[e_l/F_m]$ where e_k and e_l denote the nonterminal hyperedges in H'_{k-1} and G_{l-1}, respectively. Choosing now $FIRST = H'_{k-1}$, $LINK = G_{l-1}$, and $LAST = F_m$ and using the notation introduced in definition 2.1, we get $H = FIRST \otimes (LINK \otimes LAST)$.

Since the hyperedge-replacement grammar under consideration is typed and the hyperedges e_k and e_l possess the same label, e_k and e_l are hyperedges of the same type, say of type $(\hat{m}, \hat{n})$. Thus, $LINK$ and $LAST$ are of the same type, namely of type $(\hat{m}, \hat{n})$. Since $LINK$ is an $A(\hat{m}, \hat{n})$-handled $(\hat{m}, \hat{n})$-hypergraph, for each $i \in \mathbb{N}$, $LINK^i$ is defined and turns out to be $A(\hat{m}, \hat{n})$-handled. Since $FIRST$ is $A(\hat{m}, \hat{n})$-handled and $LAST$ is a $(\hat{m}, \hat{n})$-hypergraph, for $i \in \mathbb{N}$, $FIRST \otimes (LINK^i \otimes LAST)$ can be constructed.

In the following, we will show that, for $i \in \mathbb{N}$, $FIRST \otimes (LINK^i \otimes LAST)$ belongs to the language L generated by the hyperedge-replacement grammar HRG: We use the derivation $Z \stackrel{*}{\Rightarrow} FIRST$, a derivation $A^\bullet \stackrel{*}{\Rightarrow} LINK^i$ (composed by derivations $A^\bullet \stackrel{*}{\Rightarrow} LINK$), and the derivation $A^\bullet \stackrel{*}{\Rightarrow} LAST$.

Claim 1. For each $i \in \mathbb{N}$, there is a derivation $A^\bullet \stackrel{*}{\Rightarrow} LINK^i$.

Proof of claim 1 (by induction on i). By definition, $LINK^0 = A(\hat{m}, \hat{n})^\bullet$. Therefore, there is a derivation $A^\bullet \stackrel{0}{\Rightarrow} LINK^0$. Suppose that the statement is true for some $i \geq 0$. Now $LINK^{i+1} = LINK \otimes LINK^i$. By choice of $LINK$, there is a derivation $A^\bullet \stackrel{*}{\Rightarrow} LINK$ such that $LINK$ is $A(\hat{m}, \hat{n})$-handled with handle e_k. By the inductive hypothesis, there is a derivation $A^\bullet \stackrel{*}{\Rightarrow} LINK^i$. The embedding of this derivation into $LINK$ yields the derivation $LINK \stackrel{*}{\Rightarrow} LINK[e_k/LINK^i]$ with

$LINK[e_k/LINK^i] = LINK \otimes LINK^i = LINK^{i+1}$. Therefore, we get a derivation $A^\bullet \stackrel{*}{\Longrightarrow} LINK \stackrel{*}{\Longrightarrow} LINK^{i+1}$. This completes the inductive proof.

Now, for $i \in \mathbb{N}$, a derivation $Z \stackrel{*}{\Longrightarrow} FIRST \otimes (LINK^i \otimes LAST)$ can be constructed according to the following rules:

(1) Embed the derivation $A^\bullet \stackrel{*}{\Longrightarrow} LAST$ into $LINK^i$.
    This yields a derivation $LINK^i \stackrel{*}{\Longrightarrow} LINK^i \otimes LAST$.
(2) Embed the derivation $A^\bullet \stackrel{*}{\Longrightarrow} LINK^i \stackrel{*}{\Longrightarrow} LINK^i \otimes LAST$ into $FIRST$.
    This yields a derivation $FIRST \stackrel{*}{\Longrightarrow} FIRST \otimes (LINK^i \otimes LAST)$.
(3) Compose the obtained derivation with the derivation $Z \stackrel{*}{\Longrightarrow} FIRST$.

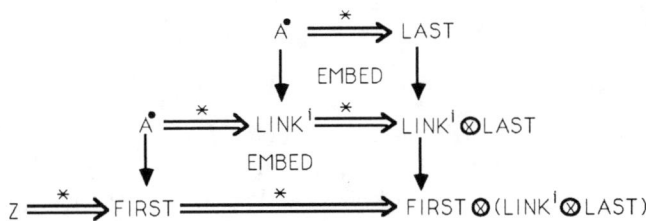

Hence, for $i \in \mathbb{N}$, $FIRST \otimes (LINK^i \otimes LAST)$ belongs to the language L generated by the hyperedge-replacement grammar HRG.

To complete the proof, we have to show claim 2 (see below) and verify the additional requirements.

Claim 2. Let $HRG = (N, T, P, Z)$ be a proper hyperedge-replacement grammar and c, max, and n the numbers chosen above. Then we have

(1) For each direct derivation $H \Longrightarrow H'$ in HRG, intsize$(H') \leq$ max $\cdot$ intsize(H).
(2) For each $A \in N$ and each derivation $A^\bullet \stackrel{m}{\Longrightarrow} H$ of length m in HRG,
    intsize$(H) \leq$ max^m and size$(H) \leq$ max$^m + c$.
(3) If $H \in L(HRG)$ and size$(H) >$ max$^n + c$,
    then the length of each derivation of H in HRG is greater than n.

Proof of claim 2. (1) Let $H \Longrightarrow H'$ be a direct derivation in HRG. Then at most all hyperedges of H are replaced simultaneously by at most the maximal number max of internal items of right-hand sides of productions. This implies intsize$(H') \leq |INT_H| +$ max $\cdot |E_H| \leq$ max $\cdot$ intsize(H).
(2) Let $A^\bullet \stackrel{m}{\Longrightarrow} H$ be a derivation of length m. By statement (1), intsize$(H) \leq$ max$^m \cdot$ intsize$(A^\bullet) =$ max^m and size$(H) =$ intsize$(H) +$ extsize$(A^\bullet) \leq$ max$^m + c$ because intsize$(A^\bullet) = 1$ and extsize$(A^\bullet) \leq c$.
(3) Let $Z \stackrel{m}{\Longrightarrow} H$ be a derivation of length m. By statement (2), max$^m + c \geq$ size(H). Now size$(H) >$ max$^n + c$ implies $m > n$.

Now the proof may be completed as follows. Since $H \in L(HRG)$ and $\text{size}(H) > p = \max^n + c$, the length of the derivation $der : Z \Longrightarrow H_1 \Longrightarrow \ldots H_m = H$ — considered at the beginning — is greater than the number n of nonterminals in the grammar. Hence the decomposition of H into $FIRST$, $LINK$, and $LAST$ — as mentioned above — is possible. By choice of k, there is a derivation of $LINK \otimes LAST$ is of length $(m - k) + 1 \leq n + 1$. Therefore, $\text{size}(LINK \otimes LAST) \leq \max^{n+1} + c = q$. Moreover, $\text{extsize}(LINK) \leq r$ because HRG is a grammar of order r. Finally, $LINK$ is nontrivial because HRG is a grammar without single productions (and thus cycle-free). This completes the proof. $\square$

We continue this section by the discussion of an example illustrating the pumping property.

2.4 Example (Non-Context-Free String Languages)

As shown in chapter I, the string-graph language $L = \{(a^n b^n c^n)^\bullet | n \geq 1\}$ can be generated by a hyperedge-replacement grammar of order 4, i.e., $L = \{(a^n b^n c^n)^\bullet | n \geq 1\}$ is a hyperedge-replacement language of order 4. It possesses the pumping property. This may be seen as follows: A string graph $(a^n b^n c^n)^\bullet$ is a $(1,1)$-hypergraph of the following form:

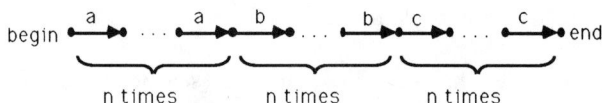

For $n \geq 3$, the string graph$(a^n b^n c^n)^\bullet$ can be decomposed as indicated below.

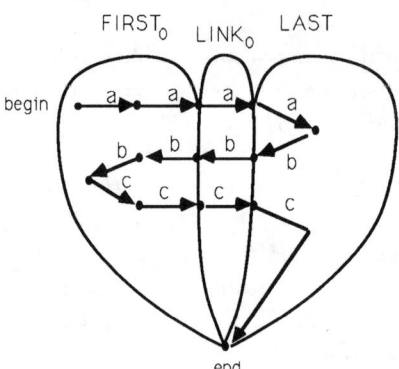

Fig. 2.1. Decomposition of the string graph $(a^4 b^4 c^4)^\bullet$

$FIRST$ is a (1,1)-hypergraph containing the distinguished nodes, *begin* and *end*, of the string graph as distinguished nodes. It consists of 3 chains of edges of length $n-2$, an a-chain, a b-chain, and a c-chain, where the a-chain is attached to the distinguished *begin*-node and the c-chain is attached to the end of the b-chain. Moreover, it may be seen as (2,2)-handled, where the first pair of tentacles is attached to the end of the a-chain and the beginning of the b-chain and the second pair of tentacles is attached to the end of the c-chain and the distinguished *end*-node. It is composed with the $LINK$-component with respect to the (2,2)-handle. The $LINK$-component consists of an a-edge, a b-edge, and a c-edge. Moreover, it possesses a (2,2)-handle which is attached to the target of the a-edge, the source of the b-edge, the target of the c-edge and the distinguished *end*-node. Finally, the $LAST$-component consists of an a-edge, a b-edge, and a c-edge where the b-edge is attached to the a-edge and the c-edge ends in the distinguished *end*-node. Note that neither $FIRST_0$ ($FIRST$ without the (2,2)-handle) nor $LINK_0$ ($LINK$ without the (2,2)-handle) nor $LAST$ is connected. Moreover, $LINK$ is non-trivial.

The pumped (1,1)-hypergraphs have the following shape:

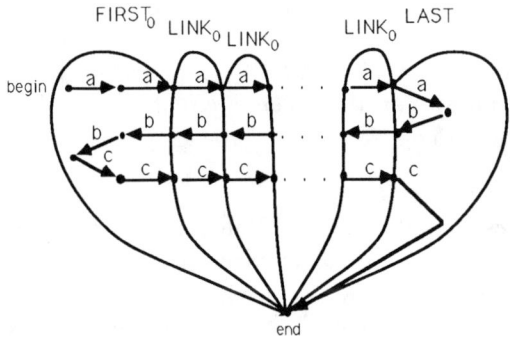

Fig. 2.2. A pumped (1,1)-hypergraph

Obviously, each resulting (1,1)-hypergraph is a string graph of the string-graph language $L = \{(a^n b^n c^n)^\bullet | n \geq 1\}$.

2.5 Corollary (Finiteness Problem)

For hyperedge-replacement grammars, the *Finiteness Problem* is decidable, i.e., there is an algorithm to determine whether a given hyperedge-replacement grammar generates a finite or infinite number of non-isomorphic hypergraphs.

Proof

Let HRG be a proper hyperedge-replacement grammar and p and q be the constants defined in the proof of theorem 2.3. Then $L(HRG)$ contains an infinite number of non-isomorphic hypergraphs if and only if $L(HRG)$ contains a hypergraph H with $p < \text{size}(H) \leq p + q$. This may be seen as follows.

If H is a hypergraph in $L(HRG)$ with $p + q \geq \text{size}(H) > p$, then, by the pumping lemma, H can be written as $H = FIRST \otimes LINK \otimes LAST$ such that $LINK$ is non-trivial and for all $k \geq 0$, $FIRST \otimes LINK^k \otimes LAST$ is in $L(HRG)$. By non-triviality of $LINK$, these hypergraphs are pairwise distinct. Hence, there is an infinite number of non-isomorphic hypergraphs in $L(HRG)$.

Conversely, if the number of non-isomorphic hypergraphs in $L(HRG)$ is infinite, then there are arbitrary "large" hypergraphs in $L(HRG)$; in particular, there is a hypergraph $H \in L(HRG)$ with $\text{size}(H) > p + q$. By the pumping lemma, this hypergraph can be written as $FIRST \otimes LINK \otimes LAST$ such that $\text{size}(LINK \otimes LAST) \geq q$, $\text{intsize}(LINK) > 1$, and for all $k \geq 0$, $H^{(k)} = FIRST \otimes LINK^k \otimes LAST$ is in $L(HRG)$. In particular, $H^{(0)}$ is in $L(HRG)$ and $\text{size}(H) > \text{size}(H^{(0)}) > p$. If $\text{size}(H^{(0)}) > p + q$, we repeat the procedure until we eventually find a hypergraph H' in $L(HRG)$ with $p + q \geq \text{size}(H') > p$.

Now we may precede as follows. By corollary 1.6, we may test all (non-isomorphic) hypergraphs $H \in \mathcal{H}_T$ with $p < \text{size}(H) \leq p + q$ for membership in $L = L(HRG)$. If there is such a hypergraph, then $L(HRG)$ contains clearly an infinite number of non-isomorphic hypergraphs; if not, then there are no hypergraphs of size greater than p in L, so that the number of non-isomorphic hypergraphs is finite. □

One of the main uses of results like the Pumping Lemma is to prove that specific hypergraph languages are not hyperedge-replacement languages — a task which is rather difficult in general. We derive now a theorem from the Pumping Lemma which applies very nicely to show that specific hypergraph languages cannot be generated by hyperedge-replacement grammars.

2.6 Theorem (Linear-Growth Theorem)

Let L be an infinite hyperedge-replacement language. Then there exist an infinite sequence of hypergraphs in L, say $H_0, H_1, H_2, \ldots$, and constants $c, d \in \mathbb{N}$ with $c + d > 0$ such that for all $i \geq 0$,

$$|V_{H_{i+1}}| = |V_{H_i}| + c \quad \text{and} \quad |E_{H_{i+1}}| = |E_{H_i}| + d.$$

Proof

The desired sequence of hypergraphs can be obtained by pumping up a sufficiently large hypergraph H_0 in L. The constant c can be chosen to be the number of internal nodes of $LINK$ and the constant d can be chosen as the number of hyperedges in $LINK$ minus 1. Because $LINK$ is non-trivial, we get $c \neq 0$ or $d \neq 0$. □

2.7 Example (Complete Graphs)

The set of all complete graphs cannot be generated by a hyperedge-replacement grammar because their growth with respect to the number of hyperedges is not linear as required by the Linear-Growth Theorem.

2.8 Example (Square Grids)

The set of all square grids of the form

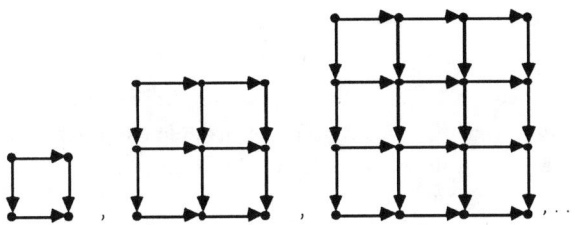

cannot be generated by a hyperedge-replacement grammar because they grow too fast.

2.9 Example (String Graphs)

The string-graph language $\{(a^{n^2})^\bullet | n \geq 1\}$ cannot be generated by a hyperedge-replacement grammar because the growth of the number of edges is not linear as required by the Linear-Growth Theorem.

3. Applications of the Pumping Lemma

In this section, we present some consequences of the Pumping Lemma for hyperedge-replacement languages concerning the connectivity, the clique size, and the minimum degree of its (hyper)graphs. In particular, it turns out that for hyperedge-replacement languages of simple graphs the connectivity, the clique size, as well as the minimum degree is bounded. For simplicity, all results are formulated for simple graphs. But let us mention that one can get similar results for (simple) hypergraphs.

3.1 Definition (Simplicity)

A graph $G \in \mathcal{G}_C$ is *simple* if there are no *multiple edges* with the same label, i.e., for all $e, e' \in E_G$, $s_G(e) = s_G(e')$, $t_G(e) = t_G(e')$, and $l_G(e) = l_G(e')$ implies $e = e'$, and there are no *loops*, i.e., for all $e \in E_G$, $s_G(e) \neq t_G(e)$.

3.2 Definition (Connectivity)

The *connectivity* of a graph G, $\mathrm{conn}(G)$, is the minimum number of nodes whose removal disconnects G into at least two non-empty components or reduces G to a single node.

3.3 Theorem (Connectivity Theorem I)

Let L be a hyperedge-replacement language of order r the members of which are simple graphs. Then for all $G \in L$ (except perhaps a finite number of non-isomorphic graphs), $\mathrm{conn}(G) \leq r$.

Proof

Let L be a hyperedge-replacement language of order r the members of which are simple and p and q be the constants occurring in the Pumping Lemma. Then each graph $G \in L$ with $|V_G| > p + q$ can be written as $FIRST \otimes LINK \otimes LAST$ such that $\mathrm{size}(LINK \otimes LAST) \leq q$, $\mathrm{extsize}(LINK) \leq r$, $\mathrm{intsize}(LINK) > 1$, and for $k \in \mathbb{N}$, $FIRST \otimes LINK^k \otimes LAST$ is in L.

Let V be the set of external nodes of $LINK$ and V' be the corresponding set of nodes in $FIRST \otimes (LINK \otimes LAST)$. Then the removal of V' from $FIRST \otimes (LINK \otimes LAST)$ yields at least two non-empty components: Since $|V_G| > p + q$ and $LINK \otimes LAST$ has at most q nodes, the remainder of the $FIRST$-part has more than p nodes. Since $LINK$ has at least one internal node, the remainder of the $LINK \otimes LAST$-part has at least one node. (The last statement results from the fact that $\mathrm{intsize}(LINK) > 1$ and that the members of L are simple graphs. If $LINK$ would have no internal nodes, then for all $k \in \mathbb{N}$, $LINK^k$ and $LINK$ would have the same number of nodes. By $\mathrm{intsize}(LINK) > 1$, $LINK$ would contain at least one "terminal" edge and $LINK^k$ would contain at least k "terminal" edges. Since the number of simple graphs with a fixed set of nodes is finite, pumping would yield non-simple graphs.)

Since the number of external nodes in $LINK$ is bounded by r, the minimum number of nodes whose removal disconnects G is bounded by r, as well. Thus, for all graphs G with $|V_G| > p + q$, $\mathrm{conn}(G) \leq r$. Furthermore, there is only a finite number of simple graphs with $|V_G| \leq p + q$. This completes the proof. □

Remark

Each hyperedge-replacement language L of simple graphs is of *bounded connectivity*, i.e., there exists a natural number $k \in \mathbb{N}$ such that $\mathrm{conn}(H) \leq k$ for all $G \in L$. This may be seen as follows. Each hyperedge-replacement language L is of order r for some $r \in \mathbb{N}$. By the Connectivity Theorem I, $\mathrm{conn}(G) \leq r$ for all $G \in L$ (except perhaps a finite number of non-isomorphic graphs). Choosing now r' to be the maximum connectivity of the execptions, we get $\mathrm{conn}(G) \leq \max\{r, r'\}$ for all $G \in L$.

Besides the Connectivity Theorem I, a criterion concerning the connectivity of the graphs as well as the connectivity of their subgraphs turns out to be useful.

3.4 Theorem (Connectivity Theorem II)

Let L be a hyperedge-replacement language of simple graphs. Then there is a natural number $k \in I\!N$ such that for all $G \in L$ and all $G' \subseteq G$, $\text{conn}(G') \leq k$.

Proof

Let L is a hyperedge-replacement language. Then the set $\text{sub}(L)$ of all (0,0)-subgraphs of graphs in L is a hyperedge-replacement language as well. By the Connectivity Theorem I, there is a natural number $k \in I\!N$ such that for all $G'_0 \in \text{sub}(L)$, $\text{conn}(G'_0) \leq k$. Since for each $G \in L$ and each subgraph $G' \subseteq G$, the underlying (0,0)-subgraph G'_0 is a member of $\text{sub}(L)$ and a graph and its underlying (0,0)-graph are of the same connectivity, we get $\text{conn}(G') = \text{conn}(G'_0) \leq k$. □

3.5 Definition (Clique Size)

The *clique size* of a graph G, $\text{cliquesize}(G)$, is the maximum size of the cliques in G. (A clique is a complete subgraph of G; the size of a clique is given by the number of nodes.)

3.6 Theorem (Clique-Size Theorem)

Let L be a hyperedge-replacement language of simple graphs. Then there is a natural number $k \in I\!N$ such that for all $G \in L$, $\text{cliquesize}(G) \leq k$.

Proof

By the Connectivety Theorem II, there is a natural number $k \in I\!N$ such that for all $G \in L$ and all $G' \subseteq G$, $\text{conn}(G') \leq k$. Since for $G \in L$, each clique G' of G is of size $|V_{G'}|$ and of connectivity $\text{conn}(G') = |V_{G'}| - 1$ and $\text{conn}(G') \leq k$, $\text{cliquesize}(G) \leq k+1$. □

3.7 Definition (Degree)

The *degree* of a node v in G, $d_G(v)$, is the number of incoming and outgoing edges to and from v. The *degree* of a graph G, $\text{degree}(G)$, is the maximum degree of its nodes. The *minimum degree* of G, $\text{mindegree}(G)$, is the minimum of the degrees of its nodes.

3.8 Theorem (Minimum-Degree Theorem)

Let L be a hyperedge-replacement language of simple graphs. Then there is a natural number $k \in I\!N$ such that for all $G \in L$, $\text{mindegree}(G) \leq k$.

Proof

Let L be a hyperedge-replacement language of simple graphs and p and q be the natural numbers occurring in the Pumping Lemma. Then each $G \in L$ with size$(G) > p$ can be written as $FIRST \otimes LINK \otimes LAST$ such that size$(LINK \otimes LAST) \leq q$, intsize$(LINK) > 1$, and for $k \in \mathbb{N}$, $FIRST \otimes LINK^k \otimes LAST$ is in L. Since all graphs in L are simple and intsize$(LINK) > 1$, $LINK$ must have an internal node. (Otherwise, pumping would yield non-simple graphs.) Since the number of nodes in $LINK \otimes LAST$ is bounded by q and $LINK \otimes LAST$ is a simple graph (a consequence of the simplicity of G), each internal node v of $LINK$ is of degree $d_{LINK}(v) \leq q - 1$. Furthermore, for each internal node v of $LINK$, there is a corresponding node v' in $G = FIRST \otimes LINK \otimes LAST$ with $d_G(v') = d_{LINK}(v)$. Thus, mindegree$(G) \leq q - 1$ for all $G \in L$ with size$(G) > p$. Moreover, mindegree$(G) \leq p - 1$ for all $G \in L$ with size$(G) \leq p$. Hence, mindegree$(H) \leq \max\{p, q\} - 1$ for all $G \in L$. □

3.9 Definition (Diameter)

The *diameter* of a connected graph G, diam(G), is the maximal distance between two of its nodes:
$$\text{diam}(G) = \max_{v,v' \in V_G} \text{dist}(v, v')$$
where dist$(v, v') = \min\{\text{length}(p)|\ p$ is a simple path in G joining v and $v'\}$.

3.10 Theorem (Diameter Theorem)

Let L be an infinite hyperedge-replacement language of simple, connected graphs. Moreover, let L be of bounded degree. Then there is a natural number $k \in \mathbb{N}$ such that for each natural number $m \in \mathbb{N}$, there exists a graph $M \in L$ with
$$|V_M| \geq m \quad \text{and} \quad \text{diam}(M) \geq \frac{|V_M|}{k}.$$

Proof

Let L be a hyperedge-replacement language of simple, connected graphs and p and q be the natural numbers occurring in the Pumping Lemma. Since L is infinite, there exists a graph $G \in L$ with $p < \text{size}(G) \leq p + q$ (see corollary 2.5). By the Pumping Lemma, G can be written as $FIRST \otimes LINK \otimes LAST$ such that size$(LINK \otimes LAST) \leq q$, intsize$(LINK) > 1$, and, for $n \in \mathbb{N}$, $FIRST \otimes LINK^n \otimes LAST$ is in L.

Since L is a set of simple graphs, $LINK$ possesses at least one internal node. (Otherwise, pumping would yield non-simple graphs.)

Since L is of bounded degree, the handle of $LINK$ is not allowed to be attached to external nodes, only. (If the handle of $LINK$ is attached to external nodes only, then each pumping step creates a new node and an edge connecting it with an external node.

Since the number of external nodes is bounded, the degree of one external node would grow beyond any bound.) Hence $LINK$ possesses internal attachment nodes.

Since L is a set of connected graphs, there is an $n \geq 1$, a set $ATT(e)'$ of attachment nodes, and a corresponding set EXT' of external nodes in $LINK^n$ such that for each attachment node $att(e)_i$ in $ATT(e)'$, there is a path connecting $att(e)_i$ and the corresponding node ext_i, there is no path connecting $att(e)_i$ with an non-important external node, and there is no path connecting ext_i with an non-important attachment node.

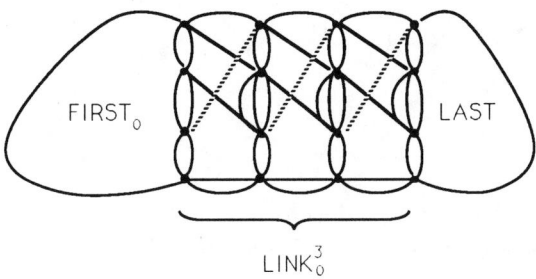

(An external node ext_{i_0} is said to be non-important, if there is a sequence of indices $i_0, \ldots, i_n$ such that $ext_{i_0} = att(e)_{i_1}$, $ext_{i_1} = att(e)_{i_2}$, ..., $ext_{i_n} = att(e)_{i_0}$. If an attachment node would be connected with a node of this type, the degree of this node would grow beyound any bound.)

For $m \in I\!N$, consider the graph $M = FIRST \otimes LINK^{2n \cdot m} \otimes LAST$. Then

$$|V_M| \geq 2n \cdot m \geq m \quad \text{and} \quad \text{diam}(M) \geq m.$$

By choice of G, $|V_G| \leq \text{size}(G) \leq p + q$. Moreover, $G = FIRST \otimes LINK \otimes LAST$ and $|V_{LINK}| \leq \text{size}(LINK \otimes LAST) \leq q$. Therefore, $|V_M| \leq p + q(2n \cdot m) \leq 2q(2n \cdot m)$ and

$$\text{diam}(M) \geq m \geq \frac{|V_M|}{4qn}.$$

□

Remark

1. The requirement that L is of bounded degree is essential. For example, the set $WHEEL$ of all wheels with at least 3 spokes is an infinite set of simple, connected graphs with unbounded degree, but bounded diameter: For a wheel $W(n)$ with n spokes, degree$(W(n)) = n$, $|V_{W(n)}| = n + 1$, and diam$(W(n)) = 2$.

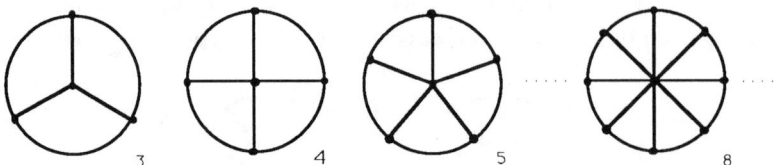

Fig. 3.1. Wheels

The set $WHEEL = \{W(n) | n \geq 3\}$ can be generated by the hyperedge-replacement grammar of order 3. But the quotient of $|V_{W(n)}|$ and diam$(W(n))$, $\frac{n+1}{2}$, grows beyond every bound.

2. An analogous result for node-replacement languages in the sense of Janssens and Rozenberg can be found in [JR 81].

3.11 Example (Snails)

The set of all graphs of the form

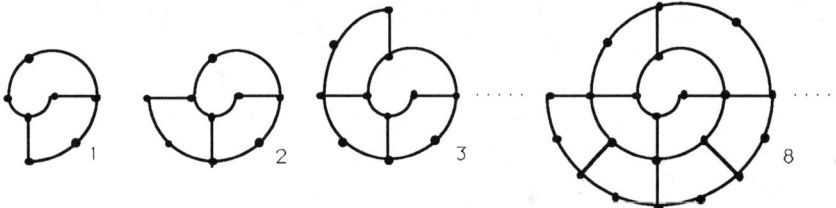

Fig. 3.2. Snails

called *snails*, cannot be generated by a hyperedge-replacement grammar although the connectivity and the degree are bounded (for each snail S, conn$(S) = 2$ and degree$(S) \leq 4$) and their growth with respect to the number of nodes and hyperedges is linear. The set $SNAIL$ of snails forms an infinite set of graphs of bounded degree and every snail S is simple and connected. If $SNAIL$ would be a hyperedge-replacement language, then, by the Diameter Theorem, there would exist a constant k such that for each $m \in \mathbb{N}$, there exists a snail S with $|V_S| \geq m$ and diam$(S) \geq \frac{|V_S|}{k}$. But such a constant does not exist.

The Connectivitiy Theorem, the Minimum-Degree Theorem, as well as the Diameter Theorem (all derived from the Pumping Lemma for hyperedge-replacement languages) apply very nicely to show that specific well-known sets of simple graphs cannot be generated by hyperedge-replacement grammars.

3.12 Theorem

The following sets of simple graphs cannot be generated by a hyperedge-replacement grammar:

(1) the set of all graphs;
(2) the set of all complete graphs;
(3) the set of all bipartite graphs;
(4) the set of all Eulerian graphs;
(5) the set of all Hamiltonian graphs;
(6) the set of all regular graphs;
(7) the set of all planar graphs;
(8) the set of all square grids;
(9) the set of all snails.

Proof

Statements (1)-(6) follow directly from the Connectivity Theorem and the Minimum-Degree Theorem, respectively. Each complete graph is a graph, Hamiltonian, and regular, each complete graph with odd number of nodes is Eulerian, and each complete bipartite graph is bipartite. On the other hand, for a complete graph K_n with $n \geq 1$ nodes, $\text{conn}(K_n) = n - 1 = \text{mindegree}(K_n)$, and, for a complete bipartite graph $K_{m,n}$ whose node sets have m and n nodes ($m, n \geq 1$), $\text{conn}(K_{m,n}) = \min\{m, n\} = \text{mindegree}(K_{m,n})$. Thus, the sets (1)-(6) are of unbounded connectivity and unbounded minimum degree.

Statement (7) follows from the fact that hyperedge-replacement languages L are of bounded *tree-width*. (In Lautemann [La 88a], it is shown that that hyperedge-replacement languages are of bounded decomposability. Since Lautemann's notion of "decomposability" corresponds to the notion of "tree-width" introduced by Robertson and Seymour, the boundedness of the tree-width follows directly from the boundedness of the decomposability.) On the other hand, each $n \times n$-grid has tree-width n (see Robertson and Seymour [RS 86]) and is planar. Thus, the set of planar graphs is of unbounded tree-width.

Statement (8) follows directly from the Linear-Growth Theorem (the number of nodes (and edges) grows too fast) as well as the Diameter Theorem (for an $n \times n$-grid $G(n)$, $|V_{G(n)}| = n^2$ and $\text{diam}(G(n)) = 2(n - 1)$. Therefore, the quotient of $|V_{G(n)}|$ and $\text{diam}(G(n))$ grows beyond every bound).

Statement (9) follows from the Diameter Theorem 3.10: the quotient of $|V_{S(n)}|$ and $\text{diam}(S(n))$ grows beyond every bound. Note that the other theorems cannot applied because the set of snails is of bounded connectivity, bounded degree, and the growth of the number of nodes and edges is linear. □

4. Parikh's Theorem for HRL's

We now present a result, called Parikh's Theorem, which relates hyperedge-replacement languages to semilinear sets and adapts Parikh's Theorem for context-free string languages to hyperedge-replacement languages.

Parikh's Theorem for context-free string languages was published originally by Parikh in [Pa 61] and was republished in [Pa 66] due to its importance and the inaccessibility of the original publication. It states that counting the occurrences of symbols in words of a context-free language yields a semilinear set. The proof given in [Pa 66] involves a complicated rearrangement of derivation trees. Essentially the same proof may be found in the books of Ginsburg [Gi 66] and Salomaa [Sa 73]. In [Gr 72], Greibach showed still another proof, using a Kleene-type characterization of context-free languages due to Gruska [Gr 71] in terms of an iterated substitution operator. In [Go 77], Goldstine has shown that a slightly strengthened form of the classical Pumping Lemma for context-free languages can be used to give a simplified proof of Parikh's Theorem. It should be stressed that his proof is conceptually the same as Parikh's original proof; it is somewhat clearer because it makes use of a generalized version of the Pumping Lemma instead of manipulating derivations or derivation trees.

Parikh's, Greibach's, as well as Goldstine's proofs could be adapted: Derivation trees are introduced in chapter II, a Kleene-type characterization for hyperedge-replacement languages is presented in chapter III, and a Pumping Lemma is formulated and proved in the previous section. We present a very short proof which directly makes use of Parikh's Theorem for context-free string languages.

4.1 Definition (Parikh Mapping)

Let $T = \{a_1, \ldots, a_n\}$ be an alphabet and $\psi : \mathcal{H}_T \to I\!N^n$ [1]) be the mapping given by

$$\psi(H) = (\#_{a_1}(H), \ldots, \#_{a_n}(H)),$$

where $\#_{a_i}(H)$ denotes the number of a_i-labeled hyperedges in $H \in \mathcal{H}_T$. Then ψ is termed a *Parikh mapping*. For any language $L \subseteq \mathcal{H}_T$, $\psi(L)$ denotes the set $\psi(L) = \{\psi(H) | H \in L\}$.

---

[1]) For $n \geq 1$, $I\!N^n$ denotes the Cartesian product of $I\!N$ with itself n times. For elements $x = (x_1, \ldots, x_n)$ and $y = (y_1, \ldots, y_n)$ in $I\!N^n$ and c in $I\!N$, $x + y = (x_1 + y_1, \ldots, x_n + y_n)$, $x - y = (x_1 - y_1, \ldots, x_n - y_n)$, and $cx = (cx_1, \ldots, cx_n)$.

4.2 Definition (Linear and Semilinear Sets)

A set $S \subseteq \mathbb{N}^n$ is *linear* if S is of the form

$$S = \left\{ x_0 + \sum_{i=1}^{k} c_i x_i \mid c_1, \ldots, c_k \in \mathbb{N} \right\},$$

where $k \geq 1$ and $x_1, \ldots, x_k \in \mathbb{N}^n$. $S \subseteq \mathbb{N}^n$ is *semilinear* if it is the finite union of linear sets.

The fundamental result concerning the distribution of labeled hyperedges in hypergraphs is presented in the following theorem.

4.3 Theorem (Parikh's Theorem)

For any hyperedge-replacement language L, the set $\psi(L)$ is semilinear.

Proof

Let L be a hyperedge-replacement language and $HRG = (N, T, P, Z)$ be a generating hyperedge-replacement grammar. By corollary 1.10, we may assume that HRG is proper. Then we construct a context-free string grammar HRG_{str} as follows: Let $str : \mathcal{H}_{N \cup T} \rightarrow (N \cup T)^*$ be a mapping assigning a string $str(H) = l_H(e_1) \ldots l_H(e_n)$ to a hypergraph H with hyperedges $e_1, \ldots, e_n$ and let $HRG_{str} = (N, T, str(P), str(Z))$ with $str(P) = \{(A, str(R)) \mid (A, R) \in P\}$. Then $\psi(L(HRG)) = \psi_{str}(L(HRG_{str}))$ where ψ_{str} denotes the usual Parikh mapping for string languages. By Parikh's Theorem for context-free string languages, the set $\psi_{str}(L(HRG_{str}))$ is semilinear. Consequently, the set $\psi(L(HRG)) = \psi(L)$ is semilinear. □

Remark

1. An explicit proof based on derivation trees is given in [Ha 89b].
2. For proving Parikh's Theorem for hyperedge-replacement languages, one may use the Kleene-Type Characterization Theorem presented in chapter III (2.3). Obviously, (1) finiteness of a language L implies semilinearity of $\psi(L)$. If we can show that (2) semilinearity of $\psi(K)$ and $\psi(L)$ implies semilinearity of $\psi(SUB_A(K, L))$ and (3) semilinearity of $\psi(L)$ implies semilinearity of $\psi(L^A)$, then the Characterization Theorem implies that $\psi(L)$ is semilinear for each hyperedge-replacement language.

Like counting the number of hyperedges (with suitable label), counting the number of nodes in hypergraphs of a hyperedge-replacement language yields a semilinear set.

4.4 Definition (Modified Parikh Mapping)

Let $T = \{a_1, \ldots, a_n\}$ be an alphabet and $\psi' : \mathcal{H}_T \to \mathbb{N}^{n+1}$ be the mapping given by

$$\psi'(H) = (|V_H|, \#_{a_1}(H), \ldots, \#_{a_n}(H)),$$

where $\#_{a_i}(H)$ denotes the number of a_i-labeled hyperedges in H. Then ψ' is termed a *modified Parikh mapping*. For any language $L \subseteq \mathcal{H}_T$, $\psi'(L)$ denotes the set $\psi'(L) = \{\psi'(H) | H \in L\}$.

4.5 Corollary (Modified Parikh Theorem)

For any hyperedge-replacement language L, the set $\psi'(L)$ is semilinear.

Proof

Let L be a hyperedge-replacement language. Then we consider a modified language $L' = \{H' | H \in L\}$ where, for $H \in L$, H' is obtained from H by attaching a (0,1)-edge with a label *node* (not in T) to each node in H. Obviously, L' is a hyperedge-replacement language as well (attach hyperedges to all nodes of the axiom and to the internal nodes of the right-hand sides). By theorem 4.3, $\psi(L')$ is semilinear. On the other hand, for $H' \in L'$, $\psi(H') = (\#_{node}(H), \#_{a_1}(H), \ldots, \#_{a_n}(H)) = (|V_H|, \#_{a_1}(H), \ldots, \#_{a_n}(H)) = \psi'(H)$. Therefore, $\psi'(L)$ is semilinear. □

Remark

There are several languages L, such as the set of all graphs and the set of all snails (investigated in section 3), which have the semilinearity property but are not hyperedge-replacement languages.

5. Bibliographic Note

The Pumping Lemma presented in section 2 is based on the Pumping Lemma for edge-replacement languages given in Kreowski [Kr 79]. A hyperedge-replacement version was first given in [HK 87c].

Chapter V
Generative Power of HRG's

This chapter is devoted to a subtler view of the order of a hyperedge-replacement grammar and the resulting generative power. In particular, hyperedge-replacement grammars whose generated hypergraphs are ordinary graphs or string graphs are objects of interest.

For each hyperedge-replacement grammar, the maximum number of tentacles involved in the replacement of a hyperedge plays an important role: it is closely related to the order introduced in chapter IV. The order turns out to restrict the generative power of hyperedge-replacement grammars in the following way. Let $\mathcal{HRL}_k$ for some $k \in \mathbb{N}$ be the subclass of $\mathcal{HRL}$ which comprises languages generated by hyperedge-replacement grammars up to the order k. Then, for example, the set of all k-trees is in $\mathcal{HRL}_k$ but not in $\mathcal{HRL}_{k-1}$. In other words, the family $(\mathcal{HRL}_k)_{k \in \mathbb{N}}$ forms an infinite hierarchy of classes of hypergraph languages, which remains proper even if restricted to graph languages. Furthermore, hyperedge-replacement grammars seem to be an interesting generative mechanism for string languages. Let $\mathcal{SL}_k$ denote the subclass of $\mathcal{HRL}_k$ which contains all string-graph languages of $\mathcal{HRL}_k$. Then the family $(\mathcal{SL}_{2k})_{k \in \mathbb{N}}$ forms an infinite hierarchy of classes of string-graph languages, which starts with the class of context-free string languages (represented as string-graph languages).

The chapter is organized as follows: In section 1, we present several examples for graph-generating hyperedge-replacement grammars and investigate the relationship to ordinary edge-replacement grammars. In section 2, we study the graph-generating power of hyperedge-replacement grammars. Accordingly, in sections 3 and 4, we present some string-graph-generating grammars, investigate the relationship to context-free string grammars, and study the string-graph-generating power of hyperedge-replacement grammars.

1. Graph-Generating Grammars of Small Order

In this section, we will investigate graph-generating hyperedge-replacement grammars of order 2 and compare their generative power with the one of edge-replacement grammars.

1.1 Definition (Graph Languages)

A hypergraph language L is said to be a *graph language* if all $H \in L$ are graphs. The class of all graph languages is denoted by $\mathcal{L}_{GRAPH}$.

As demonstrated already in chapter I, hyperedge-replacement grammars may be used to generate sets of ordinary graphs. Given an arbitrary hyperedge-replacement grammar, it is easy to decide whether or not the grammar generates a set of graphs.

1.2 Theorem

For hyperedge-replacement grammars, it is decidable whether or not all members of the generated language are graphs.

Proof

Let HRG be a hyperedge-replacement grammar. By the Reducedness Theorem, we may construct an equivalent reduced grammar HRG'. Now the reduced grammar generates a set of graphs if and only if all terminal labeled hyperedges occurring in the grammar are $(1,1)$-edges. Hence, there is an algorithm to determine if $L(HRG)$ is a graph language. □

1.3 Example (Discrete Graphs, Stars, Trees, Series-Parallel Graphs, etc.)

The following sets of simple graphs can be generated by hyperedge-replacement grammars of order 0, 1, and 2, respectively:

- the set of all totally disconnected (discrete) graphs;
- the set of all stars;
- the set of all trees;
- the set of all series-parallel graphs;
- the set of all maximal outerplanar graphs.

The axiom and the productions of the grammars look as follows.

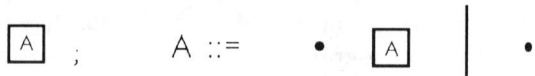

Fig. 1.1. Axiom and productions of $HRG_{DISCRETE}$

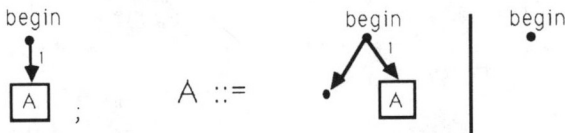

Fig. 1.2. Axiom and productions of HRG_{STAR}

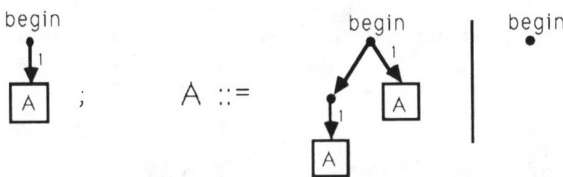

Fig. 1.3. Axiom and productions of HRG_{TREE}

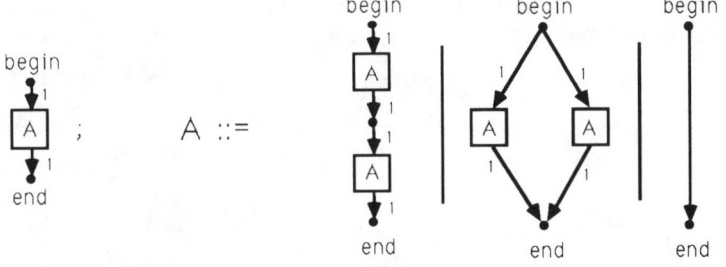

Fig. 1.4. Axiom and productions of HRG_{SP}

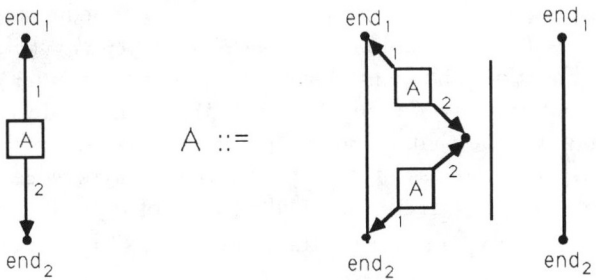

Fig. 1.5. Axiom and productions of HRG_{MOPS}

In the following, we will restrict ourselves to graph-generating hyperedge-replacement grammars. Within this class of grammars, there is the class of edge-replacement grammars (see, e.g., [Kr 79, HK 83+87a])

1.4 Definition (Edge-Replacement Grammars)

A hyperedge-replacement grammar $HRG = (N, T, P, Z)$ is an *edge-replacement grammar* if all hyperedges in Z are (1,1)-edges and all right-hand sides of productions in P are (1,1)-graphs. The class of all edge-replacement grammars is denoted by $\mathcal{ERG}$. The class of all languages generated by an edge-replacement grammar is denoted by $\mathcal{ERL}$.

Remark

Edge-replacement grammars are hyperedge-replacement grammars of order 2; on the other hand, they generate graph languages. Hence we have

$$\mathcal{ERL} \subseteq \mathcal{HRL}_2 \cap \mathcal{L}_{GRAPH}.$$

In the following, we will show that hyperedge-replacement grammars of order 2 generating graph languages and edge-replacement grammars are of the same generative power.

1.5 Theorem

$$\mathcal{HRL}_2 \cap \mathcal{L}_{GRAPH} = \mathcal{ERL}.$$

Proof

Let $HRG = (N, T, P, Z)$ be a hyperedge-replacement grammar of order 2 generating a set of graphs. Without loss of generality, we may assume that HRG is a typed and reduced grammar without empty productions. By typedness of HRG, there is a function $ltype : N \to \mathbb{N} \times \mathbb{N}$ such that for all $A \in N$, $ltype(A) = (m, n)$ with $m + n \leq 2$. By the Type-Modification Theorem (chapter I, 4.4), the grammar can be modified in such a way that nonterminals of type (2,0) or (0,2) become nonterminals of type (1,1). Therefore, we may assume that the nonterminal hyperedges are of type (1,1), (1,0), (0,1), or (0,0). By reducedness of HRG, all terminal hyperedges are of type (1,1). By the absense of empty productions, for all $A \in N$ of type $(0,0)$ and all derivations $A^{\bullet} \stackrel{*}{\Longrightarrow} G$ to a terminal hypergraph G, the node set of G is non-empty. (In the case $(l(Z), frame(Z)) \in P$, $frame(Z) \in L(HRG) \cap \mathcal{L}_{GRAPH}$, i.e., $frame(Z)$ has at least one node, and $l(Z) \in N$ is of type $\neq (0,0)$.)

In the following, we construct a hyperedge-replacement grammar $HRG' = (N, T, P', Z')$ in which all nonterminal hyperedges are of type (1,1). The construction is based on operations c and c' which modify the types of hyperedges and hypergraphs, respectively.

For $H \in \mathcal{H}_C$, let $c(H)$ be the hypergraph $(V, E_H, s, t, l_H, begin_H, end_H)$ with

$V = V_H \cup \{v(e) | e \in E_H \text{ with } type(e) = (0,0)\}$,
$s(e) = s_H(e)$ and $t(e) = t_H(e)$ if $type(e) = (m,n)$ for some $m, n \geq 1$,
$s(e) = t(e) = s_H(e)$ if $type(e) = (1,0)$,
$s(e) = t(e) = t_H(e)$ if $type(e) = (0,1)$,
$s(e) = t(e) = v(e)$ if $type(e) = (0,0)$.

For $H \in \mathcal{H}_C$, let $c'(H)$ be the hypergraph $(V, E_H, s_H, t_H, l_H, begin, end)$ with

$V = V_H$, $begin = begin_H$, and $end = end_H$ if $type(H) = (m,n)$ for $m, n \geq 1$,
$V = V_H \cup \{v\}$, $begin = begin_H$, and $end = v$ if $type(H) = (1,0)$,
$V = V_H \cup \{v\}$, $begin = v$, and $end = end_H$ if $type(H) = (0,1)$,
$V = V_H \cup \{v, v'\}$, $begin = v$, and $end = v'$ if $type(H) = (0,0)$.

For $H \in \mathcal{H}_C$ and $v \in V_H$, let $c_v(H)$ be the hypergraph $(V_H, E_H, s_H, t_H, l_H, begin, end_H)$ with $begin = v$.

Now let $HRG' = (N, T, P', Z')$ be the hyperedge-replacement grammar with

- $P' = \{(A, c'(c(R))) \mid (A, R) \in P \text{ and } type(R) \neq (0,0)\} \cup$
  $\{(A, c'(c_v(c(R)))) \mid (A, R) \in P, type(R) = (0,0), \text{ and } v \in INT_{c(R)}\}$
- $Z' = c(Z)$.

Then $L(HRG') = L(HRG)$. This may be seen as follows. If $H \in \mathcal{H}_C$, $e \in E_H$, and $repl : \{e\} \to \mathcal{H}_C$ with $repl(e) = R$ is a base for replacement in H, then

- $c(H[e/R]) = c(H)[e/c'(c(R))]$ if $type(R) \neq (0,0)$
- $c(H[e/R]) = c(H)[e/c'(c_v(c(R)))]$ if $type(R) = (0,0)$ and $v \in INT_{c(R)}$.

From this follows (by induction on the length of derivations) that for each derivation $Z \stackrel{*}{\Rightarrow} H$ in HRG, there is a derivation $Z' \stackrel{*}{\Rightarrow} H'$ in HRG' with $H' = c(H)$ and, on the other hand, for each derivation $Z' \stackrel{*}{\Rightarrow} H'$ in HRG', there is a derivation $Z \stackrel{*}{\Rightarrow} H$ in HRG with $c(H) = H'$. Since c is the identity on terminal hypergraphs (all terminal hyperedges are (1,1)-edges), this proves that $L(HRG) = L(HRG')$.

Moreover, by construction, HRG' is an edge-replacement grammar. This completes the proof. □

2. The Graph-Generating Power of HRG's

This section is devoted to a subtler view of the order of a hyperedge-replacement grammar and the resulting generative power. By definition of the order of a hyperedge-replacement language, we have

$$\mathcal{HRL}_0 \subseteq \mathcal{HRL}_1 \subseteq \mathcal{HRL}_2 \subseteq \ldots \subseteq \mathcal{HRL}_k \subseteq \ldots.$$

In the following, we will show that all of the inclusions are proper. For this purpose, we will use the Pumping Lemma for hyperedge-replacement languages of order k ($k \in I\!N$).

There are several sets of graphs which can be generated by a grammar of small order. For example, the set of all discrete graphs can be generated by a grammar of order 0, the set of all trees can be generated by a grammar of order 1, and the set of series-parallel graphs can be generated by a grammar of order 2. Intuitively, it might be clear, that these sets cannot be generated by a grammar of lower order. In the following, for each natural number $k \in I\!N$, we will present sets of graphs that can be generated by a grammar of order k, but not by a grammar of lower order. In particular, for $k \geq 1$, we will consider

- the set of all k-grids,
- the set of all k-bipartite graphs,
- the set of all (partial) k-trees,
- the set of all graphs of bandwidth $\leq k$, and
- the set of all graphs of cyclic bandwidth $\leq k$.

It turns out that the first four sets of graphs can be generated by a grammar of order k, but not by a grammar of order $k - 1$, and that the last one can be generated by a grammar of order $2k$, but not by a grammar of order $2k - 1$. As a consequence, we get a proper language hierarchy.

2.1 Example (k-Grids)

For $k \geq 1$, the set $kGRID$ of all $k \times n$-grids (with $n \geq 2$) of the form

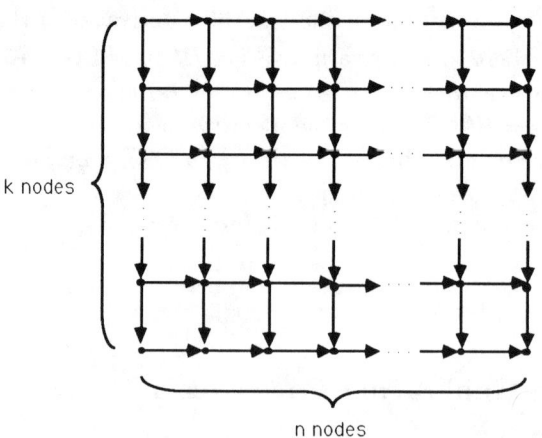

Fig. 2.1. A k-grid

can be generated by the grammar HRG_{kGRID} with axiom and productions as given in Fig. 2.2.

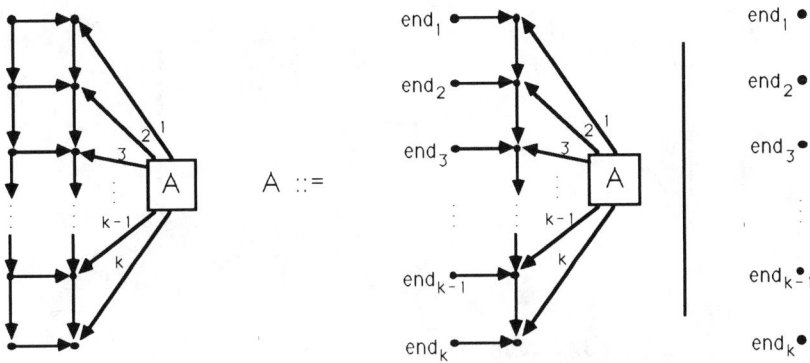

Fig. 2.2. Axiom and productions of HRG_{kGRID}

Obviously, HRG_{kGRID} is a grammar of order k. Thus, $kGRID$ can be generated by a grammar of order k. Making use of the Pumping Lemma, it can be shown that $kGRID$ cannot be generated by a grammar of order $k-1$ (Assume $kGRID$ is a language of order $k-1$. Then, by the Pumping Lemma, each sufficiently large k-grid G belonging to the language $kGRID$ can be decomposed into a $FIRST$-component, a $LINK$-component with at most $k-1$ external nodes, and a $LAST$-component such that the composition of $FIRST$, $LAST$, and n samples of $LINK$ for each natural number n yields also a k-grid. But for each such decomposition of G, pumping yields a non-grid, a contradiction.)

2.2 Example (k-Bipartite Graphs)

For $k \geq 1$, the set $kBIP$ of all *k-bipartite graphs* can be generated by a grammar HRG_{kBIP} of order k (c.f. chapter I, 3.5). Since $kBIP$ contains an infinite number of graphs of of connectivity k, $kBIP$ cannot be generated by a grammar of order $k-1$ (c.f. the Connectivity Theorem).

2.3 Example (k-Trees)

For $k \geq 1$, the set of all *k-trees* (see Rose [Ro 74]) is recursively defined as follows:
(1) Each complete graph with k nodes is a k-tree.
(2) Given a k-tree $T_k(n)$ on n nodes, a k-tree on $n+1$ nodes is obtained when the $(n+1)$-th node is made adjacent to each node of a k-clique in $T_k(n)$.

For arbitrary but fixed positive k, one can easily find a hyperedge-replacement grammar HRG_{kTREE} of order k generating the set of all k-trees. The grammar simulates the recursive construction of a k-tree: As axiom we choose a complete graph with k nodes and an additional $(0, k)$-hyperedge attached to the k nodes (indicating that there is a k-clique). The "generating" production generates a new node new, k edges connecting new with the external nodes, and $k+1$ hyperedges indicating the old k-clique and the

k arising k-cliques. The "terminating" production allows to remove a hyperedge. For $k = 2$, the axiom and the productions may be illustrated as follows.

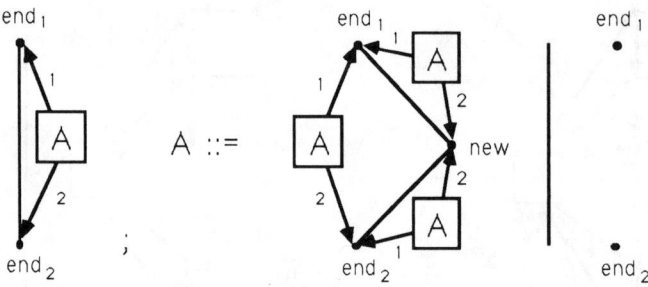

Fig. 2.3. Axiom and Productions of HRG_{2TREE}

Furthermore, for $k \geq 2$, the addition of the "edge-removing" production which allows to remove an ordinary edge yields a hyperedge-replacement grammar HRG_{pkTREE} of order k generating the set of all partial k-trees.

Thus, for $k \geq 1$, the set $kTREE$ of all k-trees can be generated by a grammar of order k. By the Connectivity Theorem, $kTREE$ cannot be generated by a grammar of order $k - 1$. (Suppose $kTREE$ is a language of order $k - 1$. Then, except perhaps a finite number, all elements in $kTREE$ are of connectivity $\leq k - 1$. On the other hand, each k-tree with at least $k + 1$ nodes is of connectivity k, a contradiction.) Similarly, for $k \geq 2$, the set $pkTREE$ of all partial k-trees can be generated by a grammar of order k, but not by a grammar of order $k - 1$.

2.4 Example (Graphs of Bandwidth $\leq k$)

For $k \geq 1$, a graph G is said to be of *bandwidth* $\leq k$ if there is a bijective mapping $f : V_G \to \{1, 2, \ldots, |V_G|\}$, such that for all $e \in E_G$,

$$|f(s_G(e)) - f(t_G(e))| \leq k.$$

For $k \geq 1$, there is a hyperedge-replacement grammar HRG_{kBW} of order k which generates all (simple) graphs of bandwidth $\leq k$ with at least k nodes. The axiom is a complete graph with k nodes and one hyperedge having k tentacles attached to the k nodes. The "generating" production produces a new node, connects it to the original nodes of the hyperedge, and produces a new hyperedge attached to the "last" $k - 1$ nodes as well as to the new node; the "hyperedge-removing" production allows us to remove the hyperedge; finally, the "edge-removing" production allows us to remove an ordinary edge. The axiom and the main productions may be illustrated as follows.

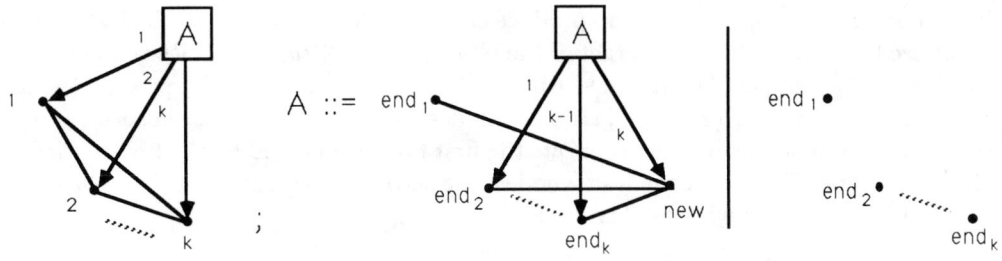

Fig. 2.4. Axiom and productions of HRG_{kBW}

Thus, for $k \geq 1$, the set kBW of all (simple) graphs of bandwidth $\leq k$ (with at least k nodes) can be generated by a grammar of order k. Since kBW contains an infinite number of non-isomorphic graphs of connectivity k, kBW cannot be generated by a grammar of order $k-1$ (c.f. Connectivity Theorem).

2.5 Example (Graphs of Cyclic Bandwidth $\leq k$)

For $k \geq 1$, a graph G is said to be of *cyclic bandwidth* $\leq k$ if there is a bijective mapping $f : V_G \to \{1, 2, \ldots, |V_G|\}$, such that for all $e \in E_G$,

$$\min\Big\{|f(s_G(e)) - f(t_G(e))|\,,\, |V_G| - |f(s_G(e)) - f(t_G(e))|\Big\} \leq k.$$

The set of all (simple) graphs of cyclic bandwidth $\leq k$ with at least $3k$ nodes can be generated by a hyperedge-replacement grammar HRG_{kCBW} of order $2k$. The axiom is a graph of bandwidth k with $3k$ nodes and one hyperedge having $2k$ tentacles attached to the "first k nodes" as well as to the "last k nodes".

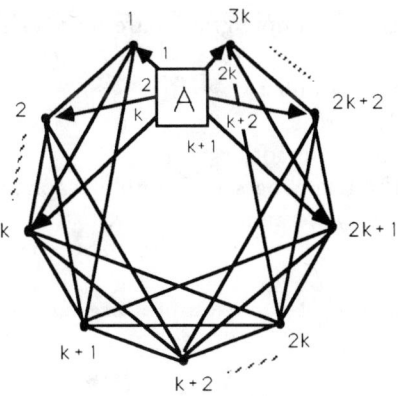

Fig. 2.5. Axiom of HRG_{kCBW}

The "node-generating" production produces a new node, connects it to the last k nodes (that are the nodes which are target of the $(k+1)th, (k+2)th, \ldots, (2k)th$ tentacle), and produces a new hyperedge attached with its first k tentacles to the first k nodes, and with its other k tentacles to the last $k-1$ nodes as well as to the last generated node. The "cycle-closing" production connects the first node (indicated by the first tentacle of the single hyperedge) with the last k nodes, the second node with the last $k-1$ nodes, ..., and the kth node with the last node.

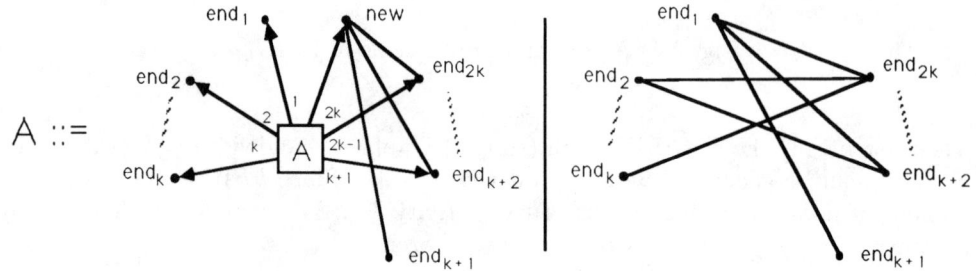

Fig. 2.6. Productions of HRG_{kCBW}

Finally, an "edge-removing" production allows us to remove an ordinary edge.

Thus, for $k \geq 1$, the set $kCBW$ of all (simple) graphs of cyclic bandwidth $\leq k$ (with at least $3k$ nodes) can be generated by a grammar of order $2k$. Since $kCBW$ contains an infinite number of non-isomorphic graphs of connectivity $2k$, $kCBW$ cannot be generated by a grammar of order $2k-1$ (c.f. Connectivity Theorem).

2.6 Summary

For $k \geq 1$, the following sets of simple graphs are in $\mathcal{HRL}_k - \mathcal{HRL}_{k-1}$:
- the set of all k-grids;
- the set of all k-bipartite graphs;
- the set of all (partial) k-trees;
- the set of all graphs of bandwidth $\leq k$.

Furthermore, for $k \geq 1$, the following set of simple graphs is in $\mathcal{HRL}_{2k} - \mathcal{HRL}_{2k-1}$:
- the set of all graphs of cyclic bandwidth $\leq k$.

As an immediate consequence of the examples presented above, we get the following hierarchy theorem.

2.7 Hierarchy Theorem

1. $\mathcal{HRL}_{k-1} \subset \mathcal{HRL}_k$ for all $k \geq 1$.
2. $\mathcal{HRL}_{k-1} \cap \mathcal{L}_{GRAPH} \subset \mathcal{HRL}_k \cap \mathcal{L}_{GRAPH}$ for all $k \geq 1$.

Remark

As a consequence of the Hierarchy Theorem, the number of external nodes in the right-hand sides of productions cannot be bounded without reducing the generative power. The situation may be illustrated by the following diagram.

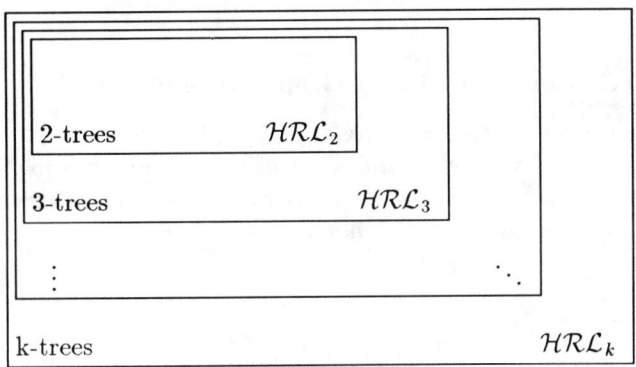

3. String-Graph-Generating Grammars of Small Order

In this section, we will investigate string-graph-generating hyperedge-replacement grammars of order 2 and compare their generative power with the one of context-free string grammars.

3.1 Definition (String-Graph Languages)

A hypergraph language L is said to be a *string-graph language* if all $H \in L$ are string graphs. The class of all string-graph languages is denoted by $\mathcal{L}_{STRING}$.

As demonstrated already in chapter I, hyperedge-replacement grammars can be used to generate languages of string-like structure. This seems to be quite attractive, because it provides a context-free mechanism for generating certain non-context-free string languages. Given an arbitrary hyperedge-replacement grammar, it is easy to decide whether or not the grammar generates a string-graph language.

3.2 Theorem

For hyperedge-replacement grammars, it is decidable whether or not all members of the generated language are string graphs.

Proof

Let $HRG = (N, T, P, Z)$ be a hyperedge-replacement grammar of order r. It can be shown that the property STR given by $STR(H)$ if and only if H is a string graph is $\mathcal{HRG}_r$-compatible in the sense of definition 2.1 of chapter VI. Therefore, by theorem 4.1 in chapter VI, it is decidable whether or not STR holds for all $H \in L(HRG)$; i.e., it is decidable whether all $H \in L(HRG)$ are string graphs. □

3.3 Definition (Context-Free String-Graph Grammars)

A hyperedge-replacement grammar $HRG = (N, T, P, Z)$ is said to be a *context-free string-graph grammar*, if the right-hand sides of the productions in P as well as the axiom Z are string graphs. The class of all string-graph languages generated by a context-free string-graph grammar is denoted by $\mathcal{CFL}$.

Remark

1. Each context-free string grammar $G = (N, T, P, S)$ (without λ-rules) induces a context-free string-graph grammar $G^\bullet = (N, T, P^\bullet, S^\bullet)$ with $P^\bullet = \{(A, r^\bullet) | (A, r) \in P\}$ such that the string-graph language $L(G^\bullet)$ generated by $G^\bullet$ is obtained from the string language $L(G)$ generated by G just by string-to-string-graph transformation:

$$L(G^\bullet) = \{w^\bullet | w \in L(G)\}.$$

In this sense, hyperedge-replacement grammars generalize context-free string grammars.
2. Context-free string-graph grammars are hyperedge-replacement grammars of order 2; on the other hand, they generate string-graph languages. Hence we have

$$\mathcal{CFL} \subseteq \mathcal{HRL}_2 \cap \mathcal{L}_{STRING}.$$

In the following, we will show that hyperedge-replacement grammars of order 2 generating string-graph languages and context-free string-graph grammars are of the same generative power.

3.4 Theorem

$$\mathcal{HRL}_2 \cap \mathcal{L}_{STRING} = \mathcal{CFL}.$$

Proof

Let $L \in \mathcal{HRL}_2 \cap \mathcal{L}_{STRING}$. If $L = \emptyset$, then L can be generated by a context-free string-graph grammar with an empty set of productions. Otherwise, there is an edge-replacement grammar $HRG = (N, T, P, Z)$ of order 2 generating L (c.f. Theorem 1.5). Without loss of generality, we may assume that HRG is reduced and does not contain empty productions. Since L is a non-empty set of string graphs and HRG is a reduced edge-replacement grammar without empty productions, Z is a chain graph and, for each

$(A, R) \in P$, R is a chain graph, as well. (A (1,1)-graph G is said to be a *chain graph* if it is of the form $G = (\{v_0, v_1, \ldots, v_n\}, \{e_1, \ldots, e_n\}, s, t, l, v_0, v_n)$ where $v_0, v_1, \ldots, v_n$ are pairwise distinct, $s(e_i) = v_{i-1}$ and $t(e_i) = v_i$ or $s(e_i) = v_i$ and $t(e_i) = v_{i-1}$ for $i = 1, \ldots, n$.)

Thus, it remains to show that the "chain-graph" grammar HRG can be modified into an equivalent context-free string-graph grammar HRG'. By reducedness of HRG, for each $A \in N$, there is a derivation $Z \stackrel{*}{\Longrightarrow} F$ from the axiom to a chain graph F containing an edge with label A and there is a derivation $A^\bullet \stackrel{*}{\Longrightarrow} G$ from the handle $A^\bullet$ to a terminal chain graph. Then G must already be a string graph or a reversed string graph, i.e., a string graph in which the begin node and the end node are exchanged. Moreover, all chain graphs derived from $A^\bullet$ are string graphs or all chain graphs derived from $A^\bullet$ are reversed string graphs. Thus, there is a mapping $dir : N \to \{\downarrow, \uparrow\}$ such that $dir(A) = \downarrow$ if all derived graphs are string graphs and $dir(A) = \uparrow$ otherwise.

We will use two operations r and r' on chain graphs. The operation r reverses an edge e in G if $l_G(e) \in N$ and $dir(l_G(e)) = \uparrow$; the operation r' exchanges the begin and the end node. More formally, for a chain graph G, let $r(G) = (V_G, E_G, s, t, l_G, begin_G, end_G)$ with $s(e) = t_G(e)$ and $t(e) = s_G(e)$ if $l_G(e) \in N$ and $dir(l_G(e)) = \uparrow$ and $s(e) = s_G(e)$ and $t(e) = t_G(e)$ otherwise and let $r'(G) = (V_G, E_G, s_G, t_G, l_G, end_G, begin_G)$. Then the grammar $HRG' = (N, T, P', Z')$ with

- $P' = \{(A, r(R)) \mid (A, R) \in P \text{ and } dir(A) = \downarrow\} \cup$
  $\{(A, r'(r(R))) \mid (A, R) \in P \text{ and } dir(A) = \uparrow\}$
- $Z' = r(Z)$

is a context-free string-graph grammar and $L(HRG') = L(HRG)$. This may be seen as follows. If G is a chain graph, e is an edge in G with $l_G(e) \in N$, and R is a chain graph, then we have

- $r(G[e/R]) = r(H)[e/r(R)]$ if $dir(l_G(e)) = \downarrow$ and
- $r(G[e/R]) = r(H)[e/r'(r(R))]$ if $dir(l_G(e)) = \uparrow$.

Consequently for each derivation $Z \stackrel{*}{\Longrightarrow} G$ by P, there is a derivation $r(Z) \stackrel{*}{\Longrightarrow} r(G)$ by P', and vice versa. Moreover $r(G) = G$ for $G \in \mathcal{G}_T$. Thus, $L = L(HRG) = L(HRG')$.

Furthermore, we have the following. If $A \in N$ and $A^\bullet \stackrel{*}{\Longrightarrow} G \in \mathcal{G}_T$ is a derivation by P to a string graph, then $dir(A) = \downarrow$, there is a derivation $A^\bullet = r(A^\bullet) \stackrel{*}{\Longrightarrow} r(G)$ by P', and $r(G) = G$ is a string graph. If $A \in N$ and $A^\bullet \stackrel{*}{\Longrightarrow} G \in \mathcal{G}_T$ is a derivation by P to a reversed string graph, then $dir(A) = \uparrow$, there is a derivation $A^\bullet = r'(r(A^\bullet)) \stackrel{*}{\Longrightarrow} r'(r(G))$ by P', and $r'(r(G)) = r'(G)$ is a string graph.

By reducedness of HRG' (the reducedness of HRG implies that of HRG'), each chain graph occurring in the grammar HRG' is a string graph. Thus HRG' is a context-free string-graph grammar. This completes the proof. □

4. The String-Graph-Generating Power of HRG's

There are several sets of string graphs which can be generated by a grammar of small order. E.g., for each context-free string language L, the induced string-graph language $L^\bullet = \{w^\bullet | w \in L\}$ can be generated by a hyperedge-replacement grammar of order 2. Furthermore, for several non-context-free string languages, e.g., $\{a^n b^n c^n | n \geq 1\}$, the induced string-graph language can be generated by a hyperedge-replacement grammar of order ≥ 4. In the following, for each natural number $k \in \mathbb{N}$, we will present some string-graph languages that can be generated by a grammar of order $2k$, but not by a grammar of lower order. In particular, for $k \geq 1$, we will consider the string-graph languages

- $\{(w^k)^\bullet \mid w \in T^+\}$ $(|T| > 1)$;
- $\{(a_1^n b_1^n a_2^n b_2^n \ldots a_k^n b_k^n)^\bullet \mid n \geq 1\}$;
- $\{(a_1^n b_1^n a_2^n b_2^n \ldots a_k^n)^\bullet \mid n \geq 1\}$.

It turns out that these sets of string graphs induced by non-context-free string languages can be generated by a grammar of order $2k$, but not by a grammar of order $2k - 1$. As a consequence, we get a proper language hierarchy.

4.1 Example

The string-graph language $L = \{(a^m b^n c^m d^n)^\bullet \mid m, n \geq 1\}$ can be generated by the hyperedge-replacement grammar HRG with the axiom $S(1,1)^\bullet$ and the productions

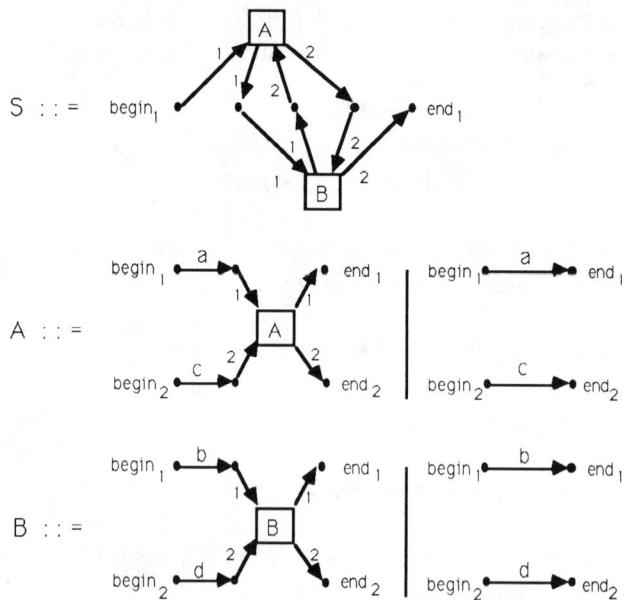

Fig. 4.1. Productions of HRG

Thus, L is a hyperedge-replacement language of order 4. By the Pumping Lemma, it turns out that L is not a language of order 3.

4.2 Example

For $k \geq 1$, the string-graph language $W^k = \{(w^k)^\bullet | w \in T^+\}$ ($|T| \geq 2$) can be generated by the hyperedge-replacement grammar HRG_{W^k} of order $2k$. The axiom and the productions are as follows.

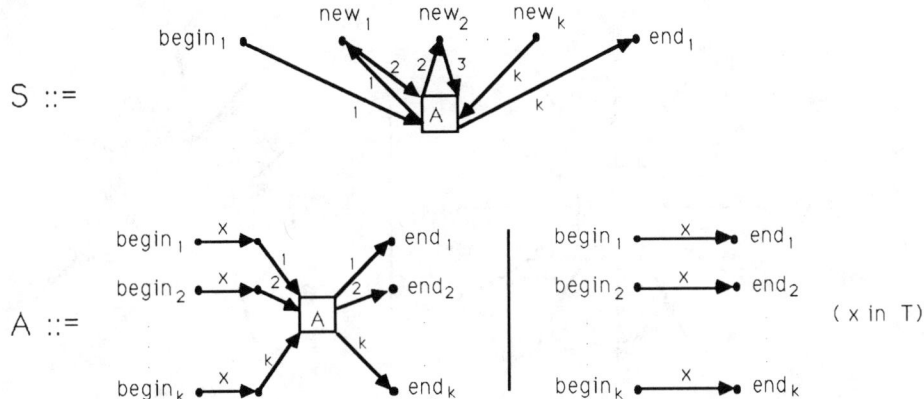

Fig. 4.2. Axiom and productions of HRG_{W^k}

Thus, W^k is a string-graph language of order $2k$. Making use of the Pumping Lemma, it can be shown that W^k is not a string-graph language of order $2k - 1$. (Assume W^k is a language of order $2k - 1$. Then, by the Pumping Lemma, each sufficiently large string graph $(w^k)^\bullet$ belonging to the language W^k can be decomposed into a *FIRST*-component, a *LINK*-component with at most $2k - 1$ external nodes, and a *LAST*-component such that the composition of *FIRST*, *LAST*, and n samples of *LINK* for each natural number n yields also a member of W^k. But for each such decomposition of $(w^k)^\bullet$, the *LINK*-component contains at most $k - 1$ parts of the string graph $(w^k)^\bullet$; so pumping yields a graph not belonging to W^k, a contradiction.)

4.3 Example

For $k \geq 1$ and symbols $a_i, b_i \in C$ ($i = 1, \ldots, k$), the string-graph language

$$L_k = \{(a_1^n b_1^n a_2^n b_2^n \ldots a_k^n b_k^n)^\bullet \mid n \geq 1\}$$

can be generated by a hyperedge-replacement grammar HRG_k of order $2k$. For $k = 6$, the productions are as follows:

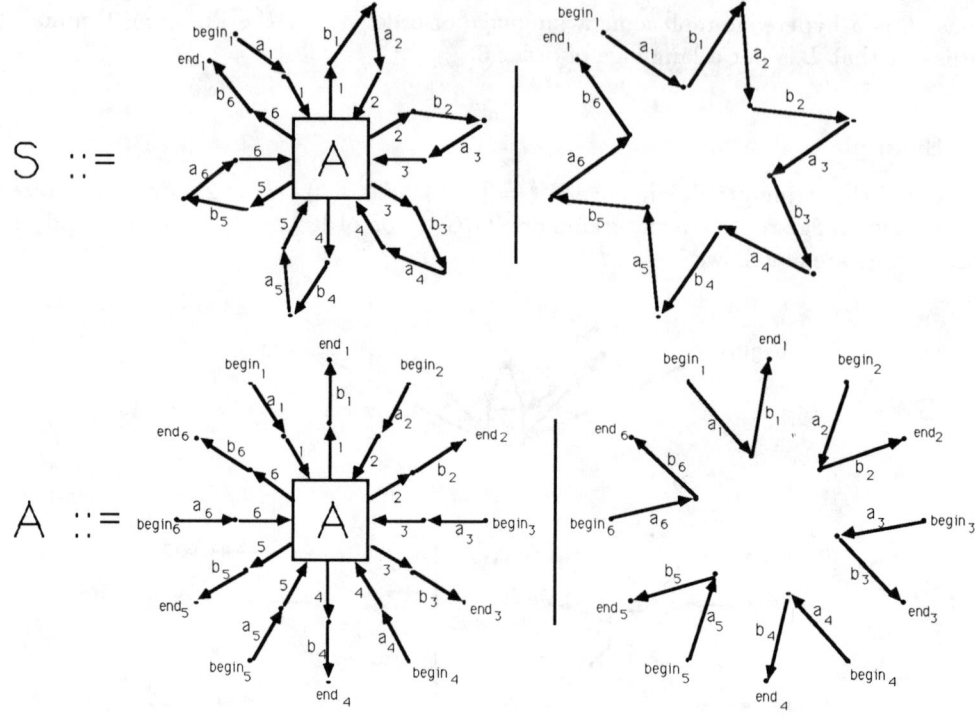

Fig. 4.3. Productions of HRG_6

Thus, L_k is a string-graph language of order $2k$. By the Pumping Lemma, it can be shown that L_k is not a string-graph lanuage of order $2k-1$.

In a similar way, it can be shown that for $k \geq 1$, the string-graph language

$$L'_k = \{(a_1^n b_1^n a_2^n b_2^n \ldots a_k^n)^\bullet \mid n \geq 1\}$$

can be generated by a hyperedge-replacement grammar HRG'_k of order $2k$. (For $k = 2$, $a_1 = a$, $b_1 = b$, and $a_2 = c$, the productions are given in chapter I, 3.6.) Again, by the Pumping Lemma, it can be shown that L'_k is not a string-graph lanuage of order $2k-1$.

4.4 Summary

For $k \geq 1$, the following string-graph languages are in $\mathcal{HRL}_{2k} - \mathcal{HRL}_{2k-1}$:

- $\{(w^k)^\bullet \mid w \in T^+\}$ ($|T| > 1$);
- $\{(a_1^n b_1^n a_2^n b_2^n \ldots a_k^n b_k^n)^\bullet \mid n \geq 1\}$;
- $\{(a_1^n b_1^n a_2^n b_2^n \ldots a_k^n)^\bullet \mid n \geq 1\}$.

4.5 Hierarchy Theorem

1. $\mathcal{HRL}_{2k-1} \cap \mathcal{L}_{STRING} \subset \mathcal{HRL}_{2k} \cap \mathcal{L}_{STRING}$ for all $k \geq 1$.
2. $\mathcal{HRL}_{2k} \cap \mathcal{L}_{STRING} = \mathcal{HRL}_{2k+1} \cap \mathcal{L}_{STRING}$ for all $k \geq 1$.

Proof

1. As already shown, for $k \geq 1$, the string-graph language $W^k = \{(w^k)^\bullet | w \in T^+\}$ ($|T| > 1$) is a language of order $2k$, but not of order $2k-1$.

2. Let $L \in \mathcal{L}_{STRING}$ be a hyperedge-replacement language of order $2k+1$ and $HRG = (N, T, P, Z)$ a typed, wellformed, and reduced hyperedge-replacement grammar of order $2k+1$ generating L. Then we will construct an equivalent grammar $HRG' = (N, T, P', Z')$ of lower order. By reducedness of HRG, for each $A \in N$, there is a derivation $Z \stackrel{*}{\Longrightarrow} \bar{F}$ where $\bar{F}$ is terminal up to one hyperedge e with label A. Moreover, there is a derivation $A^\bullet \stackrel{*}{\Longrightarrow} G$ to some terminal hypergraph G. Embedding of the derivation into G yields a derivation $\bar{F} \stackrel{*}{\Longrightarrow} \bar{G}$ with $\bar{G} \in \mathcal{H}_T$. Since all terminal hypergraphs generated by HRG are string graphs, $\bar{G}$ is a string graph. By well-formedness of HRG, the image of G in $\bar{G}$ is isomorphic to G. Therefore, we may assume that G is a subgraph of $\bar{G}$. Since $\bar{G}$ is a string graph and G is a subgraph of G, we have the following degree properties.

- $d_G^-(v) = d_G^+(v) = 1$ for $v \in INT_G$,
- $0 \leq d_G^-(v) \leq 1$ and $0 \leq d_G^+(v) \leq 1$ for $v \in EXT_G$.

(For a graph G, $d_G^-(v)$ and $d_G^+(v)$ denote the indegree and the outdegree of v in G, respectively.) Moreover, for two derivations $A^\bullet \stackrel{*}{\Longrightarrow} G$, $A^\bullet \stackrel{*}{\Longrightarrow} G'$ with $G, G' \in \mathcal{G}_T$, $type(G) = type(G')$, say (m, n), and corresponding external nodes have the same degree, i.e., $d_G^-(ext_{G,i}) = d_{G'}^-(ext_{G',i})$ and $d_G^+(ext_{G,i}) = d_{G'}^+(ext_{G',i})$ for $i \in [m+n]$. (Suppose, some corresponding external nodes have different indegree or outdegree, then the embedding of the derivations into $\bar{F}$ would yield derivations $\bar{F} \stackrel{*}{\Longrightarrow} \bar{G} \in \mathcal{G}_T$ and $\bar{F} \stackrel{*}{\Longrightarrow} \bar{G}' \in \mathcal{G}_T$ where some corresponding nodes in $\bar{G}$ and $\bar{G}'$ have different indegree or outdergree. On the other hand, $\bar{G}$ and $\bar{G}'$ are string graphs, a contradiction.)

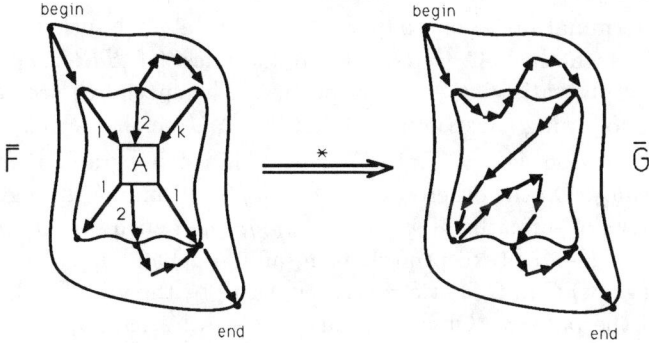

Fig. 4.4. A derivation in HRG

Given a derivation $A^\bullet \overset{*}{\Rightarrow} G \in \mathcal{G}_T$, two types of external nodes play a specific role, nodes $v \in EXT_G$ with $d_G^-(v) = d_G^+(v) = 0$ and nodes $v \in EXT_G$ with $d_G^-(v) = d_G^+(v) = 1$. In the first case, the derivation $A^\bullet \overset{*}{\Rightarrow} G$ does not produce any edge incident to v. The same holds for each other derivation $A^\bullet \overset{*}{\Rightarrow} G'$ to a terminal graph G'. In this sense, v is irrelevant in each derivation starting from $A^\bullet$, and one may be tempted to remove the tentacle of the hyperedge e of $A^\bullet$ attached to v. In the second case, the derivation $A^\bullet \overset{*}{\Rightarrow} G$ produces two edges incident with v. The same holds for each other derivation $A^\bullet \overset{*}{\Rightarrow} G'$ to a terminal graph F'. Therefore, in all derivations starting from $A^\bullet$, the required incoming edge as well as the required outgoing edge for v is generated. Considering a derivation $Z \overset{*}{\Rightarrow} \bar{F}$ with some hyperedge e with label A, the hyperedges $e' \in E_{\bar{F}-\{e\}}$ do not produce any edge incident with v. In this sense, v is irrelevant to them and one may attempt to remove all tentacles of hyperedges attached to v, delete the node, and generate it at the moment when the first edge for it shall be generated.

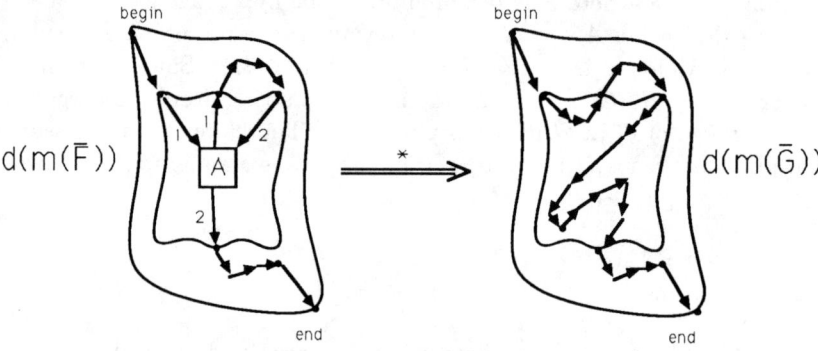

Fig. 4.5. A derivation in HRG'

This observation is the basis for our construction. We proceed as follows: We construct a new grammar $HRG' = (N, T, P', Z')$ with the help of operations m, m'_A ($A \in N$), and d which modify the types of the hyperedges and the hypergraphs and delete arising isolated internal nodes, respectively.

For $A \in N$ with $ltype(A) = (m,n)$ (for some $m, n \in \mathbb{N}$), choose a hypergraph $\bar{F} \in \mathcal{H}_{N \cup T}$ which is terminal up to one hyperedge e with label A such that $Z \overset{*}{\Rightarrow} \bar{F}$, and a graph $G \in \mathcal{G}_T$ such that $A^\bullet \overset{*}{\Rightarrow} G$. (By reducedness of HRG, we can effectively construct hypergraphs satisfying these properties. The special choices of $\bar{F}$ and G do not influence the following constructions.) Let $\bar{F} \overset{*}{\Rightarrow} \bar{G}$ be the derivation obtained by embedding the derivation $A^\bullet \overset{*}{\Rightarrow} G$ into $\bar{F}$. Then $\bar{G}$ is a string graph, i.e., there is path p from $begin_{\bar{G}}$ to $end_{\bar{G}}$. On the other hand, $\bar{G} = \bar{F}[e/G]$. Running through the path, one finds that it consists of subpaths $p_1, q_1, p_2, \ldots, p_k, q_k, p_{k+1}$ such that $p_1, p_2, \ldots, p_{k+1}$ are non-empty paths in $\bar{F} - \{e\}$ (except perhaps p_1 and p_{k+1}) and $q_1, \ldots, q_k$ are non-empty paths in (the image of) G in $\bar{G}$. For $i = 1, \ldots, k$, let u_i be the initial endpoint and v_i the final endpoint of the path q_i. Obviously, the nodes $u_1, \ldots, u_k, v_1, \ldots, v_k$ are external nodes of G. Moreover, they are pairwise distinct. Now let $ltype'(A) = (k, k)$ be the new type of A and $\varphi_A : [k+k] \to [m+n]$ be the mapping with $\varphi_A(i) = j$ if $u_i = ext_j$ and $\varphi_A(k+i) = j$ if $v_i = ext_j$ ($i \in [k]$).

For $H \in \mathcal{H}_C$, let $m(H)$ be the hypergraph $(V_H, E_H, s, t, l_H, begin_H, end_H)$ with

$$s(e) = att_H(e)_{\varphi_{l_H(e)}(1)} \ldots att_H(e)_{\varphi_{l_H(e)}(k)} \text{ and}$$
$$t(e) = att_H(e)_{\varphi_{l_H(e)}(k+1)} \ldots att_H(e)_{\varphi_{l_H(e)}(k+k)}$$

if $l_H(e) \in N$ and $ltype'(l_H(e)) = (k,k)$ ($k \in \mathbb{N}$) and $s(e) = s_H(e)$ and $t(e) = t_H(e)$ otherwise.

Accordingly, for a hypergraph $H \in \mathcal{H}_C$ and a symbol $A \in N$, let $m'_A(H)$ be the hypergraph $(V_H, E_H, s_H, t_H, l_H, begin, end)$ with

$$begin = ext_{H,\varphi_A(1)} \ldots ext_{H,\varphi_A(k)} \text{ and}$$
$$end = ext_{H,\varphi_A(k+1)} \ldots ext_{H,\varphi_A(k+k)}$$

if $type(H) = ltype(A)$ and $ltype'(A) = (k,k)$ and $begin = begin_H$ and $end = end_H$ otherwise.

Finally, let $d(H)$ be the hypergraph $(V, E_H, s, t, l, begin_H, end_H)$ with

$$V = V_H - \{v \in INT_H | d_H^-(v) = d_H^+(v) = 0\},$$
$$s(e) = s_H(e) \text{ and } t(e) = t_H(e) \text{ for } e \in E_H.$$

Now let $HRG' = (N, T, P', Z')$ be the hyperedge-replacement grammar with

- $P' = \{(A, d(m'_A(m(R)))) \mid (A,R) \in P\}$
- $Z' = d(m(Z))$.

Then $L(HRG') = L(HRG)$. This may be seen as follows. If $H \in \mathcal{H}_C$, $e \in E_H$, and $repl : \{e\} \to \mathcal{H}_C$ with $repl(e) = R$ is a base for replacement in H, then

- $d(m(H[e/R])) = d(m(H))[e/d(m'_{l_H(e)}(m(R)))]$.

From this follows (by induction on the length of derivations) that for each derivation $Z \stackrel{*}{\Rightarrow} H$ in HRG, there is a derivation $Z' \stackrel{*}{\Rightarrow} H'$ in HRG' with $H' = d(m(H))$ and, on the other hand, for each derivation $Z' \stackrel{*}{\Rightarrow} H'$ in HRG', there is a derivation $Z \stackrel{*}{\Rightarrow} H$ in HRG with $d(m(H)) = H'$. Since m is the identity on terminal hypergraphs and d is the identity on string graphs, this proves that $L(HRG) = L(HRG')$.

Furthermore, HRG' is a grammar of order $\leq 2k$. This may be seen as follows. By assumption, HRG is a grammar of order $2k+1$, i.e., $extsize(R) \leq 2k+1$ for all $(A,R) \in P$. By construction of HRG', $extsize(R')$ is even and $\leq extsize(R)$ for all $(A,R') \in P'$ corresponding to $(A,R) \in P$. Thus, $extsize(R') \leq 2k$ for all $(A,R') \in P'$. This completes the proof. □

Remark

As a consequence of the Hierarchy Theorem, the number of external nodes in the right-hand sides of productions cannot be bounded without reducing the string-graph-generating power.

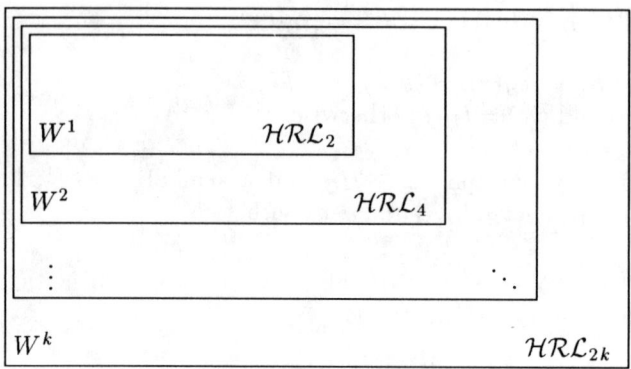

5. Bibliographic Note

Most of the results concerning the generative power are formulated, but not proved in [HK 87c].

Chapter VI

Graph-Theoretic Aspects of HRL's

Graph grammars and graph languages are motivated from a wide spectrum of applications, so that for the last 20 years, many researchers have felt encouraged to introduce and to investigate an enormous variety of graph-rewriting mechanisms (see the proceedings of the four graph grammar workshops [CER 79, ENR 83, ENRR 87, and EKR 91] as a survey on theory and applications). As a class of grammars defines and generates a class of languages, but does not tell much about these languages in general, it is hard to find a class of graph grammars with nice decidability properties and desirable structural results.

At least two approaches are more promising: Boundary node-label-controlled graph grammars [RW 86a+b] and edge-replacement grammars [HK 83+87a, Co 90a]. In both cases, the generative mechanisms and powers are of context-free nature, and several — especially graph-theoretic — properties are decidable for the generated graph languages. The investigation of decision problems concerning graph languages (generated by edge- or hyperedge-replacement grammars) is continued in this chapter and a quite general criterion for decidability is given. Roughly speaking: whenever a graph-theoretic property is "compatible" with the derivation process of hyperedge-replacement grammars in a well-defined manner, then for each given hyperedge-replacement grammar, the questions

(1) Is there a graph in the generated language satisfying this property?
(2) Do all graphs in the generated language satisfy this property?

are decidable.

The chapter is organized as follows: In section 1, graph-theoretic properties like total disconnectedness, connectedness, existence of Eulerian paths and cycles, and k-edge-colorability are discussed and it is shown that these properties can be easily tested for a graph provided that a derivation of the graph is known. In section 2, a formal definition of compatibility is given and the graph properties investigated in section 1 are shown to be compatible. The set of compatible graph properties turns out to be closed under Boolean operations. In section 3, we present a linear-time algorithm saying that given a compatible property $PROP_0$, for each hyperedge-replacement grammar

HRG and each hypergraph $H \in L(HRG)$ with derivation tree $T(H)$, we can decide $PROP_0(H)$ in linear time with respect to the size of $T(H)$. In section 4, we state a so-called metatheorem saying that given a compatible property $PROP_0$, for each hyperedge-replacement grammar HRG, the questions whether $PROP_0$ holds for some resp. for all hypergraphs $H \in L(HRG)$ are decidable. Furthermore, in section 5, we present a so-called Filter Theorem saying that for each compatible property $PROP_0$ and each hyperedge-replacement grammar HRG, effectively a grammar HRG_{PROP_0} can be constructed generating the set of all hypergraphs from $L(HRG)$ satisfying the property $PROP_0$. The construction in the Filter Theorem may be used whenever one wants to decide the existential- and the universal problem for $PROP_0$ mentioned above as well as if one wants to decide the except-a-finite-number problem and the finite-number problem for $PROP_0$. In sections 6 and 7, some non-compatible graph-theoretic properties as well as unsolvable graph-theoretic problems are discussed. Finally, in section 8, some remarks on related research are given.

The considerations are based on the following assumption.

General Assumption

In the following, we assume that each hyperedge-replacement grammar and each edge-replacement grammar under consideration is completely typed and well-formed. In this case, $A^\bullet$ denotes the handle induced by the symbol A and its type.

1. Some Compatible Graph-Theoretic Properties

A hyperedge-replacement grammar, as a generating device, specifies a hypergraph language. Unfortunately, the generating process never produces more than a finite subset of the language explicitly (and even this may consume much time). Hence, one may wonder what the hyperedge-replacement grammar can tell us about the generated language. As a matter of fact, by the Context-Freeness Lemma, we have the following nice situation. Given a hyperedge-replacement grammar and an arbitrary terminal hypergraph H with derivation $A^\bullet \Longrightarrow R \stackrel{*}{\Longrightarrow} H$, we get a decomposition of H into "smaller" components which are derivable from the handles of the hyperedges in R. If one is interested in graph-theoretic properties of derived hypergraphs, one may ask how a certain property of a derived hypergraph depends on properties of the components and of the involved hypergraph R. If a property is "compatible" with the derivation process of hyperedge-replacement grammars, i.e., if it can be tested for each derived hypergraph H by testing the property (or related properties) for the components and composing the results to a result for H, then a hyperedge-replacement grammar can tell us whether (1) there is a hypergraph in the generated language having this property and whether (2) all hypergraphs in the generated language have this property.

In this section, we turn to several graph-theoretic properties and show that they are "compatible" with the replacement process of hyperedges. A formal definition of compatibility as well as a metatheorem saying that compatibility implies decidability of the questions (1) and (2) are given in the next section. We are going to have a close look at connectedness, existence of Eulerian paths and cycles, having a k-bounded degree, and edge-colorability. To get accustomed to our kind of investigations, we first consider the question whether or not a given hypergraph H is *totally disconnected*, i.e., whether or not $E_H = \emptyset$.

Total Disconnectedness

Given a hyperedge-replacement grammar $HRG = (N, T, P, Z)$, a hypergraph $H \in \mathcal{H}_T$, and a derivation of the form $A^\bullet \Longrightarrow R \overset{*}{\Longrightarrow} H$ in HRG, there is a simple method for testing whether H is totally disconnected or not. The proposed method makes use of the fact that H can be obtained from R by replacing each hyperedge $e \in E_R$ by the result $H(e)$ of its fibre.

1.1 Theorem (Total Disconnectedness)

Let $HRG = (N, T, P, Z)$ be a hyperedge-replacement grammar, $A^\bullet \Longrightarrow R \overset{*}{\Longrightarrow} H$ a derivation in HRG with $A \in N \cup T$ and $H \in \mathcal{H}_T$, and for $e \in E_R$, $l_R(e)^\bullet \overset{*}{\Longrightarrow} H(e)$ the fibre of $R \overset{*}{\Longrightarrow} H$ induced by e. Then H is totally disconnected if and only if $H(e)$ is totally disconnected for all $e \in E_R$.

Proof

Without loss of generality, we can assume that $H = REPLACE(R, repl)$ with $repl(e) = H(e) \subseteq H$ for all $e \in E_R$. If H is totally disconnected, i.e., $E_H = \emptyset$, then $E_{H(e)} = \emptyset$ for all $e \in E_R$. Conversely, if $H(e)$ is totally disconnected for all $e \in E_R$, then $E_H = \sum_{e \in E_R} E_{H(e)} = \emptyset$, i.e., H is totally disconnected. □

To simplify the technicalities, we restrict our following considerations to the class of edge-replacement grammars. Remember that a hyperedge-replacement grammar is an edge-replacement grammar if the hyperedges in the axiom are $(1,1)$-edges and the right-hand sides of the productions are $(1,1)$-graphs.

Connectedness

Now we are going to discuss the question "Is G connected?" for a graph $G \in \mathcal{G}_T$ given by a derivation $A^\bullet \Longrightarrow R \overset{*}{\Longrightarrow} G$ in an edge-replacement grammar $ERG = (N, T, P, Z)$ in terms of the fibres $l_R(e)^\bullet \overset{*}{\Longrightarrow} G(e)$ induced by the edges of R. Obviously, a graph G is connected whenever R is connected and $G(e)$ is connected for all $e \in E_R$. The converse relationship does not hold, as the following example shows.

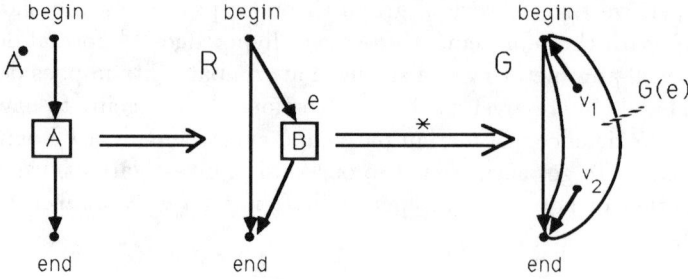

Fig. 1.1. A derivation of the form $A^{\bullet} \Longrightarrow R \stackrel{*}{\Longrightarrow} G$

Consider the derivation $A^{\bullet} \Longrightarrow R \stackrel{*}{\Longrightarrow} G$ in Fig 1.1 in which R (consisting of a terminal edge as well as a nonterminal edge e) is connected and the derived graph G (consisting of three terminal edges) is also connected. The graph $G(e)$ (marked by the "half-moon") derived from the handle of e is not connected. It is "semi-connected" in the following sense: each node of $G(e)$ is joined with $begin_{G(e)} = begin$ or $end_{G(e)} = end$; addition of an edge between $begin_{G(e)}$ and $end_{G(e)}$ would yield a connected graph. Note that the removal of the edge $e \in E_R$ (whose handle derives the non-connected graph $G(e)$) from the connected graph R yields a connected graph $R' = R - \{e\}$, again. The connection of the nodes $v_1, v_2 \in V_{G(e)} \subseteq V_G$ is given by three edges, the edge joining the nodes v_1 and $begin_{G(e)} = begin$ in $G(e)$, the edge outside from $G(e)$ connecting $begin$ and end, and the edge joining $end = end_{G(e)}$ and v_2 in $G(e)$.

The example shows that — beside the property "connectedness" — the property "semi-connectedness" is needed to characterize connectedness of graphs derived from handles. In the following, a (1,1)-graph G is said to be *semi-connected* if each node $v \in V_G - \{begin_G, end_G\}$ is joined with $begin_G$ or end_G. It is called *connected* if each node $v \in V_G - \{begin_G, end_G\}$ is joined with $begin_G$ and end_G.

1.2 Theorem (Connectedness)

Let $ERG = (N, T, P, Z)$ be an edge-replacement grammar, $A^{\bullet} \Longrightarrow R \stackrel{*}{\Longrightarrow} G$ a derivation in ERG with $A \in N \cup T$ and $G \in \mathcal{G}_T$, and for $e \in E_R$, $l_R(e)^{\bullet} \stackrel{*}{\Longrightarrow} G(e)$ the fibre of $R \stackrel{*}{\Longrightarrow} G$ induced by e. Then G is connected if and only if $R - \{e \in E_R | G(e) \text{ is not connected}\}$ is connected and $G(e)$ is semi-connected for all $e \in E_R$. G is semi-connected if and only if $R - \{e \in E_R | G(e) \text{ is not connected}\}$ is semi-connected and $G(e)$ is semi-connected for all $e \in E_R$.

Proof

Without loss of generality, we may assume that $V_R \subseteq V_G$ and $G = REPLACE(R, repl)$ with $repl(e) = G(e) \subseteq G$ for all $e \in E_R$. Let G be connected. Then $G(e)$ is semi-connected for each $e \in E_R$, which may be seen as follows: If for some $e \in E_R$, $G(e)$ would not be semi-connected, then there would be a connected component of $G(e)$

neither containing $begin_{G(e)}$ nor $end_{G(e)}$ which would be a connected component in G as well. Moreover, $R' = R - \{e \in E_R | G(e)$ is not connected$\}$ turns out to be connected: For $v_1, v_2 \in V_R \subseteq V_G$ there exists a path p in G which joins v_1 and v_2 [1]. Running through the path, some nodes of R are visited, say $w_0, \ldots, w_n$. Cutting p in these nodes, one gets a sequence of paths $p_1, \ldots, p_n$ (where p_i connects w_{i-1} and w_i for $i = 1, \ldots, n$). For each $i = 1, \ldots, n$, there exists $e_i \in E_R$ such that p_i belongs to $G(e_i)$. Obviously, e_i connects w_{i-1} and w_i for $i = 1, \ldots, n$. Thus, the edges $e_1, \ldots, e_n$ form a path from v_1 to v_2 in R. Note that $e_1, \ldots, e_n \in E_{R'}$, because the graphs $G(e_1), \ldots, G(e_n)$ are semi-connected as well as begin-end connected, and hence connected.

Conversely, let $R' = R - \{e \in E_R | G(e)$ is not connected$\}$ be connected and $G(e)$ be semi-connected for all $e \in E_R$. Let $v_1, v_2 \in V_G$. Three cases may occur.
Case 1. $v_1, v_2 \in V_R$. Then R has a path from v_1 to v_2 consisting, say, of edges $e_1, \ldots, e_n$, and, $G(e_i)$, for $i = 1, \ldots, n$ has a path p_i connecting $begin_{G(e_i)}$ and $end_{G(e_i)}$. Therefore, the sequence of paths $p_1, \ldots, p_n$ forms a path p from v_1 to v_2 in G.
Case 2. $v_1 \in INT_{repl(e)}$ (for some $e \in E_R$) and $v_2 \in V_R$. By semi-connectedness of $repl(e)$, there is a node $v_1' \in EXT_{repl(e)}$ such that v_1 and v_1' are joined by a path in $repl(e)$. Moreover, v_1' and v_2 are joined by a path in G (cf. case 1). Thus, there is a path from v_1 to v_2 in G.
Case 3. $v_i \in INT_{repl(e_i)}$ for some $e_i \in E_R$ ($i = 1, 2$). Using the same arguments as in case 2, there is a node $v_i' \in EXT_{repl(e_i)}$, such that v_i and v_i' are joined by a path in $repl(e_i)$ ($i = 1, 2$). Moreover, v_1' and v_2' are joined by a path in G (cf. case 1). Thus, there is a path from v_1 to v_2 in G.
Consequently, G is connected. This completes the proof of the first statement.

The second statement can be proved in a similar way. □

For expressing the interrelations between the statements concerning connectedness and semi-connectedness we make use of an index set I, a predicate $CONN$ defined on pairs (G, x) with $G \in \mathcal{G}_C$ and $x \in I$, and a predicate $CONN'$ defined on triples $(R, assign, x)$, with $R \in \mathcal{G}_C$, $assign : E_R \to I$, and $x \in I$, respectively:

- $I = \{\text{co}, \text{semico}\}$,
- $CONN(G, \text{co})$ if and only if G is connected,
  $CONN(G, \text{semico})$ if and only if G is semi-connected,
- $CONN'(R, assign, \text{co})$ if and only if
  $R - \{e \in E_R | assign(e) \neq \text{co}\}$ is connected,
  $CONN'(R, assign, \text{semico})$ if and only if
  $R - \{e \in E_R | assign(e) \neq \text{co}\}$ is semi-connected.

Now the theorem can be reformulated as follows.

---

[1] A *path* is meant to be a sequence $p - e_1, e_2, \ldots, e_n$ of edges such that for $1 \leq i < n$, e_i and e_{i+1} are adjacent.

1.3 Corollary (Connectedness)

Let $ERG = (N, T, P, Z)$ be an edge-replacement grammar, $A^\bullet \Longrightarrow R \stackrel{*}{\Longrightarrow} G$ a derivation in ERG with $A \in N \cup T$ and $G \in \mathcal{G}_T$, and for $e \in E_R$, $l_R(e)^\bullet \stackrel{*}{\Longrightarrow} G(e)$ the fibre of $R \stackrel{*}{\Longrightarrow} G$ induced by e. Then for $x \in \{\text{co}, \text{semico}\}$, $CONN(G, x)$ holds if and only if there is a mapping $assign : E_R \to \{\text{co}, \text{semico}\}$ such that $CONN'(R, assign, x)$ as well as $CONN(G(e), assign(e))$ for all $e \in E_R$.

Proof

Let $CONN(G, x)$ with $x = \text{co}$ ($x = \text{semico}$) be satisfied. Then, by theorem 1.2, $R - \{e \in E_R | G(e) \text{ is not connected}\}$ is connected (semi-connected) and $G(e)$ is semi-connected for all $e \in E_R$. Now choose $assign : E_R \to I$ by $assign(e) = \text{co}$ if and only if $G(e)$ is connected ($e \in E_R$). Then $CONN'(R, assign, x)$ is satisfied. Moreover, $CONN(G(e), \text{semico})$ holds for all $e \in E_R$ and, by choice of $assign$, $CONN(G(e), \text{co})$ holds for all $e \in E_R$ with $assign(e) = \text{co}$.

Conversely, let $assign : E_R \to I$ be a mapping such that $CONN'(R, assign, \text{co})$ ($CONN'(R, assign, \text{semico})$) and $CONN(G(e), assign(e))$ for $e \in E_R$ hold. Then $R - \{e \in E_R | G(e) \text{ is not connected}\} \supseteq R - \{e \in E_R | assign(e) \neq \text{co}\}$ is connected (semi-connected) and $G(e)$ is semi-connected for all $e \in E_R$. By theorem 1.2, $CONN(G, \text{co})$ ($CONN(G, \text{semico})$) holds. □

Eulerian Paths and Cycles

We are going to discuss the questions "Has G an Eulerian path from $begin_G$ to end_G?" and "Has G an Eulerian cycle?" These questions may be reformulated as "Is it possible to find a path that starts in $begin_G$, traverses each edge of the graph exactly once, goes through all nodes, and ends in end_G?" and "Is it possible to find a cycle that traverses each edge of the graph exactly once, goes through all nodes, and ends in the starting node?" These questions may be handled using the well-known graph-theoretic fact that a graph G has an Eulerian path from $begin_G$ to end_G if and only if it is connected and $begin_G$ and end_G are the only nodes with odd degree and that G has an Eulerian cycle if and only if G is connected and every node of G has even degree (see, e.g., Harary [Ha 72], Gibbons [Gi 85]). The problem whether G is connected or not can be handled as in 1.2. Hence it remains to find criterions for testing whether or not every node of G has even degree, except $begin_G$ and end_G, and whether or nor every node of G has even degree. The "even-degree property" (as well as the "even-degree-except-$begin$-and-end property") of a graph G with derivation $A^\bullet \Longrightarrow R \stackrel{*}{\Longrightarrow} G$ can be characterized in terms of the fibres $l_R(e)^\bullet \stackrel{*}{\Longrightarrow} G(e)$. The characterization is based on the following observation. Let R be a graph and v be a node in R. If an edge $e \in E_R$ outgoing from $v \in V_R$ is replaced by some graph $G(e)$, then the degree of $begin_{G(e)}$ has to be taken into account whenever the degree of a node $v \in V_R \subseteq V_G$ is considered; accordingly, the degree of $end_{G(e)}$ has to be taken in consideration if e is incoming into the node v. Now the $d_G(v)$ can be determined by summing up the degrees $d_{G(e)}(begin_{G(e)})$ for all edges $e \in s_R^{-1}(v)$

outgoing from $v \in V_R$ and the degrees $d_{G(e)}(end_{G(e)})$ for all edges $e \in t_R^{-1}(v)$ incoming into $v \in V_R$.

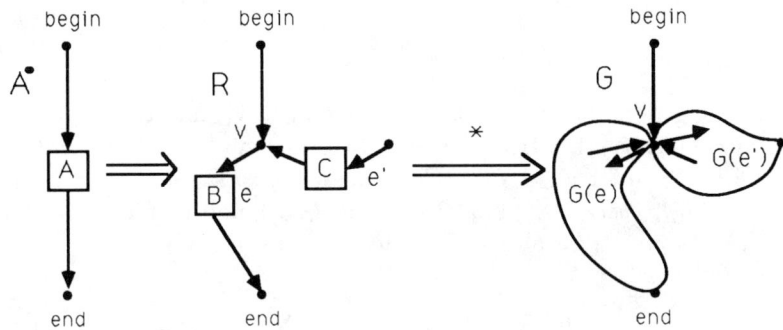

Fig. 1.2. A derivation of the form $A^\bullet \Longrightarrow R \overset{*}{\Longrightarrow} G$

With respect to the question "Do all nodes of a graph G have even degree?" it is useful to know for a graph $G(e)$ whether or not the degree of all internal nodes is even, the degree of the begin node is even or odd, and the degree of the end node is even or odd. For determining whether or not all nodes of G have even degree, i.e., whether $d_G(v) \bmod 2 = 0$ for all $v \in V_G$, we have to consider the nodes $v \in V_R \subseteq V_G$ as well as the nodes $v \in V_{G(e)} \subseteq V_G$ in the graphs $G(e)$ derived from $e \in E_R$. Since the graph R may contain edges which are replaced in the derivation of G, we have to use the values $d_{G(e)}(begin_{G(e)}) \bmod 2$ and $d_{G(e)}(end_{G(e)}) \bmod 2$ of the graphs $G(e)$ ($e \in E_R$). Thus, the "auxiliary" property concerning R used to compose the results of the components $G(e)$, is more complicated than the "main" property.

Let $G, R \in \mathcal{G}_C$ be (1,1)-graphs, $assign : E_R \to I$ a mapping from the edge set E_R to the index set $I = [0,1] \times [0,1]$ [2], and $i, j \in [0,1]$. Then

- $EVEN(G,(i,j))$ denotes the fact that $d_G(begin_G) \bmod 2 = i$, $d_G(end_G) \bmod 2 = j$, and $d_G(v) \bmod 2 = 0$ for all $v \in INT_G$.
- $EVEN'(R, assign, (i,j))$ denotes the fact that $ASSIGN(begin_R) \bmod 2 = i$, $ASSIGN(end_R) \bmod 2 = j$, and $ASSIGN(v) \bmod 2 = 0$ for all $v \in INT_R$ where, for $v \in V_R$, $ASSIGN(v) = \sum_{e \in s_R^{-1}(v)} assign(e)_1 + \sum_{e \in t_R^{-1}(v)} assign(e)_2$ and $assign_1, assign_2 : E_R \to [0,1]$ are the projections of the mapping $assign$ to the first and the second component, respectively.

1.4 Theorem (Eulerian Paths and Cycles)

Let $ERG = (N, T, P, Z)$ be an edge-replacement grammar, $A^\bullet \Longrightarrow R \overset{*}{\Longrightarrow} G$ a derivation in ERG with $A \in N \cup T$ and $G \in \mathcal{G}_T$, and for $e \in E_R$, $l_R(e)^\bullet \overset{*}{\Longrightarrow} G(e)$ the fibre of

---

[2] For $m, n \in \mathbb{N}$ with $m \leq n$, $[m,n]$ denotes the set $[m,n] = \{i \mid m \leq i \leq n\}$.

$R \overset{*}{\Longrightarrow} G$ induced by e. Then for $i,j \in [0,1]$, $EVEN(G,(i,j))$ is true if and only if there is a mapping $assign : E_R \to [0,1] \times [0,1]$ such that $EVEN'(R, assign, (i,j))$ as well as $EVEN(G(e), assign(e))$ for all $e \in E_R$ are true.

Proof

Without loss of generality, we may assume that $V_R \subseteq V_G$ and $G(e) \subseteq G$ for all $e \in E_R$. Suppose $EVEN(G,(i,j))$ is true. Then $d_G(begin_G) \bmod 2 = i$, $d_G(end_G) \bmod 2 = j$, and $d_G(v) \bmod 2 = 0$ for $v \in INT_G$. Choosing $assign : E_R \to [0,1] \times [0,1]$ by $assign(e) = (d_{G(e)}(begin_{G(e)}) \bmod 2, d_{G(e)}(end_{G(e)}) \bmod 2)$ for $e \in E_R$, we obtain $EVEN(G(e), assign(e))$ for all $e \in E_R$. Moreover, for $v \in V_R$,

$$ASSIGN(v) \bmod 2 = \Big(\sum_{e \in s_R^{-1}(v)} assign(e)_1 + \sum_{e \in t_R^{-1}(v)} assign(e)_2 \Big) \bmod 2$$

$$= \Big(\sum_{e \in s_R^{-1}(v)} d_{G(e)}(begin_{G(e)}) + \sum_{e \in t_R^{-1}(v)} d_{G(e)}(end_{G(e)}) \Big) \bmod 2$$

$$= d_G(v) \bmod 2.$$

Since, by assumption, $d_G(begin_G) \bmod 2 = i$, $d_G(end_G) \bmod 2 = j$, and $d_G(v) \bmod 2 = 0$ for $v \in INT_R$, we obtain $ASSIGN(begin_R) \bmod 2 = i$, $ASSIGN(end_R) \bmod 2 = j$, and $ASSIGN(v) \bmod 2 = 0$ for $v \in INT_R$, i.e., $EVEN'(R, assign, (i,j))$ is satisfied.

Conversely, let $assign : E_R \to [0,1] \times [0,1]$ be a mapping such that $EVEN'(R, assign, (i,j))$ as well as $EVEN(G(e), assign(e))$ for all $e \in E_R$ are true. Then, for $v \in V_G$,

$$d_G(v) \bmod 2 = \Big(\sum_{e \in s_R^{-1}(v)} d_{G(e)}(begin_{G(e)}) + \sum_{e \in t_R^{-1}(v)} d_{G(e)}(end_{G(e)}) \Big) \bmod 2$$

$$= \Big(\sum_{e \in s_R^{-1}(v)} assign(e)_1 + \sum_{e \in t_R^{-1}(v)} assign(e)_2 \Big) \bmod 2$$

$$= ASSIGN(v) \bmod 2.$$

By assumption, we have $ASSIGN(begin_R) \bmod 2 = i$, $ASSIGN(end_R) \bmod 2 = j$, and $ASSIGN(v) \bmod 2 = 0$ for all $v \in INT_R$. Therefore, we get $d_G(begin_G) \bmod 2 = i$, $d_G(end_G) \bmod 2 = j$, and $d_G(v) \bmod 2 = 0$ for $v \in INT_R$. Hence, $EVEN(G,(i,j))$ is satisfied. □

Remark

With respect to the questions "Has G an Eulerian cycle?" and "Has G an Eulerian path from $begin_G$ to end_G?" we get the following relations: G has an Eulerian cycle if and only if $CONN(G, \text{co})$ and $EVEN(G,(0,0))$. G has an Eulerian path connecting $begin_G$ and end_G if and only if $CONN(G, \text{co})$ and $EVEN(G,(1,1))$.

k-Bounded Degree

In this subsection we will investigate the question "Is the degree of G bounded by k ?". A graph G is said to be *k-bounded* (for some $k \in \mathbb{N}$) if the degree of G is bounded by k, i.e., $d_G(v) \leq k$ for all $v \in V_G$. Similar to the "even-degree property" investigated in 1.4, the "k-boundedness property" of a graph G with derivation $A^\bullet \Longrightarrow R \stackrel{*}{\Longrightarrow} G$ can be characterized in terms of the fibres $l_R(e)^\bullet \stackrel{*}{\Longrightarrow} G(e)$. This characterization is based on the observation that k-boundedness of G is induced by k-boundedness of the $G(e)$, provided that for each $v \in V_R$, the sum of the degrees of the begin nodes of the $G(e)$ for which e is outgoing from $v \in V_R$ and the end nodes of the $G(e)$ for which e is incoming into $v \in V_R$ is bounded by k.

Let $G, R \in \mathcal{G}_C$ be (1,1)-graphs, $assign : E_R \to I$ a mapping from the edge set E_R to the index set $I = [0, k] \times [0, k]$, and $i, j \in [0, k]$ (for some $k \in \mathbb{N}$). Then

- $BOUNDED(G, (i, j))$ denotes the fact that
  $\max_{v \in V_G} d_G(v) \leq k$, $d_G(begin_G) = i$, and $d_G(end_G) = j$.
- $BOUNDED'(R, assign, (i, j))$ denotes the fact that
  $\max_{v \in V_R} ASSIGN(v) \leq k$, $ASSIGN(begin_R) = i$, and $ASSIGN(end_R) = j$
  where, for $v \in V_R$, $ASSIGN(v) = \sum_{e \in s_R^{-1}(v)} assign(e)_1 + \sum_{e \in t_R^{-1}(v)} assign(e)_2$.

1.5 Theorem (k-Boundedness)

Let $ERG = (N, T, P, Z)$ be an edge-replacement grammar, $A^\bullet \Longrightarrow R \stackrel{*}{\Longrightarrow} G$ a derivation in ERG with $A \in N \cup T$ and $G \in \mathcal{G}_T$, and for $e \in E_R$, $l_R(e)^\bullet \stackrel{*}{\Longrightarrow} G(e)$ the fibre of $R \stackrel{*}{\Longrightarrow} G$ induced by e. For $i, j \in [0, k]$, $BOUNDED(G, (i, j))$ holds if and only if there is a mapping $assign : E_R \to [0, k] \times [0, k]$ such that $BOUNDED'(R, assign, (i, j))$ as well as $BOUNDED(G(e), assign(e))$ for all $e \in E_R$.

Proof

Without loss of generality, we may assume that $V_R \subseteq V_G$ and $G(e) \subseteq G$ for all $e \in E_R$. Suppose $BOUNDED(G, (i, j))$ holds. Then $\max_{v \in V_{G(e)}} d_{G(e)}(v) \leq k$ for $e \in E_R$, i.e., $G(e)$ is k-bounded for $e \in E_R$. Choosing $assign : E_R \to [0, k] \times [0, k]$ by $assign(e) = (d_{G(e)}(begin_{G(e)}), d_{G(e)}(end_{G(e)}))$ for $e \in E_R$, $BOUNDED(G(e), assign(e))$ is true for all $e \in E_R$. Moreover, for $v \in V_R$,

$$ASSIGN(v) = \sum_{e \in s_R^{-1}(v)} assign(e)_1 + \sum_{e \in t_R^{-1}(v)} assign(e)_2$$

$$= \sum_{e \in s_R^{-1}(v)} d_{G(e)}(begin_{G(e)}) + \sum_{e \in t_R^{-1}(v)} d_{G(e)}(end_{G(e)})$$

$$= d_G(v).$$

By assumption, $\max_{v \in V_G} d_G(v) \leq k$, $d_G(begin_G) = i$, and $d_G(end_G) = j$. Thus, we obtain $\max_{v \in V_R} ASSIGN(v) \leq k$, $ASSIGN(begin_R) = i$, and $ASSIGN(end_R) = j$, i.e., $BOUNDED'(R, assign, (i,j))$ is satisfied.

Conversely, let $assign : E_R \to [0,k] \times [0,k]$ be a mapping such that $BOUNDED'(R, assign, (i,j))$ as well as $BOUNDED(G(e), assign(e))$ for all $e \in E_R$ hold. Then for $e \in E_R$ and $v \in INT_{G(e)}$, $d_G(v) = d_{G(e)}(v) \leq k$ and for $v \in V_R \subseteq V_G$,

$$d_G(v) = \sum_{e \in s_R^{-1}(v)} d_{G(e)}(begin_{G(e)}) + \sum_{e \in t_R^{-1}(v)} d_{G(e)}(end_{G(e)})$$

$$= \sum_{e \in s_R^{-1}(v)} assign(e)_1 + \sum_{e \in t_R^{-1}(v)} assign(e)_2$$

$$= ASSIGN(v)$$

Thus, $\max_{v \in V_G} d_G(v) = \max \{\max_{e \in E_R} \max_{v \in INT_{G(e)}} d_{G(e)}(v), \max_{v \in V_R} d_G(v)\}$
$\leq \max \{k, \max_{v \in V_R} ASSIGN(v)\}$. By assumption, we have $\max_{v \in V_R} ASSIGN(v) \leq k$, $ASSIGN(begin_R) = i$, and $ASSIGN(end_R) = j$. Consequently, $\max_{v \in V_G} d_G(v) \leq k$, $d_G(begin_G) = i$, and $d_G(end_G) = j$, i.e., $BOUNDED(G, (i,j))$ is satisfied. □

k-Edge-Colorability

In this subsection we will consider the problem of coloring the edges of a graph G such that no two adjacent edges are uniformly colored. Such a distribution of colors is called an edge-coloring of G. Similar to the k-boundedness investigated in 1.5, the k-edge-colorability of a graph G with derivation $A^{\bullet} \Longrightarrow R \stackrel{*}{\Longrightarrow} G$ can be characterized in terms of the fibres $l_R(e)^{\bullet} \stackrel{*}{\Longrightarrow} G(e)$. This characterization is based on the observation that the k-edge-coloring of G is induced by the k-edge-coloring of the $G(e)$ provided that for each $v \in V_R$, the cardinality of the union of the color sets $C_{G(e)}(begin_{G(e)})$ — the set of colors used for the edges in $G(e)$ incident with $begin_{G(e)}$ — for which e is outgoing from $v \in V_R$ and $C_{G(e)}(end_{G(e)})$ — set of colors used for the edges in $G(e)$ incident with $end_{G(e)}$ — for which e is incoming into $v \in V_R$ is equal to the degree of v in V_G and also is bounded by k.

To recall the notion of edge-colorability, let G be a graph, $k \in \mathbb{N}$, and C be a set with k elements. A mapping $c_G : E_G \to C$ is a k-edge-coloring of G if $c_G(e) \neq c_G(e')$ for each pair $e, e' \in E_G$ of adjacent edges. G is said to be k-edge-colorable if there is a k-edge-coloring of G.

Let $G, R \in \mathcal{G}_C$ be (1,1)-graphs, $assign : E_R \to I$ be a mapping from the edge set E_R to the index set $I = \mathcal{P}(C) \times \mathcal{P}(C)$ [3], and $X, Y \subseteq C$. Then

---

[3] For a set A, $\mathcal{P}(A)$ denotes the power set of A.

- $COLOR(G,(X,Y))$ denotes the fact that there is a k-edge-coloring c_G of G such that $C_G(begin_G) = X$ and $C_G(end_G) = Y$ where for $v \in V_G$, $C_G(v)$ is the color set $C_G(v) = \{c_G(e) | e \in s_G^{-1}(v) \cup t_G^{-1}(v)\}$.
- $COLOR'(R, assign, (X,Y))$ refers to the fact that $|ASSIGN(v)| = ASSIGN^\#(v) \leq k$ [4] for all $v \in V_R$, $ASSIGN(begin_R) = X$, and $ASSIGN(end_R) = Y$ where for $v \in V_R$, $ASSIGN(v) = \bigcup_{e \in s_R^{-1}(v)} assign(e)_1 \cup \bigcup_{e \in t_R^{-1}(v)} assign(e)_2$ and $ASSIGN^\#(v) = \sum_{e \in s_R^{-1}(v)} |assign(e)_1| + \sum_{e \in t_R^{-1}(v)} |assign(e)_2|$.

1.6 Theorem (k-Edge-Colorability)

Let $ERG = (N, T, P, Z)$ be an edge-replacement grammar, $A^\bullet \Longrightarrow R \stackrel{*}{\Longrightarrow} G$ a derivation in ERG with $A \in N \cup T$ and $G \in \mathcal{G}_T$, and for $e \in E_R$, $l_R(e)^\bullet \stackrel{*}{\Longrightarrow} G(e)$ the fibre of $R \stackrel{*}{\Longrightarrow} G$ induced by e. For $X, Y \subseteq C$, $COLOR(G,(X,Y))$ holds if and only if there is a mapping $assign : E_R \to \mathcal{P}(C) \times \mathcal{P}(C)$ such that $COLOR'(R, assign, (X,Y))$ as well as $COLOR(G(e), assign(e))$ for all $e \in E_R$.

Proof

Without loss of generality, we may assume that $V_R \subseteq V_G$ and $G(e) \subseteq G$ for all $e \in E_R$. Suppose $COLOR(G,(X,Y))$ holds. Let $c_G : E_G \to C$ be a k-edge-coloring of G. Because $G(e) \subseteq G$, the restriction of c_G to $E_{G(e)}$ defines an appropriate k-edge-coloring $c_{G(e)}$ of each $G(e)$. Choosing $assign : E_R \to \mathcal{P}(C) \times \mathcal{P}(C)$ by $assign(e) = (C_{G(e)}(begin_{G(e)}), C_{G(e)}(end_{G(e)}))$ for $e \in E_R$, $COLOR(G(e), assign(e))$ becomes true for each $e \in E_R$. Furthermore, for $v \in V_R \subseteq V_G$,

$$ASSIGN(v) = \bigcup_{e \in s_R^{-1}(v)} assign(e)_1 \cup \bigcup_{e \in t_R^{-1}(v)} assign(e)_2$$
$$= \bigcup_{e \in s_R^{-1}(v)} C_{G(e)}(begin_{G(e)}) \cup \bigcup_{e \in t_R^{-1}(v)} C_{G(e)}(end_{G(e)})$$
$$= C_G(v).$$

By assumption, $|C_G(v)| \leq k$ for all $v \in V_G$, $C_G(begin_G) = X$, and $C_G(end_G) = Y$. Thus, $|ASSIGN(v)| \leq k$ for $v \in V_R$, $ASSIGN(begin_R) = X$, and $ASSIGN(end_R) = Y$. Moreover, $|ASSIGN(v)| = |C_G(v)| = ASSIGN^\#(v)$ for $v \in V_R$, because c_G is an edge-coloring of G. Hence, $COLOR(R, assign, (X,Y))$ holds.

Conversely, let $assign : E_R \to \mathcal{P}(C) \times \mathcal{P}(C)$ be a mapping such that $COLOR'(R, assign, (X,Y))$ as well as $COLOR(G(e), assign(e))$ for all $e \in E_R$ hold. Then for each $e \in E_R$, there is a k-edge-coloring $c_{G(e)} : E_{G(e)} \to C$ of $G(e)$ with $C_{G(e)}(begin_{G(e)}) = assign(e)_1$ and $C_{G(e)}(end_{G(e)}) = assign(e)_2$. Thus, for $v \in V_R$,

---

[4] For a set A, $|A|$ denotes the number of elements in A.

$$C_G(v) = \bigcup_{e \in s_R^{-1}(v)} C_{G(e)}(begin_{G(e)}) \cup \bigcup_{e \in t_R^{-1}(v)} C_{G(e)}(end_{G(e)})$$

$$= \bigcup_{e \in s_R^{-1}(v)} assign(e)_1 \cup \bigcup_{e \in t_R^{-1}(v)} assign(e)_2$$

$$= ASSIGN(v).$$

By assumption, $|ASSIGN(v)| = ASSIGN^\#(v) \leq k$ for $v \in V_R$, $ASSIGN(begin_R) = X$, and $ASSIGN(end_R) = Y$. Consequently, $|C_G(v)| \leq k$ for $v \in V_R$, $C_G(begin_G) = X$, and $C_G(end_G) = Y$. Define now $c_G : E_G \to C$ by $c_G(e') = c_{G(e)}(e')$ for $e \in E_R$ and $e' \in E_{G(e)}$. Then c_G becomes an edge-coloring of G because for $e \in E_R$, $c_{G(e)}$ is an edge-coloring and for $v \in V_R \subseteq V_G$, $|C_G(v)| = |ASSIGN(v)| = ASSIGN^\#(v)$. Hence, $COLOR(G,(X,Y))$ is satisfied. □

2. A General View of Compatible Predicates

All examples given in section 1 follow a simple scheme. Roughly speaking, a predicate $PROP_0$ holds for $H \in \mathcal{H}_C$ which is derivable from a handle $A^\bullet$ starting with the production (A, R) if and only if R fulfills some auxiliary predicate $PROP_0'$ and $PROP_0$ holds for all $H(e)$, $e \in E_R$. As the above mentioned example concerning connectedness demonstrates, this view is oversimplified for most applications. To check $PROP_0$ for H, one may have to check some other related properties for the $H(e)$ (with respect to the connectedness of H, some of the $H(e)$ are allowed to be semi-connected). Therefore, we use families of properties indexed by some finite set I and we need a mapping $assign$ which determines the property from the family to be checked for each $H(e)$.

2.1 Definition (Compatible Predicates [1])

1. Let $\mathcal{C} \subseteq \mathcal{HRG}$, I a finite set, called the index set, $PROP$ a decidable predicate defined on pairs (H, i), with $H \in \mathcal{H}_C$ and $i \in I$, and $PROP'$ a decidable predicate on triples $(R, assign, i)$, with $R \in \mathcal{H}_C$, a mapping $assign : E_R \to I$, and $i \in I$. Then $PROP$ is called $(\mathcal{C}, PROP')$-compatible if for all $HRG = (N, T, P, Z) \in \mathcal{C}$ and all derivations $A^\bullet \Longrightarrow R \stackrel{*}{\Longrightarrow} H$ with $A \in N \cup T$ and $H \in \mathcal{H}_T$, and for all $i \in I$, $PROP(H,i)$ holds if and only if there is a mapping $assign : E_R \to I$ such that $PROP'(R, assign, i)$ holds and $PROP(H(e), assign(e))$ holds for all $e \in E_R$.
2. A predicate $PROP_0$ on $\mathcal{H}_C$ is called $\mathcal{C}$-compatible if predicates $PROP$ and $PROP'$ and an index i_0 exist such that $PROP$ is $(\mathcal{C}, PROP')$-compatible and $PROP_0 = PROP(-, i_0)$. ($PROP(-, i_0)$ denotes the unary predicate given by $PROP(-, i_0)(H) = PROP(H, i_0)$ for all $H \in \mathcal{H}_C$.)

---

[1] All considered predicates are assumed to be *closed under isomorphisms*, i.e., for a predicate $PROP_0$ defined on hypergraphs, if $H \cong H'$ for some $H, H' \in \mathcal{H}_C$, then $PROP_0(H)$ holds if and only if $PROP_0(H')$ holds.

Remark

1. Intuitively, a property is compatible if it can be tested for a large hypergraph with a long fibre by checking the smaller components of the corresponding shorter fibres. Such a property must be closed under isomorphisms because the derivability of hypergraphs is independent of the representation of nodes and hyperedges.

2. More general, one may consider a family of finite index sets $I_{(m,n)}$ ($m, n \in \mathbb{N}$), a decidable predicate $PROP$ defined on pairs (H, i) with $H \in \mathcal{H}_C$ and $i \in I_{type(H)}$, and a decidable predicate $PROP'$ on triples $(R, assign, i)$ with $R \in \mathcal{H}_C$, a mapping $assign$ assigning an index $assign(e) \in I_{type(e)}$ to each $e \in E_R$, and $i \in I_{type(H)}$.

Various explicit examples of compatible predicates were discussed in section 1.

2.2 Example (Compatible Predicates)

1. The predicate $DISCO_0$ given by
   - $DISCO_0(H)$ if and only if H is totally disconnected

is $\mathcal{HRG}$-compatible: Take a one-element index set $I = \{i_0\}$ and the predicates $DISCO$ and $DISCO'$ given by $DISCO(H, i_0)$ if and only if H is totally disconnected and $DISCO'(R, assign, i_0)$ if and only if $R \in \mathcal{H}_C$. Then, by theorem 1.1, $DISCO$ is $(\mathcal{HRG}, DISCO')$-compatible and $DISCO_0 = DISCO(-, i_0)$ is $\mathcal{HRG}$-compatible.

2. The predicates $CONN_0$ and $CONN_1$ given for (1,1)-graphs $G \in \mathcal{G}_C$ by
   - $CONN_0(G)$ if and only if G is connected,
   - $CONN_1(G)$ if and only if G is semi-connected

are $\mathcal{ERG}$-compatible (cf. Theorem 1.2).

3. The predicates $EVEN_0$ and $EVEN_1$ given for (1,1)-graphs $G \in \mathcal{G}_C$ by
   - $EVEN_0(G)$ if and only if every node of G has even degree,
   - $EVEN_1(G)$ if and only if every node of G has even degree,
     except $begin_G$ and end_G

are $\mathcal{ERG}$-compatible (cf. Theorem 1.4). Moreover, the predicates $EULERPATH$ and $EULERCYCLE$ given by
   - $EULERPATH(G)$ if and only if G has an Eulerian path
   - $EULERCYCLE(G)$ if and only if G has an Eulerian cycle

are $\mathcal{ERG}$-compatible, provided that the conjunction of $\mathcal{ERG}$-compatible predicates is $\mathcal{ERG}$-compatible.

4. For $k \in \mathbb{N}$, the predicates $kBOUNDED$ and $kCOLOR$ given by
   - $kBOUNDED(G)$ if and only if G is k-bounded
   - $kCOLOR(G)$ if and only if G has a k-edge-coloring

are $\mathcal{ERG}$-compatible, provided that the disjunction of $\mathcal{ERG}$-compatible predicates is $\mathcal{ERG}$-compatible (cf. Theorems 1.5 and 1.6).

The examples in 2.2 show that the question of closedness of $\mathcal{C}$-compatibility is very important. In fact, $\mathcal{C}$-compatibility is closed under Boolean operations.

2.3 Theorem (Closure Under Boolean Operations)

Let $\mathcal{C} \subseteq \mathcal{HRG}$ and $PROP_{10}$, $PROP_{20}$ be $\mathcal{C}$-compatible predicates. Then the predicates $(\neg PROP_{10})$, $(PROP_{10} \wedge PROP_{20})$, and $(PROP_{10} \vee PROP_{20})$ defined by

- $(\neg PROP_{10})(H)$ if and only if $\neg PROP_{10}(H)$.
- $(PROP_{10} \wedge PROP_{20})(H)$ if and only if $PROP_{10}(H) \wedge PROP_{20}(H)$,
- $(PROP_{10} \vee PROP_{20})(H)$ if and only if $PROP_{10}(H) \vee PROP_{20}(H)$,

are $\mathcal{C}$-compatible.

Proof

Let for $j = 1, 2$, $PROP_{j0}$ be a $\mathcal{C}$-compatible predicate, $PROP_j$, $PROP'_j$ the corresponding predicates, I_j the index set, and i_j the index such that $PROP_{j0} = PROP_j(-, i_j)$.

1. For proving the $\mathcal{C}$-compatibility of $(PROP_{10} \wedge PROP_{20})$, we define new predicates $PROP$ and $PROP'$ derived from the given ones and show the $(\mathcal{C}, PROP')$-compatibility of $PROP$ using the compatibility of the old ones. Let

- $I = I_1 \times I_2$,
- $PROP(H, (j_1, j_2)) \iff PROP_1(H, j_1) \wedge PROP_2(H, j_2)$, and
- $PROP'(R, assign, (j_1, j_2)) \iff PROP'_1(R, assign_1, j_1) \wedge PROP'_2(R, assign_2, j_2)$
  where $assign_1$, $assign_2$ are the projections of $assign$ to the first and the second component, respectively.

For $H \in \mathcal{H}_\mathcal{C}$, $(PROP_{10} \wedge PROP_{20})(H) \iff PROP_{10}(H) \wedge PROP_{20}(H) \iff PROP_1(H, i_1) \wedge PROP_2(H, i_2) \iff PROP(H, (i_1, i_2))$, i.e., $(PROP_{10} \wedge PROP_{20}) = PROP(-, (i_1, i_2))$. It remains to be shown that $PROP$ is $(\mathcal{C}, PROP')$-compatible. This can be proved by the following reasoning for a derivation $A^\bullet \Longrightarrow R \overset{*}{\Longrightarrow} H$ with $A \in N \cup T$ and $H \in \mathcal{H}_T$: By definition of $PROP$, the $(\mathcal{C}, PROP'_1)$-compatibility of $PROP_1$, and the $(\mathcal{C}, PROP'_2)$-compatibility of $PROP_2$, we obtain

$PROP(H, (j_1, j_2))$
$\iff PROP_1(H, j_1) \wedge PROP_2(H, j_2)$
$\iff$ (A) $\begin{cases} \exists\, assign_1 : E_R \to I_1, \exists\, assign_2 : E_R \to I_2 : \\ PROP'_1(R, assign_1, j_1) \wedge PROP'_2(R, assign_2, j_2) \\ \wedge \bigwedge_{e \in E_R} PROP_1(H(e), assign_1(e)) \wedge \bigwedge_{e \in E_R} PROP_2(H(e), assign_2(e)). \end{cases}$

Choosing $assign : E_R \to I$ as $assign(e) = (assign_1(e), assign_2(e))$ for all $e \in E_R$, $PROP(H(e), assign(e))$ for $e \in E_R$ as well as $PROP'(R, assign, (j_1, j_2))$ become true. Conversely, if for some mapping $assign : E_R \to I$, $PROP(H(e), assign(e))$ (for $e \in E_R$) as well as $PROP'(R, assign, (j_1, j_2))$ hold, then we obtain (A) choosing $assign_1$ and $assign_2$ as the projections of $assign$ to the first and the second component, respectively. Hence $PROP$ is $(\mathcal{C}, PROP')$-compatible and $(PROP_{10} \wedge PROP_{20}) = PROP(-, (i_1, i_2))$ is $\mathcal{C}$-compatible.

2. For proving the $\mathcal{C}$-compatibility of $(PROP_{10} \vee PROP_{20})$, we define new predicates $PROP$ and $PROP'$ as follows.

- $I = (I_1 \cup \{*\}) \times (I_2 \cup \{*\})$.

- $PROP(H,(j_1,j_2)) \iff PROP_1(H,j_1) \vee PROP_2(H,j_2)$,
  $PROP(H,(j_1,*)) \iff PROP_1(H,j_1)$,
  $PROP(H,(*,j_2)) \iff PROP_2(H,j_2)$,
  $PROP(H,(*,*)) \iff H \in \mathcal{H}_C$, where $j_1 \in I_1$ and $j_2 \in I_2$.

- $PROP'(R, assign, (j_1, j_2))$
  $\iff PROP'_1(R, assign_1, j_1)$ and $assign_2(e) = *$ for all $e \in E_R$ or
  $\qquad PROP'_2(R, assign_2, j_2)$ and $assign_1(e) = *$ for all $e \in E_R$,
  $PROP'(R, assign, (j_1, *))$
  $\iff PROP'_1(R, assign_1, j_1)$ and $assign_2(e) = *$ for all $e \in E_R$,
  $PROP'(R, assign, (*, j_2))$
  $\iff PROP'_2(R, assign_2, j_2)$ and $assign_1(e) = *$ for all $e \in E_R$,
  $PROP'(R, assign, (*,*)) \iff R \in \mathcal{H}_C$
  where $assign_1$, $assign_2$ are the projections of $assign$ to the first and the second component, respectively, and $j_1 \in I_1$ and $j_2 \in I_2$.

Clearly, the new predicates are decidable since the original ones are. For $H \in \mathcal{H}_C$, $(PROP_{10} \vee PROP_{20})(H) \iff PROP_{10}(H) \vee PROP_{20}(H) \iff PROP_1(H, i_1) \vee PROP_2(H, i_2) \iff PROP(H, (i_1, i_2))$, i.e., $(PROP_{10} \vee PROP_{20}) = PROP(-, (i_1, i_2))$. It remains to be shown that $PROP$ is $(\mathcal{C}, PROP')$-compatible. This can be proved by the following reasoning for a derivation $A^\bullet \Longrightarrow R \stackrel{*}{\Longrightarrow} H$ with $A \in N \cup T$ and $H \in \mathcal{H}_T$.

Case 1. $j_1 \in I_1$ and $j_2 \in I_2$.

Let $PROP(H,(j_1,j_2))$ be satisfied. Then $PROP_1(H,j_1)$ or $PROP_2(H,j_2)$ is satisfied. In the first case, there is a mapping $assign_1 : E_R \to I_1$ such that $PROP'_1(R, assign_1, j_1)$ and $PROP_1(H(e), assign_1(e))$ for $e \in E_R$ become true. Choosing $assign : E_R \to I$ by $assign(e) = (assign_1(e), *)$, $PROP'(R, assign, (j_1, j_2))$ and $PROP(H(e), assign(e))$ for $e \in E_R$ become true. In the second case, there is a mapping $assign_2 : E_R \to I_2$ such that $PROP'_2(R, assign_2, j_2)$ and $PROP_2(H(e), assign_2(e))$ for $e \in E_R$ become true. Choosing $assign : E_R \to I$ by $assign(e) = (*, assign_2(e))$, $PROP'(R, assign, (j_1, j_2))$ and $PROP(H(e), assign(e))$ for $e \in E_R$ become true.

Conversely, let $assign : E_R \to I$ be a mapping such that $PROP'(R, assign, (j_1, j_2))$ and $PROP(H(e), assign(e))$ (for $e \in E_R$) hold. Then $PROP'_1(R, assign_1, j_1)$ and $assign_2(e) = *$ for $e \in E_R$ or $PROP'_2(R, assign_2, j_2)$ and $assign_1(e) = *$ for $e \in E_R$. In the first case, $PROP_1(H(e), assign_1(e))$ for all $e \in E_R$. In the second case, $PROP_2(H(e), assign_2(e))$ for all $e \in E_R$. By the compatibility of $PROP_1$ and $PROP_2$, $PROP_1(H, j_1)$ or $PROP_2(H, j_2)$ holds, i.e., $PROP(H, (j_1, j_2))$ is satisfied.

Similarly, the cases
Case 2. $j_1 \in I_1$ and $j_2 = *$,
Case 3. $j_1 = *$ and $j_2 \in I_2$,
Case 4. $j_1 = *$ and $j_2 = *$
can be handled. Hence $PROP$ is $(\mathcal{C}, PROP')$-compatible and $(PROP_{10} \vee PROP_{20}) = PROP(-, (i_1, i_2))$ is $\mathcal{C}$-compatible.

3. For deriving the $\mathcal{C}$-compatibility of $(\neg PROP_{10})$, we define new predicates $PROP$ and $PROP'$ and show the $(\mathcal{C}, PROP')$-compatibility of $PROP$. Let

- $I = \mathcal{P}(I_1)$,
- $PROP(H, X)$
$$\iff \bigwedge_{x \in X} PROP_1(H, x) \wedge \bigwedge_{x \notin X} \neg PROP_1(H, x),$$
- $PROP'(R, assign, X)$
$$\iff \bigwedge_{x \in X} \bigvee_{a \in M(assign)} PROP_1'(R, a, x) \wedge \bigwedge_{x \notin X} \bigwedge_{a \in M(assign)} \neg PROP_1'(R, a, x)$$
where $M(assign) = \{a : E_R \to I_1 \mid a(e) \in assign(e) \text{ for } e \in E_R\}$.

Then the $(\mathcal{C}, PROP')$-compatibility of $PROP$ can be proved by the following reasoning for a derivation $A^\bullet \Longrightarrow R \stackrel{*}{\Longrightarrow} H$ with $A \in N \cup T$ and $H \in \mathcal{H}_T$. By the definition of $PROP$ and the $(\mathcal{C}, PROP_1')$-compatibility of $PROP_1$,

$PROP(H, X)$
$$\iff \bigwedge_{x \in X} PROP_1(H, x) \wedge \bigwedge_{x \notin X} \neg PROP_1(H, x)$$
$$\iff \bigwedge_{x \in X} \bigvee_{a: E_R \to I_1} [\, PROP_1'(R, a, x) \wedge \bigwedge_{e \in E_R} PROP_1(H(e), a(e)) \,]$$
$$\wedge \bigwedge_{x \notin X} \neg \bigvee_{a: E_R \to I_1} [\, PROP_1'(R, a, x) \wedge \bigwedge_{e \in E_R} PROP_1(H(e), a(e)) \,].$$

Let $PROP(H, X)$ be satisfied. Choosing $assign : E_R \to I$ by $assign(e) = \{i \in I_1 \mid PROP_1(H(e), i)\}$ for all $e \in E_R$, we get $PROP(H(e), assign(e))$ for all $e \in E_R$. Moreover, for each $x \in X$, there is a mapping $a : E_R \to I_1$ such that $PROP'(R, a, x)$ and $a(e) \in assign(e)$ for all $e \in E_R$. For each $x \notin X$, there is no mapping $a : E_R \to I_1$ such that $PROP_1'(R, a, x)$ and $a(e) \in assign(e)$ for all $e \in E_R$. Thus, $PROP_1'(R, assign, X)$ is satisfied.

Conversely, if $PROP'(R, assign, X)$ and $PROP(H(e), assign(e))$ $(e \in E_R)$ hold for some mapping $assign : E_R \to I$, then we have

(A) $\displaystyle\bigwedge_{x\in X}\bigvee_{a\in M(assign)} PROP'_1(R,a,x) \wedge \bigwedge_{e\in E_R}\bigwedge_{x\in assign(e)} PROP_1(H(e),x)$

$\displaystyle\Longrightarrow \bigwedge_{x\in X}\bigvee_{a\in M(assign)} [\, PROP'_1(R,a,x) \wedge \bigwedge_{e\in E_R} PROP_1(H(e),a(e)) \,]$

$\displaystyle\Longrightarrow \bigwedge_{x\in X} PROP_1(H,x)$

(B) $\displaystyle\bigwedge_{x\notin X}\bigwedge_{a\in M(assign)} \neg PROP'_1(R,a,x) \wedge \bigwedge_{e\in E_R}\bigwedge_{x\notin assign(e)} \neg PROP_1(H(e),x)$

$\displaystyle\Longrightarrow \bigwedge_{x\notin X}\bigwedge_{a: E_R\to I_1} [\, \neg PROP'_1(R,a,x) \vee \bigvee_{e\in E_R} \neg PROP_1(H(e),a(e)) \,]$

(For a mapping $a: E_R \to I_1$, two cases may occur. In the case $a\in M(assign)$, $\neg PROP_1(R,a,x)$ holds. In the case $a\notin M(assign)$, $a(e)\notin assign(e)$ for some $e\in E_R$ and, hence, $\neg PROP_1(H(e),a(e))$ holds for some $e\in E_R$.)

$\displaystyle\Longrightarrow \bigwedge_{x\notin X}\neg \bigvee_{a: E_R\to I_1} [\, PROP'_1(R,a,x) \wedge \bigwedge_{e\in E_R} PROP_1(H(e),a(e)) \,]$

$\displaystyle\Longrightarrow \bigwedge_{x\notin X} \neg PROP_1(H,x).$

By (A) and (B), $PROP(H,X)$ becomes satisfied. This completes the proof of the $(\mathcal{C}, PROP')$-compatibility of $PROP$.

Finally, we will show how the $\mathcal{C}, PROP'$-compatibility of $PROP$ induces the $\mathcal{C}$-compatibility of $(\neg PROP_{10})$. Obviously,

$(\neg PROP_{10})(H) \iff \neg PROP_{10}(H) \iff \neg PROP_1(H,i_1)$

$\displaystyle\iff \bigvee_{X\subseteq I_1 \text{ with } i_1\notin X} [\, \bigwedge_{x\in X} PROP_1(H,x) \wedge \bigwedge_{x\notin X} \neg PROP_1(H,x) \,]$

$\displaystyle\iff \bigvee_{X\subseteq I_1 \text{ with } i_1\notin X} PROP(H,X).$

The $(\mathcal{C}, PROP')$-compatibility of $PROP$ implies the $\mathcal{C}$-compatibility of $PROP(-,X)$ for all $X\subseteq I_1$. Since the disjunction of $\mathcal{C}$-compatible predicates yields a $\mathcal{C}$-compatible predicate, $\neg PROP_{10}$ becomes $\mathcal{C}$-compatible. $\square$

2.4 Example (Compatible Predicates)

The predicates $EULERPATH$, $EULERCYCLE$, $kBOUNDED$, and $kCOLOR$ given by
- $EULERPATH(G)$ if and only if $CONN_0(G) \wedge EVEN_1(G)$,
- $EULERCYCLE(G)$ if and only if $CONN_0(G) \wedge EVEN_0(G)$,
- $kBOUNDED(G)$ if and only if $\bigvee_{0\leq i,j\leq k} BOUNDED(G,(i,j))$,
- $kCOLOR(G)$ if and only if $\bigvee_{X,Y\subseteq C} COLOR(G,(X,Y))$

are $\mathcal{ERG}$-compatible.

In the following, we define so-called proper compatible predicates and show that for each compatible family of properties, we may effectively construct a proper compatible family of properties such that each property of the first family may be expressed by properties of the second family. Each proper compatible family of properties induces a decomposition of set of all hypergraphs (of the same type) into a finite number of non-empty, pairwise disjoint sets of hypergraphs with the same property. All members of such a set behave equally with respect to other properties whenever they are inserted into the same context. This is the reason for the close relationship between compatible and finite properties in the sense of Lengauer and Wanke [LW 88]. This relationship is investigated in [HKL 92].

2.5 Definition (Proper Compatible Predicates)

A $(\mathcal{C}, PROP')$-compatible predicate $PROP$ is said to be *proper*, if for all $H \in \mathcal{H}_\mathcal{C}$, there exists a unique index $i \in I$ such that $PROP(H, i)$, and for all $R \in \mathcal{H}_\mathcal{C}$ and all mappings $assign : E_R \to I$, there exists a unique index $i \in I$ such that $PROP'(R, assign, i)$.

2.6 Theorem (Proper Compatible Predicates)

Let $\mathcal{C} \subseteq \mathcal{HRG}$ and $PROP_0$ be a $\mathcal{C}$-compatible predicate. Then there are an index set $I!$, predicates $PROP!$, $PROP!'$, and a subset $I_0 \subseteq I!$ such that $PROP!$ is a proper $(\mathcal{C}, PROP!')$-compatible predicate and $PROP_0 = \bigvee_{i \in I_0} PROP!(-, i)$.

Proof

Let $PROP_0$ be $\mathcal{C}$-compatible. Then there exist an index set I, predicates $PROP$, $PROP'$, and an index $i_0 \in I$, such that $PROP$ is $(\mathcal{C}, PROP')$-compatible and $PROP_0 = PROP(-, i_0)$. In the following, we define an new index set $I!$, new predicates $PROP!$ and $PROP!'$, and an index set $I_0 \subseteq I$ satisfying the conditions mentioned above: Let

- $I! = \mathcal{P}(I)$,
- $PROP!(H, X)$
  $$\iff \bigwedge_{x \in X} PROP(H, x) \wedge \bigwedge_{x \notin X} \neg PROP(H, x),$$
- $PROP!'(R, assign, X)$
  $$\iff \bigwedge_{x \in X} \bigvee_{a \in M(assign)} PROP'(R, a, x) \wedge \bigwedge_{x \notin X} \bigwedge_{a \in M(assign)} \neg PROP'(R, a, x)$$
  where $M(assign) = \{a : E_R \to I \mid a(e) \in assign(e) \text{ for } e \in E_R\}$,
- $I_0 = \{X \in I! \mid X \subseteq I \text{ with } i_0 \in X\}$.

Then, by the proof given in 2.3, $PROP!$ is $(\mathcal{C}, PROP!')$-compatible and, by the definition of $PROP!$ and I_0, $PROP_0 = PROP(-, i_0) = \bigvee_{X \in I_0} PROP!(-, X)$. It remains to be shown the properness. For $H \in \mathcal{H}_\mathcal{C}$, consider $X = \{i \in I \mid PROP(H, i) \text{ is satisfied}\}$. Then $PROP!(H, X)$ is satisfied and if $PROP!(H, X) = PROP!(H, X')$, then $X = X'$.

For $R \in \mathcal{H}_C$ and $assign : E_R \to I!$, consider $X = \{i \in I | PROP'(R, a, i)$ for some $a \in M(assign)\}$. Then $PROP!'(R, assign, X)$ is satisfied and if $PROP!'(R, assign, X) = PROP!'(R, assign, X')$, then $X = X'$. This completes the proof. □

3. Efficient Analysis of Graph Properties

In this section we consider compatible hypergraph properties $PROP_0$ and show that whenever a hypergraph $H \in L(HRG)$ and a derivation (or a derivation tree $T(H)$) of H is known, then we can decide $PROP_0(H)$ in linear time with respect to the size of $|T(H)|$ of $T(H)$.

3.1 Theorem (Efficient Analysis)

Let $PROP_0$ be $\mathcal{C}$-compatible for some class $\mathcal{C}$ of hyperedge-replacement grammars. Then for all $HRG \in \mathcal{C}$, all $H \in L(HRG)$, and all derivation trees $T(H)$ of H, it can be decided in $O(|T(H)|)$ time whether $PROP_0(H)$ holds. (The constant factor depends on HRG and $PROP_0$.)

Proof

Let $PROP_0$ be $\mathcal{C}$-compatible for some class $\mathcal{C}$ of hyperedge-replacement grammars. Then by theorem 2.5, we may assume that there are an index set I, predicates $PROP$, $PROP'$, and an index set $I_0 \subseteq I$ such that

$$PROP_0 = \bigvee_{i \in I_0} PROP(-, i)$$

as well as the other the conditions in theorem 2.5 are satisfied. Given $H \in \mathcal{H}_C$ and a derivation tree $T(H)$ of H (for some $HRG \in \mathcal{C}$), we process in a bottom-up fashion:
1. For each leaf l of $T(H)$ respresenting the hypergraph $H(l)$ in $L(HRG)$, choose the index $i \in I$ for which $PROP(H(l), i)$ holds and let $i(l) = i$. (By choice of $PROP$, there exists uniquely one index with this property.)
2. For a node v with label $e^\bullet$, outgoing hyperedge with label (A, R), and direct descendants $v_1, \ldots, v_m$ with labels $e_1^\bullet, \ldots, e_m^\bullet$, the index $i(v)$ of v is determined from the indices $i(v_1), \ldots, i(v_m)$ of the nodes $v_1, \ldots, v_m$ as follows: Choose the index $i \in I$ for which $PROP'(R, assign, i)$ with $assign(e_j) = i(v_j)$ for $e_j \in \{e_1, \ldots, e_m\}$ holds and let $i(v) = i$. Note that $e_1, \ldots, e_m$ are the hyperedges in R. (By choice of $PROP'$, there exists uniquely one index with this property.)

This procedure yields an index $i(v)$ for each node v in the derivation tree. By the $(\mathcal{C}, PROP')$-compatibility of $PROP$, the index $i(v)$ of a node v in the derivation tree $T(H)$ is i if and only if $PROP(H(v), i)$ holds ($H(v)$ denotes the hypergraph represented by the subtree with v as root). This may be seen as follows: For leaves, the claim follows immediately from 1. Consider now a node v with (A, R)-labeled outgoing hyperedge and direct descendants $v_1, \ldots, v_m$ with labels $e_1^\bullet, \ldots, e_m^\bullet$, respectively. Assume that the statement holds for the nodes $v_1, \ldots, v_m$. Let $H(v_1), \ldots, H(v_m)$ be the hypergraphs represented by the subtrees with $v_1, \ldots, v_m$ as roots, respectively, and $i(v_1), \ldots, i(v_m)$ the corresponding indices. Then, by the induction hypothesis, $PROP(H(v_1), i(v_1)), \ldots, PROP(H(v_m), i(v_m))$ hold. Let $assign : \{e_1, \ldots, e_m\} \to I$ be the mapping with $assign(e_j) = i(v_j)$ for $j = 1, \ldots, m$. Then, by choice of i, $PROP'(R, assign, i)$ is satisfied. Now the $(\mathcal{C}, PROP')$-compatibility of $PROP$ implies that $PROP(H, i)$ with $H = REPLACE(R, repl)$ and $repl(e_j) = H(e_j)$ (for $j = 1, \ldots, m$) holds. On the other hand, H is the hypergraph represented by the node v.

Let us consider the original hypergraph H with derivatin tree $T(H)$. Then $H = H(root)$, where $root$ denotes the root of $T(H)$. By the considerations above, $PROP(H, i(root))$ is satisfied. On the other hand, $PROP_0(H)$ holds if and only if $\bigvee_{i \in I_0} PROP(H, i)$. Therefore,

$$PROP_0(H) \text{ holds if and only if } i(root) \in I_0.$$

To see that the procedure takes linear time, let us mention that for each hyperedge-replacement grammar HRG, the size of the handles represented by leaves of $T(H)$ as well as the size of the right-hand sides is bounded by a constant depending on HRG, and the index set I is finite. Therefore, each procedure call "DETERMINE INDEX" takes constant time. DETERMINE INDEX is called once for each node of the derivation tree $T(H)$. Therefore, the cost to determine the index $i(root)$ is $O(n)$, where n is the number of nodes in the derivation tree $T(H)$. □

4. A Metatheorem for Graph-Theoretic Decision Problems

Given a (hyper)graph property $PROP_0$ and a class $\mathcal{C}$ of hyperedge-replacement grammars, we are going to study two types of questions for all $HRG \in \mathcal{C}$: "Does $PROP_0$ hold for some $H \in L(HRG)$?" and "Does $PROP_0$ hold for all $H \in L(HRG)$?". Both questions turn out to be decidable, provided that $PROP_0$ is $\mathcal{C}$-compatible. We call this result "metatheorem" because of its generic character: Whenever one can prove the compatibility of a property (and we have given various examples in section 2), one gets a particular decision result for this property as corollary of the metatheorem.

4.1 Theorem (Metatheorem for Decision Problems)
Let $PROP_0$ be $\mathcal{C}$-compatible with respect to some class $\mathcal{C}$ of hyperedge-replacement grammars. Then for all $HRG \in \mathcal{C}$, it is decidable whether
(1) $PROP_0$ holds for some $H \in L(HRG)$;
(2) $PROP_0$ holds for all $H \in L(HRG)$.

Proof

Let $PROP_0$ be $\mathcal{C}$-compatible for some class $\mathcal{C}$ of hyperedge-replacement grammars and $PROP$ and $PROP'$ the corresponding predicates over the index set I such that $PROP$ is $(\mathcal{C}, PROP')$-compatible and $PROP_0 = PROP(-, i_0)$ for some $i_0 \in I$. Let $HRG = (N, T, P, Z) \in \mathcal{C}$. Then the main task of the proof is to construct the sets

- $V_{PROP,i} = \{A \in N \cup T \mid \exists H \in \mathcal{H}_T : A^\bullet \underset{P}{\overset{*}{\Longrightarrow}} H \text{ and } PROP(H, i)\}$

for all $i \in I$. Then the decision problem reduces to checking whether $l(Z) \in V_{PROP,i_0}$.

For constructing $V_{PROP,i}$, we define sets $V_{PROP,i,k}$ for $k \in \mathbb{N}$ recursively as follows:

- $V_{PROP,i,0} = \{A \in T \mid PROP(A^\bullet, i) \text{ is satisfied}\}$,
- $V_{PROP,i,k+1} = V_{PROP,i,k} \cup \{A \in N \mid \exists (A, R) \in P, \exists assign : E_R \to I : \\ PROP'(R, assign, i) \text{ and } l_R(e) \in V_{PROP,i,k} \text{ for } e \in E_R\}$.

Since $V_{PROP,i,k} \subseteq V_{PROP,i,k+1} \subseteq N \cup T$ for all $i \in I$ and $k \in \mathbb{N}$ and $N \cup T$ is finite, there is some $l \in \mathbb{N}$ such that $V_{PROP,i,l} = V_{PROP,i,l+1}$. Obviously, all $V_{PROP,i,k}$ up to the smallest possible l can be constructed effectively. Hence, it remains to be shown that $V_{PROP,i} = V_{PROP,i,l}$, which is an immediate consequence of the following two claims.

Claim 1. $V_{PROP,i,k} \subseteq V_{PROP,i}$ for all $i \in I$ and $k \in \mathbb{N}$.

Proof of claim 1 (by induction on k). The statement is trivially true for $k = 0$. Assume that it is true for k, and let A be in $V_{PROP,i,k+1}$. If A is also in $V_{PROP,i,k}$, the inductive step is trivial. If A is in $V_{PROP,i,k+1} - V_{PROP,i,k}$, then there is a production $(A, R) \in P$ such that $l_R(e) \in V_{PROP,i,k}$ for all $e \in E_R$ and $PROP'(R, assign, i)$ for some mapping $assign : E_R \to I$. By the inductive hypothesis, $l_R(e) \in V_{PROP,i}$ for all $e \in E_R$. Therefore, there is a derivation $l_R(e)^\bullet \overset{*}{\Longrightarrow} H(e)$ for some $H(e) \in \mathcal{H}_T$ with $PROP(H(e), assign(e))$. Joint embedding of these derivations into R yields a derivation $R \overset{*}{\Longrightarrow} H$ where $H \in \mathcal{H}_T$. Moreover, there is a direct derivation $A^\bullet \Longrightarrow R$ by the production (A, R). Composing these derivations, we get a derivation $A^\bullet \overset{*}{\Longrightarrow} H$ where $H \in \mathcal{H}_T$. Since $PROP$ is $(\mathcal{C}, PROP')$-compatible, $PROP(H, i)$ is satisfied. Altogether, it turns out that $A \in V_{PROP,i}$. This proves Claim 1.

Claim 2. $V_{PROP,i} \subseteq V_{PROP,i,l}$.

Proof of claim 2. $A \in V_{PROP,i}$ means that there is a derivation $A^\bullet \overset{*}{\Longrightarrow} H$ with $H \in \mathcal{H}_T$ and $PROP(H, i)$. Thus, we prove the following statement by induction on the number of derivation steps.

If $A \in N \cup T$ and $A^\bullet \overset{*}{\Longrightarrow} H$ for some $H \in \mathcal{H}_T$ with $PROP(H, i)$, then $A \in V_{PROP,i,l}$.

For each zero-step derivation $A^\bullet \overset{0}{\Longrightarrow} H$ with $H \in \mathcal{H}_T$ and $PROP(H,i)$, $H \cong A^\bullet$, $A \in T$, and $PROP(A^\bullet, i)$ is satisfied. Thus, $A \in V_{PROP,i,0} \subseteq V_{PROP,i,l}$. Assume that the statement is true for k-step derivations, and let $A^\bullet \overset{k+1}{\Longrightarrow} H$ with $H \in \mathcal{H}_T$ and $PROP(H,i)$. Then the derivation decomposes into $A^\bullet \Longrightarrow R' \overset{k}{\Longrightarrow} H$ for some $R' \in \mathcal{H}_{N \cup T}$. If the first derivation step is a dummy, then $A^\bullet \cong R'$, and $R' \overset{k}{\Longrightarrow} H$ can be modified into $A^\bullet \overset{k}{\Longrightarrow} H$. By the inductive hypothesis, this implies $A \in V_{PROP,i,l}$. Otherwise, $R' \cong R$ for some production $(A, R) \in P$ and the derivation $A^\bullet \Longrightarrow R' \overset{k}{\Longrightarrow} H$ can be modified into $A^\bullet \Longrightarrow R \overset{k}{\Longrightarrow} H$. Consider now the fibres $l_R(e)^\bullet \overset{k}{\Longrightarrow} H(e)$ of $R \overset{*}{\Longrightarrow} H$ for $e \in E_R$. By the $(\mathcal{C}, PROP')$-compatibility of $PROP$, there is some mapping $assign : E_R \to I$ such that $PROP'(R, assign, i)$ and $PROP(H(e), assign(e))$ ($e \in E_R$) are satisfied. Using the inductive hypothesis, we get $l_R(e) \in V_{PROP,i,l}$ for $e \in E_R$. By definition and choice of l, we get $A \in V_{PROP,i,l+1} = V_{PROP,i,l}$. This proves Claim 2.

Obviously, $PROP_0$ holds for all $H \in L(HRG)$ if and only if there is no $H \in L(HRG)$ such that $\neg PROP_0$ holds. By theorem 2.3, $\neg PROP_0$ is $\mathcal{C}$-compatible. Thus, the question whether $\neg PROP_0$ holds for some $H \in L(HRG)$ is decidable. Hence, the decision problem whether $PROP_0$ holds for all $H \in L(HRG)$ can be reduced to the decision problem whether $\neg PROP_0$ holds for some $H \in L(HRG)$. □

Combining the compatibility results of section 2 with theorem 4.1 one obtains a list of decidability results.

4.2 Corollary (Special Decidable Problems)

The question: "Does a given edge-replacement grammar generate some or only graphs with property $PROP_0$?" is decidable for all edge-replacement grammars and all properties in the following list:
- A graph is totally disconnected.
- A graph is connected (or semi-connected).
- All nodes of a graph have even degree.
- A graph has an Eulerian cycle (or an Eulerian path).
- The degree of a graph is bounded by k (for some $k \in \mathbb{N}$).
- A graph has an edge-coloring with at most k colors (for some $k \in \mathbb{N}$).

Remark

1. Remember that the predicate $DISCO_0$ is $\mathcal{HRG}$-compatible.
2. Although in most cases we have restricted to the class $\mathcal{ERG}$ of all edge-replacement grammars, we are convinced that our statements hold even if we consider the class of all hyperedge-replacement grammars which generate ordinary graph languages and use nonterminal hyperedges with a bounded number of tentacles. We even guess that the considered properties are compatible for arbitrary hyperedge-replacement grammars

(with a bounded number of tentacles) if their definition is properly adapted to hypergraphs (which seems easy with respect to connectedness, degree properties as well as k-edge-colorability).

3. As shown in [HKV 89], many other properties — like the existence of Hamiltonian paths and cycles, node coloring, and subcontraction — are compatible and the corresponding questions are decidable.

5. A Filter Theorem for HRL's

We continue our study of basic properties of hyperedge-replacement grammars and languages, where the central question is the following: "If L is a hyperedge-replacement language and $PROP_0$ a graph-theoretic property, is the set of all hypergraphs from L satisfying $PROP_0$ again a hyperedge-replacement language?" We demonstrate that the class of hyperedge-replacement languages is very "stable" in the sense that for all compatible properties the resulting languages are hyperedge-replacement languages. In particular, the above question gets an affirmative answer, if the property $PROP_0$ is: being connected, Eulerian, Hamiltonian, planar, or k-colorable.

5.1 Theorem (Filter Theorem)

Let $PROP_0$ be a $\mathcal{C}$-compatible predicate for some class $\mathcal{C}$ of hyperedge-replacement grammars. For every $HRG \in \mathcal{C}$, there is a hyperedge-replacement grammar HRG_{PROP_0} such that $L(HRG_{PROP_0}) = \{H \in L(HRG) | H \text{ satisfies } PROP_0\}$.

Proof

Let $PROP_0$ be $\mathcal{C}$-compatible and $PROP$ and $PROP'$ be the corresponding predicates over the index set I such that $PROP$ is $(\mathcal{C}, PROP')$-compatible and $PROP_0 = PROP(-, i_0)$ for some $i_0 \in I$. Let $HRG = (N, T, P, Z) \in \mathcal{C}$. Then, we construct a hyperedge-replacement grammar $HRG' = (N', T, P', Z')$ as follows. Let

- $N' = N \times I$;
- $P' = \{((A,i), (R, assign)) \mid (A, R) \in P,\ assign : E_R \to I,\ i \in I,$
  $PROP'(R, assign, i)$, and $PROP(l_R(e)^\bullet, assign(e))$ for $e \in E_R$ with $l_R(e) \in T$ }
  where for $R \in \mathcal{H}_C$ and $assign : E_R \to I$, $(R, assign)$ denotes the hypergraph
  $(V_R, E_R, s_R, t_R, l, begin_R, end_R)$ with $l(e) = (l_R(e), assign(e))$ if $l_R(e) \in N$ and
  $l(e) = l_R(e)$ otherwise;
- $Z' = (Z, assign)$ with $assign(e(Z)) = i_0$.

It remains to be shown that $L(HRG') = \{H \in L(HRG) | H \text{ satisfies } PROP_0\}$.

Claim 1. If $(A, i) \in N \times I$, $A^\bullet \stackrel{*}{\Longrightarrow} H \in \mathcal{H}_T$ is a derivation in HRG, and $PROP(H, i)$ holds, then there is a derivation $(A, i)^\bullet \stackrel{*}{\Longrightarrow} H$ in HRG'.

Proof of claim 1 (by induction on the number of steps in the derivation). For each zero-step derivation $A^\bullet \stackrel{0}{\Longrightarrow} H$ in HRG, $H \notin \mathcal{H}_T$. For each one-step derivation $A^\bullet \stackrel{1}{\Longrightarrow} H$ in HRG to $H \in \mathcal{H}_T$ with $PROP(H,i)$, there is a production $(A,R) \in P$ such that $H = REPLACE(R, repl)$ with $repl(e) = l_R(e)^\bullet$ for $e \in E_R$. By $(\mathcal{C}, PROP')$-compatibility of $PROP$, there is a mapping $assign : E_R \to I$ such that $PROP'(R, assign, i)$ and $PROP(l_R(e)^\bullet, assign(e))$ hold for $e \in E_R$. Hence, $((A,i),(R,assign)) \in P'$. Moreover, $(R, assign) = R$. Thus, there is a derivation $(A,i)^\bullet \stackrel{1}{\Longrightarrow} H$ in HRG'. Suppose now that the statement is true for k-step derivations. Let $A^\bullet \stackrel{k+1}{\Longrightarrow} H \in \mathcal{H}_T$ be a $(k+1)$-step derivation in HRG and $PROP(H,i)$ be satisfied. Then we can assume that the derivation is of the form $A^\bullet \Longrightarrow R \stackrel{k}{\Longrightarrow} H$ for some $(A,R) \in P$. Consider now the fibres $l_R(e)^\bullet \stackrel{k}{\Longrightarrow} H(e)$ of $R \stackrel{k}{\Longrightarrow} H$ to $e \in E_R$. Since $PROP(H,i)$ holds and $PROP$ is $(\mathcal{C}, PROP')$-compatible, there is a mapping $assign : E_R \to I$ such that $PROP'(R, assign, i)$ and $PROP(H(e), assign(e))$ hold for $e \in E_R$. By the construction of P', $((A,i),(R,assign)) \in P'$. Moreover, by the inductive hypothesis, for all $e \in E_R$ with $l_R(e) \in N$, there is a derivation $(l_R(e), assign(e))^\bullet \stackrel{*}{\Longrightarrow} H(e)$ in HRG'. Embedding these derivations into $(R, assign)$ yields a derivation $(R, assign) \stackrel{*}{\Longrightarrow} H'$. Since the hypergraphs $(R, assign)$ and R differ only in the labels of the nonterminal hyperedges and $H = REPLACE(R, repl)$ with $repl(e) = H(e)$ for $e \in E_R$, the hypergraph $H' = REPLACE((R, assign), repl)$ equals H. Thus, there is a derivation $(A,i)^\bullet \Longrightarrow (R, assign) \stackrel{*}{\Longrightarrow} H$ in HRG'.

Claim 2. If $(A,i) \in N \times I$ and $(A,i)^\bullet \stackrel{*}{\Longrightarrow} H \in \mathcal{H}_T$ is a derivation in HRG', then there is a derivation $A^\bullet \stackrel{*}{\Longrightarrow} H$ in HRG and $PROP(H,i)$ holds.

Proof of Claim 2 (by induction on the number of steps in the derivation). For each zero-step derivation $(A,i)^\bullet \stackrel{0}{\Longrightarrow} H$, $H \notin \mathcal{H}_T$. For each one-step derivation $(A,i)^\bullet \stackrel{1}{\Longrightarrow} H \in \mathcal{H}_T$, there is a production $((A,i),(R, assign))$ in P' such that H is obtained as $H = REPLACE((R, assign), repl)$ with $repl(e) = l_{(R, assign)}(e)^\bullet$ for $e \in E_{(R, assign)}$. By construction of P', (A,R) is a production in P and $assign : E_R \to I$ is a mapping such that $PROP'(R, assign, i)$ and $PROP(l_R(e)^\bullet, assign(e))$ hold for $e \in E_{R,T} = E_R$. Thus, there is a derivation $A^\bullet \stackrel{1}{\Longrightarrow} H$ in HRG and, by $(\mathcal{C}, PROP')$-compatibility of $PROP$, $PROP(H,i)$ is satisfied. Suppose that the statement is true for k-step derivations. Let $(A,i)^\bullet \stackrel{k+1}{\Longrightarrow} H \in \mathcal{H}_T$ be a $(k+1)$-step derivation in HRG'. Then we can assume that the derivation decomposes into $(A,i)^\bullet \Longrightarrow (R, assign) \stackrel{k}{\Longrightarrow} H$ for some production $((A,i),(R, assign)) \in P'$. Hence $PROP'(R, assign, i)$ and, for terminal hyperedges $e \in E_R$, $PROP(l_R(e)^\bullet, assign(e))$ hold. For nonterminal hyperedges $e \in E_{(R, assign)}$, the fibres of the derivation $(R, assign) \stackrel{k}{\Longrightarrow} H$ are of the form $(l_R(e), assign(e))^\bullet \stackrel{k}{\Longrightarrow} H(e)$. By the inductive hypothesis, for each nonterminal $e \in E_R$, there is a derivation $l_R(e)^\bullet \stackrel{*}{\Longrightarrow} H(e)$ in HRG and $PROP(H(e), assign(e))$ holds. Embedding the derivations into R yields a derivation $R \stackrel{*}{\Longrightarrow} H$ in HRG. Thus, there is a derivation $A^\bullet \Longrightarrow R \stackrel{*}{\Longrightarrow} H$ in HRG. Moreover, by $(\mathcal{C}, PROP')$-compatibility of $PROP$, $PROP(H,i)$ holds. This completes the inductive step.

By Claim 1 and 2, there is a derivation $(l(Z), i_0)^\bullet \stackrel{*}{\Longrightarrow} H$ in HRG' if and only if there is a derivation $l(Z)^\bullet \stackrel{*}{\Longrightarrow} H \in \mathcal{H}_T$ in HRG and $PROP(H, i_0)$ is satisfied. This completes the proof of the theorem. □

The Filter Theorem may be used to get further decidability results.

5.2 Corollary (Metatheorem for Decision Problems)

Let $PROP_0$ be $\mathcal{C}$-compatible with respect to some class $\mathcal{C}$ of hyperedge-replacement grammars. Then, for all $HRG \in \mathcal{C}$, it is decidable whether
(1') $PROP_0$ holds for no $H \in L(HRG)$ except perhaps a finite number;
(2') $PROP_0$ holds for all $H \in L(HRG)$ except perhaps a finite number.

Proof

By the Filter Theorem, for every hyperedge-replacement grammar $HRG \in \mathcal{C}$, we may construct hyperedge-replacement grammars HRG_{PROP_0} and $HRG_{\neg PROP_0}$ generating the sets $L(HRG_{PROP_0}) = \{H \in L(HRG) | \ H \text{ satisfies } PROP_0\}$ and $L(HRG_{\neg PROP_0}) = \{H \in L(HRG) | \ H \text{ satisfies } \neg PROP_0\}$, respectively. Now $PROP_0$ holds for a finite number of hypergraphs $H \in L(HRG)$ if and only if $L(HRG_{PROP_0})$ is finite and $PROP_0$ holds for all $H \in L(HRG)$ except perhaps a finite number if and only if $L(HRG_{\neg PROP_0})$ is finite. By the decidability of the Finiteness Problem for hyperedge-replacement grammars, we obtain the desired decidability results. □

Remark

Analogously, the Filter Theorem and the decidability of the Emptiness Problem for hyperedge-replacement grammars may be used to obtain the decidability results presented in section 4, theorem 4.1.

6. Non-Compatible Graph-Theoretic Properties

The Filter Theorem presented in section 5 can be used to show that there exist properties which are not compatible in the sense of definition 2.1.

6.1 Theorem

The predicate $SQUARE$ given for all $H \in \mathcal{H}_C$ by

$$SQUARE(H) \text{ if and only if } |V_H| = n^2 \text{ for some } n \in \mathbb{N}$$

is not $\mathcal{HRG}$-compatible.

Proof

Assume that $SQUARE$ is $\mathcal{HRG}$-compatible. Then we consider a hyperedge-replacement grammar HRG which generates the set $L(HRG) = \{DISCRETE(k)|k \geq 1\}$ of all discrete graphs. By the Filter Theorem, there is a hyperedge-replacement grammar HRG_{SQUARE} which generates $L(HRG_{SQUARE}) = \{DISCRETE(k)|k$ is square$\}$. By the Pumping Lemma (or the Linear-Growth Theorem), we know that the set of discrete graphs with square number of nodes cannot be generated by a hyperedge-replacement grammar, because their growth with respect to the number of nodes is not linear. Thus, $SQUARE$ cannot be $\mathcal{HRG}$-compatible. □

7. Unsolvable Graph-Theoretic Decision Problems

There are questions about single hypergraphs which have the same form as compatible properties, but are undecidable. We present an example of this type.

7.1 Definition (Automorphism Group)

An *automorphism* of a hypergraph $H \in \mathcal{H}_C$ is an isomorphism of the underlying (0,0)-hypergraph with itself. The set of all automorphisms of H, also called the *automorphism group* of H, is *trivial* if the identity is the only automorphism; otherwise the automorphism group of H is *non-trivial*.

7.2 Theorem

Given an arbitrary hyperedge-replacement grammar $HRG \in \mathcal{HRG}$, it is undecidable whether there is a hypergraph $H \in L(HRG)$ with non-trivial automorphism group.

Proof

For each context-free string grammar $CFG = (N, T, P, S)$ without λ-productions, we obtain an edge-replacement grammar $CFG' = (N', T', P', Z')$ as follows. Let

- $N' = N \cup T$;
- $T' = \{a'|a \in T\}$;
- $P' = \{(A, w^\bullet) \mid (A, w) \in P\} \cup \{(a, R(a)) \mid a \in T\}$
  where for $a \in T$, $R(a)$ denotes the (1,1)-graph with two parallel edges in opposite directions each labeled with a';
- $Z' = S^\bullet$.

Then there is a graph $G \in L(CFG')$ with non-trivial automorphism group if and only if $L(CFG)$ contains a palindrome. But this is undecidable, as a straightforward application of the Post Correspondence Problem shows. □

Remark

In [WW 89], Wanke and Wiegers show the following. Let $k \geq 3$ be any fixed natural number. Given an arbitrary linear hyperedge-replacement grammar $HRG \in \mathcal{HRG}$ generating a set of graphs, it is undecidable whether there is a graph $G \in L(HRG)$ having bandwidth k.

8. Related Research

In this chapter, a spectrum of graph-theoretic properties has been studied and proved to be compatible. Moreover, several decidability results for compatible properties have been presented. Related research can be found in the literature.

In the theory of node-replacement grammars and languages, one encounters specific graph properties (total disconnectedness, connectedness, planarity and Hamiltonicity etc.). In [JR 81], Janssens and Rozenberg consider node-label-controlled (NLC) graph grammars, investigate — beside some standard language theoretic decision problems — graph-theoretic decision problems, and show that the questions of the type

- Does the language of a NLC grammar contain a totally disconnected graph?
- Does it contain a connected graph, a planar graph, a Hamiltonian graph, etc.?

are undecidable. In [RW 86b], Rozenberg and Welzl restrict to boundary node-label-controlled (BNLC) graph grammars the generative power of which is of a context-free nature, study questions of the form

- If L is a BNLC language and $PROP_0$ a graph-theoretic property, is the set of all graphs L_{PROP_0} from L satisfying $PROP_0$ also a BNLC language?,

and give affirmative answers for k-colorability, connectivity, and subcontraction. Furthermore, in [Wa 91], Wanke presents algorithms for analyzing single graphs and sets of graphs generated by boundary node-label-controlled graph grammars.

In the theory of hyperedge-replacement grammars and languages, one encounters three types of graph properties that play an important role in proving decidability and structural results. The three types are called compatible, finite, and inductive graph properties. All three of them cover graph properties that are well-behaved with respect to certain operations on hypergraphs. In [LW 88], Lengauer and Wanke introduce the notion of a *finite* property $PROP_0$. It means roughly that there is only a finite number of classes of graphs that behave differently with respect to $PROP_0$ when put into all possible environments. Courcelle investigates in [Co 90a] so-called *inductive* properties. Roughly speaking, a family of predicates is inductive relative to a set of graph operations if each predicate can be tested in the following way. If a graph is given as a result of applying one of the operations, then whether the predicate holds for it can be determined by checking corresponding predicates for the arguments of the operation. Finally, in [HKV 89] — and in this book — graph properties are studied that are *compatible* with the derivation process of a class of hyperedge-replacement grammars in a certain way. In all three cases, more or less the same results have been shown. Moreover, the known examples of compatible, finite, and inductive properties are the same: k-colorability, connectedness, planarity, Hamiltonicity, etc. No wonder, because in [HKL 92] all three notions are shown to be essentially equivalent for the class of all hyperedge-replacement grammars.

The concepts and techniques considered in this chapter apply to complexity issues. Compatibility says that a property can be tested for a hypergraph derived by long fibres (starting from a handle) by testing some hypergraphs derived by shorter fibres. This observation leads to fast tests of compatible properties under specific conditions. The details are worked out — in some degree — in [Kr 87a]. Other authors use more or less the same ideas to come up with efficient solutions of particular graph problems on some types of graphs. In [Sl 82], Slisenko introduces a class of graph grammars, which can be seen as special hyperedge-replacement grammars, and gives a polynomial-time algorithm testing the existence of Hamiltonian paths in the generated graphs. Lengauer (see, e.g., [Le 87]) and Lautemann (see [La 88a]) present efficient tests for a variety of graph problems dealing with hierachical graphs and decomposition trees, respectively.

9. Bibliographic Note

The theorems presented in section 1 as well as theorem 2.3 are published in [Ha 89a]. Theorems 4.1 and 7.2 correspond to the theorems 4.3, 4.4, and 6.2 in [HKV 89]. Theorems 5.1 and 6.1 are also published in [HK 90]. A comparison of compatible, finite and inductive graph properties is given in [HKL 92].

Chapter VII
Boundedness Aspects of HRL's

Besides the decision questions considered in chapter VI, we investigate the decidability of a different type of problems concerning functions on graphs and, in particular, numeric quantities like the numbers of nodes, edges, and paths, the node degree, maximum and minimum lengths of paths and cycles, etc. The kind of question we ask for a class of grammars may be called *Boundedness Problem*. It is as follows:

(3) Is it decidable whether (or not), concerning a particular quantity, the values of all graphs generated by a grammar are bounded?

For example, we want to know whether the node degree or the number of paths grow beyond any bound within a graph language. As a main result, we show that such a Boundedness Problem is decidable for a class of hyperedge-replacement grammars if the corresponding quantity function is built up by maxima, sums, and products and if the function is compatible with the derivation process of the given grammars. Examples of this kind are the bounded-node-degree problem, the bounded-maximum-path-length problem, the bounded-maximum-number-of-paths problem and others. It should be mentioned that the only result of same nature occurring in the literature is the decidability of the bounded-degree problem for NLC grammars (see [JRW 86]).

The chapter is organized as follows: In section 1, we discuss several examples of numeric functions which are compatible with the derivation process of our grammars in a certain way. In section 2, we introduce the general notion of compatible functions and relate them with the notion of compatible predicates. In section 3, we show that the Boundedness Problem (3) corresponding to a numeric function is decidable if the function is pointwise defined as the maximum of sums and products and if it is compatible. Finally, in section 4, we present an unsolvable Boundedness Problem.

1. Some Compatible Graph-Theoretic Functions

Given a hyperedge-replacement grammar, one may be interested in the values of graph-theoretic functions of the derived hypergraphs and one may ask how a certain value of a derived hypergraph depends on values of the components determined by the derivation. A function is said to be "compatible" with the derivation process of hyperedge-replacement grammars if it can be computed for each derived hypergraph H by computing the values (or related values) for the components and composing the values to the value of H.

In this section, we take up several graph-theoretic functions and show that they are "compatible" with the replacement process of hyperedges. A formal definition of compatibility with respect to functions is given in the next section. We discuss the number of nodes and hyperedges, the number of simple paths and cycles, the length of a shortest path, the length of a longest simple path, the minimum and maximum degree, and the number of components.

Notation

Let $I\!N^\circ = I\!N + \{\diamond\}$ denote the set of all natural numbers plus a special symbol $\diamond$. We use this special symbol $\diamond$ if the considered function has no sensible integer value. We calculate with $\diamond$ as follows: For $i \in I$ and $n_i \in I\!N^\circ$,

- $\sum_{i \in I} n_i = \diamond$ and $\prod_{i \in I} n_i = \diamond$ if and only if $n_j = \diamond$ for some $j \in I$,
- $\min_{i \in I} n_i = \min_{i \in I'} n_i$ and $\max_{i \in I} n_i = \max_{i \in I'} n_i$ for $I' = \{i \in I | n_i \neq \diamond\}$, and $\min_{i \in I} n_i = \diamond$ and $\max_{i \in I} n_i = \diamond$ for $I = \emptyset$.

Number of Nodes and Hyperedges

To illustrate our kind of investigation, we first consider the computation of the number of nodes and hyperedges in a hypergraph. In the following, let $|V_H|$ denote the number of nodes, $|INT_H|$ the number of internal nodes, and $|E_H|$ the number of hyperedges in a hypergraph H. Let $A^\bullet \Longrightarrow R \stackrel{*}{\Longrightarrow} H$ be a derivation of H, and for $e \in E_R$, $l_R(e)^\bullet \stackrel{*}{\Longrightarrow} H(e)$ be the fibre of $R \stackrel{*}{\Longrightarrow} H$ induced by e. Then the node set of H consists of the nodes of R and the internal nodes of the components $H(e)$. Hence, the number of nodes in H can be computed from the number of nodes in R and the number of internal nodes in the $H(e)$ by summing up the numbers. For example, the hypergraph H in Fig. 1.1 has 8 nodes; 4 nodes are already in R, $H(e)$ and $H(e'')$ possess one internal node, each, $H(e')$ has 2 internal nodes. Even simpler, the number of hyperedges in H can be determined by the number of hyperedges in the $H(e)$ by summing up the numbers of the $H(e)$. In our example, $H(e)$ has one, $H(e')$ and $H(e'')$ possess four and two hyperedges, respectively; therefore, the whole hypergraph H has seven hyperedges.

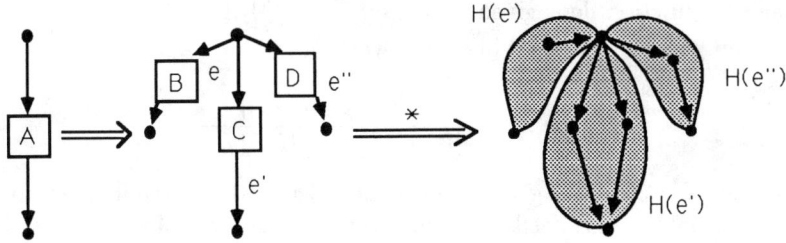

Fig. 1.1. A derivation of the form $A^\bullet \Longrightarrow R \stackrel{*}{\Longrightarrow} H$

1.1 Theorem (Number of Nodes and Hyperedges)

Let $HRG = (N, T, P, Z)$ be a hyperedge-replacement grammar, $A^\bullet \Longrightarrow R \stackrel{*}{\Longrightarrow} H$ a derivation in HRG with $A \in N \cup T$ and $H \in \mathcal{H}_T$, and for $e \in E_R$, $l_R(e)^\bullet \stackrel{*}{\Longrightarrow} H(e)$ the fibre of $R \stackrel{*}{\Longrightarrow} H$ induced by e. Then

$$|V_H| = |V_R| + \sum_{e \in E_R} |INT_{H(e)}|;$$

$$|INT_H| = |INT_R| + \sum_{e \in E_R} |INT_{H(e)}|;$$

$$|E_H| = \sum_{e \in E_R} |E_{H(e)}|.$$

Proof

Without loss of generality, we can assume that $H = REPLACE(R, repl)$ with $repl(e) = H(e) \subseteq H$ for $e \in E_R$. By definition of replacement, $V_H = V_R + \sum_{e \in E_R} INT_{H(e)}$, $E_H = \sum_{e \in E_R} E_{H(e)}$, and $EXT_H = EXT_R$. Hence, we have $INT_H = V_H - EXT_H = V_R - EXT_R + \sum_{e \in E_R} INT_{H(e)} = INT_R + \sum_{e \in E_R} INT_{H(e)}$. Now the cardinality statements with respect to the number of nodes and the number of hyperedges follow directly from the set-theoretic statements. □

Remark

1. The composed function size given by $size(H) = |V_H| + |E_H|$ can be treated similarly. It makes use of the auxiliary function intsize given by $intsize(H) = |INT_H| + |E_H|$.

$$size(H = |V_R| + \sum_{e \in E_R} intsize(H(e));$$

$$intsize(H) = |INT_R| + \sum_{e \in E_R} intsize(H(e)).$$

2. The density function dens given by $\text{dens}(H) = \frac{|E_H|}{|V_H|}$ if $|V_H| > 0$ (and $\text{dens}(H) = \diamond$ otherwise) can also be expressed in such a way:

$$\text{dens}(H) = \frac{\sum_{e \in E_R} |E_{H(e)}|}{|V_R| + \sum_{e \in E_R} |INT_{H(e)}|}.$$

The expression for computing $\text{dens}(H)$ makes use of the possibility to compute the number of internal nodes as well as the number of hyperedges of the $H(e)$'s. It does not make use of the density of some of the $H(e)$'s.

For simplifying the technicalities, we restrict our following consideration to the class of edge-replacement grammars. Remember that a hyperedge-replacement grammar is an edge-replacement grammar if and only if the hyperedges in the axiom are (1,1)-edges and the right-hand sides of the productions are (1,1)-graphs.

1.2 General Assumption

For the rest of this section, let $ERG = (N, T, P, Z)$ be a completely typed and well-formed edge-replacement grammar, $A^\bullet \Longrightarrow R \overset{*}{\Longrightarrow} G$ a derivation in ERG with $A \in N \cup T$ and $G \in \mathcal{G}_T$, and for $e \in E_R$, $l_R(e)^\bullet \overset{*}{\Longrightarrow} G(e)$ the fibre of $R \overset{*}{\Longrightarrow} G$ induced by e.

Simple Paths: Number, Minimum and Maximum Length

We are going to discuss how the number of simple paths of a graph G can be computed from the number of simple paths of the graphs $G(e)$. Considering for example the graph G in Fig. 1.2, one may observe that G contains five simple paths connecting $begin_G$ and end_G; one path is created by the edge e and lies completely in $G(e)$, the other four ones are created by the edges e' and e'' (forming a simple path connecting $begin_R$ and end_R) and are composed by a simple path of $G(e')$ joining $begin_{G(e')}$ and $end_{G(e')}$ and a simple path of $G(e'')$ joining $end_{G(e')} = begin_{G(e'')}$ and $end_{G(e'')}$. The product of the number of simple paths of $G(e')$ (joining $begin_{G(e')}$ and $end_{G(e')}$) and the number a simple paths of $G(e'')$ (joining $begin_{G(e'')}$ and $end_{G(e'')}$) describes the number of simple paths created by the simple path in R built from e' and e''. The sum of all numbers of simple paths created by a simple path in R connecting $begin_R$ and end_R describes the number of all simple paths in G connecting $begin_G$ and end_G.

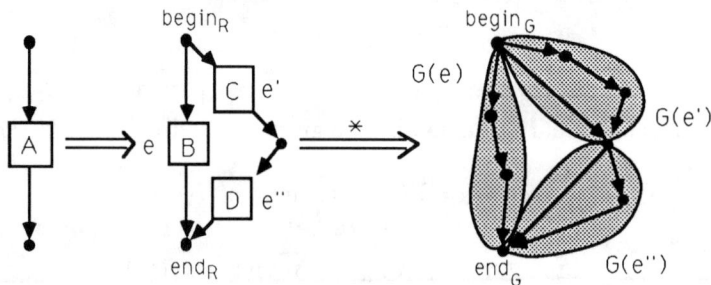

Fig. 1.2. A derivation of the form $A^\bullet \Longrightarrow R \overset{*}{\Longrightarrow} G$

Although $G(e)$ contains a path connecting $begin_G$ and end_G, this path is not a shortest one in G. $G(e')$ contains a path of length one connecting $begin_G = begin_{G(e')}$ and $end_{G(e')}$ and $G(e'')$ contains a path of length one connecting $end_{G(e')} = begin_{G(e'')}$ and $end_{G(e'')} = end_G$. Hence, the path in R connecting $begin_R$ and end_R built from e' and e'' creates a path of length two. The sum of the minimum path length of $G(e')$ (joining $begin_{G(e')}$ and $end_{G(e')}$) and the minimum path length of $G(e'')$ (joining $begin_{G(e'')}$ and $end_{G(e'')}$) describes the minimum length of paths created by the path in R built from e' and e''. The minimum of all the minimum path lengths created by paths in R connecting $begin_R$ and end_R describes the minimum length of paths in G connecting $begin_G$ and end_G. Analogously, the maximum of all the maximum simple-path lengths created by simple paths in R connecting $begin_R$ and end_R describes the the maximum length of simple paths in G connecting $begin_G$ and end_G.

We will use the following notions. Given a graph G, a *path* joining v_0 and v_n is a sequence $p = v_0, e_1, v_1, e_2, \ldots, e_n, v_n$ of alternating nodes and edges such that for $1 \leq i \leq n$, v_{i-1} and v_i are the nodes incident with e_i. If $v_0 = v_n$ then p is said to be a *cycle*. In this case, we do not distinguish p either from the cycle $v_i, e_{i+1}, \ldots, e_n, v_n, e_1, \ldots, e_i, v_i$ or from the cycle $v_i, e_i, \ldots, e_1, v_0, e_n, \ldots, e_{i+1}, v_i$. If each node appears once in a path, then the sequence is called a *simple* path. If each node appears once except that $v_0 = v_n$ and $n \geq 3$ then p is a *simple cycle*. The *length* of a path or a cycle p, denoted length(p), is the number of edges it contains. "e on p" denotes the fact that e occurs in p.

1.3 Theorem (Simple Paths: Number, Minimum and Maximum Length)

For a (1,1)-graph G, let $PATH_G$ denote the set of simple paths joining $begin_G$ and end_G and numpath(G) the number of these paths in G. Moreover, let minpath(G) and maxpath(G) denote the minimum and maximum simple-path length, respectively, if any and minpath(G) = $\diamond$ = maxpath(G) otherwise. Then

$$\text{numpath}(G) = \sum_{p \in PATH_R} \prod_{e \text{ on } p} \text{numpath}(G(e));$$

$$\text{minpath}(G) = \min_{p \in PATH_R} \sum_{e \text{ on } p} \text{minpath}(G(e));$$

$$\text{maxpath}(G) = \max_{p \in PATH_R} \sum_{e \text{ on } p} \text{maxpath}(G(e)).$$

Proof

Let G be a (1,1)-graph and $\hat{p}$ be a simple path joining $begin_G$ and end_G. Without loss of generality, we can assume that $G = REPLACE(R, repl)$ with $V_R \subseteq V_G$ and $repl(e) = G(e) \subseteq G$ for $e \in E_R$. Starting from $begin_G$ and running through $\hat{p}$, nodes of R are visited in a certain sequence $v_0, \ldots, v_n$. Decomposing $\hat{p}$ in these nodes, one gets a sequence of simple paths $p_1, \ldots, p_n$ (where p_i connects v_{i-1} and v_i for $i = 1, \ldots, n$). For $i = 1, \ldots, n$, there exists $e_i \in E_R$ such that p_i belongs to $G(e_i)$. Otherwise, if p_i

would be covered by more components, it would visit at least three nodes of R. By the same reason, e_i connects v_{i-1} and v_i (for $i = 1,\ldots,n$). Thus, $p = v_0, e_1, \ldots, e_n, v_n$ forms a simple path joining $begin_R$ and end_R and for $i = 1,\ldots,n$, p_i is a simple path joining $begin_{G(e_i)}$ and $end_{G(e_i)}$. Conversely, if $p = v_0, e_1, \ldots, e_n, v_n$ is a simple path joining $begin_R$ and end_R and for $i = 1,\ldots,n$, p_i is a simple path joining $begin_{G(e_i)}$ and $end_{G(e_i)}$, then the replacement of the edges $e_1, \ldots, e_n$ by the corresponding paths $p_1, \ldots, p_n$ yields a simple path joining $begin_G$ and end_G. Therefore,

$$PATH_G = \bigcup_{p \in PATH_R} \left\{ replace(p, path) | path(e) \in PATH_{G(e)} \right\}$$

where $replace(p, path)$ denotes the path obtained from p by replacing all edges e on p by the corresponding paths $path(e)$.

The statements about the number of simple paths as well as the minimum and maximum simple path length follow immediately from the set-theoretical statement: Since for a simple path $p \in PATH_R$, $replace(p, path) \neq replace(p, path')$ if and only if $path(e) \neq path'(e)$ for some e on p, the number of simple paths induced by p is $\prod_{e \text{ on } p} \text{numpath}(G(e))$. Since different paths in R yield different paths in G, the number of simple paths in G is the sum of the numbers of simple paths induced by some simple path in R. Since for a simple path $p \in PATH_R$, $length(replace(p, path)) = \sum_{e \text{ on } p} length(path(e))$,

$$\min_{\hat{p} \in PATH_G} length(\hat{p}) = \min_{p \in PATH_R} \sum_{e \text{ on } p} \min_{path(e) \in PATH_{G(e)}} length(path(e)).$$

Replacing min by max wherever it occurs, we obtain a corresponding statement for $\max_{\hat{p} \in PATH_G} length(\hat{p})$. Using the definition of minpath and maxpath, we can derive the claimed minimum- and maximum-statements. □

Simple Cycles: Number, Minimum and Maximum Length

The number of simple cycles, the minimum cycle length, and the maximum simple-cycle length of a graph can be determined using the computation of the number of simple paths, the minimum path length, and the maximum simple-path length, respectively. Considering for example the graph G in Fig. 1.2, G contains 6 simple cycles, one completely lying in $G(e')$, one completely lying in $G(e'')$, and four ones running through $G(e)$, $G(e')$, and $G(e'')$. The latter are composed by simple paths of $G(e)$, $G(e')$, and $G(e'')$. The product of the number of simple paths of $G(e)$, $G(e')$, and $G(e'')$ describes the number of simple cycles created by the simple cycle in R built from e, e', and e''. The sum of all numbers of simple cycles created by simple cycles in R describes the number of all composed simple cycles in G. Adding the numbers of simple cycles in the $G(e)$ ($e \in E_R$), we obtain the number of all simple cycles in G. The minimum resp. maximum simple-cycle length can be handled in a similar way.

1.4 Theorem (Simple Cycles: Number, Minimum and Maximum Length)

For a (1,1)-graph G, let $CYCLE_G$ denote the set of simple cycles and numcycle(G) the number of these cycles in G. Moreover, let mincycle(G) and maxcycle(G) denote the minimum and maximum simple-cycle length, respectively, if any and mincycle(G) = $\diamond$ = maxcycle(G) otherwise. Then

$$\text{numcycle}(G) = \sum_{c \in CYCLE_R} \prod_{e \text{ on } c} \text{numpath}(G(e)) + \sum_{e \in E_R} \text{numcycle}(G(e));$$

$$\text{mincycle}(G) = \min\left\{ \min_{c \in CYCLE_R} \sum_{e \text{ on } c} \text{minpath}(G(e)) \,,\, \min_{e \in E_R} \text{mincycle}(G(e)) \right\};$$

$$\text{maxcycle}(G) = \max\left\{ \max_{c \in CYCLE_R} \sum_{e \text{ on } c} \text{maxpath}(G(e)) \,,\, \max_{e \in E_R} \text{maxcycle}(G(e)) \right\}.$$

Proof

Let G be a (1,1)-graph and $\hat{c}$ be a simple cycle. Without loss of generality, we can assume that $G = REPLACE(R, repl)$ with $V_R \subseteq V_G$ and $repl(e) = G(e) \subseteq G$ for $e \in E_R$. Starting somewhere on $\hat{c}$ and running through $\hat{c}$, two cases may occur.
First case. The cycle $\hat{c}$ belongs to a single component, say $G(e)$.
Second case. The cycle $\hat{c}$ does not belong to a single component. Then we consider the sequence $v_0, \ldots, v_n$ of visited nodes of R. Decomposing $\hat{c}$ in these nodes, one gets a sequence of simple paths $p_1, \ldots, p_{n+1}$ (where p_i connects v_{i-1} and v_i for $i = 1, \ldots, n$ and p_{n+1} connects v_n and v_0). For $i = 1, \ldots, n+1$, there exists $e_i \in E_R$ such that p_i belongs to $G(e_i)$. Otherwise, if p_i would be covered by more components, it would visit at least three nodes of R. By the same reason, e_i connects v_{i-1} and v_i (for $i = 1, \ldots, n+1$). Thus, $c = v_0, e_1, \ldots, e_{n+1}, v_{n+1}$ forms a simple cycle in R and for $i = 1, \ldots, n+1$, p_i is a simple path joining $begin_{G(e_i)}$ and $end_{G(e_i)}$.

Conversely, if $c = v_0, e_1, \ldots, e_{n+1}, v_{n+1}$ is a simple cycle in R and for $i = 1, \ldots, n+1$, p_i is a simple path joining $begin_{G(e_i)}$ and $end_{G(e_i)}$, then the replacement of the edges $e_1, \ldots, e_{n+1}$ by the paths $p_1, \ldots, p_{n+1}$ yields a simple cycle in G. Moreover, if $e \in E_R$ and c is a simple cycle in $G(e)$, then c is a cycle in G as well. Therefore,

$$CYCLE_G = \bigcup_{c \in CYCLE_R} \left\{ replace(c, path) | path(e) \in PATH_{G(e)} \right\}$$
$$\cup \bigcup_{e \in E_R} CYCLE_{G(e)}$$

where $replace(c, path)$ denotes the cycle obtained from c by replacing all edges e on c by the corresponding simple paths $path(e)$.

The statements on the number of simple cycles as well as the minimum and maximum simple cycle length are immediate consequences of the set theoretical statement: Since for a simple cycle c in R, $replace(c, path) \neq replace(c, path')$ if and only if

$path(e) \neq path'(e)$ for some e on c, the number of simple cycles induced by c is $\prod_{e \text{ on } c} \text{numpath}(G(e))$. Different simple cycles in R yield different cycles in G. Finally, cycles belonging to different components are different. Therefore, we obtain the claimed cardinality statement from the set-theoretic statement. Since for a simple cycle $c \in CYCLE_R$, $\text{length}(replace(c, path)) = \sum_{e \text{ on } c} \text{length}(path(e))$, we get

$$\min_{\hat{c} \in CYCLE_G} \text{length}(\hat{c})$$
$$= \min \left\{ \begin{array}{l} \min_{c \in CYCLE_R} \sum_{e \text{ on } c} \min_{path(e) \in PATH_{G(e)}} \text{length}(path(e)), \\ \min_{e \in E_R} \min_{c \in CYCLE_{G(e)}} \text{length}(c) \end{array} \right\}.$$

A corresponding statement for $\max_{\hat{c} \in CYCLE_G} \text{length}(\hat{c})$ can be obtained. Using the definition of mincycle and maxcycle, we can derive the claimed minimum- and maximum-statements. □

Minimum and Maximum Degree

We continue in discussing how the minimum (maximum) degree of a graph G can be computed from the minimum (maximum) degree of the $G(e)$. With respect to the determination of the minimum (maximum) degree of a graph G is is useful to know the minimum (maximum) degree of the internal nodes of the $G(e)$ as well as the degrees of the $begin_{G(e)}$ and $end_{G(e)}$. As illustrated in Fig. 1.3, the degree $D_R(v)$ of a node $v \in V_R \subseteq V_G$ can be determined by summing up the degrees of the nodes $begin_{G(e)}$, $begin_{G(e')}$, $begin_{G(e'')}$ (e, e', and e'' are the outgoing edges from v), and $end_{G(e''')}$ (e''' is the only incoming edge in v). Building the minimum (maximum) of the $D_R(v)$ with $v \in V_R$, we obtain the minimum (maximum) degree of the nodes $v \in V_R \subseteq V_G$. Moreover, the degrees of the internal nodes of the $G(e)$ have to be taken into account.

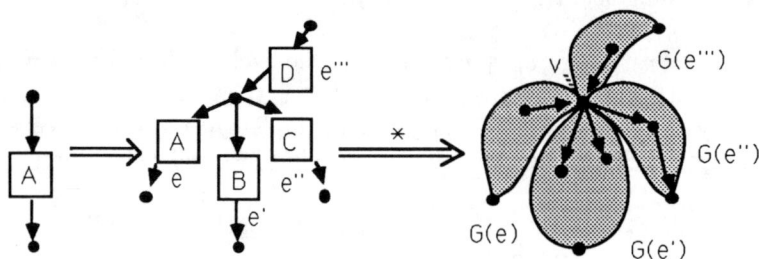

Fig. 1.3. A derivation of the form $A^{\bullet} \Longrightarrow R \stackrel{*}{\Longrightarrow} G$

1.5 Theorem (Minimum and Maximum Degree)

For a graph G, let mindegree(G) and maxdegree(G) denote the minimum and maximum degree among the nodes of G, respectively. Moreover, let minintdegree(G) denote the minimum degree among the internal nodes of G and bdegree(G) and edegree(G) the degree of $begin_G$ and end_G, respectively. Then

$$\text{mindegree}(G) = \min\left\{ \min_{v \in V_R} D_R(v) , \min_{e \in E_R} \text{minintdegree}(G(e)) \right\};$$

$$\text{minintdegree}(G) = \min\left\{ \min_{v \in INT_R} D_R(v) , \min_{e \in E_R} \text{minintdegree}(G(e)) \right\};$$

$$\text{maxdegree}(G) = \max\left\{ \max_{v \in V_R} D_R(v) , \max_{e \in E_R} \text{maxdegree}(G(e)) \right\};$$

$$\text{bdegree}(G) = D_R(begin_R) \text{ and } ; \text{edegree}(G) = D_R(end_R)$$

where, for $v \in V_R$, $D_R(v) = \sum_{e \in s_R^{-1}(v)} \text{bdegree}(G(e)) + \sum_{e \in t_R^{-1}(v)} \text{edegree}(G(e))$.

Proof

Let G be a (1,1)-graph and v be a node in G. Without loss of generality, we can assume that $G = REPLACE(R, repl)$ with $V_R \subseteq V_G$ and $repl(e) = G(e) \subseteq G$ for $e \in E_R$. Thus, the degree of v in G, $d_G(v)$, can be determined as follows:

$$d_G(v) = \begin{cases} D_R(v) & \text{if } v \in V_R \\ d_{G(e)}(v) & \text{if } v \in INT_{G(e)} \text{ for some } e \in E_R \end{cases}$$

where $D_R(v) = \sum_{e \in s_R^{-1}(v)} \text{bdegree}(G(e)) + \sum_{e \in t_R^{-1}(v)} \text{edegree}(G(e))$. By definition of the minimum degree of G and the mimimum degree of G among the internal nodes,

$$\text{mindegree}(G) = \min_{v \in V_G} d_G(v)$$

$$= \min\left\{ \min_{v \in V_R} D_R(v) , \min_{e \in E_R} \min_{v \in INT_{G(e)}} d_{G(e)}(v) \right\}$$

$$= \min\left\{ \min_{v \in V_R} D_R(v) , \min_{e \in E_R} \text{minintdegree}(G(e)) \right\};$$

$$\text{minintdegree}(G) = \min_{v \in INT_G} d_G(v)$$

$$= \min\left\{ \min_{v \in INT_R} D_R(v) , \min_{e \in E_R} \min_{v \in INT_{G(e)}} d_{G(e)}(v) \right\}$$

$$= \min\left\{ \min_{v \in INT_R} D_R(v) , \min_{e \in E_R} \text{minintdegree}(G(e)) \right\}.$$

Let maxintdegree(G) denote the maximum degree among the internal nodes of G. Then

$$\text{maxdegree}(G) = \max_{v \in V_G} d_G(v)$$

$$= \max\left\{\max_{v \in V_R} D_R(v)\,,\, \max_{e \in E_R} \max_{v \in INT_{G(e)}} d_{G(e)}(v)\right\}$$

$$= \max\left\{\max_{v \in V_R} D_R(v)\,,\, \max_{e \in E_R} \text{maxintdegree}(G(e))\right\}.$$

Since $\text{maxdegree}(G(e)) = \max\left\{\text{maxintdegree}(G(e))\,,\, \text{bdegree}(G(e))\,,\, \text{edegree}(G(e))\right\}$ and $\text{bdegree}(G(e)), \text{edegree}(G(e)) \leq \max_{v \in V_R} D_R(v)$, the last expression can be simplified to $\max\{\max_{v \in V_R} D_R(v)\,,\, \max_{e \in E_R} \text{maxdegree}(G(e))\}$. Finally, by the definition of bdegree and edegree, we get $\text{bdegree}(G) = D_R(begin_R)$ and $\text{edegree}(G) = D_R(end_R)$. This completes the proof. □

Number of Components

Finally, we will show how the number of components of a graph G can be computed provided that a derivation $A^\bullet \Longrightarrow R \overset{*}{\Longrightarrow} G$ of G with fibres $l_R(e)^\bullet \overset{*}{\Longrightarrow} G(e)$ is given. We count the number of components of the graph R' obtained from R by removing all edges e for which $\text{numpath}(G(e))$ is zero (nodes which are in the same component of R' are in the same component of G) and look for "new" components obtained by the replacement of e by $G(e)$ neither containing $s_R(e)$ nor $t_R(e)$. In our example in Fig. 1.4, $\text{numpath}(G(e))$ as well as $\text{numpath}(G(e'))$ are zero, thus R' consists of two components. e creates no new component, its created nodes belong to the component containing the source resp. the target of e, e' creates one new component with 2 nodes, all other nodes belong to the component containing the source resp. the target of e', e'' and e''' do not create new components. Therefore, G consists of 3 components.

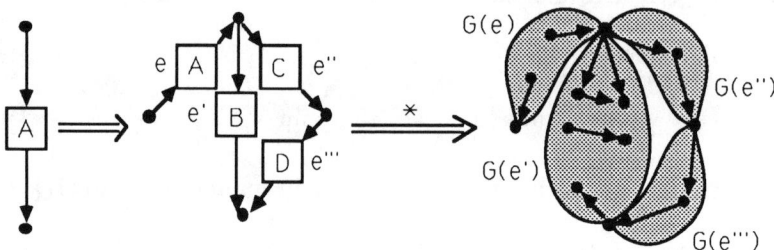

Fig. 1.4. A derivation of the form $A^\bullet \Longrightarrow R \overset{*}{\Longrightarrow} G$

1.6 Theorem (Number of Components)

For a $(1,1)$-graph G, let $\text{comp}(G)$ denote the number of connected components in G and $\text{newcomp}(G)$ denote the number of connected components neither containing begin_G nor end_G. Then

$$\text{comp}(G) = \text{comp}(R') + \sum_{e \in E_R} \text{newcomp}(G(e));$$

$$\text{newcomp}(G) = \text{newcomp}(R') + \sum_{e \in E_R} \text{newcomp}(G(e))$$

where $R' = R - \{e \in E_R | \text{numpath}(G(e)) = 0\}$.

Remark

The function value $\text{newcomp}(G)$ can be expressed directly by

$$\text{newcomp}(G) = \begin{cases} \text{comp}(G) - 1 & \text{if numpath}(G) \geq 1 \\ \text{comp}(G) - 2 & \text{otherwise.} \end{cases}$$

Proof

Without loss of generality, we can assume that $G = REPLACE(R, repl)$ with $V_R \subseteq V_G$ and $repl(e) = G(e) \subseteq G$ for $e \in E_R$.

First, let $COMP$ be a connected component in G. Then two cases may occur.
Case 1. $V_{COMP} \cap V_R = \emptyset$. Then $V_{COMP} \subseteq INT_{G(e)}$ for some $e \in E_R$, i.e., $COMP$ is a "new" component created by e neither containing $\text{begin}_{G(e)}$ nor $\text{end}_{G(e)}$.
Case 2. $V_{COMP} \cap V_R \neq \emptyset$. Then the subgraph $COMP' \subseteq R'$ with
- $V_{COMP'} = V_{COMP} \cap V_R$ and
- $E_{COMP'} = \{e \in E_R | s_R(e), t_R(e) \in V_{COMP}$ and $\text{numpath}(G(e)) \neq 0\}$

forms a connected component of R'.
Consequently, $\text{comp}(G) \leq \text{comp}(R') + \sum_{e \in E_R} \text{newcomp}(G(e))$. Analogously, we get $\text{newcomp}(G) \leq \text{newcomp}(R') + \sum_{e \in E_R} \text{newcomp}(G(e))$.

Conversely, let $COMP' \subseteq R'$ be a connected component in R'. Then for each pair of nodes $v, v' \in V_{COMP'}$, v and v' are connected in G (they are connected in R' and for $e \in E_{R'}$, $\text{numpath}(G(e)) \geq 1$). Consider now an arbitrary edge in $e \in E_R - E_{R'}$. Two cases may occur: (a) The source and target node of e are in the same component of R'. Then all nodes of $G(e)$ which are connected with $\text{begin}_{G(e)}$ or $\text{end}_{G(e)}$ are in the same component as $s_R(e)$ and $t_R(e)$. (b) The source and the target node are in different components of R'. In any case, the nodes of $G(e)$ which are connected with $\text{begin}_{G(e)}$ are in the same component as $s_R(e)$ and all nodes of $G(e)$ which are connected with $\text{end}_{G(e)}$ are in the same component as $t_R(e)$. Different components in R' yield different components in G. Moreover, for an edge $e \in E_R$, the components in $G(e)$ which neither contain $\text{begin}_{G(e)}$ nor $\text{end}_{G(e)}$ yield additional components. Thus, $\text{comp}(R') + \sum_{e \in E_R} \text{newcomp}(G(e)) \leq \text{comp}(G)$ and $\text{newcomp}(R') + \sum_{e \in E_R} \text{newcomp}(G(e)) \leq \text{newcomp}(G)$. □

2. A General View of Compatible Functions

In this section we introduce the notion of compatible functions in such a way that all functions considered in the previous section are special cases. Roughly speaking, a function f_0 on hypergraphs is said to be compatible with the derivation process of hyperedge-replacement grammars if for each hypergraph H and each of its derivation, the value of H, $f_0(H)$, can be computed from the values of some specific subhypergraphs $H(e)$ determined by the fibres of the derivation. As the examples will show, this view is oversimplified for most applications. To compute the value of H, it might be necessary to compute the values of some other related functions for the $H(e)$'s. Therefore, we use families of functions indexed by some finite set I, and we need a mapping *assign* which determines the values for the $H(e)$'s with respect to the different value functions.

2.1 Definition (Compatible Functions [1])

1. Let $\mathcal{C} \subseteq \mathcal{HRG}$, I a finite index set, VAL a set of values, $f : \mathcal{H}_\mathcal{C} \times I \to VAL$ a function on pairs $(H, i) \in \mathcal{H}_\mathcal{C} \times I$ and f' a function on triples $(R, assign, i)$ with $R \in \mathcal{H}_\mathcal{C}$, $assign : E_R \times I \to VAL$, and $i \in I$ with values in VAL. Then f is called $(\mathcal{C}, f')$-compatible if for all $HRG = (N, T, P, Z) \in \mathcal{C}$ and all derivations of the form $A^\bullet \Longrightarrow R \stackrel{*}{\Longrightarrow} H$ with $A \in N \cup T$ and $H \in \mathcal{H}_T$, and for all $i \in I$,

$$f(H, i) = f'(R, assign, i)$$

where $assign : E_R \times I \to VAL$ is given by $assign(e, j) = f(H(e), j)$ ($e \in E_R$, $j \in I$).

2. A function $f_0 : \mathcal{H}_\mathcal{C} \to VAL$ is called $\mathcal{C}$-compatible if functions f and f' and an index i_0 exist such that f is $(\mathcal{C}, f')$-compatible and $f_0 = f(-, i_0)$. ($f(-, i_0)$ denotes the function given by $f(-, i_0)(H) = f(H, i_0)$ for all $H \in \mathcal{H}_\mathcal{C}$.)

Remark

1. Intuitively, a function is compatible if it can be computed for a large hypergraph derived by a fibre by computing some values for the smaller components of the corresponding shorter fibres. Such a function must be closed under isomorphisms because the derivability of hypergraphs is independent of the representation of nodes and hyperedges.

2. $\mathcal{C}$-compatibility is concerned with the productions of the grammars in $\mathcal{C}$ and not with their axioms. Therefore, we may assume that, for each $HRG = (N, T, P, Z) \in \mathcal{C}$ and each $Z' \in \mathcal{H}_\mathcal{C}$, $HRG' = (N, T, P, Z')$ is in the class $\mathcal{C}$ as well.

---

[1] All considered functions are assumed to be *closed under isomorphisms*, i.e., for a function f_0 defined on hypergraphs, if $H \cong H'$ for some $H, H' \in \mathcal{H}_\mathcal{C}$, then $f_0(H) = f_0(H')$.

2.2 Example (Compatible Functions)

1. Let $\mathcal{C} = \mathcal{HRG}$ be the class of all hyperedge-replacement grammars, $I = \{all, int\}$, $VAL = \mathbb{N}$, and f and f' be the functions given by

   - $f(H, all) = |V_H|$;
     $f(H, int) = |INT_H|$;
   - $f'(R, assign, all) = |V_R| + \sum_{e \in E_R} assign(e, int)$;
     $f'(R, assign, int) = |INT_R| + \sum_{e \in E_R} assign(e, int)$.

By theorem 4.1, we get $f(H, all) = f'(R, assign, all)$ and $f(H, int) = f'(R, assign, int)$ with $assign(e, j) = f(H(e), j)$ for $e \in E_R$ and $j \in I$. Therefore, the function f is $(\mathcal{HRG}, f')$-compatible and the function $f_0 = f(-, all)$ concerning

- the number of nodes

is $\mathcal{HRG}$-compatible. Furthermore, the following functions on hypergraphs are $\mathcal{HRG}$-compatible:

- the number of hyperedges,
- the size,
- the density of a hypergraph.

2. Let $\mathcal{C} = \mathcal{ERG}$ be the class of all edge-replacement grammars, $I = \{np\}$ the one-element set, $VAL = \mathbb{N}$, and f and f' be the functions given by

   - $f(G, np) = \text{numpath}(G)$;
   - $f'(R, assign, np) = \sum_{p \in PATH_R} \prod_{e \text{ on } p} assign(e, np)$.

By theorem 4.3, $f(G, np) = f'(R, assign, np)$ with $assign(e, np) = f(H(e), np)$ ($e \in E_R$). Therefore, the function f is $(\mathcal{ERG}, f')$-compatible and the function $f_0 = f(-, np)$ concerning

- the number of simple paths (connecting the external nodes)

is $\mathcal{ERG}$-compatible. Furthermore, by theorems 4.3-4.6, the following functions on (1,1)-graphs are $\mathcal{ERG}$-compatible:

- the minimum-path length (of paths connecting the external nodes);
- the maximum-simple-path length (of paths connecting the external nodes);
- the number of simple cycles;
- the minimum-cycle length;
- the maximum-simple-cycle length;
- the minimum degree;
- the maximum degree;
- the number of components of a graph.

The notion of compatible functions generalizes our notion of compatible predicates (see chapter VI). More interesting, a certain type of compatible functions that are composed of minima, maxima, sums, and products induce compatible predicates of the form: the function value of a graph exceeds a given fixed integer, or the function value does not exceed a fixed integer. Consequently, we get the decidability of the problems (1) and (2) of chapter VI for these predicates as a corollary.

2.3 Definition (Special Compatible Functions)

1. A function $f : \mathcal{H}_\mathcal{C} \times I \to \mathbb{N}^\circ$ is said to be $(\mathcal{C}, \min, \max, +, \cdot)$-*compatible* if there exists a function f' such that f is $(\mathcal{C}, f')$-compatible and for each right-hand side R of some production in $\mathcal{C}$ and each $i \in I$, $f'(R, -, i)$ corresponds to an expression formed with variables $assign(e, j)$ ($e \in E_R$, $j \in I$) and constants from $\mathbb{N}$ by addition, multiplication, minimum, and maximum. The function f is $(\mathcal{C}, \max, +, \cdot)$-*compatible* if the operation min does not occur.

2. A function $f_0 : \mathcal{H}_\mathcal{C} \to \mathbb{N}^\circ$ is $(\mathcal{C}, \min, \max, +, \cdot)$-*compatible* if a function f and an index i_0 exist such that f is $(\mathcal{C}, \min, \max, +, \cdot)$-compatible and $f_0 = f(-, i_0)$. Accordingly, the function f_0 is $(\mathcal{C}, \max, +, \cdot)$-*compatible* if f is $(\mathcal{C}, \max, +, \cdot)$-compatible.

2.4 Theorem (Compatible Predicates Induce Compatible Functions)

Let $PROP_0$ be a $\mathcal{C}$-compatible predicate. Then the function $f_0 : \mathcal{H}_\mathcal{C} \to \mathbb{N}^\circ$ given by

$$f_0(H) = \begin{cases} 1 & \text{if } PROP_0(H) \text{ holds} \\ 0 & \text{otherwise} \end{cases}$$

is $(\mathcal{C}, \max, +, \cdot)$-compatible.

Proof

Let $PROP_0$ be a $\mathcal{C}$-compatible predicate, $PROP$, $PROP'$ the corresponding predicates, I the corresponding index set, and i_0 the index such that $PROP_0 = PROP(-, i_0)$. Then we define functions f, f' as follows.

$$f(H, i) = \begin{cases} 1 & \text{if } PROP(H, i) \text{ holds} \\ 0 & \text{otherwise}; \end{cases}$$

$$f'(R, assign', i) = \begin{cases} 1 & \text{if } PROP'(R, assign, i) \text{ holds for some } assign : E_R \to I \\ & \text{with } assign'(e, assign(e)) = 1 \text{ for all } e \in E_R \\ 0 & \text{otherwise.} \end{cases}$$

Obviously, $f_0(H) = f(H, i_0)$. Hence it remains to show that f is $(\mathcal{C}, f')$-compatible. Let $H \in \mathcal{H}_T$, $A^\bullet \Longrightarrow R \stackrel{*}{\Longrightarrow} H$ be a derivation of H in HRG, and for $e \in E_R$, $l_R(e)^\bullet \stackrel{*}{\Longrightarrow} H(e)$ be the fibre of $R \stackrel{*}{\Longrightarrow} H$ induced by e.

If $f(H, i) = 1$, then $PROP(H, i)$ is satisfied. By the $(\mathcal{C}, PROP')$-compatibility of $PROP$, there is a mapping $assign : E_R \to I$ such that $PROP'(R, assign, i)$ and

$PROP(H(e), assign(e))$ for $e \in E_R$ hold. Thus, $f(H(e), assign(e)) = 1$ for all $e \in E_R$. Define now $assign' : E_R \times I \to \mathbb{N}^\diamond$ by $assign'(e, j) = f(H(e), j)$ for $e \in E_R$ and $j \in I$. Then $f'(R, assign', i) = 1$.

Conversely, if $f'(R, assign', i) = 1$ with $assign'(e, j) = f(H(e), j)$ for $e \in E_R$ and $j \in I$, then there is a mapping $assign : E_R \to I$ such that $PROP'(R, assign, i)$ holds and $f(H(e), assign(e)) = 1$ for $e \in E_R$. By definition of f, $PROP(H(e), assign(e))$ holds for $e \in E_R$. Now the $(\mathcal{C}, PROP')$-compatibility of $PROP$ implies that $PROP(H, i)$ holds. Thus, $f(H, i) = 1$.

Now $f(H, i) = f'(R, assign', i)$ where $assign'(e, j) = f(H(e), j)$ for $e \in E_R$ and $i \in I$, i.e. f is $(\mathcal{C}, f')$-compatible. Moreover, $f'(R, assign', i)$ can be expressed as follows:

$$\max\left\{0, \max_{assign \in ASSIGN} \prod_{e \in E_R} assign'(e, assign(e))\right\}$$

where $ASSIGN = \{assign : E_R \to I | PROP'(R, assign, i) \text{ is satisfied}\}$. Hence, the function f is $(\mathcal{C}, \max, +, \cdot)$-compatible. □

2.5 Theorem (Compatible Functions Induce Compatible Predicates)

Let $f_0 : \mathcal{H}_\mathcal{C} \to \mathbb{N}^\diamond$ be a $(\mathcal{C}, \min, \max, +, \cdot)$-compatible function and $n \in \mathbb{N}^\diamond$ [2]. Then the predicate $PROP_0$ given for $H \in \mathcal{H}_\mathcal{C}$ by

$$PROP_0(H) \iff f_0(H) \leq n$$

is $\mathcal{C}$-compatible.

Proof

Let $f_0 : \mathcal{H}_\mathcal{C} \to \mathbb{N}^\diamond$ be a $(\mathcal{C}, \min, \max, +, \cdot)$-compatible function, f and f' the corresponding functions, I the corresponding index set, and i_0 the index such that $f_0 = f(-, i_0)$. Let $J = \{0, 1, \ldots, n\} + \{\diamond, big\}$ for $n \in \mathbb{N}$ and $J = \{\diamond, big\}$ for $n = \diamond$. Moreover, let $[-] : \mathbb{N}^\diamond \to J$ be the mapping with $[m] = big$ for $m > n$ and $[m] = m$ otherwise.

Now we define a new index set $\hat{I}$ and predicates $PROP$, $PROP'$ as follows.

- $\hat{I} = [I \to J]$ (the set of all mappings from I to J);
- $PROP(H, p) \iff [f(H, i)] = p(i)$ for $i \in I$;
- $PROP'(R, assign, p) \iff [f'(R, assign', i)] = p(i)$ for all $assign' : E_R \times I \to \mathbb{N}^\diamond$ with $[assign'(e, i)] = assign(e)(i)$ ($e \in E_R$, $i \in I$) and all $i \in I$.

Then $PROP$ is $(\mathcal{C}, PROP')$-compatible. This may be seen as follows.

First, let $PROP(H, p)$ be satisfied. Then we have $[f(H, i)] = p(i)$ for $i \in I$. By the $(\mathcal{C}, f')$-compatibility of f, $[f'(R, assign', i)] = [f(H, i)] = p(i)$ for $i \in I$ where

---

[2] We assume that for $n \in \mathbb{N}^\diamond$, $\diamond \leq n$.

$assign'(e,j) = f(H(e), j)$ for $e \in E_R$ and $j \in I$. Now choose $assign : E_R \to [I \to J]$ by $assign(e)(j) = [f(H(e),j)]$. Then $PROP(H(e), assign(e))$ holds for all $e \in E_R$. By the monotonicity of minimum, maximum, addition, and multiplication, we obtain $[f'(R, assign'', i)] = p(i)$ for all mappings $assign'' : E_R \times I \to {I\!\!N}^\circ$ with $[assign''(e,j)] = assign(e)(j)$ ($e \in E_R, j \in I$). Thus, $PROP'(R, assign, p)$ is satisfied.

Conversely, let $assign : E_R \to [I \to J]$ be a mapping such that $PROP'(R, assign, p)$ and $PROP(H(e), assign(e))$ for $e \in E_R$ hold. By the $(\mathcal{C}, f')$-compatibility of f, we have $f(H, i) = f'(R, assign', i)$ where $assign'(e, j) = f(H(e), j)$ for $e \in E_R$ and $j \in I$. By the definition of $PROP$, $[f(H(e), j)] = assign(e)(j)$ for all $e \in E_R$ and all $j \in I$. By the definition of $PROP'$, $[f'(R, assign', i)] = p(i)$ for all $i \in I$. Thus, $[f(H, i)] = [f'(R, assign', i)] = p(i)$ for all $i \in I$, i.e., $PROP(H, p)$ is satisfied.

Thus, $PROP$ is $(\mathcal{C}, PROP')$-compatible and for each $p \in [I \to J]$, the predicate $PROP(-, p)$ is $\mathcal{C}$-compatible. Furthermore, for $H \in \mathcal{H}_\mathcal{C}$,

$$PROP_0(H) \iff \bigvee_{p \in [I \to J] \text{ with } p(i_0) \leq n} PROP(H, p).$$

Since for $p \in [I \to J]$, the predicate $PROP(-, p)$ is $\mathcal{C}$-compatible and $\mathcal{C}$-compatible predicates are closed under disjunctions (see chapter VI, section 2), the predicate $PROP_0$ is $\mathcal{C}$-compatible. □

2.6 Corollary (Metatheorem for Decision Problems)

Let f_0 be $(\mathcal{C}, \min, \max, +, \cdot)$-compatible for some class $\mathcal{C}$ of hyperedge-replacement grammars and $n \in {I\!\!N}^\circ$. Then for all $HRG \in \mathcal{C}$ it is decidable whether
(1) $f_0(H) \leq n$ holds for some $H \in L(HRG)$;
(2) $f_0(H) \leq n$ holds for all $H \in L(HRG)$.

Proof

Corollary 2.6 follows immediately from the $\mathcal{C}$-compatibility of the predicate $PROP_0$ given for $H \in \mathcal{H}_\mathcal{C}$ by $PROP_0(H) \iff f_0(H) \leq n$ and the metatheorem for decision problems presented in chapter VI, section 4. □

Remark

Analogous statements hold for the relations $<$, $=$, $\geq$, and $>$.

3. A Metatheorem for Boundedness Problems

Given a graph-theoretic function f_0 and a class $\mathcal{C}$ of hyperedge-replacement grammars, we are going to study the following type of questions for all $HRG \in \mathcal{C}$: "Is it decidable whether the values of all hypergraphs generated by HRG are bounded?" The question turns out to be decidable provided that f_0 is $(\mathcal{C}, \max, +, \cdot)$-compatible. We call this result "metatheorem" because of its generic character: Whenever one can prove the $(\mathcal{C}, \max, +, \cdot)$-compatibility of a function (and we have given various examples in section 2), one gets a particular decision result for this function as corollary of the metatheorem.

3.1 Theorem (Metatheorem for Boundedness Problems)

Let f_0 be a $(\mathcal{C}, \max, +, \cdot)$-compatible function for some class $\mathcal{C}$ of hyperedge-replacement grammars. Then, for all $HRG \in \mathcal{C}$, it is decidable whether or not there is a natural number $n \in I\!N$ such that $f_0(H) \leq n$ for all $H \in L(HRG)$.

Proof [1]

Let f_0 be a $(\mathcal{C}, \max, +, \cdot)$-compatible function. Let f and f' be the corresponding functions over the index set I so that f is $(\mathcal{C}, f')$-compatible and $f_0 = f(-, i_0)$ for some index $i_0 \in I$. Let $HRG = (N, T, P, Z)$ be a completely typed and well-formed hyperedge-replacement grammar in $\mathcal{C}$. Moreover, we may assume that, for each $A \in N$, the grammar $HRG(A) = (N, T, P, A^\bullet)$ is in $\mathcal{C}$ as well (compare remark 2.1.2).

The proof is based on the following idea. We construct a directed graph D containing all relevant information on derivations in HRG and look for certain cyclic structures in D. This enables us to decide whether or not the values may grow beyond any bound.

We need first some auxiliary notions. Let $J = \{\diamond, 0, 1, big\}$ and $[-] : I\!N^\circ \to J$ be the mapping given by $[m] = big$ if $m \geq 2$ and $[m] = m$ otherwise. Given a symbol $A \in N$ and a mapping $p : I \to J$, a hypergraph $H \in \mathcal{H}_T$ is said to be an (A, p)-*hypergraph* if there is a derivation $A^\bullet \stackrel{*}{\Longrightarrow} H$ of H such that $[f(H, i)] = p(i)$ for all $i \in I$. By corollary 2.6, we can effectively determine the set

$$EXIST = \{(A, p)|\ \text{there exists an } (A, p)\text{-hypergraph }\}.$$

Furthermore, we need a function f'' which is derived from f' and is defined on hypergraphs R, functions $q : E_R \times I \to J$, and indices $i \in I$ by

$$f''(R, q, i) = [f'(R, assign, i)]$$

for some $assign : E_R \times I \to I\!N^\circ$ with $[assign(e, j)] = q(e, j)$. f'' is always defined because $assign$ can be chosen as $assign(e, j) = q(e, j)$ if $q(e, j) \in \{\diamond, 0, 1\}$ and $assign(e, j) = 2$ otherwise. The well-definedness of f'' follows from the fact that

---

[1] The proof stems from W. Vogler and can be found in [HKV 91].

$[f'(R, assign, i)] = [f'(R, assign', i)]$ if $[assign(e, j)] = [assign'(e, j)]$ for $e \in E_R$, $j \in I$ which holds for $(\mathcal{C}, \min, \max, +, \cdot)$-compatible functions.

By assumption, the function f is $(\mathcal{C}, \max, +, \cdot)$-compatible. Since multiplication distributes over addition and maximum and addition distributes over maximum, we may assume that $f'(R, -, i)$ is a maximum of sums, each formed from products of constants and variables $assign(e, j)$ ($e \in E_R$, $j \in I$). Substituting $assign(e, j)$ by $q(e, j)$, if $q(e, j) \in \{\diamond, 0, 1\}$, that means that the variables $assign(e, j)$ are kept as variables if $q(e, j) = big$, and simplifying the expression, i.e. deleting all sums that evaluate to $\diamond$, all products that evaluate to 0 and all factors that evaluate to 1, we obtain an expression $EXP(f'(R, -, i), q)$ formed as s a maximum of sums where each sum is a product of constants and variables $assign(e, j)$ ($e \in E_R$, $j \in I$), again. Let $SIMPLE(f'(R, -, i), q)$ denote the set of all $assign(e, j)$ for which one sum in $EXP(f'(R, -, i), q)$ simply is $assign(e, j)$ and $NONTRIVIAL(f'(R, -, i), q)$ denote the set of all $assign(e, j)$ for which some sum in $EXP(f'(R, -, i), q)$ contains $assign(e, j)$, but also a non-trivial factor or some other product.

We can now define the directed graph D. As node set of D we choose

$$V = \{(A, p, i) | (A, p) \in EXIST \text{ and } p(i) = big\}.$$

The set of edges of D contains two types of edges, greaterequal-edges and greater-edges, which can be given as follows. For nodes (A, p, i) and (B, p', j) there is *greaterequal-edge* [or *greater-edge*] connecting (A, p, i) and (B, p', j), denoted by $(A, p, i) \Rightarrow (B, p', j)$ [or $(A, p, i) \rightarrow (B, p', j)$] if there is a production $(A, R) \in P$ and a mapping $q : E_R \times I \rightarrow J$ such that, $p = f''(R, q, -)$, for all $e \in E_R$, $(l_R(e), q(e, -)) \in EXIST$, and there exists an $e \in E_R$ such that $l_R(e) = B$, $q(e, -) = p'$, and $assign(e, j) \in SIMPLE(f'(R, -, i), q)$ [or $assign(e, j) \in NONTRIVIAL(f'(R, -, i), q)$].

In the following, we will show that the graph D contains all information to decide whether or not some function values grow beyond any bound. It turns out that the greater-edges of D play an important role. Remember that for each (B, p', j) in D, there is at least one derivation $B^\bullet \stackrel{*}{\Rightarrow} G$ in HRG with $[f(G, -)] = p'$ and $f(G, j) \geq 2$. We will show that, whenever we have a derivation $B^\bullet \stackrel{*}{\Rightarrow} G$ in HRG with $[f(G, -)] = p'$ and $f(G, j) \geq 2$ and there is a greater-edge $(A, p, i) \rightarrow (B, p', j)$ in D, then there exists a derivation $A^\bullet \stackrel{*}{\Rightarrow} H$ in HRG with $[f(H, -)] = p$ and $f(H, i) > f(G, j)$.

Claim 1. Let (A, p, i) and (B, p', j) be nodes in D and G be a (B, p')-hypergraph.
(a) If $(A, p, i) \rightarrow (B, p', j)$, then $f(H, i) > f(G, j)$ for some (A, p)-hypergraph H.
(b) If $(A, p, i) \Rightarrow (B, p', j)$, then $f(H, i) \geq f(G, j)$ for some (A, p)-hypergraph H.

Proof of claim 1. Let $(A, p, i) \rightarrow (B, p', j)$ be a greater-edge in D and G be an arbitrary (B, p')-hypergraph. By construction of D, there is some production $(A, R) \in P$ and some $q : E_R \times I \rightarrow J$ such that, for all $e \in E_R$, $(l_R(e), q(e, -)) \in EXIST$. Moreover, there is some $e' \in E_R$ with $l_R(e') = B$ and $q(e', -) = p'$. By definition of $EXIST$, for each $e \in E_R$, there exists a derivation $l_R(e)^\bullet \stackrel{*}{\Rightarrow} H(e)$ such that $[f(H(e), -)] = q(e, -)$.

Since $l_R(e') = B$ and G is an (B, p')-hypergraph, there exists a derivation $l_R(e')^\bullet \overset{*}{\Rightarrow} G$ such that $[f(G,-)] = p'$. Joint Embedding of the derivations $l_R(e)^\bullet \overset{*}{\Rightarrow} H(e)$ for $e \in E_R - \{e'\}$ and the derivation $l_R(e')^\bullet \overset{*}{\Rightarrow} G$ — instead of $l_R(e')^\bullet \overset{*}{\Rightarrow} H(e')$ — into R yields a derivation $R \overset{*}{\Rightarrow} H$. Combining it with the direct derivation $A^\bullet \Rightarrow R$, we get a derivation $A^\bullet \overset{*}{\Rightarrow} H$. By the $(\mathcal{C}, \max, +, \cdot)$-compatibility of f, H is an (A, p)-hypergraph: Let $assign$ and $assign'$ be defined by $assign(e, -) = f(H(e), -)$ for $e \in E_R$, $assign'(e', -) = f(G, -)$ and $assign'(e, -) = f(H(e), -)$ otherwise. Then we have $[f(H, -)] = [f'(R, assign', -)] = f''(R, [assign'], -) = f''(R, [assign], -) = f''(R, q,)= p$. Moreover, by the special choice of the edges of D, $f(H, i) = f'(R, assign', i) > assign'(e', j) = f(G, j)$. [Observe that in the sum leading to the creation of $(A, p, i) \to (B, p', j)$ all remaining variables are substituted by at least 2.] Analogously, if $(A, p, i) \Rightarrow (B, p', j)$ is a greaterequal-edge in D, we get $f(H, i) \geq f(G, j)$.

In the following, we will look for special structures in D, called lasso structures. A subgraph L of D is called a *lasso structure* if it contains for each node a unique outgoing edge and each cycle contains a greater-edge. A node (A, p, i) of D is said to be *unbounded*, if, for all $n \in \mathbb{N}$, there is an (A, p)-hypergraph H with $f(H, i) > n$; otherwise it is said to be *bounded*.

Claim 2. Let L be a lasso structure in D. Then every (A, p, i) in L is unbounded.

Proof of claim 2. Assume to the contrary and let k be minimal such that, for some (A, p, i) in L, for every (A, p)-hypergraph H we have $f(H, i) \leq k$. By the above claim we have for the unique successor (B, p', j) of (A, p, i) in L and every (B, p')-hypergraph G that $f(G, j) \leq k$. By choice of k, there must exist a (B, p')-hypergraph G with $f(G, j) = k$ and we have $(A, p, i) \Rightarrow (B, p', j)$. Repeating this consideration we eventually get a lasso [13] in L whose cycle has greaterequal-edges only, a contradiction.

Claim 3. There exists a lasso structure L in D containing all unbounded (A, p, i).

Proof of claim 3. Let k be the maximal $f(H, i)$, where H is an (A, p)-hypergraph with derivation $A^\bullet \Rightarrow R \overset{*}{\Rightarrow} H$ such that (A, p, i) is bounded, but at least 2. Moreover, let $\Phi(k) = f'(R, ass_k, i) + 1$ where $ass_k(-, -) = k$. Then we define a subgraph L of D iteratively using sets OK and NOK, such that the following properties hold after each step:

(1) $OK \cup NOK = \{(A, p, i) \in V | (A, p, i) \text{ is unbounded}\}$;
(2) $OK \cap NOK = \emptyset$;
(3) $OK \subseteq V_L \subseteq OK \cup NOK$;
(4) each node in OK has a unique outgoing edge in L;
(5) each cycle of L contains a greater-edge;
(6) each maximal path of L ends with a greater-edge [14].

---

[13] If we add to a path $v_1 \ldots v_n$, which has distinct nodes by definition, an edge $v_n v_i$, $i \subset \{1, \ldots, n-1\}$, then the resulting graph is called a *lasso*.

[14] We call a path *maximal*, if its last node has outdegree 0.

Initially, let $OK = \emptyset$, $NOK = \{(A,p,i) \in V | (A,p,i)$ is unbounded$\}$, and L be the empty graph. For the iteration step, choose a derivation $A^\bullet \overset{*}{\Longrightarrow} H$ of minimal length such that H is an (A,p)-hypergraph with $f(H,i) \geq \Phi(k)$ and $(A,p,i) \in NOK$. Let (A,R) be the first production of this derivation. We have hypergraphs $H(e)$, $e \in E_R$, and some $q : E_R \times I \to J$ such that $H(e)$ is an $(l_R(e), q(e,-))$-hypergraph for $e \in E_R$. $f'(R,-,i)$ in its simplified normal form is a maximum of sums, and, by definition of k and Φ, the maximum is attained for a sum containing a variable $assign(e,j)$ such that $f(H(e),j) > k$. Put $(B,p',j) = (l_R(e), q(e,-), j)$, $OK = OK \cup \{(A,p,i)\}$, $NOK = NOK - \{(A,p,i)\}$, add to L the corresponding edge from (A,p,i) to (B,p',j) and — if necessary — (A,p,i) and/or (B,p',j). The first four conditions on L given above hold true (we have $f(H(e),j) > k$, therefore, $(B,p',j) \in OK \cup NOK$). If the new edge is a greater-edge, then each new cycle contains it, each new non-trivial maximal path ends with it $((B,p',j) \notin OK)$ or ends with a non-trivial maximal path that already existed $((B,p',j) \in OK)$. If the new edge is a greaterequal-edge, we must have $f(H(e),j) \geq \Phi(k)$, thus $(B,p',j) \in OK$, since we have chosen a shortest derivation. Hence any new non-trivial maximal path ends with an old one starting at (B,p',j). If there are new cycles, then we already had $(A,p,i) \in V_L$ and any edge leading to (A,p,i) is a greater-edge. Since the set $\{(A,p,i) \in V | (A,p,i)$ is unbounded$\}$ is finite, the construction is finished after a finite number of steps. After these steps, $OK = \{(A,p,i) \in V | (A,p,i)$ is unbounded$\}$ and $NOK = \emptyset$. Moreover, by (3), (4), and (5), $V_L = OK$, each node of L has a unique outgoing edge in L, and each cycle of L contains a greater-edge. Consequently, the constructed L is a lasso structure and, since $V_L = \{(A,p,i) \in V | (A,p,i)$ is unbounded$\}$, L contains all unbounded (A,p,i).

Now we may proceed as follows:

(1) Construct the graph D for HRG.
(2) Check for each subgraph of D whether it is a lasso structure.
(3) Check for each lasso structure L whether it contains $(l(Z), p, i_0)$ for some p.

If there is a lasso structure L in D containing $(l(Z), p, i_0)$ (for some p), then, by claim 2, $(l(Z), p, i_0)$ is unbounded, meaning that, for all $n \in \mathbb{N}$, there is an $(l(Z), p)$-hypergraph H with $f(H, i_0) > n$. Hence, for all $n \in \mathbb{N}$, there is a hypergraph $H \in L(HRG)$ with $f_0(H) > n$. Conversely, if for all $n \in \mathbb{N}$, there is a hypergraph $H \in L(HRG)$ with $f_0(H) > n$, then, for all $n \in \mathbb{N}$, there is a p and an $(l(Z), p)$-hypergraph H with $f(H, i_0) > n$. Since the number of p's is finite, we can find some p such that, for all $n \in \mathbb{N}$, there is an $(l(Z), p)$-hypergraph H with $f(H, i_0) > n$. Therefore, $(l(Z), p, i_0)$ is unbounded and, by claim 3, there exists a lasso structure containing $(l(Z), p, i_0)$. This completes the proof of the theorem. □

Combining the compatibility results of section 2 and theorem 3.1, one obtains a list of decidability results concerning boundedness problems.

3.2 Corollary

For each edge-replacement grammar ERG and each function in the following list, it is decidable whether (or not) the function values of the graphs in $L(ERG)$ grow beyond any bound.
- the number of nodes;
- the number of edges;
- the size;
- the number of simple paths (connecting the external nodes);
- the number of simple cycles;
- the maximum-simple-path length (of paths connecting the external nodes),
- the maximum-simple-cycle length;
- the maximum degree;
- the number of components of a graph.

Proof

The first eight statements follow directly from the theorems in section 1 and the metatheorem for boundedness problems. The last statement follows from theorem 1.6 and the metatheorem as follows. Theorem 1.6 makes use of $\text{comp}(R')$ and $\text{newcomp}(R')$ where R' is obtained from R by removing the edges $e \in E_R$ for which $\text{numpath}(G(e)) = 0$. It can be shown that $\text{comp}(R')$ and $\text{newcomp}(R')$ can be expressed as maxima of products. Let $\text{bec}, \text{nbec} : \mathcal{G}_C \to \mathbb{N}^\diamond$ be the functions defined by $\text{bec}(G) = 1$ if there is a path from $begin_G$ to end_G, $\text{bec}(G) = 0$ otherwise, and $\text{nbec}(G) = 1 - \text{bec}(G)$. By results of [HKV 89] and theorem 2.4, these functions are $(\mathcal{ERG}, \max, +, \cdot)$-compatible, and, thus, we may use $\text{bec}(G(e))$ and $\text{nbec}(G(e))$ when giving a formula for $\text{comp}(R')$ and $\text{newcomp}(R')$. Let, for $E \subseteq E_R$, $<E>$ denote the spanning subgraph of R with edge set E. Then

$$\text{comp}(R') = \max_{E \subseteq E_R} [\prod_{e \in E} \text{bec}(G(e)) \cdot \prod_{e \in E_R - E} \text{nbec}(G(e))] \cdot \text{comp}(<E>);$$

$$\text{newcomp}(R') = \max_{E \subseteq E_R} [\prod_{e \in E} \text{bec}(G(e)) \cdot \prod_{e \in E_R - E} \text{nbec}(G(e))] \cdot \text{newcomp}(<E>).$$

(Observe that the product of products gives 1 for exactly one E, namely the one that induces R', and 0 otherwise. Furthermore, $\text{comp}(<E>)$ and $\text{newcomp}(<E>)$ are constants.) □

Remark

1. Remember that the functions concerning the number of nodes, the number of hyperedges, and the size are $(\mathcal{HRG}, \max, +, \cdot)$-compatible.
2. Although we avoided the troublesome technicalities, we are convinced that the other considerations of this section work for more general types of hyperedge-replacement grammars as well. For example, all the statements should hold even if the class $\mathcal{ERG}$

is replaced by the class of all hyperedge-replacement grammars which generate ordinary graph languages and use hyperedges with a bounded number of tentacles as nonterminals. We even think that the considered functions are compatible for arbitrary hyperedge-replacement grammars if their definition is properly adapted to hypergraphs.

Let us mention that some problems — like the connectivity problem, the maximum-clique-size problem, and the chromatic-number problem — are trivial in the following sense: for all hyperedge-replacement grammars HRG, there is a bound (depending only on HRG) such that the function values of all graphs do not exceed the bound. This knowledge can be used to show that other boundedness problems — as the minimum-clique-covering problem and the maximum-indepentent-set problem — are decidable.

The *clique partition number* of a graph G, cliquepart(G), is the smallest number of cliques that form a partition of the node set V_G. A set of nodes in a graph G is *independent* if no two of them are adjacent. The largest number of nodes in such a set is called the *independence number* of G and is denoted by indep(G).

3.3 Theorem

For each hyperedge-replacement grammar $HRG \in \mathcal{HRG}$ generating a set of graphs, it is decidable whether the clique partition number cliquepart(G) and the independence number indep(G) of graphs G in $L(HRG)$ grows beyond any bound.

Proof

Since for each hyperedge-replacement grammar HRG, the maximum clique size is bounded in $L(HRG)$, say by cliquesize(HRG) ≥ 1, and for each $G \in L(HRG)$,

$$\frac{|V_G|}{\text{cliquesize}(HRG)} \leq \text{cliquepart}(G) \leq |V_G|,$$

the clique partition number is bounded in $L(HRG)$ if and only if the number of nodes is bounded in $L(HRG)$. Since for each hyperedge-replacement grammar HRG, the chromatic number is bounded in $L(HRG)$, say by chrom(HRG) ≥ 1 for each $H \in L(HRG)$, the maximum number of equally colored nodes in a chrom(HRG)-coloring of G, maxc(G), is a lower bound of indep(G). On the other hand, $|V_G| \leq$ chrom(HRG) $\cdot$ maxc(G). Thus,

$$\frac{|V_G|}{\text{chrom}(HRG)} \leq \text{indep}(G) \leq |V_G|.$$

Therefore, the independence number is bounded in $L(HRG)$ if and only if the number of nodes is bounded on $L(HRG)$. □

4. Unsolvable Boundedness Problems

Certainly, there are Boundedness Problems where theorem 3.1 fails. For example, we can give a function for which the corresponding Boundedness Problem is undecidable.

4.1 Theorem
Let $\mathcal{C} \subseteq \mathcal{HRG}$ be a class of hyperedge-replacement grammars such that each edge-replacement grammar with a single nonterminal is in $\mathcal{C}$. Let $\text{nod}' : \mathcal{H}_\mathcal{C} \to I\!N$ be the function with $\text{nod}'(H) = |V_H|$ if H has a non-trivial automorphism group and $\text{nod}'(H) = 0$ otherwise. Then it is undecidable whether, for a given $HRG \in \mathcal{C}$, nod' grows beyond any bound.

Proof
For each context-free string grammar $CFG = (N, T, P, S)$ without λ-productions, we obtain an edge-replacement grammar $CFG' = (N', T', P', Z')$ as follows. Let

- $N' = N \cup T$;
- $T' = \{a' | a \in T\}$;
- $P' = \{(A, w^\bullet) \mid (A, w) \in P\} \cup \{(a, R(a)) \mid a \in T\}$
  where for $a \in T$, $R(a)$ denotes the (1,1)-graph with two parallel edges in opposite directions each labeled with a';
- $Z' = S^\bullet$.

Then the function values of the graphs in $L(CFG')$ grow beyond any bound if and only if $L(CFG)$ contains palindromes of unbounded length. A well-known application of the Post Correspondence Problem (PCP) shows that it is undecidable whether a context-free string grammar generates a palindrome. This application involves context-free string grammars with one nonterminal which generate palindromes of unbounded length if they generate a palindrome at all. □

5. Related Research

In this chapter, we have been able to show that the Boundedness Problem is solvable for classes of hyperedge-replacement grammars and functions that are compatible with the derivation process and where the values of derivable graphs are composed of maxima, sums, and products of component values. Related research can be found in the literature.

In [JRW 86], Janssens, Rozenberg, and Welzl show that is it decidable for all graph languages $L(GG)$ generated by a node-label-controlled graph grammar GG, whether there is a bound n such that $\text{degree}(G) \leq n$ for all $G \in L(GG)$.

In [CM 92], Courcelle and Mosbah, present a systematic investigation of evaluations, i.e., functions that associate which every graph a value in some set VAL, say {true, false}, $I\!N$, $I\!R$, $\mathcal{P}(I\!N)$. The central result of their paper is the description, in a uniform way, of a large class of compatible evaluations. This is done in a formalism that associates logic and algebra, or more precisely, monadic second-order logic and semiring homomorphisms.

In [Se 92], Seidl investigates cost functions for tree automata and shows that for suitable semirings, it is decidable in polynimial time whether or not the costs of accepting computations is bounded. His theorems give efficient versions of the metatheorem for boundedness problems proving that boundedness of costs is decidable. The result presented in this chapter is somewhat stronger by allowing not only polynomials where $+$ and $\cdot$ or max and $+$ but also polynomials where all three operatores max, $+$, and $\cdot$ occur.

In [HK 92], Habel and Kuske present pumping lemmata for hyperedge-replacement graph languages which can be used to solve the boundedness problems with respect to the functions maxpath and minpath, assigning the maximum and the minimum length of a simple path to a graph, respectively. Roughly speaking, these lemmata say that every graph of a hyperedge-replacement language with a sufficiently large function value can be pumped up, so that each pumping step increases the function value and the result of pumping is a graph of the language. Therefore, the boundedness problems with respect to maxpath and minpath may be reduced to the problems whether there exists a graph in the hyperedge-replacement language with sufficiently large function value.

Although the metatheorem for boundedness problems applies to a variety of examples it seems to be strangely restricted. Further research should clarify the situation:

(1) We would expect that the metatheorem holds under more general or modified assumptions. In particular, we would like to know how functions given by minima or differences or divisions work.
(2) We suspect that certain combinations of arithmetic operations are not allowed. For instance, maxima and minima seem to antagonize each other — at least sometimes.
(3) Compatible functions are defined for arbitrary domains. But we have obtained significant results only for boolean and integer values. What about other domains? How can arbitrary compatibility be exploited? How do other meaningful interpretations look like?

6. Bibliographic Note

The results presented in this chapter can be found [HKV 91]. A method for solving Boundedness Problems by Pumping Lemmata will be published in [HK 92].

Chapter VIII

Extensions and Variations of HRG's

In this chapter, extensions and variations of hyperedge-replacement grammars are considered. On the one hand, one may change over to arbitrary hypergraph-replacement grammars in which hypergraphs (not only hyperedges) are replaced. On the other hand, one may equip hyperedge-replacement grammars (as well as hypergraph-replacement grammars) with application conditions or may pass over to parallel hyperedge-replacement grammars. Beside these extensions, one may modify hyperedge-replacement grammars in such a way that the generated objects are no longer hypergraphs but 2-dimensional line figures.

In section 1, hypergraph-replacement grammars in the sense of the "Berlin approach" to graph grammars (see, e.g., [EPS 73, Ro 75a, Eh 79, Kr 87b]) are considered. As in formal language theory, one may define "monotone", "context-sensitive", and "context-free" grammars. Using the same techniques as in the string case for Chomsky grammars one can show that the membership problem is not decidable for arbitrary hypergraph grammars (corresponding to type 0 grammars) but it is decidable for monotone hypergraph grammars. Somewhat surprisingly, monotone hypergraph grammars are more powerful than context-sensitive ones. Context-free hypergraph grammars turn out to be equivalent to hyperedge-replacement grammars. In this sense, hypergraph-replacement grammars generalize hyperedge-replacement grammars. In section 2, hypergraph-replacement grammars are extended by a very general notion of application conditions which can be defined separately for each production. In addition to the general concept, we study some special cases of hypergraph grammars with application conditions with respect to their generative power. In section 3, parallel hyperedge-replacement grammars — closely related to ETOL systems — are discussed. Finally, in section 4, hyperedge-replacement grammars are equipped with layout information. Therefore, the generated graphs and hypergraphs can easily be displayed as 2-dimensional (or likewise as 3-dimensional) patterns on a "screen", which is given by a layout of the initial hypergraph. In this way, the well studied graph-grammar approach of hyperedge-replacement grammars can be utilized to produce pretty patterns.

1. Hypergraph-Replacement Grammars

This section generalizes hyperedge-replacement grammars to arbitrary hypergraph-replacement grammars which can be seen as a hypergraph version of the "Berlin" graph-grammar approach (see, e.g., Ehrig [Eh 79] and Kreowski [Kr 87b]).

Informally, the approach works as follows: A hypergraph production $p = (L \supseteq K \subseteq R)$ consists of two hypergraphs L and R and a corresponding interface hypergraph K (also called gluing hypergraph) which relates some nodes and hyperedges of L to nodes and hyperedges in R. To apply a production $p = (L \supseteq K \subseteq R)$ to a hypergraph H we have to specify L as a subhypergraph of H and to make sure that the following contact condition is satisfied: Each contact node is a gluing node, where a contact node is a node in L which is source or target of a tentacle of a hyperedge in H not belonging to L. The application of a production $p = (L \supseteq K \subseteq R)$ to a hypergraph H leads to a derived hypergraph H' which can be obtained from H with specific subhypergraph L satisfying the contact condition in the following way:

- Remove all nodes and hyperedges of L which are not gluing items in H to obtain the persistent hypergraph D (which becomes a hypergraph by the contact condition).
- Add all nodes and hyperedges of R which are not gluing items — the gluing items are already in L and hence in D — such that R becomes a subhypergraph of the resulting hypergraph H'.

1.1 Definition (Productions and Derivations)

1. A *hypergraph production* $p = (L \supseteq K \subseteq R)$ consists of two hypergraphs L and R, called the *left-hand side* and the *right-hand side* of p, respectively, and an auxiliary hypergraph K, called the *gluing hypergraph*, satisfying $K \subseteq L$ and $K \subseteq R$.
2. Let H, H' be hypergraphs and $p = (L \supseteq K \subseteq R)$ be a production. Then H *directly derives* H' by p if H' is isomorphic to the hypergraph X constructed in the following four steps:

(1) CHOOSE a hypergraph morphism $h: L \to H$, called the *(left-)occurrence map*.
(2) CHECK the following *gluing condition* consisting of the *contact condition* and the *identification condition*:
   If the image of a node $v \in V_L$ under h contacts some hyperedge $e \in E_H - E_{h(L)}$, i.e., if a tentacle of e points to it, then $v \in V_K$.
   If different items $x, y \in L$ [1)] are identified by h, i.e., if $x \neq y$ but $h(x) = h(y)$, then $x, y \in K$.
(3a) REMOVE the occurrence $h(L)$ of L in H up to $h(K)$ from H yielding the *remainder* $D = H - (h(L) - h(K))$ [2)].

[1)] "$x \in L$" is short for "$x \in V_L$ or $x \in E_L$" and is used whenever nodes and hyperedges do not have to be distinguished. Similarly, "$h(x)$" is short for "$h_V(x)$ or $h_E(x)$".
[2)] " $-$ " denotes the difference of sets for nodes and hyperedges separately.

(3b) ADD the right-hand side R up to K to D yielding the *gluing* $X = D + (R - K)$ [3], whose components are defined as follows:
- $V_X = V_D + (V_R - V_K)$ and $E_X = E_D + (E_R - E_K)$,
- each node and each hyperedge keeps its label,
- each hyperedge of E_D keeps its sources and targets,
- each hyperedge of $E_R - E_K$ keeps its sources and targets provided that they are in $V_R - V_K$; otherwise sources and targets are handed over to V_D: $s_X(e) = h_V'^*(s_R(e))$ and $t_X(e) = h_V'^*(t_R(e))$ for $e \in E_R - E_K$ where $h_V' : V_R \to V_X$ is given by $h_V'(v) = v$ for $v \in V_R - V_K$ and $h_V'(v) = h_V(v)$ for $v \in V_K$.

Such a *direct derivation* is denoted by $H \Longrightarrow H'$ or $H \underset{p}{\Longrightarrow} H'$ by p.

3. A sequence of direct derivations of the form $H_0 \underset{p_1}{\Longrightarrow} \ldots \underset{p_k}{\Longrightarrow} H_k$ constitutes a *derivation* from H_0 to H_k. Such a derivation may be denoted by $H_0 \underset{P}{\overset{*}{\Longrightarrow}} H_k$ if $p_1, \ldots, p_k \in P$.

Remark

1. The occurrence map $h : L \to H$ locates the *occurrence* $h(L)$ of L in H.
2. The gluing condition ensures that D is a subhypergraph of H and that H is the "gluing" of L and D with respect to the gluing hypergraph K.
3. For $x \in K$, $d(x) = h(x)$ defines a morphism $d : K \to D$ locating $h(K)$ in D.
4. Let $X \cong H'$ and $i : X \to H'$ be the corresponding isomorphism. Then h' given by $h'(x) = i(x)$ if $x \in R - K$, and $h'(x) = i(d(x))$ otherwise, defines a morphism $h' : R \to H'$, called the *right-occurrence map*. Correspondingly, $h'(R)$ is called the *occurrence* of R in H'. Further the restriction of $i : X \to H'$ to $D \subseteq X$ defines a morphism.
5. All morphisms involved in a direct derivation can be grouped into two squares,

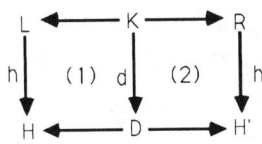

which are actually gluing diagrams in the sense of [Eh 79], 2.6. The explicit construction of the derived hypergraph given above corresponds to the gluing analysis and the gluing construction in [Eh 79], 3.7 and 3.8.
6. The definition of a direct derivation is symmetric in the following sense. Let $H \Longrightarrow H'$ be a direct derivation by $p = (L \supseteq K \subseteq R)$ based on the left-occurrence map $h : L \to H$. Let $h' : R \to H'$ be the corresponding right-occurrence map. Then there is a direct derivation $H' \Longrightarrow H$ by the *inverse production* $p^{-1} = (R \supseteq K \subseteq L)$ based on the occurrence map $h' : R \to H'$.
7. All construction may be done for node- and hyperedge-labeled hypergraphs, as well.

---

[3] "$+$" denotes the disjoint union of sets for nodes and hyperedges separately.

1.2 Example (Jungle Evaluation)

In [HKP 91], *jungle evaluation* is proposed as a hypergraph-rewriting approach to the evaluation of functional expressions and, in particular, of algebraically specified operations. Jungles — being intuitively forests of coalesced trees with shared substructures — are certain acyclic hypergraphs (or equivalently, bipartite graphs) the nodes and edges of which are labeled with the sorts and operation symbols of a signature. Jungles are manipulated and evaluated by the application of jungle rewrite rules, which generalize equations or, more exactly, term rewrite rules.

The application of the hypergraph production p given in Fig. 1.1 to the hypergraph H in Fig. 1.2 yields the hypergraph H'.

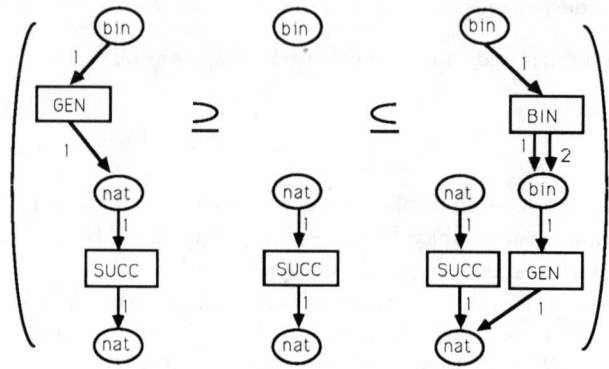

Fig. 1.1. A hypergraph production

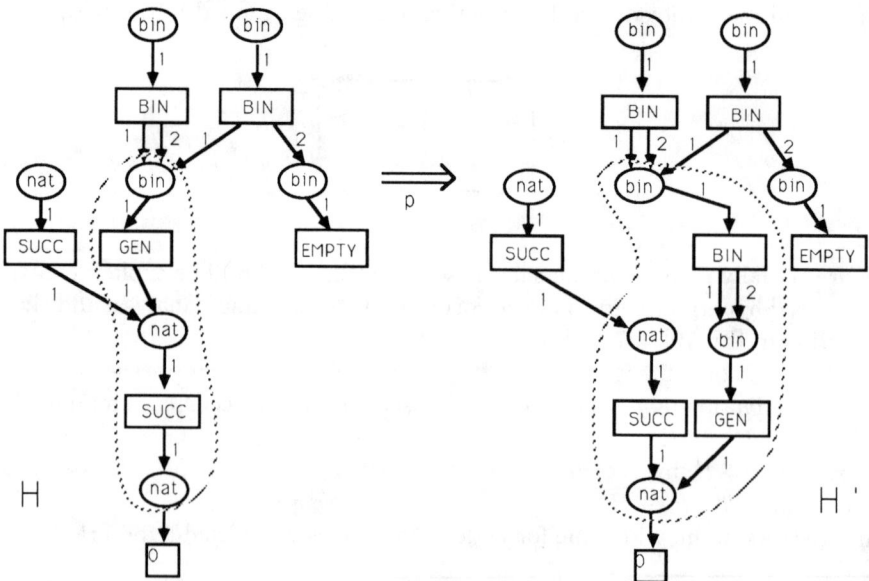

Fig. 1.2. Application of a hypergraph production

(In drawings of (node-labeled) hypergraphs, a circle represents a node and the label is inscribed in the circle.)

1.3 Definition (Hypergraph Grammars and Languages)

1. A *hypergraph grammar* is a system $HG = (N, T, P, Z)$ where $N \subseteq C$ is a set of nonterminals, $T \subseteq C$ is a set of terminals, P is a finite set of hypergraph productions, and Z is a hypergraph, called the axiom.
2. The *hypergraph language* $L(HG)$ generated by HG consists of all terminally labeled hypergraphs which can be derived from the axiom Z by applying productions of P:

$$L(HG) = \{H \in \mathcal{H}_T | Z \underset{P}{\overset{*}{\Rightarrow}} H\}.$$

1.4 Example (Graphs)

The set $GRAPH$ of all (undirected, unlabeled) *graphs* can be generated from the graph with empty node set, $\emptyset$, using a production which allows insertion of a node and a production which allows insertion of an edge between two given nodes. Note that the second production is neither context-free nor context-sensitive in the sense of definition 1.4.

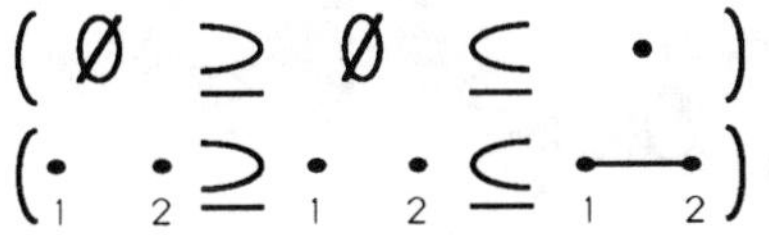

$$\begin{pmatrix} \emptyset \supseteq \emptyset \subseteq \cdot \\ \cdot_1 \ \cdot_2 \supseteq \cdot_1 \ \cdot_2 \subseteq \cdot_1 \text{—} \cdot_2 \end{pmatrix}$$

Fig. 1.3. Productions of HG_{GRAPH}

1.5 Example (Connected and Eulerian Graphs)

The set $CONN$ of all (undirected, unlabeled) *connected graphs* with at least one node can be generated from a graph with one node using a production which allows us to create a new node and to join it with a node of a connected graph using an edge and a production which allows us to join two nodes of a connected graph by an edge.

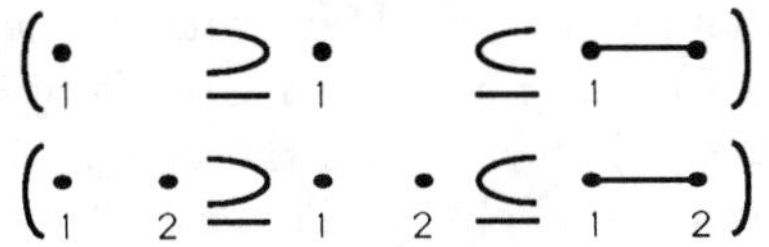

$$\begin{pmatrix} \cdot_1 \supseteq \cdot_1 \subseteq \cdot_1 \text{—} \\ \cdot_1 \ \cdot_2 \supseteq \cdot_1 \ \cdot_2 \subseteq \cdot_1 \text{—} \cdot_2 \end{pmatrix}$$

Fig. 1.4. Productions of HG_{CONN}

For generating the set $EULER$ of all (undirected, unlabeled) *Eulerian graphs* (without loops), we remember that a graph is Eulerian if and only if it is connected and every node has even degree. We make use of this relationship and equip each node with a loop whose label is "even" if the degree of the node is even and "odd" if the degree is odd. Obviously, a new node is connected to the remainder by one edge; therefore the degree is odd. Inserting a new edge between two distinct nodes changes the degree of the nodes involved: if the degree is even, it becomes odd; if it is odd, it becomes even. Removing the degree-information "even" (or the loop with label even) from a node, the degree of the node cannot be changed any more. It turns out that in a graph without even- or odd-labeled edges, all nodes have even degree. Therefore, the set of all Eulerian graphs can be generated by the grammar HG_{EULER} with the axiom

even

and productions of the type

Fig. 1.5. Productions of HG_{EULER}

where $x, y \in \{\text{even}, \text{odd}\}$, $\overline{\text{even}} = \text{odd}$, and $\overline{\text{odd}} = \text{even}$.

1.6 Example (Complete and Hamiltonian Graphs)

The set $COMPLETE$ of all *complete graphs* (with at least three nodes) can be generated from a complete graph with three nodes using the following idea. Given a graph with a directed Hamiltonian cycle, assume that the edges on the cycle are labeled by *out* (except one distinguished edge with label *beg*) and all other edges are labeled by *in*. Then we may preceed as follows: We start with the *beg*-edge, create a new node, connect it with the target of the *beg*-edge, and label it by *start*. We run through the cycle and connect all nodes on the cycle with the new node. At the end, we create an edge with label *out* and one with label *beg*. The *beg*-edge allows us to continue in this way or to finish. The grammar $HG_{COMPLETE}$ with the axiom

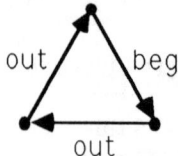

and the productions

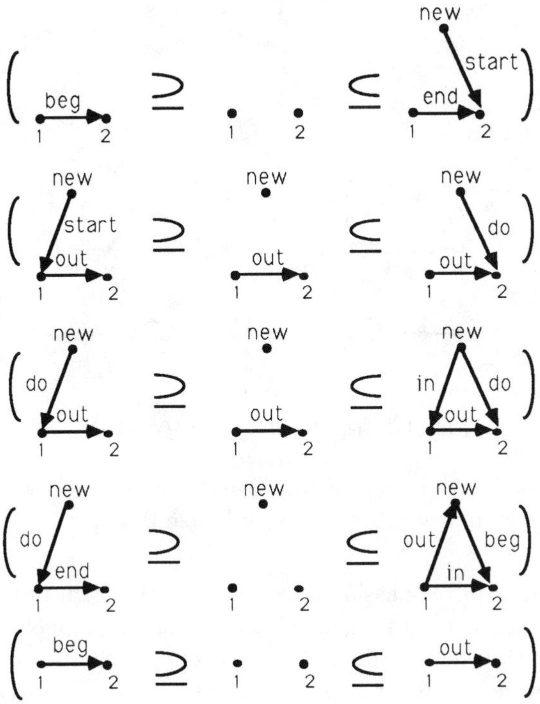

$$\left(\begin{array}{c}\text{beg}\\ \bullet\!\!\xrightarrow{}\!\!\bullet\\ 1\quad 2\end{array} \supseteq \begin{array}{c}\bullet\quad\bullet\\ 1\quad 2\end{array} \subseteq \begin{array}{c}\text{new}\\ \diagdown\text{start}\\ \text{end}\searrow\\ 1\quad 2\end{array}\right)$$

$$\left(\begin{array}{c}\text{new}\\ \diagup\text{start}\\ \text{out}\searrow\\ 1\quad 2\end{array} \supseteq \begin{array}{c}\text{new}\\ \bullet\\ \text{out}\\ 1\quad 2\end{array} \subseteq \begin{array}{c}\text{new}\\ \diagdown\text{do}\\ \text{out}\searrow\\ 1\quad 2\end{array}\right)$$

$$\left(\begin{array}{c}\text{new}\\ \text{do}\diagup\\ \text{out}\searrow\\ 1\quad 2\end{array} \supseteq \begin{array}{c}\text{new}\\ \bullet\\ \text{out}\\ 1\quad 2\end{array} \subseteq \begin{array}{c}\text{new}\\ \text{in}\triangle\text{do}\\ \text{out}\\ 1\quad 2\end{array}\right)$$

$$\left(\begin{array}{c}\text{new}\\ \text{do}\diagup\\ \text{end}\searrow\\ 1\quad 2\end{array} \supseteq \begin{array}{c}\text{new}\\ \bullet\\ \bullet\quad\bullet\\ 1\quad 2\end{array} \subseteq \begin{array}{c}\text{new}\\ \text{out}\triangle\text{beg}\\ \text{in}\\ 1\quad 2\end{array}\right)$$

$$\left(\begin{array}{c}\text{beg}\\ \bullet\!\!\xrightarrow{}\!\!\bullet\\ 1\quad 2\end{array} \supseteq \begin{array}{c}\bullet\quad\bullet\\ 1\quad 2\end{array} \subseteq \begin{array}{c}\text{out}\\ \bullet\!\!\xrightarrow{}\!\!\bullet\\ 1\quad 2\end{array}\right)$$

Fig. 1.6. Productions of $HG_{COMPLETE}$

generates the set of complete graphs in which a Hamiltonian cycle is indicated by the edge labels *out* and all edges not on the cycle are labeled by *in*. If we add productions which allow replacement of *out*-edges as well as *in*-edges by usual (unlabeled) ones, we obtain a grammar which generates the set of all (unlabeled) complete graphs. If we add a production which allows deletion of *in*-edges, we obtain a grammar which generates the set $HAMILTON$ of all *Hamiltonian graphs*.

1.7 Example (Square Grids)

Using similar ideas, one can show that the set of all *square grids* can be generated by a (hyper)graph grammar.

1.8 Example (Snails)

The set $SNAIL$ of all *snails* (see chapter IV) can be generated marking the "outer" edges by *out* and the "topical" one by *top*. If an outer edge follows the topical one, we create two new nodes and three new edges, two labeled by *out*, one by *top*; the old top-edge and the old *out*-edge become usual edges. To finish the derivation process, the topical edge gets the label *out*. As axiom we choose the snail with one cell.

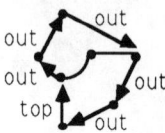

The productions look as follows:

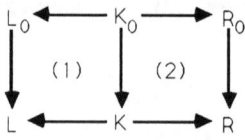

Fig. 1.7. Productions of HG_{SNAIL}

If we add a production which allows replacement of *out*-edges by usual (unlabeled) edges, we obtain a grammar which derives (unlabeled) snails.

Hypergraph grammars can be classified according to the form of the productions. This yields a proper language hierarchy. Somewhat surprisingly, monotone hypergraph grammars are more powerful than context-sensitive ones. Note that in the string case, context-sensitive and monotone grammars have the same generative power.

1.9 Definition (Special Productions, Grammars, and Languages)

1. A hypergraph production $(L \supseteq K \subseteq R)$ is *context-free* if

    - L is a handle, i.e, a hyperedge together with source and target nodes,
    - K is a discrete hypergraph with $V_K = V_L$
    - R is an arbitrary hypergraph with $K \subset R$.

2. A hypergraph production $p = (L \supseteq K \subseteq R)$ is *context-sensitive* if there exists a context-free production $p_0 = (L_0 \supseteq K_0 \subseteq R_0)$, called the *core* of p, and morphisms $L_0 \to L$, $K_0 \to K$, and $R_0 \to R$ such that (1) and (2) below are gluing diagrams (pushouts [4]).

$$\begin{array}{ccccc} L_0 & \leftarrow & K_0 & \rightarrow & R_0 \\ \downarrow & (1) & \downarrow & (2) & \downarrow \\ L & \leftarrow & K & \rightarrow & R \end{array}$$

---

[4] For the definition of the category-theoretical notions (pushouts, pullbacks etc.), we refer to Arbib and Manes [AM 75]; the corresponding set-theoretical descriptions can be found in [EK 79] and [Eh 79].

3. A hypergraph production $(L \supseteq K \subseteq R)$ is *monotone* if $\text{size}(L) \leq \text{size}(R)$.
4. A hypergraph grammar is *context-free* (*context-sensitive, monotone*) if all productions are context-free (context-sensitive, monotone).
5. A hypergraph language L is *context-free* (*context-sensitive, monotone*) if there is a context-free (context-sensitive, monotone) hypergraph grammar HG generating L. The class of all context-free (context-sensitive, monotone) hypergraph languages is denoted by $\mathcal{CFHL}$ ($\mathcal{CSHL}$, $\mathcal{MHL}$). The class of all hypergraph languages generated by arbitrary hypergraph grammars is denoted by $\mathcal{HL}$.

Remark

1. By definition, every context-free hypergraph grammar is context-sensitive, every context-sensitive hypergraph grammar is monotone, and every monotone hypergraph grammar is a hypergraph grammar. Consequently,

$$\mathcal{CFHL} \subseteq \mathcal{CSHL} \subseteq \mathcal{MHL} \subseteq \mathcal{HL}.$$

2. Note that there is a 1-1-correspondence between context-free hypergraph grammars and hyperedge-replacement grammars without empty productions: For a hyperedge-replacement grammar $HRG = (N, T, P, Z)$ without empty productions there is an equivalent context-free hypergraph grammar $HG = (N, T, hg(P), Z)$ with $hg(P) = \{hg(p) | p \in P\}$ where for $p = (A, R)$, $hg(p) = (L \supseteq K \subseteq R)$ denotes the hypergraph production for which L is the handle induced by the symbol A and the type of R and K is the frame of L. Conversely, for each context-free hypergraph-grammar $HG = (N, T, P, Z)$, there is an equivalent hyperedge-replacement grammar $HRG = (N, T, hrg(P), Z)$ without empty productions with $hrg(P) = \{hrg(p) | p \in P\}$ where for $p = (L \supseteq K \subseteq R)$, $hrg(p) = (l_L(e), R')$ denotes the hyperedge-replacement production obtained from p by choosing the label of the hyperedge $e \in E_L$ as left-hand side and the hypergraph $R' = (V_R, E_R, s_R, t_R, l_R, s_L(e), t_L(e))$ induced by R and L as right-hand side.
3. For each string grammar $G = (N, T, P, S)$ without empty productions, there is a hypergraph grammar $G^\bullet = (N, T, P^\bullet, S^\bullet)$ such that $L(G^\bullet) = \{w^\bullet | w \in L(G)\}$.
4. Using the same methods as in the string case, it can be shown that, for monotone hypergraph grammars, the Membership Problem is decidable.

Concerning the generative power of hypergraph grammars we obtain the following hierarchy where the inclusions are strict:

1.10 Theorem (Generative Power)

$$\mathcal{CFHL} \subset \mathcal{CSHL} \subset \mathcal{MHL} \subset \mathcal{HL}.$$

Proof

1. The string-graph language $\{(a^{n^2})^\bullet | n \geq 1\}$ is in $\mathcal{CSHL}$ but not in $\mathcal{CFHL}$ according to the Pumping Lemma for hyperedge-replacement grammars (see chapter IV, section 3).

2. The graph language $GRAPH$ of all graphs is in $\mathcal{MHL}$ but not in $\mathcal{CSHL}$. To show this we assume $GRAPH = L(CSHG)$ for some context-sensitive hypergraph grammar $CSHG = (N, T, P, Z)$. Then the context-free hypergraph grammar $CFHG = (N, T, core(P), Z)$ with $core(P) = \{p_0 | p_0$ is the core of some $p \in P\}$ generates the set $L(CFHG) \supseteq L(CSHG) = GRAPH$. Since $GRAPH$ is of unbounded connectivity, $L(CFHG)$ is also of unbounded connectivity, a contradiction to the Connectivity Theorem for hyperedge-replacement grammars (see chapter IV, section 4).

3. Due to a result by Uesu in [Ue 78], $\mathcal{HL}$ is the class of all recursively enumerable hypergraph languages. On the other hand, each set in $\mathcal{MHL}$ is recursive. Therefore, there exist languages in $\mathcal{HL}$ which are not in $\mathcal{MHL}$. □

2. Hypergraph-Replacement Grammars with Application Conditions

In each graph-grammar approach it is defined how and under which conditions graph productions can be applied to a given "mother graph" in order to obtain a derived "daughter graph" (see [KR 90] for a comparative study). The conditions under which productions can be applied are called application conditions. Usually, the application condition is inherent to each specific graph grammar approach and applies in a uniform way to all productions of a graph grammar within this approach. We propose allowing different application conditions for different productions in order to be more flexible using graph grammars for the design of systems in all kinds of application areas. Although the generative power of most of the known general graph-grammar approaches is sufficient to generate any recursively enumerable set of graphs, it is often convenient to have specific application conditions for each production. Such application conditions, on the one hand, include context conditions like the existence or non-existence of certain nodes, edges, or paths in the mother or the daughter graph as well as cardinallity restrictions concerning the number of incoming or outgoing edges. On the other hand, they also include embedding restrictions concerning the morphisms from the left- and right-hand side of the production to the mother and the daughter graph, respectively. Context conditions in the sense above were informally used in Montanari [Mo 70] and Rosenfeld and Milgram [RM 72] and the use of morphisms between graphs is essential to the "Berlin" approach to graph grammars. We combine these concepts, leading to a very general but mathematically simple notion of application conditions for productions.

Informally, the application of a hypergraph production $p = (L \supseteq K \subseteq R)$ with application condition $A(p)$ to a hypergraph H means:

(1) CHOOSE an occurrence of L in H.
(2) CHECK the contact condition and the identification condition.
(2') CHECK the application condition $A(p)$.
(3) REPLACE (the image of) L by R.

Note that the contact condition is a specific application condition, which always has to be satisfied. It guarantees that the result is again a hypergraph. In some cases it is useful to allow "right-hand" application conditions concerning the occurrence of the right-hand side R of the production in the derived hypergraph ("the derived hypergraph has the property $PROP$"). Then we also have to check this condition.

2.1 Definition (Application Conditions)

1. For $X \in \mathcal{H}_C$, let $\mathcal{MOR}_X$ denote the class of all morphisms starting from the hypergraph X.
2. Given a hypergraph production $p = (L \supseteq K \subseteq R)$, an *application condition* for p is a pair $A(p) = (A_L(p), A_R(p))$ of decidable subsets $A_L(p) \subseteq \mathcal{MOR}_L$ and $A_R(p) \subseteq \mathcal{MOR}_R$. $A(p)$ is said to be *left-sided* if $A_R(p) = \mathcal{MOR}_R$ and *right-sided* if $A_L(p) = \mathcal{MOR}_L$. If $A(p)$ is left-sided (right-sided) we write $A(p) = A_L(p)$ ($A(p) = A_R(p)$).
3. A *hypergraph grammar with application conditions* $HGA = (N, T, P, A, Z)$ consists of a hypergraph grammar $HG = (N, T, P, Z)$, called the hypergraph grammar *underlying* HGA, and a set $A = \{A(p) | p \in P\}$ of application conditions $A(p)$ for $p \in P$.
4. A *direct derivation* in $HGA = (N, T, P, A, Z)$ is a direct derivation $H \Longrightarrow H'$ by a production $p = (L \supseteq K \subseteq R)$ in P such that, for the occurring morphisms $L \to H$ and $R \to H'$, $L \to H \in A_L(p)$ and $R \to H' \in A_R(p)$.

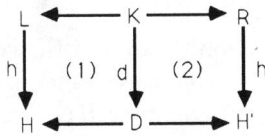

5. The *hypergraph language* $L(HGA)$ induced by HGA consists of all terminally labeled hypergraphs which are derivable in HGA (i.e. with application conditions) from the axiom Z.

Remark

1. Decidability of the subset $A_L(p)$ ($A_R(p)$) means that there is an algorithm which for each hypergraph morphism $L \to H$ ($R \to H'$) decides whether it belongs to $A_L(p)$ ($A_R(p)$) or not. We assume decidability of $A_L(p)$ and $A_R(p)$ in order to be able to decide for each direct derivation $H \Longrightarrow H'$ (by p) in the underlying grammar HG whether it is also a derivation in HGA.
2. By construction, $L(HGA) \subseteq L(HG)$ holds for each grammar HGA with application conditions and underlying grammar HG. It turns out that the corresponding hypergraph language classes $\mathcal{HLA}$ and $\mathcal{HL}$ are equal.
3. Each left-sided application condition $A_L(p)$ induces an *equivalent* right-sided application condition $A_L^{-1}(p) = \{R \to H' | \exists H \Longrightarrow H'$ by p with occurrence maps $L \to H$ and $R \to H'$ such that $L \to H \in A_L(p)\}$. Conversely, each right-sided condition $A_R(p)$ induces an equivalent left-sided condition $A_R^{-1}(p)$. As a consequence, each general application condition $A(p) = (A_L(p), A_R(p))$ can be represented by an equivalent left-sided

condition $A_L(p) \cap A_R^{-1}(p)$ or an equivalent right-sided condition $A_R(p) \cap A_L^{-1}(p)$. This shows that for theoretical reasons it is sufficient to use only left-sided or only right-sided conditions. For practical reasons, however, it is convenient to use the general case.

2.2 Classification of Application Conditions

Application conditions in general can be classified into *context conditions* concerning the class of admissible hypergraphs and *embedding conditions* concerning set-theoretical properties of hypergraph morphisms. The context conditions may require the existence of some items like nodes, hyperedges, or paths or the non-existence of such items. They are called *positive* in the first and *negative* in the second case. If the items under consideration are included in a given neighborhood of the image of L in H (or image of R in H') the conditions may be called *local* and otherwise *global*. Typical positive context conditions are the existence of nodes or hyperedges with specific labels in the mother hypergraph H or daughter hypergraph H'. Typical negative context conditions are the non-existence of nodes or hyperedges with specific labels, cardinality restrictions (the number of outgoing tentacles is bounded by the constant c), and forbidden structures in the sense of Wankmüller [Wa 82+83]. A typical local context condition is the contact condition. Typical global context conditions are the existence or non-existence of a cycle in H or H' or a path between nodes in the image of L or R. Typical embedding conditions are the injectivity of $L \to H$ or $R \to H'$ and the identification condition.

The gluing condition, which is a conjunction of the contact condition and the identification condition, is an application condition which is satisfied if and only if there is a direct derivation in the underlying grammar HG (see [Eh 79]). Hence, it is not necessary to require one of these conditions separately in the set A of application conditions of a grammar HGA.

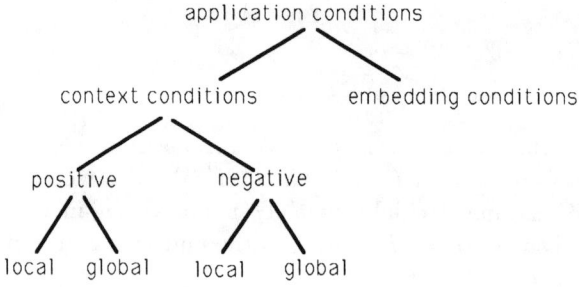

Fig. 2.1. Classification of application conditions

In [EH 86], so-called *concrete context conditions* are investigated and it is shown that context-free hypergraph grammars with concrete context conditions are equivalent to context-sensitive hypergraph grammars without application conditions. As a consequence, the corresponding hypergraph languages and classes of hypergraph languages $CFHLA$ and $CSHL$ are equal.

Concerning the generative power of hypergraph grammars with application conditions, we can show the following result:

2.3 Theorem (Generative Power)

Let $CFHLA$ be the class of languages generated by context-free hypergraph grammars with concrete context conditions and HLA be the class of languages generated by hypergraph grammars with application conditions. Then

$$CFHL \subset CFHLA \subset HL \quad \text{and} \quad HL = HLA.$$

Proof

The string-graph language $\{(a^{n^2})^\bullet | n \geq 1\}$ is in $CFHLA = CSHL$ but not in $CFHL$. The graph language $COMPLETE$ of all complete graphs is in HL but not in $CFHLA = CSHL$. By definition, $HL \subseteq HLA$. Due to a result by Uesu in [Ue 78], HL is the class of all recursively enumerable hypergraph languages. Since all application conditions are decidable, HLA cannot include any other language. □

2.4 Concluding Remark

1. Using hypergraph grammars without application conditions as basic model, the only way to incorporate context conditions is to include the concrete context in the left- and right-hand sides of the productions. The version of application conditions presented here is much more general. In particular, it includes negative context conditions and can be seen as a formalization of application conditions for graph grammar productions which were given in Montanari [Mo 70] and Rosenfeld and Milgram [RM 72].

2. Although the notion of application conditions is mathematically precise, it still allows all kinds of mathematical formalisms to define specific subclasses. We only have required decidability, but we propose to use the methods from formal language theory, logic, algebra, or graph theory in order to define specific subclasses according to the application in mind. It is interesting to study other special cases of application conditions in addition to concrete context conditions.

3. Programmed graph grammars in the sense of Bunke [Bu 79+82] provide also a way to restrict applications of productions. While the application conditions concern single productions, programmed graph grammars restrict possible sequences of productions to be applied in a derivation sequence by suitable control graphs. It depends on the kind of application which method should be taken, and it may also be useful to combine both of them.

3. Parallel Hyperedge-Replacement Grammars

In this section, parallel hyperedge-replacement grammars are introduced. They may be seen as a hypergraph version of ETOL systems (see, e.g. Herman and Rozenberg [HR 75]). This kind of systems is based on simultaneous context-free rewriting. Moreover, in a ETOL-system, the production set is divided into subsets, called tables. At each derivation step of the rewriting process, only productions belonging to the same table can be used. The underlying biological motivation is that different sets of rules may be needed at different developmental stages. Let us mention that, in addition, the set of symbols is divided into a set of nonterminal symbols and a set of terminal symbols.

3.1 Definition (Parallel Hyperedge-Replacement Grammars)

1. A *parallel hyperedge-replacement grammar*, also called a *hypergraph-ETOL-system*, is a system $PHRG = (N, T, \mathcal{P}, Z)$, where N and T are finite sets of labels, $\mathcal{P}$ is a finite set of finite production sets over N, called the set of *tables*, and $Z \in \mathcal{H}_N$ is the axiom.
2. The *hypergraph language* $L(PHRG)$ generated by $PHRG$ consists of all terminally labeled hypergraphs which can be derived from Z if in each derivation step all hyperedges are replaced applying productions of one production set P of $\mathcal{P}$ [1]:

$$L(PHRG) = \{H \in \mathcal{H}_T \mid Z \underset{\mathcal{P}}{\overset{*}{\Longrightarrow}} H\}.$$

Remark

For a parallel grammar $PHRG = (N, T, \mathcal{P}, Z)$, it may be required that for each $P \in \mathcal{P}$ and each $A \in N$ there is at least one production $p \in P$ with $lhs(p) = A$.

The relationship between parallel hyperedge-replacement grammars and usual hyperedge-replacement grammars is formulated in theorem 3.2.

3.2 Theorem

1. Let $HRG = (N, T, P, Z)$ be a usual hyperedge-replacement grammar. Then the parallel hyperedge-replacement grammar $PHRG = (N, T, \{P\}, Z)$ generates the same language as HRG, i.e., $L(HRG) = L(PHRG)$.

---

[1] Given a direct derivation $H \underset{P}{\Longrightarrow} H'$ by the "full" base $prod : E_H \to P$, we write $H \underset{P}{\Longrightarrow} H'$ provided that the fullness is of interest. If $H_0 \underset{P_1}{\Longrightarrow} H_1 \underset{P_2}{\Longrightarrow} \ldots \underset{P_k}{\Longrightarrow} H_k$ is a derivation from H_0 to H_k and $P_1, P_2 \ldots, P_k \in \mathcal{P}$, then we write $H_0 \overset{*}{\Longrightarrow} H_k$ or $H_0 \underset{\mathcal{P}}{\overset{*}{\Longrightarrow}} H_k$ provided that $\mathcal{P}$ is of interest.

2. Let $PHRG = (N, T, \mathcal{P}, Z)$ be a parallel hyperedge-replacement grammar. Then the usual hyperedge-replacement grammar $HRG = (N, T, \bigcup_{P \in \mathcal{P}} P, Z)$ generates a language including the language of $PHRG$, i.e., $L(PHRG) \subseteq L(HRG)$.

Proof

The first statement follows immediately from the existence of canonical derivations and the possibility of sequentializing parallel derivations (see, e.g., [Kr 87b]). The second statement follows from the fact that each derivation in $PHRG$ is a parallel derivation in HRG. □

3.3 Theorem (Generative Power)

Let $\mathcal{PHRL}$ be the class of languages generated by parallel hyperedge-replacement grammars. Then

$$\mathcal{HRL} \subset \mathcal{PHRL}.$$

Proof

By theorem 3.2, $\mathcal{HRL} \subseteq \mathcal{PHRL}$. The set $STAR = \{STAR(n^2) | n \geq 1\}$ of all star graphs $STAR(n^2)$ with n^2 edges starting from a single node is in $\mathcal{PHRL}$. By the Linear-Growth Theorem (see chapter IV), it can be shown that $STAR$ is not in $\mathcal{HRL}$. □

4. Figure-Generating Grammars Based on Hyperedge Replacement

The systematic generation and manipulation of artificial pictures and patterns is one of the most challenging tasks of computer science. Among the various attempts, syntactic proposals in which classes of patterns are described by grammars are found in the literature (see, e.g., Feder [Fe 68+71], Shaw [Sh 69], Pfaltz and Rosenfeld [PR 69], Fu [Fu 74+82], Stiny and Gips [St 75, Gi 75], Gonzalez and Thomason [GT 78], Maurer, Rozenberg, and Welzl [MRW 82], Bunke [Bu 83], Dassow [Da 89], Prusinkiewicz and Hanan [Pr 86+87, PH 89]).

In this section, we discuss an approach to pattern generation based on hyperedge replacement. Hyperedge-replacement grammars provide a simple, well-studied method for generating graphs and hypergraphs. For pattern generation, we consider hyperedge-decorated figures consisting of points, lines, and hyperedges — instead of hypergraphs consisting of nodes and hyperedges — as objects, replace hyperedges by hyperedge-decorated figures, and interpret the generated figures as patterns. In this way, the approach of hyperedge-replacement grammars can be utilized for the generation of surprisingly rich and pretty patterns, which may be considered as kinds of collages combining bits of pictures (as opposed to patterns drawn and computed pixel by pixel).

4.1 Assumption

We assume that the reader is familiar with the elementary notions of Euclidean geometry (see, e.g., Coxeter [Co 89]). $I\!R$ denotes the set of real numbers and $I\!R^2$ the Euclidean space of dimension 2. $I\!R^2$ is equipped with the ordinary distance function dist : $I\!R^2 \times I\!R^2 \to I\!R$.

In the following, we choose so-called figures as terminal structures of interest. To generate sets of figures, they are decorated by hyperedges in intermediate steps. Each hyperedge has a label and an ordered finite set of tentacles, each of which is attached to a point, and is a place holder for a figure or — recursively — for another decorated figure. Each decorated figure has a sequence of pin points. If a hyperedge is replaced by a decorated figure, the decorated figure is transformed in such a way that the images of the pin points of the latter match with the points attached to the hyperedge.

4.2 Definition (Hyperedge-Decorated Figures)

1. Let N be an arbitrary, but fixed alphabet, called a set of *labels*. A *hyperedge-decorated figure* over N is a system $F = (POINT, LINE, EDGE, att, lab, pin)$ where $POINT \subseteq I\!R^2$ is a finite set of *points*, $LINE \subseteq \mathcal{P}(I\!R^2)$ is a finite set of *lines*, where each line connects two, not necessarily different, points of $POINT$, $EDGE$ is a finite set of *hyperedges*, $att : EDGE \to POINT^*$ is a mapping assigning a sequence $att(e)$ of points to each $e \in EDGE$, $lab : EDGE \to N$ is a mapping assigning a label $lab(e)$ to each $e \in EDGE$, and $pin \in POINT^*$ is a sequence of *pin points*. The components of F are also denoted by $POINT_F, LINE_F, EDGE_F, att_F, lab_F$, and pin_F, respectively.
2. The class of all decorated figures over N is denoted by $\mathcal{F}_N$; the set of all decorated figures $F \in \mathcal{F}_N$ with $EDGE_F = \emptyset$ is denoted by $\mathcal{F}$.
3. Two decorated figures $F, F' \in \mathcal{F}_N$ are said to be *isomorphic*, denoted by $F \cong F'$, if the underlying figures without hyperedges are equal and if there is a bijective mapping $f : EDGE_F \to EDGE_{F'}$ such that $att_F(e) = att_{F'}(f(e))$ and $lab_F(e) = lab_{F'}(f(e))$ for all $e \in EDGE_F$.

Remark

1. We are mainly interested in the generation of patterns, which are usually infinite sets of points. On the other hand, we suggest the use of grammatical methods, which concern rule-based rewriting of finite objects. To bridge this gap, we have introduced the notion of a (decorated) figure consisting of a finite set of points and a finite set of lines (where we assume that each line has some finite description even if it is an infinite set of points). So a figure can be the object of rewriting and, at the same time, represent a potentially infinite pattern by the union of the points of the lines.
2. Figures without hyperedges consist of points and lines in the plane. In a similar way, more general types of figures, e.g., figures of points, lines, and areas, colored figures, higher-dimensional figures etc., may be treated.
3. There is a close relationship between hyperedge-decorated figures and hypergraphs: For each hyperedge-decorated figure $F \in \mathcal{F}_N$, there is hypergraph $H(F) \in \mathcal{H}_{N \cup \{\square\}}$ given

by $(POINT_F, LINE_F \cup EDGE_F, s, t, l, pin_F)$, where s assigns the empty sequence to each line and each hyperedge and t assigns the sequence of the points connected by the line to each line $l \in LINE_F$ and the sequence $att(e)$ to each hyperedge $e \in EDGE_F$, and l assigns the invisable label □ to each line $l \in LINE_F$ and $lab(e)$ to each hyperedge $e \in EDGE_F$. On the other hand, each hypergraph $H \in \mathcal{H}_{N \cup T}$ with nodes and hyperedges may be equipped with layout information such that we get a figure $F(H) \in \mathcal{F}_{N \cup T}$ with points, lines, and hyperedges.

4.3 Example

An example of a decorated figure is given in Fig. 4.1.

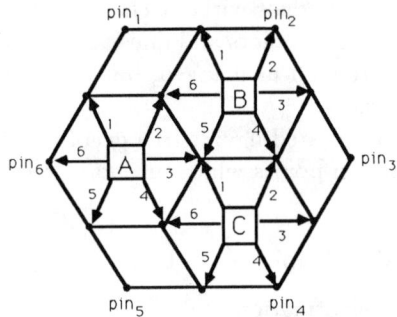

Fig. 4.1. A hyperedge-decorated figure

Hyperedges in decorated figures serve as place holders for (decorated) figures. Hence the key construction is the replacement of some hyperedges in a decorated figure by (decorated) figures. While a hyperedge is attached to some points according to our conventions, a (decorated) figure has got some pin points. If there is a transformation which maps the pin points to the attached points of the hyperedge, the hyperedge may be replaced by the transformed (decorated) figure. The formal definition of hyperedge replacement makes use of three simpler constructions on decorated figures: hyperedge removal, transformation, and addition.

4.4 Definition (Operations on Decorated Figures)

1. Let $F \in \mathcal{F}_N$ and $B \subseteq EDGE_F$. Then the *removal* of B from F yields the decorated figure $F - B = (POINT_F, LINE_F, EDGE_F - B, att, lab, pin_F)$ with $att(e) = att_F(e)$ and $lab(e) = lab_F(e)$ for all $e \in EDGE_F - B$.

2. Let $F \in \mathcal{F}_N$ and $t : \mathbb{R}^2 \to \mathbb{R}^2$ be a mapping which will be referred to as a transformation. Then the *transformation* of F by t yields the decorated figure $t(F) = (t(POINT_F), t(LINE_F), EDGE_F, att, lab_F, pin)$ with $att(e) = t(att_F(e))$ for all $e \in EDGE_F$, and $pin = t(pin_F)$ [1].

3. Let $F \in \mathcal{F}_N$ and $Y \subseteq \mathcal{F}_N$. Then the *addition* of Y to F yields the decorated figure $F+Y$ with $POINT_{F+Y} = POINT_F \cup \bigcup_{R \in Y} POINT_R$, $LINE_{F+Y} = LINE_F \cup \bigcup_{R \in Y} LINE_R$, $EDGE_{F+Y} = EDGE_F + \sum_{R \in Y} EDGE_R$, $att_{F+Y}(e) = att_F(e)$ and $lab_{F+Y}(e) = lab_F(e)$ for all $e \in EDGE_F$ and $att_{F+Y}(e) = att_R(e)$ and $lab_{F+Y}(e) = lab_R(e)$ for $R \in Y$ and $e \in EDGE_R$, and $pin_{F+Y} = pin_F$.

Remark

1. Removal removes some hyperedges without changing anything else.
2. The transformation transforms points and lines according to t. The set of hyperedges is not changed, their labels remain unchanged, but the hyperedges are attached to the transformed attached points.
3. The addition of a set of decorated figures to a decorated figure F is asymmetric with respect to the choice of the pin points which are borrowed from F.

4.5 Definition (Hyperedge Replacement)

Let $TRANS$ be a set of transformations.
Let $F \in \mathcal{F}_N$, $B \subseteq EDGE_F$, and $(repl, trans)$ be a pair of mappings $repl : B \to \mathcal{F}_N$, $trans : B \to TRANS$ with $att(e) = trans(e)(pin_{repl(e)})$ for all $e \in B$. Then the *replacement* of B in F by $(repl, trans)$ yields the decorated figure

$$REPLACE(F, repl, trans) = (F - B) + Y(B)$$

where $Y(B) = \{trans(e)(repl(e)) | e \in B\}$ denotes the set of decorated figures determined by $(repl, trans)$.

Remark

1. Hyperedge replacement is a simple construction where some hyperedges are removed, the associated decorated figures are transformed in such a way that the images of the pin points match the points attached to the corresponding hyperedges, and the transformed decorated figures are added. Note that the pin points may restrict the choice of possible transformations.
2. The transformed decorated figures replacing hyperedges are fully embedded into the resulting decorated figure, but their pin points loose their status.

---

[1] The mapping $t : \mathbb{R}^2 \to \mathbb{R}^2$ can be extended to the following mappings:
- $t : \mathcal{P}(\mathbb{R}^2) \to \mathcal{P}(\mathbb{R}^2)$ by $t(X) = \{t(x)|x \in X\}$ for $X \subseteq \mathbb{R}^2$,
- $t : \mathcal{P}(\mathcal{P}(\mathbb{R}^2)) \to \mathcal{P}(\mathcal{P}(\mathbb{R}^2))$ by $t(Y) = \{t(y)|y \in Y\}$ for $Y \subseteq \mathcal{P}(\mathbb{R}^2)$,
- $t : (\mathbb{R}^2)^* \to (\mathbb{R}^2)^*$ by $t(x_1 \ldots x_n) = t(x_1) \ldots t(x_n)$ for $x_i \in \mathbb{R}^2$, $i = 1, \ldots, n$.

In the following, figure grammars are introduced as figure-manipulating and figure language-generating devices. Based on hyperedge replacement, one can derive (decorated) figures from decorated figures by applying productions of a simple form. A production is given by a label $A \in N$ and a decorated figure $R \in \mathcal{F}_N$. It may be applied to a hyperedge e with label A provided that there is a transformation from a given set $TRANS$ of admissible transformations which maps the pin points of R to the attached points of e. The result of the application is obtained by replacing the hyperedge by the transformed image of R. More generally, several productions may be applied in parallel.

Various kinds of transformations may be considered, e.g., identical transformations, isometries, central dilatations, similarity transformations, affine transformations, ect. Depending on the kind of transformations allowed, one may derive fewer or more figures from figures by applying productions. Hence, we have to indicate what kind of transformations are considered.

4.6 General Assumption

Let $TRANS$ be an arbitrary, but fixed, set of mappings $t : \mathbb{R}^2 \to \mathbb{R}^2$, called the set of admissible *transformations*.

4.7 Definition (Productions and Derivations)

1. Let N be a set of labels. A *production* over N is a pair $p = (A, R)$ with $A \in N$ and $R \in \mathcal{F}_N$. A is called the *left-hand side* of p and is denoted by $lhs(p)$. R is called the *right-hand side* and is denoted by $rhs(p)$.
2. Let $F \in \mathcal{F}_N$, $B \subseteq EDGE_F$, and P be a set of productions over N. Then a pair $(prod, trans)$ of mappings $prod : B \to P$ and $trans : B \to TRANS$ is called a *base* on B in F if $lab_F(e) = lhs(prod(e))$ and $att_F(e) = trans(e)(pin_{rhs(prod(e))})$ for all $e \in B$.
3. Let $F, F' \in \mathcal{F}_N$ and $(prod, trans)$ be a base on B in F. Then F *directly derives* F' by $(prod, trans)$ if $F' \cong REPLACE(F, repl, trans)$ with $repl(e) = rhs(prod(e))$ for all $e \in B$. A direct derivation is denoted by $F \Longrightarrow F'$ by $(prod, trans)$, $F \Longrightarrow_P F'$, or $F \Longrightarrow F'$.
4. A sequence of direct derivations of the form $F_0 \Longrightarrow_P F_1 \Longrightarrow_P \ldots \Longrightarrow_P F_k$ is called a *derivation* from F_0 to F_k and is denoted by $F_0 \Longrightarrow_P^* F_k$ or $F_0 \Longrightarrow^* F_k$.

Using the introduced concepts of productions and derivations, figure grammars and figure languages can be introduced in the usual way.

4.8 Definition (Figure Grammars and Languages)

1. A *figure grammar* is a system $FG = (N, P, Z)$ where N is a finite set of *nonterminals*, P is a finite set of *productions* over N, and $Z \in \mathcal{F}_N$ is the *axiom*.
2. The *figure language* generated by FG consists of all figures which can be derived from Z by applying productions of P:

$$L(FG) = \{F \in \mathcal{F} \mid Z \underset{P}{\overset{*}{\Rightarrow}} F\}.$$

Remark

1. The axiom of a figure grammar plays an essential role: it determines the placement of the generated figures in the plane.
2. The figure language generated by FG depends on the set of admissible transformations. To emphasize this aspect, we sometimes write $L_{TRANS}(FG)$ instead of $L(FG)$ to denote the figure language generated by FG with respect $TRANS$. Let us mention that $TRANS \subseteq TRANS'$ implies $L_{TRANS}(FG) \subseteq L_{TRANS'}(FG)$.
3. Figure grammars are based on the replacement of hyperedges. The generated objects are figures in the sense of definition 4.1. To emphasize these aspects, figure grammars sometimes are called figure-generating hyperedge-replacement grammars.

4.9 Example (Inscribed Squares)

Let us consider the figure grammar $FG_{SQUARE} = (\{A\}, P, Z)$ where Z denotes the figure

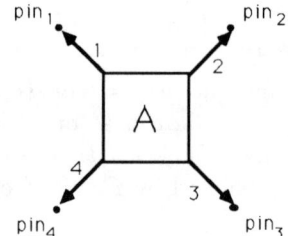

and P consists of two productions given in a kind of Backus-Naur-Form:

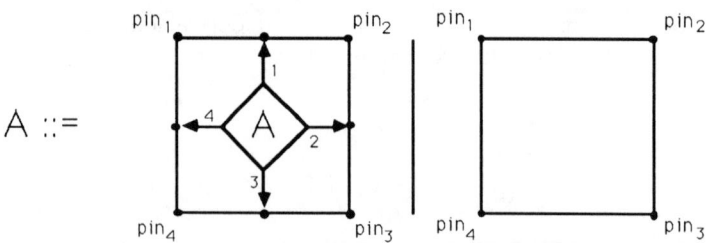

Fig. 4.2. Productions of FG_{SQUARE}

Starting from the figure Z, the first production can be applied to the single hyperedge in Z provided that we allow the translation of the right-hand side to the region of the hyperedge. Obviously, the resulting figure again possesses only one hyperedge which is labeled by A. Now the first production (or the second production) may be applied provided that it is allowed to contract, rotate and translate the right-hand side. Allowing the set $SIMILAR$ of similarity transformations only, a derivation in the figure grammar has the following shape:

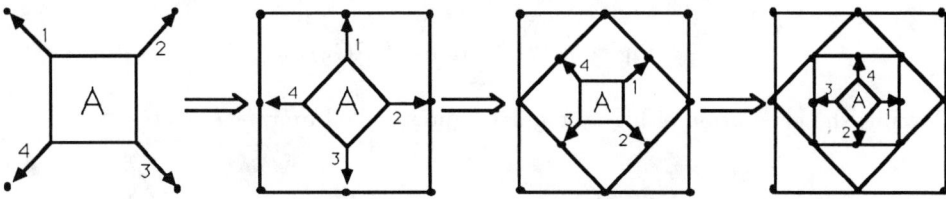

Fig. 4.3. A derivation in FG_{SQUARE}

The figures generated by FG_{SQUARE} (with respect to $SIMILAR$) are of the form

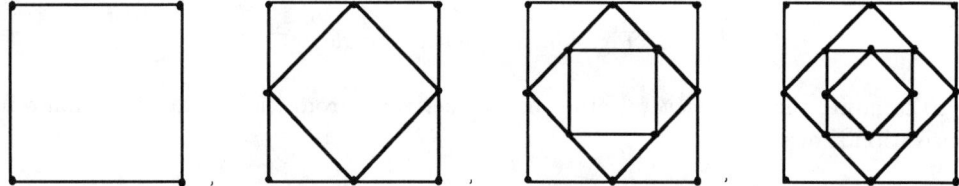

Fig. 4.4. Inscribed squares

4.10 Example (Sierpinski Triangles)

The figure grammar $FG_{SIER} = (\{A\}, \{p_1, p_2\}, Z)$ with the axiom

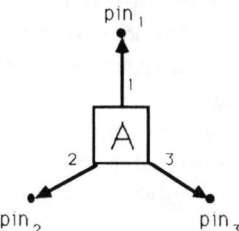

and the productions

A ::=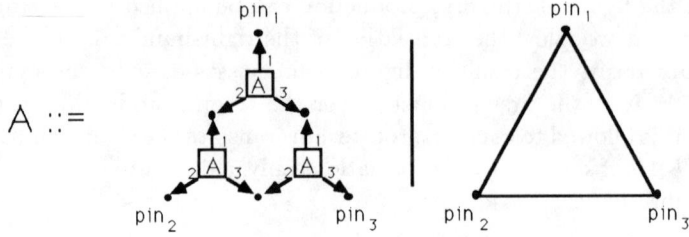

Fig. 4.5. Productions of FG_{SIER}

allows us the generation of highly regular figures, called *Sierpinski triangles*.

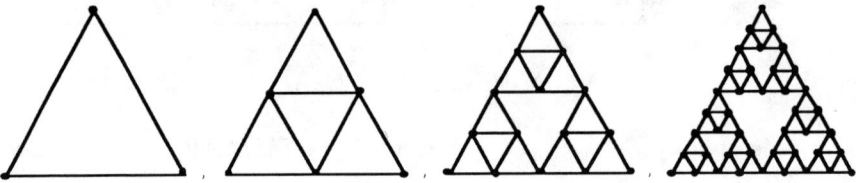

Fig. 4.6. Sierpinski triangles

Furthermore, there are several other figures derivable from the axiom as the following derivation shows.

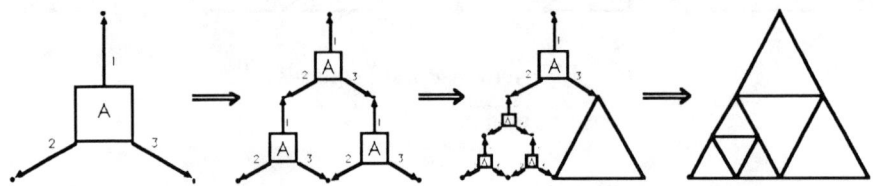

Fig. 4.7. A derivation in FG_{SIER}

Note that in the second derivation step of the derivation only two of three hyperedges are replaced. Moreover, different productions are used in this derivation step. If one is interested in generating the Sierpinski triangles only, then one has to use the ETOL-mode of rewriting, i.e. for this example,

(1) Replace all hyperedges in each step.
(2) Use one of the productions only in each step.

Therefore, it is important to consider parallel figure grammars in addition to the usual ones. In parallel figure-generating grammars, we have sets of production sets; in each derivation step we choose one set and replace all hyperedges by applying productions of this set. (A formal definition is given in [HK 88].) With respect to our example, the parallel figure grammar $PFG_{SIER} = (\{A\}, \{\{p_1\}, \{p_2\}\}, Z)$ in which the "generating" production p_1 and the "terminating" production p_2 are in different production sets generates only the Sierpinski triangles.

4.11 Concluding Remark

1. Several results known for hyperedge-replacement grammars can be adapted to figure languages generated by figure grammars. In [HK 88], it is shown that the Context-Freeness Lemma, the Fixed-Point Theorem, as well as the Pumping Lemma can be formulated for figure grammars. The Fixed-Point Theorem provides an alternative mechanism for generating figure languages described by figure-generating grammars. The Pumping Lemma provides information on the structure of complex figures generated by a grammar and may be used to show that certain kinds of figure languages cannot be generated by a figure grammar.

2. The approach for pattern generation based on figure grammars seems to be attractive in two respects: It covers various interesting examples and it promises the prospect of rich results. But more work has to be done to get a clearer picture of figure grammars.
(1) Beside the figure grammar, the kind of transformations for adapting a figure to the region of a hyperedge plays an important role. We have concentrated our considerations to affine transformations. Which other transformations will work? How does the restriction (or generalization) of the transformation concept influence the generative power?
(2) The figures considered in this section are of a simple form. More general types of figures seem to be of interest, e.g., figures of points, lines and areas, colored figures, higher-dimensional figures, etc. Which type of figures should be investigated?
(3) Another interesting type of extension involves moving points and lines after they have been generated. Up to now, all points and lines keep their place in the plane.

3. Figure grammars — as introduced above — may be seen to be context-free figure-replacement grammars. According to the general approach of hypergraph-replacement grammars, one may define arbitrary figure-replacement grammars in which figures in figures are replaced by figures.

4. Figure grammars can be extended to parallel figure grammars in order to obtain more expressive power. A formal definition can be found in [HK 88].

5. The further study should include the following topics:
(1) The notion of a shape grammar (see, e.g., Stiny [St 75], Gips [Gi 75], and Lauzzana and Pocock-Williams [LP 88]) provides another well-known way to describe patterns syntactically. How are they related to figure grammars?
(2) Maurer, Rozenberg, and Welzl [MRW 82] introduce the concept of chain grammars that generate sets of strings which can be interpreted as line drawings. In a similar, more sophisticated way, Prusinkiewicz and Hanan [Pr 86+87, PH 89] use L-systems. How are these approaches related to figure grammars?

(3) In [HK 91], we suggeste to define fractal patterns by infinite derivations as well as by generated languages where the first way seems to be more flexible and less redundant. But the relationship between fractal geometry and figure grammars concerns the patterns described by generated languages. What about infinite derivations in this respect?

5. Bibliographic Note

Hypergraph grammars were used in [HKP 91] to describe the evaluation of functional expressions, and in particular, of algebraically specified operations. Graph grammars with application conditions were investigated in [EH 86]. Figure grammars and parallel figure grammars were introduced in [HK 88]. A generalization to collage grammars can be found in [HK 91].

Conclusion

The theory of graph grammars forms a well-motivated area of theoretical computer science. It was originally attempted to attack some fundamental problems in the area of picture processing (see, e.g., Rosenfeld and Milgram [RM 72] and Pfaltz [Pf 72]), and subsequently the development of the theory was motivated (and influenced) by various application areas such as databases, incremental compilers, data flow analysis, operational semantics, abstract data types, data structures and developmental biology (see, e.g.,[Eh 79, Na 79]). Due to the diversity of motivations, the theory of graph grammars considers a very wide spectrum of graph rewriting systems (see, e.g., [CER 79, ENR 83, ENRR 87, and EKR 91]), where rather different kinds of questions are posed for different models. Thus, although by now some models possess a quite well-developed mathematical theory (see, e.g., [Eh 79, JR 80 a+b, Ja 83]) or a successful range of applications (see, e.g., [Na 79, CER 79, ENR 83, ENRR 87, and EKR 91]), in general the theory of graph grammars would benefit from more "coherence".

The theory of hyperedege-replacement grammars, the basic model considered in this book, is an attempt to build up systematically a theory for manipulating highly structured objects. The goal of these investigations is twofold: On the one hand, to built up a formal theory based on "simple and natural" assumptions, on the other hand, to propose one model of graph grammars for a variety of problems. The work may be seen as part of a systematic investigation of hyperedge-replacement grammars as well as a counterpart to the investigations on node-label controlled graph grammars considered by Dirk Janssens and Grzegorz Rozenberg (see, e.g., [JR 80a+b, Ja 83]).

This book consists mainly of two types of investigation:

First, problems with respect to the generating processes and generative power of hyperedge-replacement grammars. In chapter III, a Kleene-Type Characterization and a Fixed-Point Theorem are stated; they provide alternative mechanisms for generating hyperedge-replacement languages. In chapter IV, a Pumping Lemma for hyperedge-replacement languages is stated and used to prove results on the generative power of hyperedge-replacement grammars. In particular, in chapter V, it is shown that their generative power depends strongly on the so-called order, which is an upper bound for the number of "tentacles" a non-terminal hyperedge may have. The order induces an infinite hierarchy of classes of hypergraph languages, which remains infinite even if one considers graph or string(-graph) languages.

Secondly, some decidability problems with respect to hyperedge-replacement languages are investigated, for example in chapters VI and VII questions of the form

(1) Is there a hypergraph in the generated language satisfying the property P?
(2) Do all hypergraphs in the generated language satisfy the property P?
(3) Are the values of all hypergraphs in the generated language bounded?

are shown to be decidable for a class of hyperedge-replacement grammars if the corresponding graph-theoretic property P is "compatible" or if the corresponding quantity function f is "compatible" with the derivation process of the given grammars and is built up by maxima, sums and products.

Bibliography

[AU 72] A.V. Aho, J.D. Ullman: The Theory of Parsing, Translation, and Compiling, Vol. I: Parsing, Prentice-Hall, Englewood-Cliffs, New Jersey 1972.

[AM 75] M.A. Arbib, E.G. Manes: Arrows, Structures, and Functors, Academic Press, New York 1975.

[BPS 61] Y. Bar-Hillel, M. Perles, E. Shamir: On Formal Properties of Simple Phrase-Structure Grammars, Zeitschrift für Phonetik, Sprachwissenschaft und Kommunikationsforschung 14, 143-177, 1961.

[BC 87] M. Bauderon, B. Courcelle: Graph Expressions and Graph Rewriting, Math. Systems Theory 20, 83-127, 1987.

[Be 73] C. Berge: Graphs and Hypergraphs, North Holland, Amsterdam 1973.

[Br 83] F.J. Brandenburg: On the Complexity of the Membership Problem of Graph Grammars, in M. Nagl, J. Perl (Eds.): Graphtheoretic Concepts in Computer Science, Trauner Verlag, Linz, 40-49, 1983.

[Bu 79] H. Bunke: Programmed Graph Grammars, Lect. Not. Comp. Sci. 73, 155-166, 1979.

[Bu 82] H. Bunke: On the Generative Power of Sequential and Parallel Programmed Graph Grammars, Computing 29, 89-112, 1982.

[Bu 83] H. Bunke: Graph Grammars as a Generative Tool in Image Understanding, Lect. Not. Comp. Sci. 153, 8-19, 1983.

[CER 79]   V. Claus, H. Ehrig, G. Rozenberg (Eds.): Graph Grammars and Their Application to Computer Science and Biology, Lect. Not. Comp. Sci. 73, 1979.

[CR 92]   A. Corradini, F. Rossi: Hyperedge Replacement Jungle Rewriting for Term Rewriting Systems and Logic Programming, to appear in Theor. Comp. Sci.

[Co 87]   B. Courcelle: An Axiomatic Definition of Context-Free Rewriting and its Application to NLC Graph Grammars, Theor. Comp. Sci. 55, 141-181, 1987.

[Co 90a]   B. Courcelle: The Monadic Second-Order Logic of Graphs I: Recognizable Sets of Finite Graphs, Inform. Comput. 85, 12-75, 1990.

[Co 90b]   B. Courcelle: The Monadic Second-Order Logic of Graphs IV: Definability Properties of Equational Graphs, Annals of Pure and Applied Logic 49, 193-255, 1990.

[Co 90c]   B. Courcelle: Graph Rewriting: An Algebraic and Logical Approach, in J. van Leeuwen (Ed.): Handbook of Theoretical Computer Science, Vol. B, Elsevier, Amsterdam, 193-242, 1990.

[CER 91]   B. Courcelle, J. Engelfriet, G. Rozenberg: Context-Free Handle-Rewriting Hypergraph Grammars, Lect. Not. Comp. Sci. 532, 253-268, 1991.

[CM 92]   B. Courcelle, M. Mosbah: Monadic Second-Order Evaluations on Tree-Decomposable Graphs, Lect. Not. Comp. Sci. 570, 13-24, 1992, to appear in Theor. Comp. Sci.

[Co 89]   H.S.M. Coxeter: Introduction to Geometry, Second Edition, Wiley Classics Library Edition, John Wiley & Sons, New York 1989.

[Da 89]   J. Dassow: Graph-Thoeretic Properties and Chain Code Picture Languages, J. Inf. Process. Cybern. EIK 25, 8/9, 423-433, 1989.

[DG 78]   P. Della Vigna, C. Ghezzi: Context-Free Graph Grammars, Inform. Contr. 37, 207-233, 1978.

[Eh 79]   H. Ehrig: Introduction to the Algebraic Theory of Graph Grammars, Lect. Not. Comp. Sci. 73, 1-69, 1979.

[EH 86]   H. Ehrig, A. Habel: Graph Grammars with Application Conditions, in G. Rozenberg, A. Salomaa (Eds.): The Book of L, Springer-Verlag, Berlin, 87-100, 1986.

[EK 79]   H. Ehrig, H.-J. Kreowski: Pushout-Properties: An Analysis of Gluing Constructions for Graphs, Math. Nachr. 91, 135-149, 1979.

[EKR 91]   H. Ehrig, H.-J. Kreowski, G. Rozenberg (Eds.): Graph Grammars and Their Application to Computer Science, Lect. Not. Comp. Sci. 532, 1991.

[ENR 83]   H. Ehrig, M. Nagl, G. Rozenberg (Eds.): Graph Grammars and Their Application to Computer Science, Lect. Not. Comp. Sci. 153, 1983.

[ENRR 87] H. Ehrig, M. Nagl, G. Rozenberg, A. Rosenfeld (Eds.): Graph Grammars and Their Application to Computer Science, Lect. Not. Comp. Sci. 291, 1987.

[EPS 73]   H. Ehrig, M. Pfender, H.J. Schneider: Graph Grammars: An Algebraic Approach, Proc. of the IEEE Conf. on Automata and Switching Theory, Iowa City 1973, 167-180, 1973.

[En 89]   J. Engelfriet: Context-Free NCE Graph Grammars, Lect. Not. Comp. Sci. 380, 148-161, 1989.

[En 91]   J. Engelfriet: A Characterization of Context-Free NCE Graph Languages by Monadic Second-Order Logic on Trees, Lect. Not. Comp. Sci. 532, 311-327, 1991.

[EH 91a]   J. Engelfriet, L.M. Heyker: The String Generating Power of Context-Free Hypergraph Grammars, Journ. Comp. Syst. Sci. 43, 328-360, 1991.

[EH 91b]   J. Engelfriet, L.M. Heyker: The Term Generating Power of Context-Free Hypergraph Grammars, Lect. Not. Comp. Sci. 532, 328-344, 1991.

[EL 88]   J. Engelfriet, G. Leih: Nonterminal Bounded NLC Graph Grammars, Theor. Comp. Sci. 59, 309-315, 1988.

[EL 89]   J. Engelfriet, G. Leih: Linear Graph Grammars: Power and Complexity, Inform. Comput. 81, 88-121, 1989.

[EL 90]   J. Engelfriet, G. Leih: Complexity of Boundary Graph Languages, RAIRO Theoretical Informatics and Applications 24, 267-274, 1990.

[ELR 88]   J. Engelfriet, G. Leih, G. Rozenberg: Apex Graph-Grammars and Attribute Grammars, Acta Informatica 25, 537-571, 1988.

[ELR 91]   J. Engelfriet, G. Leih, G. Rozenberg: Nonterminal Separation in Graph Grammars, Theor. Comp. Sci. 82, 95-111, 537-571, 1991.

[ER 90]   J. Engelfriet, G. Rozenberg: A Comparison of Boundary Graph Grammars and Context-Free Hypergraph Grammars, Inform. Comput. 84, 163-206, 1990.

[FKZ 76]   R. Farrow, K. Kennedy, L. Zucconi: Graph Grammars and Global Program Data Flow Analysis, Proc. 17th Ann. IEEE Symp. on Found. of Comp. Sci., Houston, 42-56, 1976.

[Fe 68]   J. Feder: Languages of Encoded Line Patterns, Inform. Contr. 13, 230-244, 1968.

[Fe 71]   J. Feder: Plex Languages, Inform. Sci. 3, 225-241, 1971.

[Fr 78]   R. Franck: A Class of Linearly Parsable Graph Grammars, Acta Informatica 10, 175-201, 1978.

[Fu 74]   K.S. Fu: Syntactic Methods in Pattern Recognition, Academic Press, New York 1974.

[Fu 82]   K.S. Fu: Syntactic Pattern Recognition and Applications, Prentice-Hall, Englewood Cliffs, New Jersey, 1982.

[Gi 85]   A. Gibbons: Algorithmic Graph Theory, Cambridge University Press, Cambridge 1985.

[Gi 66]   S. Ginsburg: The Mathematical Theory of Context-Free Languages, McGraw-Hill, New York 1966.

[GR 62]   S. Ginsburg, G. Rice: Two Families of Languages Related to ALGOL, Journ. ACM 9, 350-371, 1962.

[Gi 75]   J. Gips: Shape Grammars and Their Uses, Artifical Perception, Shape Generation and Computer Aesthetics, Birkhäuser Verlag, Basel 1975.

[Go 77]   J. Goldstine: A Simplified Proof of Parikh's Theorem, Discrete Math. 19, 235-239, 1977.

[GT 78]   R.C. Gonzalez, M.G. Thomason: Syntactic Pattern Recognition, Addison-Wesley, Reading, Mass. 1978.

[Gr 72]   S.A. Greibach: A Generalization of Parikh's Semilinear Theorem, Discrete Math. 2, 347-355, 1972.

[Gr 71]   J. Gruska: A Characterization of Context-Free Languages, Journ. Comp. Syst. Sci. 5, 353-364, 1971.

[Ha 89a]   A. Habel: Graph-Theoretic Properties Compatible with Graph Derivations, Lect. Not. Comp. Sci. 344, 11-29, 1989.

[Ha 89b]   A. Habel: Hyperedge Replacement: Grammars and Languages, Ph.D. Thesis, Bremen 1989.

[HK 83]   A. Habel, H.-J. Kreowski: On Context-Free Graph Languages Generated by Edge Replacement, Lect. Not. Comp. Sci. 153, 143-158, 1983.

[HK 87a]   A. Habel, H.-J. Kreowski: Characteristics of Graph Languages Generated by Edge Replacement, Theor. Comp. Sci. 51, 81-115, 1987.

[HK 87b]   A. Habel, H.-J. Kreowski: May We Introduce to You: Hyperedge Replacement, Lect. Not. Comp. Sci. 291, 15-26, 1987.

[HK 87c]   A. Habel, H.-J. Kreowski: Some Structural Aspects of Hypergraph Languages Generated by Hyperedge Replacement, Lect. Not. Comp. Sci. 247, 207-219, 1987.

[HK 88]   A. Habel, H.-J. Kreowski: Pretty Patterns Produced by Hyperedge Replacement, Lect. Not. Comp. Sci. 314, 32-45, 1988.

[HK 90]   A. Habel, H.-J. Kreowski: Filtering Hyperedge-Replacement Languages Through Compatible Properties, Lect. Not. Comp. Sci. 411, 107-120, 1990.

[HK 91]   A. Habel, H.-J. Kreowski: Collage Grammars, Lect. Not. Comp. Sci. 532, 411-429, 1991.

[HKL 92]   A. Habel, H.-J. Kreowski, C. Lautemann: A Comparison of Compatible, Finite, and Inductive Graph Properties, to appear in Theor. Comp. Sci.

[HKP 91]   A. Habel, H.-J. Kreowski, D. Plump: Jungle Evaluation, Fundamenta Informaticae XV, 37-60, 1991.

[HKV 89]   A. Habel, H.-J. Kreowski, W. Vogler: Metatheorems for Decision Problems on Hyperedge Replacement Graph Languages, Acta Informatica 26, 657-677, 1989.

[HKV 91]   A. Habel, H.-J. Kreowski, W. Vogler: Decidable Boundedness Problems for Sets of Graphs Generated by Hyperedge Replacement, Theor. Comp. Sci. 89, 33-62, 1991.

[HK 92]   A. Habel, S. Kuske: Soving Boundedness Problems by Pumping Lemmata, in preparation.

[Ha 69]   F. Harary: Graph Theory, Addison-Wesley, Reading, Mass., 1969.

[HR 75]   G.T. Herman, G. Rozenberg: Developmental Systems and Languages, North Holland/American Elsevier, New York 1975.

[HU 69]   J.E. Hopcroft, J.D. Ullman: Formal Languages and Their Relation to Automata, Addison-Wesley, Reading, Mass. 1969.

[Ja 83]   D. Janssens: Node Label Controlled Graph Grammars, Ph.D. Thesis, Antwerp 1983.

[JKRE 82]   D. Janssens, H.-J. Kreowski, G. Rozenberg, H. Ehrig: Concurrency of Node-Label-Controlled Graph Transformations, Techn. Report 82-38, Antwerp 1982.

[JR 80a]   D. Janssens, G. Rozenberg: On the Structure of Node-Label-Controlled Graph Languages, Inform. Sci. 20, 191-216, 1980.

[JR 80b]   D. Janssens, G. Rozenberg: Restrictions, Extensions and Variations of NLC Grammars, Inform. Sci. 20, 217-244, 1980.

[JR 81]   D. Janssens, G. Rozenberg: Decision Problems for Node Label Controlled Graph Grammars, Journ. Comp. Syst. Sci. 22, 144-177, 1981.

[JR 82]   D. Janssens, G. Rozenberg: Graph Grammars with Neighbourhood-Controlled Embedding, Theor. Comp. Sci. 21, 55-74, 1982.

[JR 86]   D. Janssens, G. Rozenberg: Neighbourhood-Uniform NLC Grammars, Computer Vision, Graphics, and Image Processing 35, 131-151, 1986.

[JRW 86]   D. Janssens, G. Rozenberg, E. Welzl: The Bounded Degree Problem for NLC Grammars is Decidable, Journ. Comp. Syst. Sci. 33, 415-422, 1986.

[Ka 83]   M. Kaul: Parsing of Graphs in Linear Time, Lect. Not. Comp. Sci. 153, 206-218, 1983.

[Ka 86]   M. Kaul: Syntaxanalyse von Graphen bei Präzedenz-Graph-Grammatiken, Ph.D. Thesis, Report MIP-8610, Passau 1986.

[Kl 56]   S.C. Kleene: Representation of Events in Nerve Nets and Finite Automata, in C. Shannon, J. McCarthy (Eds.): Automata Studies, Annales of Math. Studies 34, Princeton, New Jersey, 3-40, 1956.

[Kr 77a]   H.-J. Kreowski: Manipulationen von Graphmanipulationen, Ph.D. Thesis, Berlin 1977.

[Kr 77b]   H.-J. Kreowski: Transformations of Derivation Sequences in Graph Grammars, Lect. Not. Comp. Sci. 56, 275-286, 1977.

[Kr 79]   H.-J. Kreowski: A Pumping Lemma for Context-Free Graph Languages, Lect. Not. Comp. Sci. 73, 270-283, 1979.

[Kr 86]   H.-J. Kreowski: Rule Trees Represent Derivations in Edge Replacement Systems, in G. Rozenberg, A. Salomaa (Eds.): The Book of L, Springer-Verlag, Berlin, 217-232, 1986.

[Kr 87a]   H.-J. Kreowski: Rule Trees Can Help to Escape Hard Graph Problems, Techn. Report, Bremen 1987.

[Kr 87b]   H.-J. Kreowski: Is Parallelism Already Concurrency? Part 1: Derivations in Graph Grammars, Lect. Not. Comp. Sci. 291, 343-360, 1987.

[KR 84]   H.-J. Kreowski, G. Rozenberg: Note on Node-Rewriting Graph Grammars, Information Processing Letters 18, 21-24, 1984.

[KR 90]   H.-J. Kreowski, G. Rozenberg: On Structured Graph Grammars, Part I and II, Inform. Sci. 52, 185-210 and 221-246, 1990.

[La 88a]   C. Lautemann: Decomposition Trees: Structured Graph Representation and Efficient Algorithms, Lect. Not. Comp. Sci. 299, 28-39, 1988.

[La 88b]   C. Lautemann: Efficient Algorithms on Context-Free Graph Languages, Lect. Not. Comp. Sci. 317, 362-378, 1988.

[La 90]   C. Lautemann: The Complexity of Graph Languages Generated by Hyperedge Replacement, Acta Informatica 27, 399-421, 1990.

[La 91]   C. Lautemann: Tree Automata, Tree Decomposition, and Hyperedge Replacement, Lect. Not. Comp. Sci. 532, 520-537, 1991.

[LP 88]   R.G. Lauzzana, L. Pocock-Williams: A Rule System for Analysis in the Visual Arts, Leonardo, Vol. 21, No. 4, 445-452, 1988.

[Le 87]   T. Lengauer: Efficient Algorithms for Finding Minimum Spanning Forests of Hierarchically Defined Graphs, Journ. of Algorithms 8, 260-284, 1987.

[LW 88]   T. Lengauer, E. Wanke: Efficient Analysis of Graph Properties on Context-Free Graph Languages, Lect. Not. Comp. Sci. 317, 379-393, 1988.

[Li 85]   U. Lichtblau: Decompilation of Control Structures by Means of Graph Transformations, Lect. Not. Comp. Sci. 185, 284-297, 1985.

[Li 90]   U. Lichtblau: Flußgraphgrammatiken, Ph.D. Thesis, Techn. Report 3/90, Oldenburg 1990.

[Li 91]   U. Lichtblau: Recognizing Rooted Context-Free Flowgraph Languages in Polynomial Time, Lect. Not. Comp. Sci. 532, 538-548, 1991.

[MR 87]   M.G Main, G. Rozenberg: Handle NLC Grammars and R.E. Languages, Journ. Comp. Syst. Sci. 35, 195-205, 1987.

[MR 90]   M.G Main, G. Rozenberg: Edge-Label Controlled Graph Grammars, Journ. Comp. Syst. Sci. 40, 188-228, 1990.

[MRW 82]   H.A. Maurer, G. Rozenberg, E. Welzl: Using String Languages to Describe Picture Languages, Information and Control 54, 155–185, 1982.

[Mo 70]   U. Montanari: Separable Graphs, Planar Graphs and Web Grammars, Inform. Contr. 16, 243-267, 1970.

[MR 87]   U. Montanari, F. Rossi: An Efficient Algorithm for the Solution of Hierarchical Networks of Constraints, Lect. Not. Comp. Sci. 291, 440-457, 1987.

[Na 79a]   M. Nagl: Graph-Grammatiken, Vieweg, Braunschweig 1979.

[Na 79b]   M. Nagl: A Tutorial and Bibliographical Survey on Graph Grammars, Lect. Not. Comp. Sci. 73, 70-126, 1979.

[Na 87]   M. Nagl: Set Theoretic Approaches to Graph Grammars, Lect. Not. Comp. Sci. 291, 41-54, 1987.

[Pa 61]   R.J. Parikh: Language Generating Devices, Quarterly Progress Report, No. 60, Research Laboratory of Electronics, M.I.T., 199-212, 1961.

[Pa 66]   R.J. Parikh: On Context-Free Languages, Journ. ACM 13, 570-581, 1966.

[Pa 72]   T. Pavlidis: Linear and Context-Free Graph Grammars, Journ. ACM 19, 1, 11-23, 1972.

[PR 69]   J.L. Pfaltz, A. Rosenfeld: Web Grammars, Proc. Int. Joint Conf. Art. Intelligence, 609-619, 1969.

[Pr 71]   T.W. Pratt: Pair Grammars, Graph Languages and String-to-Graph Translations, Journ. Comp. Syst. Sci. 5, 560-595, 1971.

[Pr 86]   P. Prusinkiewicz: Graphical Applications of L-Systems, Proc. of Graphics Interface'86 — Vision Interface'86, 247-253, 1986.

[Pr 87]   P. Prusinkiewicz: Applications of L-Systems to Computer Imagery, Lect. Not. Comp. Sci. 291, 534-548.

[PH 89]   P. Prusinkiewicz, J. Hanan: Lindenmayer Systems, Fractals, and Plants, Lect. Not. in Biomathematics 79, Springer-Verlag, New York 1989.

[RS 86] N. Robertson, P.D. Seymour: Graph Minors II, Algorithmic Aspects of Tree Width, Journ. of Algorithms 7, 309-322, 1986.

[Ro 74] D.J. Rose: On Simple Characterizations of k-Trees, Discrete Math. 7, 317-322, 1974.

[RM 72] A. Rosenfeld, D. Milgram: Web Automata and Web Grammars, Machine Intelligence 7, 307-324, 1972.

[RW 86a] G. Rozenberg, E. Welzl: Boundary NLC Graph Grammars — Basic Definitions, Normal Forms, and Complexity, Inform. Contr. 69, 136-167, 1986.

[RW 86b] G. Rozenberg, E. Welzl: Graph Theoretic Closure Properties of the Family of Boundary NLC Graph Languages, Acta Informatica 23, 289-309, 1986.

[Sa 73] A. Salomaa: Formal Languages, Academic Press, New York 1973.

[Se 92] H. Seidl: Finite Tree Automata with Cost Functions, Lect. Not. Comp. Sci. 581, 279-299, 1992.

[Sh 69] A.C. Shaw: A Formal Description Schema as a Basis for Picture Processing Systems, Inform. Contr. 14, 9-52, 1969.

[Sl 82] A.O. Slisenko: Context-Free Graph Grammars as a Tool for Describing Polynomial-time Subclasses of Hard Problems, Information Processing Letters 14, 52-56, 1982.

[St 75] G. Stiny: Pictorial and Formal Aspects of Shape and Shape Grammars, Birkhäuser Verlag, Basel 1975.

[SM 80] I. Suzuki, T. Murata: Stepwise Refinements of Transitions and Places, Informatik-Fachberichte 52, Springer-Verlag, Berlin, 136-141, 1980.

[Tu 83] G. Turán: On the Complexity of Graph Grammars, Acta Cybern. 6, 271-281, 1983.

[Ue 78] T. Uesu: A System of Graph Grammars which Generates all Recursively Enumerable Sets of Labelled Graphs, Tsukuba J. Math. 2, 11-26, 1978.

[Va 79]   R. Valette: Analysis of Petri Nets by Stepwise Refinements, Journ. Comp. Syst. Sci. 18, 35-46, 1979.

[Vo 90]   W. Vogler: On Hyperedge Replacement and BNLC Graph Grammars, Lect. Not. Comp. Sci. 411, 78-93, 1990.

[Wa 89]   E. Wanke: Algorithmen und Komplexitätsanalyse für die Verarbeitung hierarchisch definierter Graphen und hierarchisch definierter Graphfamilien, Ph.D. Thesis, Paderborn 1989.

[Wa 91]   E. Wanke: Algorithms for Graph Problems on BNLC Structured Graphs, Inform. Comput. 94, 93-122, 1991.

[WW 89]   E. Wanke, M. Wiegers: Undecidability of the Bandwidth Problem on Linear Graph Languages, Information Processing Letters 33, 193-197, 1989.

[Wa 82]   F. Wankmüller: Charakterisierung von Graphklassen durch verbotene Strukturen und Reduktionen, Ph.D. Thesis, Dortmund 1982.

[Wa 83]   F. Wankmüller: Characterization of Graph Classes by Forbidden Structures and Reductions, Lect. Not. Comp. Sci. 153, 405-414, 1983.

[Yn 71]   M.K. Yntema: Cap Expressions for Context-Free Languages, Inform. Contr. 18, 311-318, 1971.

List of Symbols

Symbol	Usage	Meaning.
$\in$	$a \in A$	a is an element of A.
$\subseteq$	$A \subseteq B$	A is a subset of B.
		(Set A is contained in set B, possibly $A = B$).
$\subset$	$A \subset B$	A is a proper subset of B.
$\cup$	$A \cup B$	Union of sets A and B.
$\cap$	$A \cap B$	Intersection of sets A and B.
$+$	$A + B$	Disjoint union of sets A and B.
$-$	$A - B$	A less B.
		(The elements of A are not in B).
$\sum$	$\sum_{i=1}^{n} A_i$	Disjoint union of sets A_i ($i = 1, \ldots, n$).
$\times$	$A \times B$	Cartesian Product of A and B.
		(The set of all pairs (a, b) where $a \in A$ and $b \in B$).
$\emptyset$		The empty set.
$\mathcal{P}$	$\mathcal{P}(A)$	Powerset of A.
		(the set of all subsets of A).
$|\ |$	$|A|$	Cardinality of set A.
		(i.e. the number of elements in A).
λ		The empty string.
$\cdot$	$u \cdot v$	Concatenation of strings u and v.
$*$	A^*	Set of all strings over A, including λ.
$+$	A^+	Set of all strings over A, except λ.
$|\ |$	$|w|$	Length of string w.
$\mathbb{N}$	$n \in \mathbb{N}$	Set of all natural numbers including zero.
$[n]$	$k \in [n]$	k is an element of $\{1, 2, \ldots n\}$.
$[m, n]$	$k \in [m, n]$	k is an element of $\{m, m+1, \ldots, n\}$.
$\to$	$f : A \to B$	Mapping from A to B.
$\circ$	$f \circ g$	Composition of f and g.

Symbol	Meaning.
C	A set of labels (or colors).
H	A multi-pointed hypergraph.
V	The set of nodes (or vertices).
E	The set of hyperegdes.
$s : E \to V^*$	The source mapping.
$t : E \to V^*$	The target mapping.
$att : E \to V^*$	The attachment mapping.
$begin \in V^*$	The sequence of begin nodes.
$end \in V^*$	The sequence of end nodes.
$ext \in V^*$	The sequence of external nodes.
$ATT(e)$	The set of attachment nodes of e.
EXT	The set of external nodes.
INT	The set of internal nodes.
$type_H(e)$	The type of e in H.
$rel_H(e)$	The relation of e in H.
$type(H)$	The type of H.
$rel(H)$	The relation of H.
$e^\bullet, A^\bullet$	Induced handles.
$H \subseteq H'$	H is a subhypergraph of H'.
$f : H \to H'$	f is a hypergraph morphism from H to H'.
$H \cong H'$	H and H' are isomorphic.
$repl : B \to \mathcal{H}_C$	A base for replacement.
$REPLACE(H, repl)$	The result of replacement.
$H[e/R]$	The result of the replacement of e in H by R.
$prod : B \to P$	A production base.
$H \xRightarrow[P]{*} H'$	A derivation from H to H' by P.
HRG	A hyperedge-replacement grammar.
$L(HRG)$	The language generated by HRG.
$\mathcal{H}_C$	The class of all multi-pointed hypergraphs over C.
$\mathcal{G}_C$	The class of all multi-pointed graphs over C.
$\mathcal{HRG}$	The class of all hyperedge-replacement grammars.
$\mathcal{ERG}$	The class of all edge-replacement grammars.
$\mathcal{HRL}$	The class of all hyperedge-replacement languages.
$\mathcal{ERL}$	The class of all edge-replacement languages.

Index

Aho, A.V., 74 ff
algebraic approach, 39, 170
Arbib, M.A., 176
application condition, 179
A-substitution, 64
attachment node, 7
automorphism, 142
automorphism group, 142, 167
axiom, 18

bandwidth, 104
Bar-Hillel, Y., 78
base for replacement, 14
Bauderon, M., 5, 38, 69
begin node, 10
Berge, C., 8
Berlin approach, 39, 170
bipartite graph, 10, 22, 93, 103
BNLC grammar, 39, 117
Boolean operation, 130
boundary NLC grammar, 39, 117
Boundedness Problem, 145, 161
Brandenburg, F.J., 5, 39
Bunke, H., 181, 183

cellular graph grammar, 38
Characterization Theorem, 64
chain graph, 109
chemical structure, 9, 20
clique-partition number, 166
clique size, 89
Clique-Size Theorem, 89
Claus, V., 5

closure
– under Boolean operations, 130
– under isomorphisms, 13, 128, 156
– under iterated X-substitution, 61
– under X-substitution, 56
collage grammar, 192
color, 7
coloring, 126
compatible
– function, 156
– predicate, 128
complete graph, 87, 93, 174
completely typed, 27
completely well-formed, 30
component of a hypergraph, 154
composition of hypergraphs, 78
– iterated, 78
connected graph, 120, 173
connectivity, 88
Connectivity Theorem, 88, 89
contact condition, 170
context-free
– hypergraph grammar, 177
– hypergraph production, 176
– string grammar, 31
– string-graph grammar, 108
Context-Freeness Lemma, 48
context-sensitive, 176
control-flow graph, 19
Courcelle, B., 5, 38, 40, 69, 143, 168
Coxeter, H.S.M., 184
cycle, 149, 150
cycle-free grammar, 77
cyclic bandwidth, 105

Dassow, J., 183
decision problem, 136, 141, 156
decompsition of a derivation, 49
degree, 89, 125, 152
Della Vigna, P., 5, 35
density of a hypergraph, 148
derivation, 17, 18, 44, 170, 179, 187
– direct, 17, 44, 170, 179, 187
– dummy, 44
– parallel, 44, 182
– sequential, 44
– valid, 44
derivation sequence, 18, 44, 170, 187
derivation tree, 51
– result of a, 51
– root of a, 51
diameter, 90
Diameter Theorem, 90
direct derivation, 17, 44, 170
discrete hypergraph, 98, 119
dummy derivation, 44

edge, 7, 12
edge coloring, 126
edge-label controlled, 41
edge replacement, 5
edge-replacement grammar, 100, 113
edge-replacement language, 100
Ehrig, H., 5, 39, 169 ff, 192
ELC grammar, 41
Embedding Lemma, 47
– generalized version, 47
embedding of a derivation, 47
empty production, 74
Emptiness Problem, 73
end node, 10
Engelfriet, J., 5, 40
equal up to isomomorphism, 48
equation system, 67, 68
equivalent grammar, 18
ETOL system, 182
Eulerian
– cycle, 122
– graph, 93, 173
– path, 122
external node, 10

external size, 80

Farrow, R., 19
Feder, J., 5, 20, 32, 183
fibre of a derivation, 49
figure, 184
– hyperedge-decorated, 184
figure grammar, 188
figure language, 188
Filter Theorem, 139
finite graph property, 143
finite hypergraph language, 13
finite production set, 77
Finiteness Problem, 85
fixed point, 67
Fixed-Point Theorem, 69
flow diagram, 9
flow-graph grammar, 19
Franck, R., 5
frame, 11
Fu, K.S., 183
function
– compatible, 156
functional expression, 8, 172

generated language, 18, 173, 179
generative power, 97 ff, 177, 181, 183
Gibbons, G., 122
Ginsburg, S., 55, 67, 94
Gips, J., 183, 191
Ghezzi, C., 5, 35
gluing condition, 170
gluing diagram, 39, 171
gluing hypergraph, 170
Goldstine, J., 94
Gonzalez, R.C., 183
grammar, 18
– completely typed, 27
– completely well-formed, 30
– cycle-free, 77
– proper, 77
– reduced, 72
– repetition-free, 28
– typed, 26
– usual, 25
– well-formed, 28

– with application conditions, 179
– without empty productions, 74
– without single productions, 76
graph, 12, 93, 173
– bipartite, 10, 22, 93, 103
– complete, 87, 93, 174
– connected, 120, 173
– Eulerian, 93, 173
– Hamiltonian, 93, 174
– maximal outerplanar, 98
– multi-pointed, 12
– planar, 93
– regular, 93
– semi-connected, 120
– simple, 87
graph grammar
– cellular, 38
– context-free, 31
– edge-label controlled, 41
– node-label controlled, 39
– edge-replacement, 100
– node-replacement, 39
graph language, 98
graph property
– compatible, 128
– finite, 143
– inductive, 143
Greibach, S.A., 94
grid, 87, 93, 102, 175
Gruska, J., 55, 63, 94

Habel, A., 5, 95, 134, 144, 168, 172, 192
Hamiltonian graph, 93, 174
Hanan, J., 183, 191
handle, 11, 51
handle NLC grammar, 40
Harary, F., 122
Herman, G.T., 182
Heyker, L.M., 5
hierarchical networks, 37
Hierarchy Theorem, 106, 113
homogeneous language, 13
Hopcroft, J.E., 72 ff, 78
HRG, 5
HRL, 56
hyperedge, 6, 7

– repetition-free, 28
hyperedge-decorated figure, 184
hyperedge replacement, 5, 14, 186
hyperedge-replacement grammar, 18
– completely typed, 27
– completely well-formed, 30
– cycle-free, 77
– parallel, 182
– proper, 77
– reduced, 72
– repetition-free, 28
– typed, 26
– usual, 25
– well-formed, 28
– without empty productions, 74
– without single productions, 76
hyperedge-replacement language, 18
hypergraph, 7
– directed, 7
– hyperedge-labeled, 7
– labeled, 8
– multi-pointed, 10
– node-labeled, 8
– repetition-free, 28
hypergraph grammar, 173
– context-free, 177
– context-sensitive, 177
– monotone, 177
– with application conditions, 179
hypergraph morphism, 12
hypergraph production, 170
– context-free, 176
– context-sensitive, 176
– monotone, 75, 177
hypergraph language, 13, 18
– context-free, 177
– context-sensitive, 177
– finite, 13
– homogeneous, 13
– monotone, 177

identification condition, 170
independence number, 166
independent set of nodes, 166
inductive graph property, 143
internal node, 10

internal size, 80
inverse production, 171
isomorphic, 12
isomorphism, 12
iterated substituion, 59
iterated composition, 78

Janssens, D., 5, 39, 92, 143, 167
Joint-Embedding Lemma, 47
– generalized version of, 47
jungle, 172
jungle evaluation, 172

Kaul, M., 5
Kennedy, K., 19
Kleene, S.C., 63
Kleene-Type Characterization, 63, 64
Kreowski, H.-J., 5, 47, 53, 78, 96, 134, 144, 168, 169 ff, 178, 192
Kuske, S., 168
k-bipartite, 22, 103
k-bounded, 125
k-edge-coloring, 126
k-grid, 102
k-tree, 103

label, 7
labeling, 7, 8
language, 13
– closed under isomorphism, 13
– finite, 13
– homogeneous, 13
language family, 68
Lautemann, C., 5, 40, 93, 134, 144
Lauzzana, R.G., 191
least fixed point, 67
left-hand side of a production, 17, 170
length of a derivation, 18, 44
length of a path/cycle, 149
length of a string, 7
Leih, G., 5, 40
Lichtblau, U., 5, 20
Lengauer, T., 5, 38, 134, 143, 144
Linear-Growth Theorem, 86
linear set, 95
loop, 87

Main, M.G., 40, 41
Manes, E.G., 176
maximal outerplanar graph, 98
Maurer, H.A., 183, 191
Membership Problem, 75
Metatheorem
– for Boundedness Problems, 161
– for Decision Problems, 136, 141, 160
(m,n)-edge, 7
(m,n)-graph, 12
(m,n)-handle, 11
(m,n)-hypergraph, 10
Milgram, D., 178, 181
minimum degree, 89
Minimum-Degree Theorem, 89
monotone, 75, 177
– grammar, 177
– production, 177
Montanari, U., 5, 37, 178
morphism, 12
Mosbah, M., 168
multi-pointed, 10
multiple edge, 87
Murata, T., 16

Nagl, M., 5
neighborhood uniform, 39
NLC grammar, 39
– boundery, 39
– context-free, 39
– Church-Rosser, 39
– handle, 40
– neighborhood-uniform, 39
NCE grammar, 40
node, 7
– attachment, 7
– source, 7
– target, 7
– external, 10
– internal, 10
node-label controlled grammar, 39
node replacement, 5
node-replacement grammar, 31
nonterminal, 17, 18
non-trivial automorphism group, 142
NUNLC grammar, 39

occurrence, 170, 171
occurrence map, 170
order of a grammar, 79
order of a language, 79

parallel derivation, 44, 182
parallel grammar, 182
Parikh, R.J., 94
Parikh mapping, 94
Parikh's Theorem, 94
path, 149
– Eulerian, 122
Pavlidis,T., 5, 34
Perles, M., 83
Petri net, 9
Pfaltz, J.L., 173
Pfender, M., 169
plex grammar, 32
Plump, D., 172, 192
Pocock-Williams, L., 191
Post Correspondence Problem, 142, 167
Pratt, T.W., 5, 35
production, 17, 18, 170, 187
– empty, 74
– single, 76
production base, 44
proper compatible predicate, 134
proper grammar, 77
property
– compatible, 128
– finite, 143
– inductive, 143
Prusinkiewicz, P., 183, 191
Pumping Lemma, 80

quotient hypergraph, 29

reduced grammar, 72
Reducedness Theorem, 72
relation
– of a hyperedge, 7
– of a hypergraph, 10
repetition-free
– grammar, 28
– hyperedge, 28
– hypergraph, 28

replacement
– of hyperedges, 14, 186
– of hypergraphs, 170
Restriction Lemma, 46
– generalized version, 46
restriction of a derivation, 46
result of a derivation tree, 51
right-hand side of a production, 17, 170
Rice, G., 55
Robertson, N., 93
root of a derivation tree, 51
Rose, D.J., 103
Rosen, B.K., 169
Rosenfeld, A., 5, 178, 181, 183
Rossi, F., 5, 37
Rozenberg, G., 5, 39 ff, 92, 143, 167, 178, 182, 183, 191

Salomaa, A., 94
Schneider, H.J., 169
Seidl, H., 168
semi-connected, 120
semilinear set, 95
semi-structured program, 19
sequential derivation, 44
sequentialization, 45
Sequentialization Theorem, 45
series-parallel graph, 98
Seymour, P.D., 93
Shamir, E., 78
Shaw, A.C., 183
simple graph, 87
simple path/cycle, 149
single production, 76
singleton, 11
Sierpinski triangle, 189
size of a hypergraph, 80
Slisenko, A.O., 36, 144
snail, 92, 93, 175
solution of an equation system, 67
source, 7
square, 188
square grid, 87, 93, 175
subhypergraph, 12
star, 30, 98
star-replacement grammar, 30

Stiny, G., 183, 191
string, 7
string graph, 12
string-graph grammar, 108
string-graph language, 107
substitution, 56
– iterated, 59
Suzuki, I., 16
system of equations, 67, 68

target, 7
tentacle of a hyperedge, 6
terminal, 18
Thomason, M.G., 183
totally disconnected, 98, 119
transformation, 186
tree, 98, 103
tree-width, 93
trivial automorphism group, 142
Turán, G., 5, 39
type
– of a hyperedge, 7
– of a hypergraph, 10
type function, 26
typed grammar, 26
Type-Modification Theorem, 27
Typification Theorem, 26

Uesu, T., 178, 181
Ullman, J.D., 72 ff, 78
unsolvable problem, 142, 167
usual grammar, 25

Valette, R., 16
valid derivation, 44
vertex, 7
Vogler, W., 5, 40, 144, 161, 168

Wanke, E., 5, 38, 134, 143
Wankmüller, F., 180
well-formed grammar, 28
Well-Formedness Theorem, 28
Welzl, E., 5, 39, 143, 167, 183, 191
wheel, 92
Wiegers, M., 143

X-substitution, 56

– iterated, 59
$X(m, n)$-handle, 78
$X(m, n)$-handled, 78

Yntema, M.K., 55, 63

Zucconi, L., 19

Lecture Notes in Computer Science

For information about Vols. 1–559
please contact your bookseller or Springer-Verlag

Vol. 560: S. Biswas, K. V. Nori (Eds.), Foundations of Software Technology and Theoretical Computer Science. Proceedings, 1991. X, 420 pages. 1991.

Vol. 561: C. Ding, G. Xiao, W. Shan, The Stability Theory of Stream Ciphers. IX, 187 pages. 1991.

Vol. 562: R. Breu, Algebraic Specification Techniques in Object Oriented Programming Environments. XI, 228 pages. 1991.

Vol. 563: A. Karshmer, J. Nehmer (Eds.), Operating Systems of the 90s and Beyond. Proceedings, 1991. X, 285 pages. 1991.

Vol. 564: I. Herman, The Use of Projective Geometry in Computer Graphics. VIII, 146 pages. 1992.

Vol. 565: J. D. Becker, I. Eisele, F. W. Mündemann (Eds.), Parallelism, Learning, Evolution. Proceedings, 1989. VIII, 525 pages. 1991. (Subseries LNAI).

Vol. 566: C. Delobel, M. Kifer, Y. Masunaga (Eds.), Deductive and Object-Oriented Databases. Proceedings, 1991. XV, 581 pages. 1991.

Vol. 567: H. Boley, M. M. Richter (Eds.), Processing Declarative Kowledge. Proceedings, 1991. XII, 427 pages. 1991. (Subseries LNAI).

Vol. 568: H.-J. Bürckert, A Resolution Principle for a Logic with Restricted Quantifiers. X, 116 pages. 1991. (Subseries LNAI).

Vol. 569: A. Beaumont, G. Gupta (Eds.), Parallel Execution of Logic Programs. Proceedings, 1991. VII, 195 pages. 1991.

Vol. 570: R. Berghammer, G. Schmidt (Eds.), Graph-Theoretic Concepts in Computer Science. Proceedings, 1991. VIII, 253 pages. 1992.

Vol. 571: J. Vytopil (Ed.), Formal Techniques in Real-Time and Fault-Tolerant Systems. Proceedings, 1992. IX, 620 pages. 1991.

Vol. 572: K. U. Schulz (Ed.), Word Equations and Related Topics. Proceedings, 1990. VII, 256 pages. 1992.

Vol. 573: G. Cohen, S. N. Litsyn, A. Lobstein, G. Zémor (Eds.), Algebraic Coding. Proceedings, 1991. X, 158 pages. 1992.

Vol. 574: J. P. Banâtre, D. Le Métayer (Eds.), Research Directions in High-Level Parallel Programming Languages. Proceedings, 1991. VIII, 387 pages. 1992.

Vol. 575: K. G. Larsen, A. Skou (Eds.), Computer Aided Verification. Proceedings, 1991. X, 487 pages. 1992.

Vol. 576: J. Feigenbaum (Ed.), Advances in Cryptology - CRYPTO '91. Proceedings. X, 485 pages. 1992.

Vol. 577: A. Finkel, M. Jantzen (Eds.), STACS 92. Proceedings, 1992. XIV, 621 pages. 1992.

Vol. 578: Th. Beth, M. Frisch, G. J. Simmons (Eds.), Public-Key Cryptography: State of the Art and Future Directions. XI, 97 pages. 1992.

Vol. 579: S. Toueg, P. G. Spirakis, L. Kirousis (Eds.), Distributed Algorithms. Proceedings, 1991. X, 319 pages. 1992.

Vol. 580: A. Pirotte, C. Delobel, G. Gottlob (Eds.), Advances in Database Technology – EDBT '92. Proceedings. XII, 551 pages. 1992.

Vol. 581: J.-C. Raoult (Ed.), CAAP '92. Proceedings. VIII, 361 pages. 1992.

Vol. 582: B. Krieg-Brückner (Ed.), ESOP '92. Proceedings. VIII, 491 pages. 1992.

Vol. 583: I. Simon (Ed.), LATIN '92. Proceedings. IX, 545 pages. 1992.

Vol. 584: R. E. Zippel (Ed.), Computer Algebra and Parallelism. Proceedings, 1990. IX, 114 pages. 1992.

Vol. 585: F. Pichler, R. Moreno Díaz (Eds.), Computer Aided System Theory – EUROCAST '91. Proceedings. X, 761 pages. 1992.

Vol. 586: A. Cheese, Parallel Execution of Parlog. IX, 184 pages. 1992.

Vol. 587: R. Dale, E. Hovy, D. Rösner, O. Stock (Eds.), Aspects of Automated Natural Language Generation. Proceedings, 1992. VIII, 311 pages. 1992. (Subseries LNAI).

Vol. 588: G. Sandini (Ed.), Computer Vision – ECCV '92. Proceedings. XV, 909 pages. 1992.

Vol. 589: U. Banerjee, D. Gelernter, A. Nicolau, D. Padua (Eds.), Languages and Compilers for Parallel Computing. Proceedings, 1991. IX, 419 pages. 1992.

Vol. 590: B. Fronhöfer, G. Wrightson (Eds.), Parallelization in Inference Systems. Proceedings, 1990. VIII, 372 pages. 1992. (Subseries LNAI).

Vol. 591: H. P. Zima (Ed.), Parallel Computation. Proceedings, 1991. IX, 451 pages. 1992.

Vol. 592: A. Voronkov (Ed.), Logic Programming. Proceedings, 1991. IX, 514 pages. 1992. (Subseries LNAI).

Vol. 593: P. Loucopoulos (Ed.), Advanced Information Systems Engineering. Proceedings. XI, 650 pages. 1992.

Vol. 594: B. Monien, Th. Ottmann (Eds.), Data Structures and Efficient Algorithms. VIII, 389 pages. 1992.

Vol. 595: M. Levene, The Nested Universal Relation Database Model. X, 177 pages. 1992.

Vol. 596: L.-H. Eriksson, L. Hallnäs, P. Schroeder-Heister (Eds.), Extensions of Logic Programming. Proceedings, 1991. VII, 369 pages. 1992. (Subseries LNAI).

Vol. 597: H. W. Guesgen, J. Hertzberg, A Perspective of Constraint-Based Reasoning. VIII, 123 pages. 1992. (Subseries LNAI).

Vol. 598: S. Brookes, M. Main, A. Melton, M. Mislove, D. Schmidt (Eds.), Mathematical Foundations of Programming Semantics. Proceedings, 1991. VIII, 506 pages. 1992.

Vol. 599: Th. Wetter, K.-D. Althoff, J. Boose, B. R. Gaines, M. Linster, F. Schmalhofer (Eds.), Current Developments in Knowledge Acquisition - EKAW '92. Proceedings. XIII, 444 pages. 1992. (Subseries LNAI).

Vol. 600: J. W. de Bakker, C. Huizing, W. P. de Roever, G. Rozenberg (Eds.), Real-Time: Theory in Practice. Proceedings, 1991. VIII, 723 pages. 1992.

Vol. 601: D. Dolev, Z. Galil, M. Rodeh (Eds.), Theory of Computing and Systems. Proceedings, 1992. VIII, 220 pages. 1992.

Vol. 602: I. Tomek (Ed.), Computer Assisted Learning. Proceedings, 1992. X, 615 pages. 1992.

Vol. 603: J. van Katwijk (Ed.), Ada: Moving Towards 2000. Proceedings, 1992. VIII, 324 pages. 1992.

Vol. 604: F. Belli, F.-J. Radermacher (Eds.), Industrial and Engineering Applications of Artificial Intelligence and Expert Systems. Proceedings, 1992. XV, 702 pages. 1992. (Subseries LNAI).

Vol. 605: D. Etiemble, J.-C. Syre (Eds.), PARLE '92. Parallel Architectures and Languages Europe. Proceedings, 1992. XVII, 984 pages. 1992.

Vol. 606: D. E. Knuth, Axioms and Hulls. IX, 109 pages. 1992.

Vol. 607: D. Kapur (Ed.), Automated Deduction – CADE-11. Proceedings, 1992. XV, 793 pages. 1992. (Subseries LNAI).

Vol. 608: C. Frasson, G. Gauthier, G. I. McCalla (Eds.), Intelligent Tutoring Systems. Proceedings, 1992. XIV, 686 pages. 1992.

Vol. 609: G. Rozenberg (Ed.), Advances in Petri Nets 1992. VIII, 472 pages. 1992.

Vol. 610: F. von Martial, Coordinating Plans of Autonomous Agents. XII, 246 pages. 1992. (Subseries LNAI).

Vol. 611: M. P. Papazoglou, J. Zeleznikow (Eds.), The Next Generation of Information Systems: From Data to Knowledge. VIII, 310 pages. 1992. (Subseries LNAI).

Vol. 612: M. Tokoro, O. Nierstrasz, P. Wegner (Eds.), Object-Based Concurrent Computing. Proceedings, 1991. X, 265 pages. 1992.

Vol. 613: J. P. Myers, Jr., M. J. O'Donnell (Eds.), Constructivity in Computer Science. Proceedings, 1991. X, 247 pages. 1992.

Vol. 614: R. G. Herrtwich (Ed.), Network and Operating System Support for Digital Audio and Video. Proceedings, 1991. XII, 403 pages. 1992.

Vol. 615: O. Lehrmann Madsen (Ed.), ECOOP '92. European Conference on Object Oriented Programming. Proceedings. X, 426 pages. 1992.

Vol. 616: K. Jensen (Ed.), Application and Theory of Petri Nets 1992. Proceedings, 1992. VIII, 398 pages. 1992.

Vol. 617: V. Mařík, O. Štěpánková, R. Trappl (Eds.), Advanced Topics in Artificial Intelligence. Proceedings, 1992. IX, 484 pages. 1992. (Subseries LNAI).

Vol. 618: P. M. D. Gray, R. J. Lucas (Eds.), Advanced Database Systems. Proceedings, 1992. X, 260 pages. 1992.

Vol. 619: D. Pearce, H. Wansing (Eds.), Nonclassical Logics and Information Proceedings. Proceedings, 1990. VII, 171 pages. 1992. (Subseries LNAI).

Vol. 620: A. Nerode, M. Taitslin (Eds.), Logical Foundations of Computer Science – Tver '92. Proceedings. IX, 514 pages. 1992.

Vol. 621: O. Nurmi, E. Ukkonen (Eds.), Algorithm Theory – SWAT '92. Proceedings. VIII, 434 pages. 1992.

Vol. 622: F. Schmalhofer, G. Strube, Th. Wetter (Eds.), Contemporary Knowledge Engineering and Cognition. Proceedings, 1991. XII, 258 pages. 1992. (Subseries LNAI).

Vol. 623: W. Kuich (Ed.), Automata, Languages and Programming. Proceedings, 1992. XII, 721 pages. 1992.

Vol. 624: A. Voronkov (Ed.), Logic Programming and Automated Reasoning. Proceedings, 1992. XIV, 509 pages. 1992. (Subseries LNAI).

Vol. 625: W. Vogler, Modular Construction and Partial Order Semantics of Petri Nets. IX, 252 pages. 1992.

Vol. 626: E. Börger, G. Jäger, H. Kleine Büning, M. M. Richter (Eds.), Computer Science Logic. Proceedings, 1991. VIII, 428 pages. 1992.

Vol. 628: G. Vosselman, Relational Matching. IX, 190 pages. 1992.

Vol. 629: I. M. Havel, V. Koubek (Eds.), Mathematical Foundations of Computer Science 1992. Proceedings. IX, 521 pages. 1992.

Vol. 630: W. R. Cleaveland (Ed.), CONCUR '92. Proceedings. X, 580 pages. 1992.

Vol. 631: M. Bruynooghe, M. Wirsing (Eds.), Programming Language Implementation and Logic Programming. Proceedings, 1992. XI, 492 pages. 1992.

Vol. 632: H. Kirchner, G. Levi (Eds.), Algebraic and Logic Programming. Proceedings, 1992. IX, 457 pages. 1992.

Vol. 633: D. Pearce, G. Wagner (Eds.), Logics in AI. Proceedings. VIII, 410 pages. 1992. (Subseries LNAI).

Vol. 634: L. Bougé, M. Cosnard, Y. Robert, D. Trystram (Eds.), Parallel Processing: CONPAR 92 – VAPP V. Proceedings. XVII, 853 pages. 1992.

Vol. 635: J. C. Derniame (Ed.), Software Process Technology. Proceedings, 1992. VIII, 253 pages. 1992.

Vol. 636: G. Comyn, N. E. Fuchs, M. J. Ratcliffe (Eds.), Logic Programming in Action. Proceedings, 1992. X, 324 pages. 1992. (Subseries LNAI).

Vol. 637: Y. Bekkers, J. Cohen (Eds.), Memory Management. Proceedings, 1992. XI, 525 pages. 1992.

Vol. 639: A. U. Frank, I. Campari, U. Formentini (Eds.), Theories and Methods of Spatio-Temporal Reasoning in Geographic Space. Proceedings, 1992. XI, 431 pages. 1992.

Vol. 640: C. Sledge (Ed.), Software Engineering Education. Proceedings, 1992. X, 451 pages. 1992.

Vol. 641: U. Kastens, P. Pfahler (Eds.), Compiler Construction. Proceedings, 1992. VIII, 320 pages. 1992.

Vol. 642: K. P. Jantke (Ed.), Analogical and Inductive Inference. Proceedings, 1992. VIII, 319 pages. 1992. (Subseries LNAI).

Vol. 643: A. Habel, Hyperedge Replacement: Grammars and Languages. X, 214 pages. 1992.